AF605801

BOCCACCIO'S FLORENCE

Politics and People in His Life and Work

Fresco on the vault of the Guild Hall, Palace of Judges and Notaries, Via del Proconsolo 34, Florence

ELSA FILOSA

Boccaccio's Florence

Politics and People in His Life and Work

UNIVERSITY OF TORONTO PRESS
Toronto Buffalo London

Toronto Buffalo London
utorontopress.com
Printed in the U.S.A.

ISBN 978-1-4875-0580-6 (cloth)
ISBN 978-1-4875-3273-4 (EPUB)
ISBN 978-1-4875-3272-7 (PDF)

Library and Archives Canada Cataloguing in Publication

Title: Boccaccio's Florence : politics and people in his life and work / Elsa Filosa.
Names: Filosa, Elsa, author.
Series: Toronto Italian studies.
Description: Series statement: Toronto Italian studies | Includes bibliographical references and index.
Identifiers: Canadiana (print) 2022018285X | Canadiana (ebook) 20220182884 | ISBN 9781487505806 (cloth) | ISBN 9781487532734 (EPUB) | ISBN 9781487532727 (PDF)
Subjects: LCSH: Boccaccio, Giovanni, 1313–1375 – Criticism and interpretation. | LCSH: Politics in literature. | LCSH: History in literature. | LCSH: Florence (Italy) – Politics and government – To 1421. | LCSH: Florence (Italy) – History – To 1421.
Classification: LCC PQ4293.H5 F56 2022 | DDC 853/.1–dc23

We wish to acknowledge the land on which the University of Toronto Press operates. This land is the traditional territory of the Wendat, the Anishnaabeg, the Haudenosaunee, the Métis, and the Mississaugas of the Credit First Nation.

University of Toronto Press acknowledges the financial support of the Government of Canada, the Canada Council for the Arts, and the Ontario Arts Council, an agency of the Government of Ontario, for its publishing activities.

Funded by the Government of Canada
Financé par le gouvernement du Canada
Canada

To my brother Brizio,
my cousin Saso,
my sister-by-choice Sara,
and to my lifelong friends
Giuly, Giacomo, Susy, Dani,
Zia Dora, Betta, Rosa, Simo,
Stef and Gibo, who are always with us all.

Contents

Illustrations and Tables

Illustrations

Tables

Acknowledgments

This work has been ten years in the making, during which time I have had the privilege to be supported by distinguished research institutions, universities, colleagues, and dear friends.

Most of the research and writing of this book was undertaken at the Villa I Tatti, The Harvard University Center for Italian Renaissance Studies in Florence, while I was an Andrew W. Mellon fellow there in 2015–16. My first thank you goes to this institution and to the anonymous committee that chose my project as one of the fifteen to be awarded that year, together with Lino Pertile, who was in his last year of directorship at that time. Also, I am most grateful to the two people who recommended me for this fellowship, Paolo Cherchi and Ron Witt, whose generosity during my graduate years at the University of North Carolina, Chapel Hill, will be always fondly remembered.

The year at I Tatti was all the more productive and formative because of the people who were there with me: the director Alina Payne, whose enthusiasm and creativity were contagious, and my fellow scholars, with whom I engaged in many stimulating and constructive discussions. My particular gratitude goes to Davide Baldi, Francesco Bausi, Luisa Capodieci, Mariano Pérez Carrasco, Diletta Gamberini, Allen Grieco, Holly Flora, Ingrid Houssaye Michienzi, Christian Kleinbub, Jonathan Nelson, Diego Pirillo, Courtney Quaintance, and David Rosenthal. I also thank the very helpful, expert librarians and staff of the Villa I Tatti, too many to name in this brief space.

In the same years, I had the pleasure of working at the State Archive of Florence, at the Biblioteca Nazionale and in the Laurentian Library. I want to thank the friends I met at the Archive for their consistent help and discussions on Boccaccio: Nicoletta Baldini, Giuseppe Biscione, Marco Cursi, Francesca Fantappiè, Francesca Klein, Steven Milner, Emanuela Porta Casucci, Laura Regnicoli, Sergio Tognetti, and, most of all, Vieri Mazzoni, whose generosity in time and expertise was always exceptional.

I was fortunate also to spend the summer of 2017 at the Mellon Summer Institute of the Getty Research Institute, where I had far-reaching discussions on Boccaccio, Petrarch, and poetry with my dear friend Maddalena Signorini.

Many colleagues invited me to present my work at their institutions, and I am grateful to them for those opportunities and for the discussions that followed: Marco

Veglia at the University of Bologna (2013), Johannes Bartuschat at the University of Zurich (2013), Zygmunt Barański at the University of Notre Dame (2014), Valerio Cappozzo at Olemiss (2015), Giuseppe Mazzotta at Yale University (2018), Elisa Brilli at the University of Toronto (2018), and Sabrina Ferrara at the Centre d'Études Supérieures de la Renaissance in Tours (2019). I also wish to thank Teodolinda Barolini for her interest and support of this project during its early stages.

This book would not have made it to publication without the constant encouragement of all my colleagues in the Department of French and Italian at Vanderbilt University, in particular Letizia Modena, William Franke, Andrea Mirabile, and Daniela D'Eugenio. I owe a special thanks to the several chairs who were supportive in very practical ways while I was writing the book: Virginia Scott, Lynn Ramey, Robert Barsky, Laurel Schneider, and Meike Werner. I cannot express all the gratitude I have for William Caferro, chair of the Department of the Classical and Mediterranean Studies, in which I am an affiliated faculty, for the numerous conversations we had on Boccaccio and the other Florentines of the period, for the exchange of archival documents, and for his continuous support through a challenging period of my academic career. Annalisa Azzoni of the Divinity School has always been my best friend in Vandyland, and I cannot leave her out. Our administrative assistant Laura Dossett has also been a major support, as has Marion Pratt, who was at the grant office until 2018.

One reason I have never stopped working on Boccaccio is the community of scholars of Boccaccisti worldwide, active in the American Boccaccio Association (which I have the honour to serve as treasurer, and have served as secretary for two mandates) and the Ente Nazionale Giovanni Boccaccio. These scholars, like Boccaccio, have wit, joy, compassion, deep emotional connections, and understanding of the misadventures of life, all qualities that make our gatherings occasions to celebrate friendship and to work in a collaborative and enthusiastic atmosphere. I cannot name every member of the ABA, but I do want to thank Simone Marchesi for his consistent help, solid presence, and humanity; I had the pleasure to serve the association with, among others, my colleagues and friends Susanna Barsella, Valerio Cappozzo, Francesco Ciabattoni, Maggie Fritz-Morkin, Eugenio Giusti, Timothy Kircher, Victoria Kirkham, Christopher Kleinhenz, Marilyn Migiel, Kristina Olson, and Michael Papio.

A heartful thank you is due to all those who have read the manuscript and made suggestions that have improved it enormously; above all, the two anonymous readers for the University of Toronto Press. I also thank Brian Maxson and Gregorio Invrea for their readings, Daniel Solomon for his help in numerous translations, and in particular Maura High, my copy editor, whose friendship and professionalism I have enjoyed from my time at the University of North Carolina, Chapel Hill. For the final touches on my manuscript, sincere thanks is due to copy editor Judy Williams, Barb Porter in the managing editorial department, and Suzanne Rancourt in the acquisitions department at University of Toronto Press.

Last, but not least, my heart is full of gratitude for my son Giorgio, who was just a little boy when I started writing this book and is now a young man, for his sunny smile, affection, and endless joy of life.

Abbreviations

Manuscript Sources

All manuscript sources are from the State Archive of Florence (ASFi).

AEOG	*Atti dell'Esecutore degli Ordinamenti di giustizia*
ACP	*Atti del Capitani del Popolo*
AP	*Atti del Podestà*
CCCE	*Camera del Comune, Camerario, Entrata*
CCCU	*Camera del Comune, Camerario, Uscita*
CCNCE	*Camera del Comune, Notaio della Camera, Entrata*
CCNCEU	*Camera del Comune, Notaio della Camera, Entrata e Uscita*
CCSCE	*Camera del Comune, Scrivano della Camera, Entrata*
CP	*Consulte e Pratiche*
CPGNR	*Capitani di Parte Guelfa, Numeri Rossi*
CR	*Capitoli, Registri*
LF	*Libri Fabarum*
Miss	*I canc Missive I cancelleria*
PR	*Provvisioni, Registri*
SCDFOA	*Signori e Collegi, Deliberazione in Forza di Ordinaria Autorità*

Printed or Online Source

DBI	*Dizionario biografico degli italiani*, available online at: https://www.treccani.it/biografico/index.html

Unless otherwise indicated, all translations are mine. English translations from the *Decameron* are by James M. Rigg.

BOCCACCIO'S FLORENCE

Introduction

Il qual trattato nell'effetto era di cacciare alcune famiglie.

(The actual goal of the treaty was to expel certain families.)
– Franco Sacchetti, *Il Trecentonovelle*, 180

The circular fresco painted in 1366 on the vault of the Hall of the Palace of the Judges and Notaries Guild in Florence represents the leading powers of the city at that time. In the centre of the image (see the frontispiece to this book) are the emblems of the Commune (the lily), the Popolo (the cross), the Guelf Party (an eagle with a snake in its talons), and the cities of Florence and Fiesole (a red-and-white shield), along with the emblems of the four quarters from which the city's priors were chosen (Santo Spirito, San Giovanni, Santa Croce, and Santa Maria Novella) together with their four sectors each (*gonfaloni*). The next circles depict the guilds and their patron saints. The external parts of the outermost circle surround and defend the internal ones, with four principal gates, each opening onto a bridge over the moat, the four bridges leading outward in the four cardinal directions. In this way, Florence is represented through a heraldic organigram in which concentric circles depict the civic institutions, the sovereign powers that ruled the Republic (Friedman 1988).

The image of a circular city, which recalls the rose window of a Gothic church and the celestial Jerusalem, was intended to communicate a sense of perfection, harmony, and balance among the institutions that regulated political, social, and economic life – a harmony that had never been reached in real life. "The tranquil and peaceful state of the city of Florence" was in fact continuously jeopardized by opposing factions' malcontents, whose disagreements often came to a head in the conspiracies that had plagued the city since its founding. The majority of these planned and sometimes attempted coups are unknown or understudied today because in practice they had little effect on the civic life of the "City of the Lily."

The year 1360, however, saw the launch and failure of a conspiracy to overthrow the faction then in control of the city of Florence by Florentines who included members of Boccaccio's circle. The event had terrible repercussions for his friends, and for Boccaccio himself, and this study, *Boccaccio's Florence*, frames the attempted coup as one of the most transforming events of Boccaccio's life. His experiences to that point brought him into circles and activities close to the conspiracy, and his life and work afterwards were deeply affected by it.

The less profound effect of attempted coups on the civic life of Florence partly explains why the conspiracy, planned for 31 December 1360 – and timed to coincide with the renewal of terms of office for the city's priors – has provoked little interest among historians. The many books on Florentine history do not include much information about the plot, with the exception of Gene Brucker's *Florentine Politics and Society (1343–1378)*, which provides an illuminating, albeit short, analysis of the events in question. Nonetheless, contemporary chronicles record the "secret treaty" in detail, showing the strong impact the conspiracy had at the time: Matteo Villani gives the most accurate report; Marchionne di Coppo Stefani sees this event as a rekindling of the resentments of the faction involved; Donato di Neri argues that the coup was organized by members of the wool guild, who could not trade their product after the embargo on Porto Pisano in 1357. The conspiracy and its suppression were not soon forgotten by Florentines, either. Franco Sacchetti refers to it over fifteen years later: "It is true that not long before 1360, there was in Florence a conspiracy made by several citizens, and two of them were beheaded; the goal of that conspiracy was to expel some families from the city" ("Ed è vero che poco tempo innanzi del 1360 era stato un trattato in Firenze di molti cittadini, e furonno due dicapitati; il qual trattato nell'effetto era di cacciare alcune famiglie"; Sacchetti, *Trecentonovelle* 1970, 180).

The chroniclers did not give the same account, or the same interpretation, of the facts. Either they did not want, or they were unable, to say openly how matters really went. And indeed, on first impression, this does seem to be an ambiguous event, engineered by a heterogeneous group of leaders, with goals that seem unclear in terms of the forces operating in the turbulent climate of Florentine politics and the contemporary situation in Italy (Klein 1988). Looked at more closely, however, it emerges as a last, desperate attempt by the leaders of international banking and trading economic enterprises to avoid financial ruin. Leaders such as the Bardi and Frescobaldi, whose families were settled in the part of Florence known as Oltrarno and were affiliated with the bankers' or merchants' guilds, were under great pressure in the late 1330s to lend money to King Edward III of England and finance Florence in its war against Lucca. To avoid bankruptcy, a series of attempts to regain power started in 1340, with a conspiracy named after the main instigators, the Bardi. These same leaders in 1342 called Walter of Brienne, the Duke of Athens, to rule Florence, because he had promised to have their debts withdrawn; and they were the ones who evicted him in 1343 when they realized he was not working in their interest. They tried to gain power again after the expulsion of the duke, with the support of the compliant Bishop of Florence, Angelo Acciaiuoli, cousin of the future grand seneschal of the Kingdom of Naples, Niccolò Acciaiuoli. Their efforts, however, did not succeed. The Florentine populace rose up against the Bardi and burned down their houses in Oltrarno; a "popular government" (1343–8) was established, and many magnates were confined outside the city walls. This new lower-class regime was swept away by the plague of 1348, resulting in a "magnate resurgence," led by the supporters of the Guelf Party, the old aristocratic party. The shift of power was effected in the tribunal's halls, with many terrorized citizens charged with being "Ghibellines or not true Guelf," the instrument of suppression being the *ammonizione*, a strong reprimand that effectively placed the accused on a blacklist. With the enforcement of the *ammonizione* in 1358, the oligarchic faction of the Guelf Party slowly but inexorably took control of the city and held it until the Ciompi Revolt in 1378.

Throughout the 1350s, the city saw much factional rivalry. It centred on two families: the Albizzi and the Ricci. The Albizzi were intransigent and extremist oligarchics, close to the Guelf Party, and they wanted to concentrate the power of the city in the hands of old nobility and old Florentine citizens; the Ricci were more liberal and open towards newly urbanized people. The continual competition between the two factions led a heterogeneous group of people to conspire against the city leaders. Their early efforts to bring changes to the city came to nothing, so they devised a new plan, to launch a coup on New Year's Eve, 1360. This plot, at the centre of this book, was their last attempt. The event might appear to be little more than a minor episode alongside the many conspiracies, riots, and secret deals that marked the history of the city. But for the twelve conspirators accused of "subverting the tranquil and peaceful state of the city of Florence," it had a tragic outcome.

For their part in the attempted coup, the Florentine Republic indicted the chief conspirators, including several close friends and neighbours of Messer Giovanni di Boccaccio da Certaldo, or, as he is most widely known, Giovanni Boccaccio, author of the *Decameron*. Two of the conspirators were executed and the others went into exile, but all found their lives and livelihoods abruptly and profoundly changed. Among the named conspirators, five were intimate friends of Boccaccio: Niccolò di Bartolo del Buono was the dedicatee of the *Comedia delle Ninfe fiorentine* and Pino de' Rossi, the recipient of the *Consolatoria*; the latter work was also written explicitly for two other conspirators, Luca di Feo Ugolini and Andrea di Tello da Lisca. Pazzino di Apardo Donati had witnessed a notary document for Boccaccio, testifying to the payment from the Commune to the ambassador *Domini Johannes Boccaccii de Certaldo*. Others among the group were his neighbours, living in Oltrarno along with Boccaccio.

This book, *Boccaccio's Florence*, is not a new biography of Giovanni Boccaccio, but a study that looks at the writer's context and at the work that came out of it;

it underscores the political relationships the writer had in Florence in the mid-1300s and invites new readings of his literary work. To draw a complete picture of what happened at that time, and the consequences for Boccaccio's life and work, I have divided the book into two parts. The first fills out the historical context and provides new information on Boccaccio's circle based on extensive archival research, and the second deals with the interconnections between the events and Boccaccio's works.

Recently, scholars have directed more attention to Boccaccio and politics. After the studies by Attilio Hortis (1875, 1879) and Francesco Macrì-Leone (1890) more than a century ago, we have started to see new contributions in the field, beginning with the seven hundredth anniversary of Boccaccio's birth in 2013. The first important conference was "Boccaccio politico," organized by Marco Veglia of the University of Bologna in 2013: the proceedings were published two years later in the official journal of the American Boccaccio Association, *Heliotropia*. In 2015, another volume appeared that established Boccaccio as a significant political figure in Florence (*The Cambridge Companion to Boccaccio*), particularly the introduction by the editors (Guyda Armstrong, Rhiannon Daniels, and Steven Milner), titled "Boccaccio as Cultural Mediator." In 2019, James Hankins added to this line of research with his essay "Boccaccio and the Political Thought of Renaissance Humanism." *Boccaccio's Florence* joins these explorations as the first monograph dedicated to Boccaccio as a historical figure immersed in the political reality of his time. As such, it contributes new material and new perspectives for our understanding of Boccaccio as man and writer.

Important archival work – including the rediscovery of several documents on Boccaccio – has been conducted by Laura Regnicoli, and historians have reconstructed more precisely the background of those years of Boccaccio's life. Examples include Vieri Mazzoni's *Accusare e proscrivere* (2010), which gives us a new understanding of the years when the practice of *ammonizione* was raging in Florence, and William Caferro's *Petrarch's War* (2018a), which portrays Boccaccio as involved in the campaign against the Ubaldini and Visconti families. My study was able to take advantage of this new information to scrutinize the Florentine years in Boccaccio's life. It investigates the political dynamics of the attempted coup of 1360, the motives behind it, and its consequences. The analysis spans the years 1340 to 1363, from the Bardi conspiracy to the date when the death sentences of some of the conspirators were commuted. The relationships between Boccaccio and this group of associates are at the heart of this book, as they and their actions deeply affected his life and writings.

I embarked on this study by necessity. In writing the Introduction to my first book (Filosa 2012), I wanted to trace the historical context in which Boccaccio's *De mulieribus claris* (*Famous Women*) was written, spanning the period from fall 1361 through 1363. At that time, after the failed coup, Boccaccio had moved back to his native Certaldo. I tried to find additional information about the conspiracy, but very little had been published. I started looking at chronicles of the time, and learned from them details about the conspiracy and the names of the conspirators, and I realized that five of them were close friends of Boccaccio. I wondered, exactly what kind of relationship did Boccaccio have with the conspirators? To what degree did these events influence his life and writings? To pursue these questions, I turned to the State Archive of Florence (ASFi) in June 2014, where I found several key documents: the scroll containing the death sentence of the conspirators (*Atti del Podestà* 1525, ff. 57r–58r); the trial proceedings (*Atti del Podestà* 1516–24); and a description of the measures undertaken by the Florentine city government (Commune) (*Provvisioni* 48, ff. 49r–131v). The fruits of this research are offered here.

In 1327, the then fourteen-year-old Giovanni Boccaccio followed his father from Florence to Naples, where Boccaccino di Chellino da Certaldo was the director of the Neapolitan branch of the Bardi Company. The father hoped the young writer would learn about business, but he was more attracted to the library of King Robert and the refinements of his court than to commercial studies. Here he composed his first works and showed early signs of his literary inclination. He returned to Florence in the winter 1340–1. In 1348, when he was thirty-five years old, the Black Death swept through Florence and Europe, and several members of his family, including his father, died during that period. Boccaccio survived, and on his father's death he assumed the legal role of *pater familias* and, as such, took care of his young half-brother and managed a sizeable inheritance from his father: several properties in Florence, Certaldo, and Capua; small farms in the countryside; property rights; and the incomes from these businesses. As a result of his local connections, he joined a select group of merchants, bankers, and old patricians, including the Del Buono, Bardi, Frescobaldi, Rossi, and Donati families. Thanks to his knowledge and devotion to the humanities and his strategic friendships, he became involved in city politics, often acting as a Florentine ambassador and cultural promoter. From a biographical standpoint, knowing about these people is crucial to understanding Boccaccio's political life. They were his friends, neighbours, political supporters, and ultimately his readers. Boccaccio's life is tied very closely to those of his friends. Their contexts and interactions are central to Boccaccio's life from 1341 through 1361, when he went into self-exile in Certaldo.

The second part of this book, "At the Intersections of Literature and Politics," analyses how the historical background reconstructed in the first part influenced the author's literary choices, particularly in three works Boccaccio wrote immediately after the conspiracy: the reassessment of *De mulieribus claris*, the *Consolatoria a Pino de' Rossi* (*Consolatory Letter to Pino de' Rossi*), and the second revision of the *Trattatello in laude di Dante* (*Life of Dante*). With what we know from the archival documents and keeping in mind the historical facts, we can now read Boccaccio's works in a new light, seeing political nuances that have been overlooked until now. In *De mulieribus claris*, Boccaccio uses the lives of famous women to instruct his readers on how friends should behave in time of conspiracy and openly condemns conspirators who carelessly name others involved. He attacks Venus, Flora, and Hercules, personages related to the mythical foundation of Florence. In the biographies presented in the book, he emphasizes the women's antityrannical motives, and depicts them as role models on how to behave in a tyrannical regime, sometimes even choosing death as an escape to freedom. Of the three works, the letter to Pino de' Rossi is probably the text in which an understanding of the historical context is most illuminating. The letter was written to Pino to console him for the sentence of exile pronounced against him for his role in the coup. Given its historical context, this letter might be seen also as a defence of Pino de' Rossi's innocence, and as a political statement against the new oligarchic regime.

The second version of *Trattatello in laude di Dante* differs from the first most obviously in its deletion of any mention in the text of the title of Dante's *Monarchia*, which had been perceived by the regime as a political threat. We see in this expurgation that Boccaccio was sensitive enough to the recent changes in the Florentine political environment – and the change in his readership – so much that they influenced his literary decisions in the second version of Dante's life.

To round out my reappraisal and rereading of works by Boccaccio that relate to this period of his life, I look at one additional piece: Day Six of the *Decameron*, the "Florentine day." The *Decameron* was written before the conspiracy of 1360, yet Day Six tells us a great deal about the people for whom Boccaccio was writing in the 1350s, who consisted largely of the entourage of his father, important members of the Arte del Cambio (bankers' guild).

This rereading of Boccaccio from a political perspective allows for a very different understanding of his literary output from the conventional ones: that it was a "religious conversion" after a visit from a monk in 1362 that caused the change in the author's style, or that the style change came about because he committed himself completely to the humanistic project proposed by the person he called his *magister*, Petrarch. What we cannot brush aside is the fact that, after experiencing bankruptcy in 1359 and the death or exile of his allies and friends, Boccaccio lost his intellectual independence. Constrained by economic difficulties and a new disadvantageous political frame, his writings had to be attuned to the traditional and moralizing oligarchic Guelf thinking and values. Moreover, he had to adhere to the cultural preferences of ecclesiastical circles, which privileged the Latin language for the *literati* over the vernacular for the *popolani*. For Boccaccio, the time for "playful" literature was over.

It is no accident that the fresco in the Palace of the Judges and Notaries (figure. I.1), painted after Boccaccio's death (sometime between 1375 and 1406), had at its centre the two "real" glories of Florence: Francesco Petrarch and Zanobi da Strada, the two poets laureate. Dante on the left and Boccaccio on the right, portrayed in profile, had more marginal roles, because after all, their works were written in the vernacular, the language of the "illiterate" *popolo*.

Figure I.1. Fresco, Palace of the Judges and Notaries Guild, Via Proconsolo 34, Florence. From left: Dante, Zanobi da Strada, Francesco Petrarch, and Giovanni Boccaccio.

PART ONE

Power and Politics in Boccaccio's Times

1 An Apprenticeship in Politics (1341–1343)

Santa Felicita Oltrarno, ov'erano capo i Bardi e' Rossi e' Frescobaldi

(Santa Felicita Oltrarno, where the leaders were the Bardi, Rossi, and Frescobaldi)
– Giovanni Villani, *Nuova Cronica*, 13.19

E questi sono i casati più cari:
Ciò sono i Bardi, Rossi, e Frescobaldi

(And these are the dearest lineages:
They are the Bardi, Rossi, and Frescobaldi)
– Antonio Pucci, *Il Centiloquio* XCI.32–3, 1373

In the years 1341–3, Giovanni Boccaccio was back in Florence, establishing himself as a writer and as manager of his family's estates and assets, at a time when the city was rife with intrigue and turmoil, from the Bardi conspiracy, to the arrival of the Duke of Athens, to the creation of the "popular government." It is during this period that Boccaccio started to make connections with people in Oltrarno who would have a great impact on his life: magnates, neighbours, members of the bankers' guild, shareholders of the Bardi, Frescobaldi, and Acciaiuoli companies, and old patricians and nobles, such as the Rossi family. These are the associates with whom he would share good and bad luck in his years in Florence. All the time he was writing, Boccaccio was deeply immersed in the city's social and political life.

From Naples to Florence: Santa Felicita in Oltrarno

In 1327, Boccaccio's father, Boccaccino di Chellino di Buonaiuto da Certaldo, moved to Naples to become the director of the Neapolitan branch of the Bardi Company. He was among the highest-paid officers of the company, both because he was an experienced merchant and because he had distinguished himself in his civic career in Florence: twice as consul for the guild of bankers, in 1322 and in 1324, and as prior, between 15 December 1322 and 15 February 1323; in 1326, he was one of the five members of the Mercanzia, the highest office in trade business. While in Naples, he succeeded in entering the Angevin court, receiving from King Robert the prestigious epithet of *consiliarius* or *cambellarius*, chamberlain. His son Giovanni, then fourteen years old, was less interested in the business than in the library of the king, who allowed him to access it. The poems he composed here are among the freshest and most exquisite of his productions. Naples and its coast was the setting for the story of the great love of his life, Fiammetta, who became the "senhal" of his poetry, as Laura did for Petrarch and Beatrice for Dante. These were probably the happiest and most formative years in Boccaccio's life.

After his father returned to Florence in 1338, Boccaccio stayed on in Naples – but not for very long. In the winter between 1340 and 1341, at the age of twenty-eight, Boccaccio moved back to Florence to join his father, who was by then living in Oltrarno. It is likely that his father recalled him to take care of family business, after the deaths of his wife, Margherita di Giandonato de' Martoli, and his heir, Giovanni's half-brother Francesco. Boccaccio gives these words to Fiammetta in his *Elegy* (59): "He was called back home by his father, who had been left with no other sons" (trans. Causa-Steindler and Mauch) ("Il padre, non essendogli rimaso altro figliuolo, il richiamò a casa sua"; *Fiamm.* V 6, 2). The mother and son may have succumbed to the epidemic that hit Florence in 1340: Giovanni Villani uses the word "pestilenza," literally plague; according to him, one-sixth of the city's population died, and no family was untouched by death (1990–1, 3.114).[1]

Boccaccio makes heartfelt, sorrowful references to this move from Naples throughout his works in this period, as in his *Elegy of Madonna Fiammetta* (II 20–1) and the *Ametus* (*Comedìa delle ninfe fiorentine*, XLIX 64–84). From the latter we read:

> But let whoever can see clearly imagine if I was to be sorrowful and bitter in heart in abandoning that gracious place. In that place are beauty, gentility, and worth, charming words, examples of virtue, and supreme pleasure along with love; there is desire that moves man to salvation; there is as much good and gaiety as man can know; there the wordly delights are fulfilled, and there sweetness is to be contemplated and enjoyed; and where I go is melancholy and eternal sadness. Here one never laughs, or rarely; and the house, dark, mute, and exceedingly sad, receives me and keeps me

1 For Boccaccino di Chellino, see Sapori 1926, 259; Zafarana 1968; Branca 1997, 14. Boccaccio's return date to Florence has been established by Branca 1976, 53–4; see also della Torre 1905, 309–13 and 342–6. Laura Regnicoli's paper (2018) reexamines the move from Naples to Certaldo and the reasons beyond it, using new archival documents. See also Santagata 2019, 77–8.

against my will, where the crude and horrible sight of a cold man, rough and miserly, saddens me ever more; so that having seen a happy day, the return to such a hostel indeed changes that sweetness into sad bitterness. (Trans. Serafini-Sauli)

(Ma pensi chi ben vede, se penoso
esser dovei e con amaro core,
quel loco abandonando grazioso.
Quivi biltà, gentilezza e valore,
leggiadri motti, essemplo di virtute,
somma piacevolezza è come amore;
quivi disio movente omo a salute,
quivi tanto di bene e d'allegrezza
quant'uom ci pote aver, quivi compite
le delizie mondane, e lor dolcezza
si vedeva e sentiva; e ov'io vado
malinconia e etterna gramezza.
Lì non si ride mai, se non di rado;
la casa oscura e muta e molto trista
me ritiene e riceve, mal mio grado;
dove la cruda e orribile vista
d'un vecchio freddo, ruvido e avaro
ognora con affanno più m'atrista
sì che l'aver veduto il giorno caro
e ritornare a così fatto ostello
rivolge ben quel dolce in tristo amaro.)

We have more historical evidence of his distress at having to return to Florence in a letter he sent to his childhood friend Niccolò Acciaiuoli, dated 28 August 1341: "I am not writing you anything about my involuntary presence in Florence, but it would be easier to show this with tears than with ink" ("Dell'essere mio in Firenze contra piacere niente vi scrivo, però che più tosto co·lagrime che con inchiostro sarebbe da dimostrare"; *Ep.* V 6). He signed it: "Your Giovanni di Boccaccio da Certaldo and Fortune's foe" ("ed inimico della Fortuna"). Such a transition from the sunny, breezy gulf of Naples to the dark, cramped, humid streets of Oltrarno, filled with dyers, woolworkers, and the acrid vapours of their boilers, must have been harsh. We can imagine how the young Boccaccio perceived the difference between the refined customs and interactions at King Robert's court and those of the merchants and workers of Florence. His father's grief, and the recent deaths of Margherita di Giandonato de' Martoli and his half-brother Francesco, must have been hard to bear, too. His father had married Margherita around 1320, when Giovanni was about seven years old. She had served as a surrogate mother to him and was Francesco's mother. This must have weighed on his heart in that home so "mute, and exceedingly sad" ("muta e molto trista"; *Comedia delle ninfe fiorentine* XLIX 77).

The Florence residence of Boccaccino di Chellino was situated in the heart of Oltrarno, bordered on one side by via di Piazza and on the other by via di Mezzo (today, via Guicciardini and via Toscanella) towards Sdrucciolo dei Pitti. Only a few steps away from their home was (and still is) the piazza with the church of Santo Spirito of the Hermits of Saint Augustine. Boccaccino's family belonged to the *popolo* who lived in the parish of Santa Felicita, in an area that was the traditional residence of families from the Val d'Elsa, where Certaldo is located, in the southernmost part of the *gonfalone* (sector) del Nicchio. The church of Santa Felicita of the Benedictine nuns was associated with the powerful and ancient magnate family of Guelf knights of the de' Rossi d'Oltrarno: the chapel to the right of the altar belonged to them and the convent's abbess was a Rossi;[2] a column erected in front of the church commemorates the victory over the Patarini heretics led by Stoldo di Berlinghiero de' Rossi in 1244. The entrance to the *gonfalone* del Nicchio was through Ponte Vecchio, where the Rossi towers still stand and the Platea de Rubeis was located, until the 1320s;[3] Boccaccio's family must have maintained close neighbourly relations with the Rossi from when they had lived in Certaldo. Indeed, when Boccaccio drew up his will in 1374, the house in which he died shared a wall with Fornaino di Andrea di Benghi de' Rossi.[4]

Oltrarno was then one of the six wards or *sestieri* of Florence, located in the southern part of the city, *ultra Arnum*, that is, across the bank of the River Arno, which originally protected the city limits from enemy incursions. Over time, Florence expanded well beyond its own natural defences, to accommodate a growing population, lured from the Florentine countryside and Tuscan rural areas by burgeoning opportunities for employment and dreams of wealth. The original Roman walls of the city were limited at first, but they started to expand in the 1200s, when the city almost doubled in size; in 1333, a third set of more extensive walls – even larger – was completed (and remained in place up until the modern era). Obviously, the expansion of the city during the 1200s was enormous. This is due to the growing importance of Florence in the world of business: the city then was one of the most important centres of commerce in Europe.

---

2 See Fiorelli Malesci 1986, esp. 159–62, 294, doc. 35; Richa 1972, vol. 9, 322–35.

3 The Platea de Rubeis was demolished by an ordinance dated 31 March 1321, to enlarge the direct route to Siena, which went straight through the *gonfalone* del Nicchio. See in this regard Sznura 1975, 119, n. 86. For the Rossi family in general, see (in addition to the most important chronicles of the time, such as those by Marchionne di Coppo Stefani and by Giovanni and Matteo Villani) Ciabani 1992, vol. 4; Ciabani 1998, 244; von Roon-Bassermann 1964; Regnicoli 2021b.

4 On the will, see Corazzini 1877, 428. The persistent physical proximity, in Certaldo and Florence, of the families da Certaldo and de' Rossi suggests to Emanuela Porta Casucci a blood relationship (Porta Casucci 2015–16, 196, n. 15).

After 1333, Oltrarno was surrounded by new walls, tracing a shape like a cone with a southward-directed point. On the other side of these walls was a moat filled by the waters of the Arno. Oltrarno was connected to the rest of the city by four bridges: the Ponte Rubaconte (today called delle Grazie), the Ponte Vecchio (built on the site of an older bridge of Roman origin), and the more recent bridges Ponte Nuovo and Santa Trinita. Each bridge was under the control of one of the four most prominent magnate families of Oltrarno: de' Bardi had control over Ponte Rubaconte; de' Rossi over Ponte Vecchio; Frescobaldi over Santa Trinita, erected by Lamberto Frescobaldi in 1252; and the Nerli family over Ponte Nuovo (today called alla Carraia). Thanks to this form of urban planning, Oltrarno was able to resist potential enemy attacks from outside the walls and be sealed off from the rest of the city by closing the bridges, creating a city within a city, an isolated fortress. This situation occurred at least twice: once, during the Bardi conspiracy of 1340 and, again, during the riot against the Duke of Athens on 26 July 1343. These historical circumstances help us understand to what extent this part of the city sensed its own distinct identity.

Oltrarno had been the last district of the city to be urbanized, and it was home to many residents who had immigrated from the countryside, the so-called *gente nuova*, who had been denounced by Dante in *Inferno* 16.73 and labelled with the moral decadence of the city: "The new crowd with their sudden profits" (trans. Hollander) ("la gente nuova e i sùbiti guadagni"). These embodied the newly enriched mercantile element, which had a profound influence on the history of Florence in the fourteenth century. At the time, as with the rest of Florence, the *sestiere* of Oltrarno was a mixture of fabulously wealthy magnates, *grassi popolani* of the major guilds, *popolani* of the minor guilds, and *popolo minuto*. This last category was composed of unorganized and unpropertied labourers, most of whom were salaried workers for the guild of wool manufacturers and merchants in the area of the church of San Frediano. Even today, many streets in this part of Florence are dedicated to them: via dei Tessitori commemorates the poor houses that had looms in constant operation, day and night; via dei Cardatori keeps alive the memory of the cardoons that combed and cleaned the wool in the area around the Gate of San Frediano; via Sant'Onofrio is named after the patron saint of dyers, whose corporation was based there for a while. After the cloth had been washed and stretched, it was dyed, for only then would it assume the value and especially the price accorded to Florentine fabrics. Via delle Caldaie included a cluster of different dyers' workshops, and it took its name from the large cauldrons in which the materials were soaked for colouring (Ciabani 1998, 217).

Oltrarno was also home to prominent magnate families, who were more or less aristocratic: some were descended from the feudal nobility of Tuscany, some not. The magnates were a juridically defined class, well known for being composed of economically powerful families. The decisive criteria for this status were not nobility or antiquity or wealth, but the behavioural pattern of the family, and more specifically their reputation for violence and ostentation. To limit their power, between 1293 and 1295, the Signoria (spurred by Giano di Bella) promulgated the Ordinances of Justice (*Ordinanze di giustizia*): the magnates were subjected to numerous restrictions and heavier penalties, and they were excluded from the priorate and the major offices, the city's executive magistracy.[5] The most prominent family in Oltrarno was that of the Bardi, together with the Rossi (who had been decorated and proud holders of "golden-spurred knighthoods," *cavalieri spron d'oro*, for generations) and the Frescobaldi.

The Bardi, who belonged to the *gonfalone* delle Scale (the easternmost sector in Oltrarno), initially settled in the Borgo Pidiglioso, home of the poorest residents in the entire city, the "lice-ridden" *pidocchiosi* who lived in hovels exposed to flooding from the Arno and landslides from the hills of San Giorgio, just beyond the Ponte Vecchio. But as their mercantile and banking activities grew and added to their wealth over the years, the Bardi built some beautiful buildings in the same area: Borgo Pidoglioso developed into Via de' Bardi. In the first half of the fourteenth century, the Bardi Company, with the Peruzzi and the Acciaiuoli companies, was considered the financial engine of the city. Over the thirteenth and fourteenth centuries, the Bardi family indeed managed to make astounding progress through the creation of a "super-company" (as defined by Edwin S. Hunt) with branches throughout the world, whose holdings would eclipse those of some modern multinational corporations.[6]

> For the Peruzzi and Acciaiuoli, the grain trade of southern Italy was the principal target and reason for being super-companies. The Peruzzi Company was not involved on the same scale in the other great commodity of medieval commerce, wool, until late in its history, while the Acciaiuoli were never a significant participant. The Bardi Company, the largest of them all, was unique in being a major player in both trades over a considerable stretch of time. (Hunt 1994, 243)

Nevertheless, 1338 marked the climax of this economic enterprise and the beginning of a decade of unforeseeable misfortunes and announced disasters. The Bardi, just like the super-company of the Peruzzi (and to some extent that of the Frescobaldi), concentrated too many of their financial assets in the hands of a single individual, the King of England, Edward III, to finance the Hundred Years'

---

5 Scholarship on the magnates is long and complicated, often contentious, and every account risks being imprecise and reductive. The major works in this historiographical tradition include Salvemini 1899; Ottokar 1962; Becker 1967–8; Guidi 1981, vol. 2, 121–9; Lansing 1991; Dameron 1992; Zorzi 1994 and 1995; and Diacciati 2011.

6 For a detailed analysis, see Hunt 1994. On Bardi, always fundamental is Sapori 1926.

War. Giovanni Villani estimates that the sums lent to Edward III by the companies of the Bardi and the Peruzzi "were worth an entire kingdom" ("valeano un reame"; 1990–1, 12.88): the final figure was about 1,365,000 florins. He continues:[7]

> This amount contained a good number of transactions made by them in favour of the said king in the past years; however it went, they were out of their mind to put so much of their own and others' money in the hands of one lord, either out of greed for new profits or in order to recoup what they had insanely lent in the past ... And this put both themselves and our city in jeopardy ... As a result, owing to their inability to cover what they owed in England and in Florence and in other places where they had business, they entirely lost their credibility and failed to repay, especially the Peruzzi, even if they did not cease thanks to the considerable possessions in Florence and in the countryside, as well as their power and status within the Commune. But because of this default ... the power and status of all the Florentine merchants were almost ruined; for sure, all the traders and every guild lost value and greatly reduced their status ... so, after the failure of the said two columns of Florence – whose power, when they were in good status, supported with their trades most of the trade of Christian merchants almost like nourishment – every merchant was as a result now suspected and mistrusted.

> (Ben avea in questa somma assai quantità di provisioni fatte a·lloro per lo detto re per li tempi passati; ma come che si fosse, fu la loro gran follia per cupidigia di guadagno o per raquistare il loro follemente prestato mettere così grosso il loro e l'altrui inn'uno signore ... E di ciò fu il grande pericolo a·lloro e alla nostra città ... E·cche n'avenne che per cagione di ciò non potendo rispondere a cui dovieno dare in Inghilterra, e in Firenze, e in altre parti dove avieno a·ffare, e del tutto perderono la credenza, e fallirono di pagamento, ispezialmente i Peruzzi, con tutto che non si cessassono per le loro grandi posessioni ch'avieno in Firenze e nel contado, e per loro grande potenzia e stato ch'avieno in Comune. Ma per questa disfalta ... molto mancò la potenzia e stato di mercatanti di Firenze; e però di tutto il Comune e·lla mercatantia e ogni arte n'abassò, e vennero in pessimo stato ... però che fallite le dette due colonne, che per la loro potenzia, quando erano in buono stato, condivano colli loro traffichi gran parte del traffico della mercantantia di Cristiani, ed erano quasi uno alimento, onde ogn'altro mercatante ne fu sospetto e male creduto.)

In reality, according to a more recent study by Edwin Hunt (1994, 207, 245–6), the two "columns" did not go bankrupt when Edward was unable to pay them

7 Even though their background and bias limit the usefulness of their records, Giovanni Villani and Marchionne di Coppo Stefani are the two most prominent chroniclers for the narrative of political history in fourteenth-century Florence. See Clarke 2007.

back: they continued, for example, to make loans during 1340–1.[8] Villani's account may well be false and biased, however compelling and reflective of a perceived reality. In the perspective offered by modern economic historians, one of the main problems was a shrinking population. In the 1340s, there was famine throughout Europe, devastating floods in Florence, and waves of pandemic before the serious outbreak of plague in 1348 that reduced the European population by as least one-third. The super-companies were trading in first-need commodities, and the decreasing demographics made them unable to exist at that size any more. No other super-company took their place afterward (Hunt 1994, 247). In sum, there was a collapse of the relationship of supply and demand.

As for the financial crisis of the Bardi, even Boccaccino di Chellino probably incurred losses. On 5 November 1339, his son Francesco sold to Francesco di Simone de' Canigiani, an associate of the Bardi Company, a house in Santa Felicita adjacent to that of the Canigiani, purchased only six years before on 31 August 1333 by the newly emancipated Francesco himself from the same Canigiani family. Boccaccino also appears to have borrowed 360 gold florins from his mother-in-law, Lippa Portinari.[9]

However this may be, as soon as Giovanni Boccaccio reached Florence, the atmosphere must have been grim in his father's household, with economic hardships compounded by the deaths of his stepmother and half-brother. Furthermore, either concurrent with or just before his arrival, Florence had witnessed what has gone down in history as the Bardi conspiracy, whose primary ringleaders were the magnates belonging to the *sestiere d'Oltrarno*: Bardi, Rossi, and Frescobaldi, helped by powerful outsider families. According to Giovanni Villani, these families organized this "great conspiracy," as the chronicler called it ("grande congiurazione"; 1990–1, 12.118–19), in reaction of the abuse of power they had suffered at the hands of the mercantile oligarchy ruling the city.

The Bardi Conspiracy of 1340

On All Saints' Day, 1 November 1340, sixteen members of the Bardi family, together with others from the Frescobaldi and the Rossi families, joined in a conspiracy against the Commune. The *casus belli* was the reelection to the office of "captain of the guards and keeper of the peace and of state of the city" (*capitano*

8 The real reasons for the bankruptcies of the super-companies have been debated largely by economic historians. See Sapori 1926; Beardwood 1931; Fryde 1949–50, 1952, 1955; and Hunt 1994.

9 On Francesco di Simone de' Canigiani, see Sapori (1926, 264); on the documentation for the house, see Agostini Muzzi (1978, 638–9, 646–7); on the borrowing of money from the mother-in-law, see Branca (1997, 53), Agostini Muzzi (1978, 649), and Regnicoli 2018.

della guardia e conservatore di pace e di stato de la città) of Jacopo de' Gabrielli da Gubbio. This office had been created in 1335 by the faction in power with the official task of guaranteeing public order. The captain had been granted unlimited authority to proceed against criminals, including immediate executive powers to dispense penal and capital justice unhampered by statutory procedures. Basically, as Giovanni Villani (1990–1, 12.39) states: "Dispensing blood justice as they saw fit, without following the statutes" ("Faccendo iustizia di sangue come li piacea, senza ordine di statute"; also, Stefani 1910, rubr. 510). The captain was always a foreigner – as was the case for many other offices, such as *podestà* (chief magistrate), *capitano del popolo* (captain of the people), and *esecutore degli ordinamenti di Giustizia* (executor of the Ordinances of Justice) – and he had at his disposal fifty horsemen and one hundred infantrymen. His office had replaced the seven *bargellini* (sergeants) established in 1334, who had served as captains of the guard, each provided with twenty-five infantrymen, one for each district (Oltrarno had two such sergeants). According to Giovanni Villani (1990–1, 12.16), the captain and his guards' true goal was to protect the governing regime and to intimidate its enemies:

> Those who ruled the city did so more to preserve and to consolidate their own status, because they feared that the new reformation of the election of the priors, set for the following January, could be contested, as certain *popolani* who were eligible for the office had been excluded.
>
> (Quelli che reggeano la città il feciono più per loro guardia e francamento di loro stato, perché dubitavano ch'a la nuova reformazione de la lezione de' priori, che·ssi dovea fare il gennaio apresso, non avesse contesa, perché certi popolani ch'erano degni d'essere al detto oficio per sette n'erano schiusi.)

He is frank in his characterization of Jacopo de' Gabrielli (12.118):

> An impetuous, cruel, and bloodthirsty man ... Like a tyrant or a tyrant's executor, he engaged in civil and criminal suits as he wished, just like the rulers had allowed, without following laws or statutes; as result he unjustly convicted the person and confiscated the property of many innocent people, and he terrified people of both the high and the low status, everyone except his own rulers, who through his stick carried out their own vendettas, as well as the occasional offences and corruption.
>
> (uomo sùbito e credule e carnefice ... Il quale a guisa di tiranno, o come esecutore di tiranni, procedea di fatto in civile e cherminale a sua volontà, come gli era posto in mano per li detti reggenti, senza seguire leggi o statuti, onde molti innocenti condannò a·ttorto inn-avere e in persona, e tenea i cittadini grandi e piccoli in grande

tremore, salvo i suoi reggenti, che col suo bastone faceano le loro vendette e talora l'offese e·lle baratterie.)

The Bardi conspiracy was thus conceived to get rid of Jacopo de' Gabrielli and his entire office, and, of course, to overturn the ruling power: "to remake the State in Florence" ("rifare in Firenze nuovo stato"; G. Villani 1990–1, 12.118).[10] The Bardi were joined by other magnates in Oltrarno, such as Frescobaldi and Rossi, but in particular they were expecting support from outside forces on foot and on horse: Count Marcovaldo, Conti Guidi, the Tarlati of Arezzo, the Pazzi of Valdarno, Ubertini and Ubaldini from the Apennines, the Guazzalotti of Prato, the Belforti of Volterra,[11] and others (G. Villani 1990–1, 12.118). The plan had been elaborated in detail, and the foreign reinforcements would have been overwhelming, but the conspiracy was unravelled by an informer. Andrea de' Bardi entrusted the secret treaty to his brother-in-law Jacopo degli Alberti, who did not hesitate to warn the priors. In the evening of All Saints' Day 1340, a warning bell rang out, and the whole city took up arms, shouting, "Long live the people and death to the traitors!" ("viva il popolo e muoiano i traditori!"). The gates of the city were barred to the allies of the conspirators.

The Oltrarno conspirators sought shelter in their own part of the city, guarding Ponte Vecchio with their weapons, particularly volleys of arrows launched from their homes and turrets on the leaders on the bridge, and they set fire to two other wooden bridges: Ponte di Santa Trinita and Ponte alla Carraia. In this way, nobody was able to cross the Arno, and Oltrarno became almost a fortified island. The Bardi and their associates dug in, waiting for outside reinforcements.

The day was saved by the *podestà* of Florence – Maffeo da Poncarale, originally from Brescia, on whom the character of Negro da Ponte Carraro, "a gentleman," was based in the *Decameron* IV.6 (Piacentini 2014, esp. 134–41) – who managed to brave the danger and cross Ponte Rubaconte on horseback with his companions. He went to negotiate with the conspirators, and with a mixture of "sensible words and polite threats" ("savie parole e cortesi minacce"; G. Villani 1990–1, 12.118), he was successful in escorting them out of the city under his protection, without allowing bloodshed, arson, or looting among the populace.

10 The anonymous writer of the *Istorie pistolesi* (1835, 345–6) echoes this version; still, the underlying motivations of the conspiracy remain unclear, but there is no doubt that they wished to abolish the Ordinances of Justice, as well as remedy their precarious economic condition. On the possible reasons behind the conspiracy, see Sapori (1926, 117–25), F.P. Tocco (2001, 50), or Najemy (2006, 134–5).

11 On 3 November 1340, Cecchino di Cacciaguerra wrote a letter to Ottaviano Belforti about this conspiracy, naming only the men who were banned: seven from the Bardi household and three from Frescobaldi's.

Only a few days later, after the conspirators had taken shelter within their properties outside Florence, the Commune delivered its verdict against them. The list included thirty-six convicted, all from Oltrarno: fifteen Bardi, thirteen Frescobaldi (among whom was Niccolò di Guido Frescobaldi, who eventually joined the plot planned for 31 December 1360), two Rossi,[12] one Nerli, and five men from the countryside.[13] Their properties within the city and in the countryside were demolished or broken.[14] But this was not the end of it. The Bardi and the Frescobaldi, together with some members of the Adimari and the Pazzi, attempted another coup just over a year later, which concluded with the beheading of Schiatta de' Frescobaldi and the conviction of his accomplices (G. Villani 1990–1, 12.119).

There is no connection between these events and Boccaccino, father of our Giovanni. Nonetheless, the proven relationships between him and the Bardi family would add anxiety in a period already difficult for economic and personal reasons. Perhaps Fiammetta, trying to keep her beloved Panfilo in Naples, refers to these events when she says that Florence is "torn by strife and war within and without, and is turbulent and filled with haughty, avaricious, and envious people and with innumerable troubles; and all these things are ill-suited to your spirit" ("tutta in arme e in guerra così cittadina come forestiere fremisce, di superba, avara e invidiosa gente fornita, e piena d'innumerabile sollecitudini: cose tutte male all'animo tuo conformi"; *Fiamm.* II 20).[15]

"Endeavour to Make One or More Friends"

Despite the unfavourable climate, Giovanni Boccaccio had to fit in with his new environment. Upon his return to Florence, he likely rekindled his friendship with his old schoolmate Zanobi da Strada, and contacted the *literates* in Florence: notaries who were also translating classics of antiquity into the vernacular, such as

12 Villani implies that the number of Rossi family members who took part was higher: Salvestrino and Roberto di Bandino de' Rossi, "plus other relatives who had a hand in it, stayed out of sight" ("più altri de' suoi consorti che vi tenieno mano, non si mostrarono"; G. Villani 1990–1, 12.118).

13 ASFi, *PR* 30, ff. 27r–v. The Commune targeted only some of the conspirators: "it was decided to proceed only against those corporals who had presented themselves in arms, and for these a summons was issued; and when they did not answer immediately, they were condemned in their possessions and in their persons as rebels and traitors to the Commune" ("solamente si procedesse contro a quelli caporali che si mostraro e furono in arme, i quali furono citati e richesti; e non comparendo subitamente furono condannati nell'avere e nelle persone, siccome ribelli e traditore del loro Comune"; G. Villani 1990–1, 12.119).

14 ASFi, *PR* 30, ff. 27v and 37r–v; G. Villani 1990–1, 12.119; *Istorie pistolesi* (1835, 348).

15 On this connection, see also Regnicoli 2018.

Filippo Ceffi, translator of Ovid's *Heroides*, or Andrea Lancia, translator of Seneca and of Virgil's *Aeneid* by request of Coppo Domenichi. Boccaccio probably also contacted his father's friend Giovanni Villani, the chronicler of the history of Florence, as well as Chancellor Ventura Monachi, who composed political and satirical sonnets, and the town crier, Antonio Pucci.[16] These were all examples of the kind of civic humanism that was later common in the Republic of Florence, of citizens who worked on behalf of the Republic and who shared a taste and passion for literature and historiography in a variety of different forms and functions.[17] Furthermore, Boccaccio was eager to meet the many "illustrious men" whom he lists in his *Zibaldone Magliabechiano* (f. 190v, published in Hortis 1879), among them Coppo di Borghese Domenichi, whom he identifies as the "greatest patriot and father of morals" ("amantissumus reipublicae et morum pater") and whose memory he also praises in other works; for example, in the *Decameron*: "a man of great and venerable authority in our time, and an illustrious person for his decorum and virtues more than for noble lineage, and worthy to be remembered forever" ("uomo di grande e reverenda auttorità ne' dì nostri, e per costume e per vertù molto più che per nobiltà di sangue chiarissimo e degno d'eterna fama"; V.9.4).[18] In his *Zibaldone Magliabechiano*, he made copies of the genealogical lists compiled by Forese Donati and Franceschino degli Albizzi (in Hortis 1879, 537). Although these highly knowledgeable friends were undoubtedly stimulating and

16 For Ventura Monachi, see Faibisoff and Robins 2019. On relations with Filippo Ceffi, see Trotta 1995. Luca Azzetta has studied the relationship between Boccaccio and Lancia (2001, 28–36). Boccaccio's cordial friendship with Pucci goes back to his earliest days in Florence, as shown by Antonio Enzo Quaglio (1976, 27–8). Several of these men had connections with one another that spanned many generations. For example, Boccaccino di Chellino was certainly a friend to Giovanni Villani – we find them both as witnesses to the marriage between Monna Selvaggia di Luto di Maso and Gherardino del fu messer Botte de' Guernieri da Certaldo in 1333 (ASFi, *Notarile Antecosimiano*, S.96; Agostini Muzzi 1978, 638) – and Villani's chronicles were often known to Boccaccio before their "publication" (Branca 1997, 59). Villani was also a friend to Andrea Lancia, who resided in the *gonfalone* delle Chiavi in San Pier Maggiore, the same one in which Boccaccino had his first home in Florence (Azzetta 2001, 18, 28). Villani is connected to several literary projects: he had commissioned a translation from Zanobi da Strada of the *Somnium Scipionis* (Billanovich 1994; Brambilla 2000); and Antonio Pucci was given permission by Villani's family to render into tercets Villani's *Nuova Cronica*. This project mostly likely never came to fruition because of a lawsuit between the sons of Antonio Pucci and those of Matteo Villani (Robins 2000, 56–8).

17 See Billanovich 1996, Hankins 2000, and the latest work of Witt (2012).

18 He is included in the *Epistles* addressed to Zanobi da Strada (VI 10, written in 1348, and IX 10, in 1353) and in the *Esposizioni*, VIII esp. litt. 68 and XVI 16. See also novellas 66 and 137 by Sacchetti (2014), and articles by Francesco Bruni (1997) and Kara Gaston (2018). Folio 190v corresponds to folio 232v, which is the page numbering from the sixteenth-century posted on the upper corner right of the parchment (Pier Giorgio Ricci and Maria Aldo Constantini follow the old page numbering).

beneficial, Boccaccio was looking for a more socially elevated audience within Florence to be his patrons.

In fourteenth-century Florence, the norms of social integration were premised on unwritten guidelines, nicely summarized by Giovanni di Pagolo Morelli, who writes in his *Memorie* (*Memories*) for his son:

> Endeavor to make one or more friends in your *gonfalone* and to do good things to them … Do your best to forge relationships with good citizens who are well loved, and powerful. And ingratiate yourself with anyone in your *gonfalone* who can help you get ahead. If you can get to him by means of a family relationship, do so. And if you cannot, then seek out his company yourself, associate with his friends, make an effort to do him favors … If you can, first look in your own *gonfalone* for a spouse, and if you can find someone there, do it there rather than someplace else. If you can't find the right person in your own *gonfalone*, look in the immediate neighborhood – don't go any further afield … But first look in your own *gonfalone*, then in the neighborhood. (Morelli 2013, 152–3, 156, trans. Baca)

> (ingegnati d'acquistare uno amico o più nel tuo gonfalone e per lui fa ciò che tu puoi di buono … ingegnati d'imparentarti con buoni cittadini e amati e potenti; e se è nel tuo gonfalone chi ti possa atare e metterti innanzi, accostati a esso. Se puoi per via di parentado, fallo; se non per questa via, usa con lui, pratica co' suoi, ingegnati di servirlo … primamente cerca nel tuo gonfalone, e se ivi puoi imparentarti, fallo più avaccio che altrove; se non puoi o non v'è quello ti bisogna o ti sodisfaccia, cerca nel quartiere; e di quivi non uscire … prima nel gonfalone, appresso nel quartiere.)

In accordance with this kind of dynamic, Giovanni Boccaccio found in Niccolò di Bartolo del Buono[19] his "only friend, and the truest example of real friendship" ("solo amico, e di vera amistà veracissimo essemplo"), as he writes in the dedication at the end of the *Comedia delle ninfe fiorentine* (L 3), the first Florence-based work in which mixed feelings emerge towards his new hometown.[20] Niccolò di Bartolo del Buono also resided in the *gonfalone* del Nicchio, but Boccaccio must have first met him in Naples, where del Buono served as agent for the Peruzzi Company from 12 March 1336 until his resignation on 15 September 1342 (Sapori 1926, 161, n. 1). In

19 On Niccolò di Bartolo del Buono, see Klein 1988; the appendix of *Accusare e proscrivere* by Mazzoni 2010, 180; and finally, Porta Casucci 2015–16, esp. 189–92.

20 The *Comedia delle ninfe fiorentine*, also titled *Ninfale d'Ameto* or simply *Ameto*, is a partially autobiographical mix of prose and verse composed between 1341 and 1342, dedicated to del Buono on his return to Florence in the second half of September 1342. Erotic novellas are narrated by a group of nymphs, and the work's narrative structure anticipates that of the *Decameron* to such an extent that in the sixteenth century it was referred to as the *piccolo Decameron* by Francesco Sansovino in his Venetian edition from 1558. A good introduction is given by Tylus 2013.

the context of Boccaccio's move, del Buono must have been an initial intermediary for him between the worlds of Naples and Florence. Gene Brucker described del Buono and Luca di Feo Ugolini as "parvenu merchants of mediocre rank" (1962, 185), and in reality del Buono was not an admirer of literary endeavours, but this did not stop Boccaccio from appealing for his patronage with a grandiose dedication, applying the encomiastic motifs typical of the court of Anjou to mercantile Florence:

> And you, my only friend, and the truest example of real friendship, Niccolò di Bartolo del Buono di Firenze, whose virtues my verses could not be sufficient to describe (and therefore I shall be silent, since they so shine by themselves that they have no need of my labors), take this rose, which was born among the thorns of my adversities, which the Florentine beauty, presenting itself to me to design with brief delight, wrenched from the rigid thistles while I dwelled in deepest gloom. And receive this the way that the good Augustus took the highly esteemed verses from Virgil, or Herennius took the like from Cicero, or from Horace, Maecenas took his, recalling to your memory the authority of Cato, who said: "When a poor friend presents you with a small gift, receive it agreeably." Indeed, I send this to you, who have such valor, avowing no other person to be my Caesar, or my Herennius or my Maecenas, except Niccolò. (*L'Ameto*, trans. Serafini-Sauli, 145)

> (E tu, o solo amico, e di vera amistà veracissimo essemplo, o Niccolò di Bartolo del Buono di Firenze, alle virtù del quale non basterieno i miei versi, e però tacciole avegna che sì per se medesime lucono che di mia fatica non hanno bisogno, prendi questa rosa, tra le spine della mia avversità nata, la quale a forza fuori de' rigidi pruni tirò la fiorentina bellezza, me nell'infimo stante delle tristizie, dando sé a me con corto diletto a disegnarsi. E questa non altrimenti ricevi che da Virgilio il buono Augusto o Erennio da Cicerone, o come da Orazio il suo Mecena prendevano i cari versi, nella memoria riducendoti l'autorità di Catone dicente: – Quando il povero amico un picciolo dono ti presenta, piacevolmente il ricevi. – Certo io a te valoroso cotale la mando, sentendo nullo altro a me essere Cesare, Erennio o Mecena, se non Niccolò.) (834–5)

Boccaccio has no qualms about using the names Caesar, Herennius, and Maecenas, or even "the good Augustus," to refer to del Buono, a merchant enrolled in the Guild of Por Santa Maria, the least exclusive of the seven major guilds in Florence (it included silk merchants, cap makers, hat makers, doublet makers, hosiers, mattress makers, and goldsmiths).[21] At the same time, he describes himself as occupying the lowest level of "poor friend," "in the lowest condition of misery," who writes his work "among the thorns of my adversities." It is fundamental to highlight that this first work composed in Florence is not dedicated to a magnate

21 For a comprehensive presentation of the guilds of Florence, see Giuliani 2006 and Artusi 2005.

but to a *popolano grasso* of his own *gonfalone*, a "parvenu," "a new man." As Emanuela Porta Casucci points out (2015–16, 191), del Buono's family was consistently engaged in the political and administrative life of the city between 1343 and 1348, which was the period of more openness towards the lower classes; these were the years of the "popular government," spanning from the fall of the Duke of Athens to the plague outbreak.[22] For example, after 1 July 1347, del Buono and others (among them, Piero di Lapo da Castiglionchio) took up the lucrative contract for the *gabella del sale* (office for the tax on salt) for four years.[23] After the plague, in unscrupulous advancement of his own interests, del Buono veered in the opposite direction. After 1350 he became an associate of the bankers from Uzzano, satellites of the Bardi super-company, and after 1352 he drew visibly closer to the Guelf aristocracy of Florentine finance, enrolling among the bankers of the Arte del Cambio in 1353 and eventually founding a private bank in 1360, only a few months before his execution.

Clearly encomiastic, in tercets, modelled on the *Caccia di Diana* (*Diana's Hunt*)[24] – which had enjoyed such success at the Anjou court of Naples – and perhaps influenced by the work of his fellow citizen and friend Antonio Pucci (*Leggiadro sermintese, pien d'amore*),[25] Boccaccio tried his hand at a *serventese* as well: in *Contento quasi ne' pensier d'amore* (*Almost happy in the thoughts of love*), he imagines "twelve damsels," all belonging to wealthy magnate families of Florence,

---

22 It would appear that del Buono enjoyed a remote connection to the da Certaldo family: Emanuela Porta Casucci claims that Vanni di Manetto del Buono, Niccolò's cousin, was related by marriage to the Velluti family from Santa Felicita, as was the da Certaldo family.

23 He was a holder, for example, of the contract of the Gabella del Sale for the city and countryside of Florence for four years after July 1347, together with a cousin, a member of the Del Bene family, and a son of the super-Guelf magnate Lapo da Castiglionchio (ASFi, *CCNCE* 1, ff. 3v, 10r, 23r–23v): see Porta Casucci 2015–16, 191, n. 5.

24 This is the first work by Giovanni Boccaccio, written in 1334 while he was in Naples. The *Caccia di Diana* is a pretext to celebrate fifty noblewomen at the core of Neapolitan society. During a hunting expedition, led by Diana, Boccaccio takes the sombre, distinctly aristocratic tradition of the *serventese* in a new and suggestive direction by means of those huntress characters, representing women who were alive and recognizable, in the miniaturist guise typical of the late Middle Ages. In Italy, the *serventese* genre had not enjoyed the same prestige as beyond the Alps except for the "pìstol disguised as a servantese," written by Dante to pay tribute to the sixty most beautiful ladies of the city ("li nomi di LX le più belle donne della cittade"), as we learn from the *Vita nuova* (II 11). On *Caccia di Diana*, see the edition by Cassell and Kirkham in English translation (*Diana's Hunt*, 1991); Saiber 2013; and Iocca's edition of *Caccia di Diana* (2016).

25 Antonio Pucci wrote his *Leggiadro sermintese, pien d'amore* (known also as *Serventese in ricordo delle belle donne ch'erano in Firenze nel 1335*) in 1335, probably inspired by Dante's lost work. Generally, Pucci's *serventese* is associated with Boccaccio's *Contento quasi nel pensier d'amore* not only because of its genre and because the same feminine characters recur, but also because the poets were close friends. In this regard, see Massera 1931; Ferreri 1970; Quaglio 1976; Bettarini Bruni 1980; Bendinelli Predelli 2006; and Banella 2015.

dancing "over beautiful flowers and beneath green foliage" ("sopra bei fiori e sotto verde fronda"; 65) and singing a ballad, *Amor, dolce signore*.[26] As in *Caccia di Diana*, the names of the beautiful women and the other characters are often identifiable. Monna Itta was the daughter of Neri de' Tornaquinci, probably wife of Piero Pantaleoni, deceased in 1354.[27] Meliana, whose real name was Emilia, was the wife of the apothecary Giovanni di Nello, who died in 1347.[28] Lisa and Pecchia were the daughters of Ranieri di Marignano de' Buondelmonti. Lisa married Simone di Chiaro Peruzzi in 1335 and died in 1363: by her request, Filippo Ceffi rendered Ovid's *Heroides* into the vernacular, and her husband, Simone, commissioned Persius's *Satires*.[29] Other recognizable women include Boccaccio's beloved Fiammetta, Monna Vanna, the beautiful woman from Lombardy, and Filippa de' Bardi, daughter of Filippozzo di Gualtierotto de' Bardi and Caterina di Vieri de' Cerchi, who married Ser Francesco Rinuccini in 1342; her son was Cino, the well-known composer of rhymes, who was devoted to Boccaccio (Filippo di Cino Rinuccini 1840, 59, 119; Branca 1990, 293, n.1). Five more women can be added to this list: Monna Lottiera, daughter of Odoaldo della Tosa, who married Nerone di Nigi Dietisalvi, elected prior many times and also gonfalonier of justice;[30]

---

26 In the collection of *Rime*, ed. Vittore Branca, it is number 69, as in the Lanza edition. This tercet is preserved in a single manuscript (MS 53 of the Accademia della Crusca in Florence), but is absent from the Bartolini collection. Roberto Leporatti's edition (2013) includes it among twenty-seven other lyrics not in Bartolini; it is assigned the number 125[a], immediately followed by ballad 125[b], which completes it, forming a polymetric. On the interesting manuscript tradition of this polymetric, see Leporatti (*Rime* 2013, 339–50). Here and elsewhere I am using Leporatti's edition.

27 This is Vittore Branca's suggestion in his notes to the Mondadori edition of *Rime* (1992, 252, n. 34). An Itta, wife of Piero Pantaleoni of the *popolo* of San Pietro del Buonconsiglio, can be found also in the *Prammatica* (2013, 355–66). Pantaleoni is described as a "pleasant man" ("piacevole uomo") in a novella by Sacchetti (1970, novella 178); according to the notes by Emilio Faccioli, he died probably in 1383.

28 On Gianni di Nello, see the bibliography by Vittore Branca in the Einaudi edition of the *Decameron* (1992, 796, n. 5). Meliana is a recurring character in Boccaccio's works: we find her in the *Comedìa delle ninfe fiorentine* (XXI 10) and in the *Amorosa visione* (XLIV 25 ff.). Billanovich suggested (1947b, 105–27) that she may be one of the narrators of the *Decameron*; if this is true, then it is darkly ironic that the second version of the novella of the Fantàsima is narrated by none other than Emilia (*Dec.* VII.1), whose cuckolded husband in the narration might be both Gianni di Lotteringhi and also the apothecary Gianni di Nello.

29 For a reconstruction of the biography of Filippo Ceffi, see the introduction by Massimo Zaggia to Ovid's *Heroides* (2009). See also Azzetta and Ceccherini 2016, and Carrai 2016. For relations between Filippo Ceffi and Giovanni Boccaccio, see Trotta 1995.

30 In his edition of the *Rime*, Branca (1992, 253, nn. 50–1) claims that Lottiera may be the Mopsa of the *Comedìa delle ninfe fiorentine* (XVI–XVII), praised as extremely beautiful and worthy of a place next to Fiammetta in the *Amorosa visione* (XLIII 79 ff.). She was praised for her beauty in the *sermentese* by Pucci and in a delicate sonnet composed by another friend of Boccaccio (CXXVI), Sennuccio del Bene. Lottiera may have been named after his illustrious relative Lottieri di Odaldo della Tosa, Bishop of Florence 1301–9.

Vanna, wife of Filippo di Bartolo Filippi, prior in 1361, probably deceased before 1363 (*Rime*, ed. Branca [1992], 253, nn. 52–4); Sismonda, daughter of Francesco Scali and wife of Francesco di Tano Baroncelli, whose father was a shareholder of the Peruzzi Company (she was also a relative of Boccaccio's father's second wife, Beatrice de' Bostichi);[31] Niccolosa, daughter of Tedice Manovelli, who married Tommaso di Tegghiaio Altoviti before 1335; and finally, Bartolomea di Giovanni, called Beatrice, who is perhaps the Bartolomea di Gherardino di Gianni who married Nastagio di Lapo Bucelli, prior, in 1347.

If the *Comedìa delle ninfe fiorentine* was dedicated to a *popolano grasso* such as Niccolò di Bartolo del Buono, this *serventese* in 1342 celebrates twelve women whose identities are not always explicit but who shared a common characteristic; among the historically identifiable characters, many were daughters of magnates (Tornaquinci, Buondelmonti, de' Bardi, della Tosa, Scali) who married very rich *popolani* engaged in politics; some of those husbands were appointed to the most coveted office, that of prior (Simone Peruzzi, Francesco Rinuccini, Nerone di Nigi Dietisalvi, Francesco Baroncelli). Niccolosa, a *popolana*, married a magnate husband.

Women at the centre of courtly literature discussing love, especially women of a higher social status – intended as the addressees of love in the *De Amore*, the very popular treatise by Andreas Capellanus – served an ennobling and transfiguring function. In reality, this commonplace of the Tuscan literary tradition was not just a topos employed to moralize, via the figure of spiritually uplifting lovers with a gentle heart. One finds the same notion governing relationships in the real world of Florence at the time. Thanks to a deliberate practice in the arrangement of marriages, these women were the point of conjunction between the magnate class and the *grassi popolani* in Florence, at least for those families who were open to the idea of a "mixed" marriage. Behind this choice, we can find specific pragmatic motivations of power. After the creation of the Ordinances of Justice between 1293 and 1295 and the legislation that ensued, magnates were excluded from the highest and most powerful governing offices of the Republic of Florence, which were now open only to the *popolani* of the major guilds.[32] As noted by Christine Klapisch-Zuber (2009, 351) in

31 See Pampaloni 1964b; Hunt 1994, 265; Regnicoli 2018, n. 50. Bice de' Bostichi, second wife of Boccaccio's father, was related to Monna Sismonda: Francesco di Tano Baroncelli was in fact her mother's cousin (see the entries by Pampaloni in *DBI* on Gherardo and Tano Baroncelli).

32 The Ordinances of Justice excluded magnates from the highest offices of the Commune, but this restriction did not extend to the Counsels of the Podestà, where a number of seats were reserved for magnates; nor did the ordinances apply to the Guelf Party or to technical assignments or prestigious diplomatic and/or ambassadorial positions, where magnates were valued for their higher status and knightly insignia.

her detailed study on marriage alliances in Florence in this time, some families, such as the Frescobaldi,[33]

> looked for sons-in-law among the *popolani* no less than among the magnates, which gave them politically active male allies from both sides. But the introduction into their home of a magnate wife and magnate allies seems to have been less profitable than bringing in a *popolana* wife and family. In Florence, it would appear that the relations formed by the introduction of a wife in the family counted more than those formed by marrying off a daughter: a brother-in-law was more directly and immediately useful than a son-in-law.
>
> The marriage strategies of the Frescobaldi seem to have been based on class solidarity with the *popolani grassi*, from whom they recruited their more useful allies, at the expense of their magnate counterparts.
>
> (cercano i loro generi tanto fra i popolani quanto fra i magnati, il che procura loro degli alleati maschi attivi di entrambi i lati. Ma l'introduzione in casa loro di una sposa magnatizia e gli alleati magnati che essa porterà loro sembrano meno redditizi di una sposa popolana e della sua famiglia. A Firenze, i legami stretti dall'ingresso di donne nella famiglia contano probabilmente più di quelli conclusi con l'uscita delle figlie: il cognato è più direttamente e immediatamente utile del genero.
>
> Le strategie matrimoniali dei Frescobaldi sembrano fondarsi su una solidarietà di classe con i popolani grassi, dove essi reclutavano i loro alleati più utili a discapito dei loro consimili magnatizi.)

After considering larger samples and different analyses, Klapish-Zuber concludes: "Bardi, Cavalcanti, Pazzi, and Rossi, just like Tornaquinci and Frescobaldi, targeted instead the Popolo (grasso), and their marriages provide evidence of class solidarity with the most prominent men of the city" (2009, 367). Gaining a son-in-law or a *grasso popolano* brother-in-law engaged in politics (even from rich newcomers) allowed the great magnate families to intrude into the magistracies of Florence and have a better control of politics. In the present context, it is worth keeping in mind that the power players of Oltrarno (the Bardi, Rossi, and Frescobaldi) exhibited a striking openness to the *grassi popolani* in their marriage choices, on one hand establishing neighbourhood alliances that unified and consolidated Oltrarno in pursuit of its specific interests, and on the other hand adding the ability to direct, at least partially, the political decisions of the city.

33 Klapisch-Zuber examines the Frescobaldi, with material from Donato Velluti's *Cronica domestica*, written between 1367 and 1370. Velluti frequently mentions Frescobaldi allies as far back as the thirteenth century. Between the end of this century and the beginning of the next one, the Velluti, who were both merchants and *popolani*, had forged alliances in particular with the Rossi, of whom they were both clients and loyal friends, and with the Petriboni, Pulci, Buondelmonti, Lucardesi, and naturally the Frescobaldi (Klapish-Zuber 2009, 349–50).

Boccaccio's *serventese*, *Contento quasi ne' pensier d'amore*, offers praise to both *grassi popolani* and magnates, and the *Comedia delle ninfe fiorentine* was dedicated to a *popolano grasso* (del Buono). With his *Amorosa visione*, however, Boccaccio plunged once again into a militant literature addressed to the highest and noblest ranks of society. A pattern of encomiastic lists can be found in the *Amorosa visione*, which in cantos XLI–XLIV blends female personages from the spheres of Naples (Fiammetta, Giovanna, Agnese, and others) and Florence (Lia from the *Comedia delle ninfe florentine*, Emilia, Lottiera, Alinora, and others) in a fusion of past and present, which amounts to more than what Branca calls "the meeting of two worlds in the imagination of Boccaccio" (1976, 61). Indeed, Boccaccio's Neapolitan past had reappeared quite literally in his Florentine present over the summer of 1342, with the arrival of Margherita, wife of Walter of Brienne, Duke of Athens, and niece of King Robert. Brienne had been invited by Florence with the highest expectations; these were subsequently dashed horribly, but in the beginning, he was certainly welcomed and wanted. The *Amorosa visione* must have been completed in the short interlude when Brienne still found favour, in the fall of 1342, during the first months of his *signoria*, and definitely before 20 January 1343, when King Robert died (his granddaughter Giovanna is introduced as still Duchess of Calabria and not as the queen, *Am. vis.* XL 14–15). The verses that praise the wife of the future "tyrant" Duke of Athens, namely, Margherita, the daughter of Philip of Taranto (*Am. vis.* XLI 40–8), would otherwise make little sense. In these verses, Boccaccio pays tribute to the aristocracy of Naples he knows so well, as well as the beautiful ladies of the magnate class of Florence and, if we accept the identifications proposed in Branca's edition, also the *popolani grassi*. After the unidentifiable and beautiful lady of Lombardy (*Am. vis.* XL 40–88), we are given a slideshow of noblewomen of Naples,[34] interspersed with the Florentine "nymphs," the beautiful and mysterious goddesses who are the protagonists of the *Comedìa delle Ninfe fiorentine* and of the *Ninfale fiesolano*;[35] an anonymous nymph from Florence is followed by Lia, Elissa, and Emilia, whom we already met in the *Comedia*. After his beloved Fiammetta, we find three members

34 Agnese di Périgord, mother of Charles of Durazzo; Margherita, wife of the Duke of Athens; Giovanna, at the time Countess of Calabria and future Queen of Naples; a noblewoman of the House of Hungary who is harder to identify, who had close relations with the House of Anjou at the time; Andrea Acciaiuoli, future dedicatee of the *De mulieribus claris*, and at the time wife of the Count of Monteoderisio, Charles of Artus, an example of mixed marriage between the magnate class of Florence and the aristocracy of Naples; Delfina of Barasso; Eleonor of Aragon; Isabel of Ibelin, cousin of Hugo IV, future dedicatee of the *Genealogia deorum gentilium*; Giovanna, daughter of Giovanni, Count of Catanzaro of the Ruffo house.

35 The "nymphs" are not simply supernatural beings; they are associated with particular women of Florence, though they cannot always be identified. For possible identifications, see Branca's notes to the *Amorosa visione* (1974) and Massera (1931) on *Contento quasi ne' pensier d'amore*. Curti (2016a and 2016b) has studied the features of the Florentine nymph, a category unique to Boccaccio.

of the magnate class: Margherita degli Asini, Lottiera della Tosa, and Alinora Gianfigliazzi. The mix of Neapolitan aristocracy, Florentine magnates, and nymphs belonging to the *popolani* is introduced in previous cantos by the comparison of the nobility of the heart against the nobility of blood (*Am. vis.* XXXIII) and the role of fortune in distributing the equal souls created by God (*Am. vis.* XXXIV). The text, so conceived, was not only encomiastic but also political, trying to promote a society where the distinction of classes was only apparent and ephemeral.

Contento quasi ne' pensier d'amore and the *Amorosa visione* are similar in several ways. *Contento quasi ne' pensier d'amore* is a polymetric composition, a series of Dantean tercets, like the *Amorosa visione*, though it ends (unusually) in a ballad. Three of the five extant copies of *Contento quasi* reproduce it alongside the *Amorosa visione* and a third work, the *Caccia di Diana*, which is also written in terza rima. The fact that these three works are collected together and share a similar style supports the reading that all three had similar purposes. They also have content in common: a sequence of beautiful women, with considerable overlap. Two of the manuscript volumes that contain these works, the *Riccardiani* 1060 and 1066 manuscripts, include them in the following order: the *Caccia di Diana*, followed by *Contento quasi ne' pensier' d'amore* and *Amor, dolce signore*, ending with *Amorosa visione*. Roberto Leporatti, in his edition of Boccaccio's *Rime*, goes so far as to suggest that this grouping was probably put together by Boccaccio himself, and that *Contento quasi ne' pensier' d'amore* should therefore not be included in the more famous collection of Boccaccio's verse, the *Rime*: "The polymetric should not be included among the *Rime* because it belongs to a different work, whose composition took place much higher up the manuscript *stemma*, so high that we cannot exclude the possibility that the author himself was responsible for it" ("Il polimetro non dovrebbe figurare tra le *Rime*, perché appartiene a un'altra opera, la cui confezione ci porta molto in alto nello stemma, tanto in alto da non potersi escludere la responsabilità dell'autore"; *Rime*, ed. Leporatti [2013], 341). Leporatti's hypothesis tallies with an observation by Victoria Kirkham on Boccaccio's signature (1998): the reason why *Caccia di Diana* and the other two works are not signed by the author is because they were conceived together with the *Amorosa visione*, cantos XV and XVI of which are structured as an acrostic that spells out the name "Giovanni di Boccaccio da Certaldo." If this hypothesis is true, if this collection of works was indeed created by Boccaccio himself, then we can imagine that it was conceived and carried out during the months that celebrated the union of the magnate class of Florence with the aristocracy of Naples through the Court of Anjou.

In sum, with the arrival of the Duke of Athens, Boccaccio dusted off the encomiastic and militant motifs he had worked with in Naples to pay tribute to his new protectors among the governing class of Florence. He maintained his links to the Court of Anjou, also thanks to Niccolò Acciaiuoli. In fact, when Florence was under the rule of the Duke of Athens, Boccaccio, together with Coppo Stefani, the father of the chronicler Marchionne, served as legal counsel to Niccolò for the construction of the Certosa on Mount Acuto (F.P. Tocco 2001, 52).

Sadly, for Boccaccio and others, the brief attempt at a Signoria in Florence under the direction of Walter of Brienne went down in history as a complete failure.

The Call and the Fall of the Duke of Athens

In the early 1340s, the political and economic state of the Republic of Florence was complicated and troubled. Relations between magnates, *popolani grassi*, and lower classes, never good at the best of times, were getting worse. It was a period of economic crisis and famine, aggravated by outbreaks of pandemic, on top of which the late 1330s marked the beginning of an unstoppable crisis for the great companies. These companies were under pressure not only from the King of England, who could not repay his debts, but also from the Commune of Florence, which embarked on a wasteful and worthless war against Pisa over the annexation of Lucca.[36]

When Florence was defeated, in October 1341, it was staggering under the massive new debt of 400,000 gold florins and out-of-pocket expenses incurred by the Balìa dei Venti (Council of Twenty), in whose hands all strategic military decisions for the war against Pisa had been placed (Paoli 1862, 7). The Florentines, however, refused to give up, and they applied for help to the pope and to King Robert of Anjou. On 22 May, they sent a letter to King Robert asking him to support Walter of Brienne as *capitano di guerra* (captain of war). The Commune designated him their military leader, informing King Robert of their decision only after the fact. Despite several attempts, however, the new captain was unable to turn the war in Florence's favour, and Lucca fell into Pisan hands for good.

As happened in moments of crisis and difficult leadership in Florentine politics, the Commune decided to elect a third party to govern the city more equitably. Walter of Brienne, despite the failure of the war for Lucca under his command, appeared to possess all the qualities of the perfect candidate: he had outstanding credentials as a Guelf, insofar as he was related to King Robert, and he was a close friend to the new and the old pope; he was already well known to Florence because he had served the city with distinction in the past as vicar to Charles of Calabria, when the latter was dictator in the 1320s. He was well liked by the magnates (among them the Bardi, Rossi, and Frescobaldi), who were supporting him in hopes of overturning the Ordinances of Justice; by the *popolani*, who were hoping for the cancellation of their debts; and by the common people, *il popolino*, the "little people," who were tired of the mismanagement of Florence's governing body. The merchants, in financial ruin, were hoping to avoid the statutory ordinances relating to bankruptcy (Sapori 1926, 147); the principal representatives on this front were the Bardi family. In his *De casibus virorum illustrium*, Boccaccio describes this historical moment in the biography of Walter of Brienne (*De cas.* IX

36 On the debts incurred in Florence for the war against Lucca, see Barbadoro 1929, 571–83. On relations between Florence and King Robert, see S. Kelly 2003, 227–35.

xxiv 5), introduced to the reader from the first lines as a man of illustrious blood but of degenerate morality ("satis claritate sanguinis conpicuus fuit, esto degener moribus"; *De cas.* IX xxiv 1):[37]

> And since the strength of the Florentines had been eroded by this aforementioned defeat and by excessive expenses, in a crowded senate on behalf of the common good they made the decision to give power with a broad licence to a man who was experienced in warfare, in order to stem the sedition of the citizens and the assaults of enemies.
>
> (Et cum iam plurimum dicta clade et importabilibus sumptibus Florentinorum essent attrite vires, frequenti senatu pro salute publica iniere Florentini consilium, ut instructo bellorum viro, qui et seditiones civium et hostium coerceret impetus, ampla cum licentia daretur imperium.)

The Commune turned to Brienne with a resolution passed on 30 May and then, on 1 June 1342, it bestowed on him the titles "Preserver and Protector of the City of Florence and Its Jurisdictions" and "General War Captain."[38] These initial resolutions did not infringe on the powers of the Commune. Nevertheless, the duke began to expand his own power: first with a decision announced on 11 July 1342 and ratified on 8 September, when, in the Public Assembly, Walter of Brienne was proclaimed Signore di Firenze, with full power for life.

Remembering these events more than fifteen years later, Boccaccio bitterly criticized the magnates, who aimed to overturn the Ordinances of Justice, and the *popolani grassi*, who were hoping to avoid repayment of money they had borrowed (*De cas.* IX xxiv 8):[39]

> And insanely choosing the tyranny of a foreigner of whom they had no experience, rather than bear the yoke of civil laws of whose custom they had experience, with

---

37 "Boccaccio's *De casibus virorum illustrium* ('The Downfall of Illustrious Men') is a nine-book encyclopedic history devoted to a review in a moralizing vein of Fortune's impact on both individual and collective destinies" (Marchesi 2013, 245). Brienne's biography was written between 1359 and 1360, years after the events described. For the dating and phases of the work's composition, see the introduction to the Mondadori edition by Pier Giorgio Ricci and Vittorio Zaccaria (1964), and see Zaccaria (2001, 34–88).

38 ASFi, *PR* 33, 15: in Paoli 1862, 63, doc. 4. On the Signoria of the Duke of Athens, see the fundamental work by Paoli 1862, Sestan 1972, and de Vincentiis 2003, 2013.

39 Boccaccio was a witness to these events. He reports that Ranieri di Giotto, captain of the Guard, had filled the city with supporters of the duke, concealing them in the houses of magnates. In other words, Walter was prepared to take the city by force if the Florentines had not handed it over themselves (*De cas.* IX xxiv 8). This detail is not recorded in the contemporary chronicles of Giovanni Villani and Marchionne di Coppo Stefani, so we infer that Boccaccio had first-hand, privileged knowledge of the events.

> little confidence in themselves, they coopted citizens in debt, of which there was at that time great abundance.
>
> (Et ignaviter eligentes potius exteri hominis tyrannidem, quam ignorabant, quam civilium legum quarum consuetudine noverant iugum ferre, minus de se confidentes, sibi cives alieno obligatos eri iunxere, quorum ea tempestate ingens erat copia.)

Boccaccio also fiercely disapproves of the festivities over the installation of the duke (*De cas.* IX xxiv 18):

> And just as if they had cast chains upon not their own liberty but rather that of another, those magnates began to celebrate the triumph over the conquered people. And those who had been in debt began to crow in celebration of their creditors' poverty; thus, the lower masses also began to rush around everywhere, to mount the Capitol of which they had no experience, everything was cracking, and they spent their holiday in vulgar and disgraceful songs.
>
> (et quasi non sue sed alterius tantum libertati iniecissent vincula, cepere magnates tripudiis subacti populi celebrare triunphos; et qui alienum es debuerant, in creditorum pauperiem debachari; sic et plebs inferior discurrere undique, et ignotum sibi Capitolium conscendere, rimari cuncta, scomatibus ignominiosis et cantibus diem agere celebrem.)

Among Brienne's first concerns was the peace with Pisa (Paoli 1862, 17–19), which did not go down well with the Tuscan Guelfs or Florentines: making peace with Pisa and withdrawing from Lucca for at least fifteen years was agreed on 9 October 1342, and ratified four days later (Sapori 1926, 148).[40] On 6 March 1343, a league was formed with the purpose of respecting the peace accords among the different parties – Florence, Pisa, and Lucca. Representing Florence were Messer Pino di Giovanni de' Rossi and the jurist Paolo di Neri Bordoni (Paoli 1862, 17–19).

Initially, Walter of Brienne showed himself to be grateful of such support, and he was particularly well disposed towards the magnates, even without giving them too much authority. One of his first governing acts came on 26 October:

---

40 According to the peace treaty between Pisa and Florence, access from Florence to the sea was to be reopened through Porto Pisano. A document drawn up by the notary ser Bartolo di ser Neri da Ruffiano, recently rediscovered and published by Sergio Tognetti (2016), lists all the business companies that had to swear allegiance to the Duke of Athens to receive important tax reductions. Among these companies were the Francesco de' Bardi Company, the de' Bardi Company, and the Banco Acciaiuoli Company.

overturning the convictions of the Bardi, Frescobaldi, Pazzi, and Nerli for the "great conspiracy" of 1340.[41] The duke was hostile, however, to the *popolani grassi*, and he tried to remove them from public offices. In so doing, he increased the privileges of the magnates. But what the latter desired more than anything else was the repeal of the Ordinances of Justice; they even stole the book in which the Ordinances were written (Paoli 1862, 37).

Soon, however, Walter of Brienne devolved into a classic tyrant. He was lustful, a "liar, greedy, a robber, monstrous, relentless, ungrateful, and wicked" ("bilinguem, avarum, detractorem, immanem, inexorabilem, ingratum, scelestum"; *De cas.* IX xxiv 27).[42] He concentrated power into his own hands, and his policies served his interests, rather than those of the city or even of a specific group. In the beginning, he favoured the magnates, but this was only to keep the necessary peace to be able to govern: peace with the neighbouring cities, peace with the countryside, and especially peace within the city. Given the dire economic straits of the Commune, the duke suspended the restitution of communal debts and *prestanze* (obligatory loan,)[43] but this move powerfully affected the super-companies, since they more than all others had financed the war for Lucca; on top of this, Brienne commissioned a new *estimo* (taxes on real estate) for city and countryside, for a total of 80,000 florins. This money was not spent on behalf of Florence but kept in his own coffers or sent abroad or spent on public festivals, all with the goal of appealing to the lower classes (Sapori 1926, 150). Everybody felt betrayed, treated like "whores," as Giovanni Villani caustically writes, eloquently capturing the disappointment of the citizens (1990–1, 13.8):

> And so, the duke was whoring and deceiving the citizens, stealing all confidence from the great men who had made him a *signore*, and stealing freedom from every authority and magistracy, all but the very name from the priors as well as the Popolo. And he abolished the office of captain of the companies of the Popolo, he removed their banners, and he dismissed every other office of the Popolo, as he wished, while he kept the company that he desired, such as innkeepers, wine sellers, wool carders, and artisans of the lower guilds, giving them consuls and rectors as they desired, dismembering the ancient orders of the guilds to which they had been subjugated in order to increase the pay for their work.

---

41 ASFi, *balie* 2, ff. 12–13v; ASFi, *PR* 32, 12: printed in Paoli 1862, 76, doc. 57.

42 The adjectives Boccaccio used recall those of the cartouche on a frescoed image of the duke, painted on the Bargello tower after his expulsion to record his infamy: "Avaricious, treacherous, and also cruel / lustful, unjust and faithless / Never did he keep his state safe" ("Avaro, traditore, e poi crudele / Lussurioso, ingiusto e spergiuro, / Giammai non tenne suo stato securo") (Yunn 2015, 183).

43 *Prestanze* were not taxes but compulsory loans to the Commune, whose payment was a precondition for the full exercise of political rights in Florence. They were generally repaid with interest.

(E così puttaneggiava e disimulava il duca co' cittadini, togliendo ogni baldanza a' grandi che·ll'aveano fatto signore, e togliendo la libertà e ogni balìa e uficio, altro che 'l nome de' priori, e al popolo; e cassò l'uficio di gonfalonieri delle compagnie del popolo, e tolse loro i gonfaloni, e ogni altro ordine e uficiali di popolo cassò, se non a suo beneplacito ritegnendosi co' beccari, vinattieri, scardassieri e artefici minuti, dando loro consoli e rettori al loro volere, dimembrando gli ordini antichi dell'arti a·ccui erano sottoposti per volere maggiori salari di loro lavorii.)

He also managed to offend the clergy, centralizing some of their privileges. But it was especially his licentious conduct and that of his mercenary troops that made him unpopular with everybody. This how Giovanni Villani describes him (1990–1, 13.8):

He and his people began to use force and wickedness and obscenity against the citizens' ladies and maidens; and among other things because of a woman he took away control of San Sebbio a' Poveri from the Calimala Guild, and gave it to others illegally. And for the sake of his love for a woman, he restored embellishments to the women of Florence, and he created a brothel for prostitutes, from which his marshal made a lot of money.

(Di donne e di donzelle di cittadini per sé e per sue genti cominciaro a·ffare di forze e villanie e di laide cose; intra·ll'altre per cagione di donna tolse a San Sebbio a' poveri, della guardia dell'arte di Calimala, e dello altrui illicitamente. E per amore di donna rendè gli ornamenti alle donne di Firenze, e fece fare il luogo comune delle femmine mondane, onde il suo maliscaldo traeva molti danari.)

Boccaccio agreed years later in the *De casibus* (IX xxiv 23–4):[44]

Hence with seduction, gifts, threats, and violence he would draw into his embrace maidens and all kinds of ladies, and he would corrupt youths, and he would allow his men all kinds of crime; in brief, with his filth, he would stain equally both human and divine affairs. And so, the unhappy citizens, who in the beginning had been made anxious, scared, and silent, now began to lament their unappreciated and lost freedom, and to desire the death and overthrow of the tyrant, and to blame their own sloth, and, if the opportunity were given, to desire to take back their previous freedom.

(Inde blanditiis, muneribus, minis et violentiis in suum concubitum virgines et quascunque matronas attrahere, adolescentes ingenuos prostrare, suis infida queque

44 This passage appears particularly relevant to my analysis in chapter 5 of the *De mulieribus claris*, especially with regard to Boccaccio's "desire for death" and to the tyrant who with "gifts, threats, and violence" rapes virgins, as in *De Virginea virgine Virginii filia*.

permictere, et breviter spurcitiis suis humana pariter et divina fedare. Quibus miseri cives initio anxii, pavidi et elingues effecti, ingemiscere male cognitam deiectamque libertatem cepere, mortem deiectionemque tyranni cupere, desidiam sua damnare, et, si via daretur, se in libertatem redigere pristinam exoptare.)

This dissatisfaction was widespread, and the definitive expulsion of the Duke of Athens took place on the day of Saint Anne, 26 July 1343. It had been heralded by three previous failed coups in early 1343, the exact dates of which are not recorded. The first is particularly important here, because it affected many who were living in Oltrarno, and some of those involved had a close relationship with Giovanni Boccaccio.

The organizer of the first attempted coup was the Bishop of Florence: Angelo Acciaiuoli, cousin to Niccolò (future grand seneschal of the kingdom of Naples), both executive members of the powerful financial company of the Acciaiuoli, which was facing bankruptcy in the same period. Many other members of the Bardi family were co-conspirators, together with Pino de' Rossi and Salvestrino de' Rossi, as well as others from the Frescobaldi family.[45] What drew together the Bardi, Rossi, and Frescobaldi was not just their residence in Oltrarno and their magnate aspirations but all their close relations with the *Regnum* of Naples and with Robert of Anjou, recently deceased on 29 January 1343; it is likely that his death had impaired their confidence in the duke.

On 26 July 1343, the fourth attempt to oust the duke was successful. Walter of Brienne, Duke of Athens and Signore of Florence, had lasted exactly eleven months. The reason this conspiracy succeeded is because all the citizens of Florence took part, confirming a local proverb: "Florence will not make a move, until all of it is in pain" ("Firenze non si muove, se tutta non si duole"; G. Villani 1990–1, 13.16, 2–3). It was carefully planned. The Adimari, Medici, and Donati ordered that on Saturday at three o'clock, when labourers were leaving their workshops, certain mercenaries would pretend to have a fight in the Mercato Vecchio and in Porta San Piero, yelling "To arms! To arms!" In fact, this was the signal for a full-scale insurrection: all the citizens, who had been alerted and were ready, rose

45 Among the Bardi family, Giovanni Villani includes Piero, Gerozzo, Iacopo, Andrea di Filippozzo, and Simone di Geri. Among the Frescobaldi who took part in the conspiracy were the Agnolo Giramonte (prior of San Iacopo) and Vieri delli Scali. Other magnates and *popolani* were the Altoviti, the Magalotti, the Strozzi, and the Mancini. Giovanni Villani reports on the other two conspiracies: the second was led by cousins Manno di Apardo Donati and Corso di Amerigo de' Donati, plotting together with Bindo, Beltramo and Mari de' Pazzi, Niccolò di Alamanno de' Medici, and Tile Benzi de' Cavicciuoli, as well as some of the Albizzi (many of whom were discovered and imprisoned by the duke). The third was led by Antonio di Baldinaccio degli Adimari and other members of the Medici family, Bordoni, Oricellai, and Aldobrandini. For all the names mentioned in this note, see G. Villani 1990–1, 13.16.

up bearing flags with the coat of arms of the Popolo and the Commune, some on foot, others on horse, yelling, "Death to the Duke and his followers! Long live the People and the Commune of Florence and freedom!" ("Muoia il duca e' suoi seguaci, e viva il popolo e 'l Comune di Firenze e libertà"; G. Villani 1990–1, 13.17). The unanimous revolt took the duke's militia completely by surprise, and they were not prepared to respond. Brienne's soldiers retreated to the piazza in front of the current Palazzo della Signoria, which the citizens immediately surrounded and besieged, blocking every movement by the duke – "and like a wicked coward, he launched into tears and lamentations" ("vilis tremensque in querelas se dedit et lacrimas"; *De cas.* IX xxiv 32). After a series of scuffles between the soldiers and the people of Florence, the duke was forced to retreat into the palace itself, where his barons had taken refuge, as well. At this point, all escape had been cut off and they were out of provisions.

Once the way had been cleared, the first course of action for Corso di Amerigo Donati (who had led the second unsuccessful coup) and his brothers was to storm the Stinche jails to free his friends and relatives imprisoned by the duke, among whom were those who had previously conspired with Corso: Manno di Apardo Donati (brother of Pazzino di Apardo Donati, who is one of the future conspirators of 1360 and a friend of Boccaccio),[46] Niccolò di Alamanno de' Medici, Tile di Guido Benzi de' Cavacciuli, Beltramo de' Pazzi (another conspirator of 1360), and many others. In this way, the rebels were able to reinforce their ranks in preparation for the assault on the Palace of the Podestà, where at the time Baglione dei Baglioni di Perugia was in office; he offered no resistance, choosing instead to flee to the Albizzi family home, where he found shelter. The Donati clan, side by side with the people, took immediate action: the Palace of the Podestà was looted of everything, including benches and windows; all documents, acts, and other writings were burned. The same looting and burning happened also in the Chamber of the Commune (Camera del Comune), to destroy any documents with the names of the exiles, the rebels, and the convicted; the acts of the Office of Commerce (Ufficiale della Mercanzia) were also burned. The destruction was targeted and deliberate: the one objective was to erase all records of convictions in judicial, criminal, and civil cases and all debts to the Commune.[47]

The situation rapidly degenerated into ruthless vendettas on behalf of the masses, who seized the opportunity to vent their anger: anyone who was hated by the people was lynched and torn to pieces ("abocconato"; G. Villani 1990–1,

---

46 Pazzino di Apardo Donati appears as a witness in a document dated 2 November 1351, which gives notice of the payment of a salary by the Commune of Florence for the embassy made by Boccaccio "in the area of Romagna and Lombardy" ("in partes Romandiole et Lombardie"; Imbriani 1882, 84).

47 For a detailed analysis of the destruction of the archives, see de Vincentiis 2003.

13.17), hung upside down, cut and quartered like a pig – "impeso per li piedi, e sparato e sbarrato come porco." Arrigo Fei, the fierce tax collector of Florence under the Duke of Athens (G. Villani 1990–1, 13.17) was butchered in this way. An eighteen-year-old boy was dismembered by the mob. Pieces of the victims' flesh were displayed on the tips of spears and swords throughout the city. Even scenes of cannibalism were reported: "Some there were so cruel, whose rage was so bestial and instinctual that they ate their flesh, whether raw or cooked" ("ed ebbevi de' sì crudeli, e con furia bestiale e tanto animosa, che mangiaro delle loro carni cruda e cotta"; G. Villani 1990–1, 13.17). We find an account of these bloody, macabre events in Boccaccio, *De cas.* IX xxiv 35–9:

> And in order that the atrocity of the rebels might temporarily be appeased, he [Brienne] ordered to be handed over to them a certain Guglielmo d'Assisi, whom he had originally designated as Protector of the Citizens, who was more savage than any beast, together with his son who was even crueller than his father. For this reason, God allowed that this man, who had already stripped many fathers of their own children for his own cruelty, might see his own son killed before his very eyes; and after this he too was killed. But it would have been more appropriate retribution if this had been allowed, for him to suffer that which he had prepared for others, for him to be ripped apart limb by limb, so that he might reach death only after a thousand wounds, he who had sought the deaths of others through a thousand tortures. This was the first victim whom Walter saw before his eyes in atonement for his own crimes, and in his presence, a certain Arrigo, the worst kind of citizen of Florence, at whose instigation property would be confiscated from the citizens, was suspended by his feet from a wooden beam like a pig and duly gutted, and finally cut into pieces.

> (Et ut paululum se postulantium atrocitas sedaretur, sicarium quendam Guilielmum assisinatem, quem conservatorem civium titularat, omni belva immaniorem, cum filio, patre truculentiore, exhiberi postulantibus iussit. Cuius ob meritum passus est Deus ut, qui plures iam parentes orbarat sua sevitia, se coram cerneret trucidari filium; quem post et ipse trucidatus est. Dignior – si permissum foret – ut quod excogitarat in alios pateretur ipse, ut membratim scilicet scerperetur, ut per mille vulnera devenisset in mortem, qui mille tormentis alienas quesierat. Hanc in expiationem suorum facinorum primam victimam in oculis suis vidit Gualtierius, quo coram et Henricus quidam, pessimus florentinus cives, cuius demonstrationibus civium sensim subtrahebat substantias, pedibus appensus tigno, more suis externatus est et postremo in frustra discerptus.)

The duke's officers were stripped of their possessions, if not of their lives. Walter of Brienne was now a prisoner of Florence, no longer a *signore.* In the end his life was spared, but only out of caution, since he had many highly placed friends. Florence was afraid of potential retaliation by the powerful French houses or their allies.

In the midst of the revolt against Brienne, magnates and the *popolani* of Oltrarno "took a common oath, sealed by a kiss on the lips" ("si giurarono insieme e baciarono in bocca"; G. Villani 1990–1, 13.17, 30–1) and barred the bridges so that nobody could get in or out. The strategy was to defend their territory and stay out of the insurrection, hoping to avoid losing their lives and their movable and fixed goods. They planned to stay neutral and then eventually support the winner. According to Giovanni Villani, the Florentines of Oltrarno acted "with the idea that, if all the ground on one side were lost, they would stay free on the other side" ("con intenzione che se tutta la terra di qua si perdesse, di tenersi francamente di là"; G. Villani 1990–1, 13.17). The day after the beginning of the rebellion, however, they sent secret messages from the Commune to seek help from the Republic of Siena. At the same time, some members of the Bardi and Frescobaldi families asked for assistance from Pisa. When the Commune and the other citizens found this out, "they were very upset" ("forte se ne turbaro"; G. Villani 1990–1, 13.17). As Marchionne di Coppo Stefani writes, only after the revolt had turned unanimously against the duke did "those of Oltrarno, who were still barred, upon hearing the citizens unanimous, cross the river on horseback, and every man ran together throughout the city" ("quelli di Oltrarno, ch'erano ancora sbarrati, udendo li cittadini d'un animo cavalcarono di qua, e la Terra si corse comunemente per ogni uomo"; 1910, rubr. 578).

As soon as Brienne was banished from Florence for good, a committee of fourteen men was created, seven magnates and seven *popolani*, led by Bishop Angelo Acciaiuoli, the cousin of Niccolò who was Boccaccio's schoolmate. Among these fourteen, others were closely linked to Boccaccio: Messer Pino de' Rossi, who had already conspired against the duke (like Rodolfo de' Bardi and Filippo Megalotti) and to whom Boccaccio dedicated the *Consolatoria a Pino de' Rossi*; Rodolfo de' Bardi, uncle of the wife of Luca di Feo Ugolini (another conspirator from 1360, whom Boccaccio addresses in the *Consolatoria a Pino de' Rossi*);[48] Simone de' Peruzzi, husband of Lisa Buondelmonti, celebrated in the *Contento quasi ne' pensier d'amore* of 1342; Giovanni de' Gianfigliazzi, from a family very dear to Boccaccio;[49] as well as Testa de' Tornaquinci, Bindo di Biligiardo della Tosa, Talano degli Adimari, all from families well known to Boccaccio (for example,

---

48 Luca di Feo Ugolini was the son of Lapa, sister to Ridolfo de' Bardi (ASFi, *Diplomatico*, Santo Spirito, 4 January 1360 according to Florentine dating practices; 1361 in common usage).

49 Boccaccio was clearly very close to the Gianfigliazzi family: Alinora, daughter of Niccolò Gianfigliazzi and wife of Pacino Peruzzi, appears in the guise of Adiona in the *Comedia delle ninfe fiorentine* and the *Amorosa visione*; the jurist Luigi Gianfigliazzi is warmly recalled in the poem dedicated to Zanobi da Strada (VII 62–5); Currado Gianfigliazzi is remembered in the novella of Chichibìo (*Dec.* VI.4); Stoldo di Matteo de' Gianfigliazzi repaid on behalf of Giovanni and Jacopo di Boccaccio da Certaldo the loan they owed to the Commune of Florence on 4 July 1364 (Regnicoli 2013a, 389, doc. 106–8).

many women celebrated in *Contento quasi ne' pensier d'amore* were from these families).[50] The drafter of the deed that created the committee was jurist Forese Rabatta, who is recalled in the *Decameron* (*Dec.* VI.5). Boccaccio had close connections with other men who took up positions in the new regime. Among the eight councillors of the priors was Bertramo di Bartolomeo de' Pazzi (another of the conspirators of 1360) (G. Villani 1990–1, 13.18), and Manno di Apardo Donati was in line to become a prior (Kohl 1992) – he was the brother of Pazzino di Apardo Donati (one of the twelve conspirators accused in 1360). Furthermore, the fourteen men were mostly directors or shareholders of companies who had joined forces in a final attempt to retain their political influence and stave off looming bankruptcies.[51] On 2 August 1343, in Santa Reparata, the Generale parlamento del Popolo (the General Parliament of the People) gave them the full authority to reform and govern the state until the end of September.

The main task facing the group and Angelo Acciaiuoli, the Bishop of Florence, was to reconstitute the different magistracies in charge of the city, including the priors, the Collegio dei Dodici (College of Twelve), and the *gonfalonieri*. Before they proceeded, under pressure from the district of San Pier Scheraggio and that of Oltrarno (representing the latter, among the fourteen, were above all Pino de' Rossi and Ridolfo de' Bardi, the uncle of Luca di Feo Ugolini), they decided to redistrict the city, dividing it no longer into *sestieri* but into *quartieri* – carving it into four large wards instead of six. The whole enterprise would have benefited those from Oltrarno, because even though they shouldered the bulk of the taxation (since they were more populated than the other *sestieri*),[52] they had only one prior. In these circumstances the four quarters of Florence were born and are still in use today, each divided into four sectors, the *gonfaloni* (see figure 1.1).

After this reorganization, the committee and the Bishop of Florence selected the priors: seventeen *popolani* and eight magnates for each quarter. Altogether they numbered one hundred.

Despite the expulsion of the tyrant and the ratification of these reforms, tensions were rising again in September 1343. Stefani observes that "the magnates

50 The fourteen men were Ridolfo de' Bardi, Pino de' Rossi, Sandro di Cenni Biliotti, Giannozzo Cavalcanti, Simone de' Peruzzi, Filippo de' Magalotti, Giovanni de' Gianfigliazzi, Bindo di Ottone Altoviti, Testa de' Tornaquinci, Marco degli Strozzi, Francesco de' Medici, Bindo di Biligiardo della Tosa, Talano degli Adimari, and Bartolo de' Ricci. See Paoli 1862, 43–9.

51 As well as the Bardi, a substantial number of the committee were involved with the Acciaiuoli company: "in addition to the Bishop … Giannozzo Cavalcanti and Bindo Altoviti could provide guarantees that they would be able to influence the choices of the committee in more pleasing directions [to the Acciaiuoli]" (F.P. Tocco 2001, 59).

52 According to Stefani's estimates (1910, rubr. 586), the district of Oltrarno paid 28,000 gold florins, San Piero Scheraggio 23,000, Borgo 12,000, San Pancrazio 13,000, Porta del Duomo 11,000, and Porta San Piero 13,000.

Figure 1.1. The four quarters of Florence

began to use force and extortion, both in the city and in the countryside, through the magistracies that they held" ("li Grandi cominciarono a fare in città e in contado forze ed istorsioni per la libertà d'ufici che avieno"; 1910, rubr. 588), and Giovanni Villani notes: "The evil magnates did not refrain, but rather they began to employ violence and murder both in the city and in the countryside, as well as false prosecutions of *popolani*" ("non si raffrenavano i malvagi grandi, ma cominciaro a·ffare delle forze e micidi in città e in contado, e di false accuse contra i popolani"; 1990–1, 13.21). The people did not tolerate this situation for long.

Bishop Angelo Acciaiuoli tried to mediate, but the magnates in Oltrarno, among whom we can imagine was also Pino de' Rossi, did not want to listen: "We shall see who will try to take away our share in the *signoria*, and who will want to banish us from Florence after we liberated her from the duke" ("Noi vedremo chi·cci torrà la parte nostra della signoria, e·cci vorrà cacciare di Firenze, che·lla francammo dal Duca"; G. Villani 1990–1, 13.19). In short, another popular insurrection erupted, commanded by three *cavalieri del popolo* (knights of the people), Giovanni della Tosa, Geri de' Pazzi, and Antonio degli Adimari. On 22 September 1343, another regime was installed, the so-called popular government, greatly expanded downward: the seats were occupied by small artisans and shopkeepers. "The majority belonged to families who had not previously held communal office. Between 1343 and 1348 the patriciate obtained less than one-third of the seats in the *Signoria*" (Brucker 1962, 105). Giovanni Villani, dismayed by so many constant reversals, quotes Dante when he writes of the Florentines: "[They] make such fine provisions / that the plans you've spun but in October / do not survive to mid-November" ("fai tanto sottili / provedimenti, ch'a mezzo novembre / non giugne quel che tu d'ottobre fili"; *Purg.* 6.143–4). He then adds: "That truly was a prophecy and verdict appropriate to our infortunate turn of events" ("E bene fu profezia e vera sentenzia in questo nostro fortuito caso"; G. Villani 1990–1, 13.19).[53]

Naturally, the magnates did not sit on the sidelines; they called for reinforcements from outside the city: "The *grandi* would have had considerable support from the counts and the Ubaldini and the Pisani, and from other tyrants from Lombardy and Romagna, and they had to take Oltrarno, since they were already in control of the bridges, and from here launch their assault on Thursday, 25 September" ("I grandi arebbero grande aiuto da' conti e Ubaldini e Pisani e d'altri tiranni di Lombardia e di Romagna, e che dovieno afforzarsi Oltrarno, ch'avieno la signoria di tutti i ponti e di qua fare cominciare l'assalto giovedì a dì XXV di settembre"; G. Villani 1990–1, 13.21). The people preempted the magnates by rising up on 24 September. In the opening stages of the confrontation, the Cavicciuli, the Donati, and the Cavalcanti, all magnates on the main side of the Arno, were defeated, after which the people's forces marched on Oltrarno, where the Bardi, Frescobaldi, Rossi, Mannelli, and Nerli were already armed and had taken possession of the bridges. Ponte Vecchio was blocked by locked gates and the adjacent armed towers of the Bardi and the Rossi, as well as by the houses of the Bardi and the Mannelli in front of the bridge. Ponte Rubaconte was impassable.

53 Dante's tercet was read as a prophecy in the context of the 1340s; Boccaccio recalls it, in his *Consolatoria a Pino de' Rossi* (§166): "God's bounty is great, and our city undergoes constant change more than any other, so that from daily experience we see confirmed the verses of our poet: that the plans you've spun but in October do not survive to mid-November" ("Infinita è la divina bontà, e la nostra città, più che altra, è piena di mutamenti, in tanto che per esperienza tutto dì veggiamo verificarsi il verso del nostro poeta: che a mezzo novembre non giugne quel che tu d'ottobre fili").

Ponte alla Carraia, monitored by the house of the Nerli, was the widest and therefore the most difficult to defend. It had been attacked not only by the people on the main side of the Arno but also by those on the other side, specifically by the *popoli* of San Frediano, of the Cuculia, and of the Fondaccio – among the most impoverished workers in Oltrarno. As soon as this bridge was captured, the Nerli and Frescobaldi were attacked by such a large number of the townspeople that they surrendered, asking for mercy; the Rossi also laid down their weapons immediately, once they discovered that the other magnates had done the same. The Bardi alone remained entrenched with a number of followers in their properties, but they were quickly surrounded on the side of Poggio San Giorgio, by the new street, Via che va a Pozzo Toscanelli – today called Sdrucciolo de' Pitti. For the Bardi, too, there was no chance of holding out against the rage of the people: They managed to escape by seeking shelter in San Niccolò, but all their mansions and houses were looted and set on fire, and the total losses were valued at 60,000 gold florins.

With the establishment of the popular government (1343–8), the magnates were once again consigned to the weak political position they had been trying to break out of with their family connections outside the city and with the *popolo grasso*. In December 1343, the members of the Bardi, Frescobaldi, Rossi, Donati, and Pazzi houses were "confined" to outside the city, "even if most of the men of these Houses, in order to relieve the people's suspicion and to escape their rage, left the city and moved to their countryside properties" ("con tutto che la maggiore parte degli uomini de' detti casati, per levare sospetto al *popolo* e fuggire la furia, se n'andarono in contado a' loro poderi ad abitare, lasciando la città"; G. Villani 1990–1, 13.28). Some members of the nobility, such as the Donati brothers, Pazzino and Manno di Apardo, were incarcerated in the Stinche prison for a short time before being expelled from the city.

In this situation, city life was likely to have been very difficult, even for Boccaccio, as he no longer enjoyed an "aristocratic" audience for his encomiastic works. After the expulsion of Walter of Brienne, Boccaccio's connections with the Bardi circle and his Angevin friendships must have been suspicious as well. Also, sometime between April 1340 and November 1343 (Regnicoli 2018), his family situation changed drastically with the second marriage of his father Boccaccino di Chellino, who brought home a very young bride, just endowed with her dowry: Bice, daughter of Ubaldino di Nepo dei Bostichi and Lore di Gherardo Baroncelli (see appendix A1.2).[54] Her maternal grandfather, Gherardo di Miccio Baroncelli, was an economically and politically active member of the Florentine Republic and an old acquaintance of Boccaccino: They were both members of the bankers' guild,

54 Recently, Laura Regnicoli located the last will of Ubaldino di Nepo de' Bostichi (2018, n. 50: ASFi, *Diplomatico*, San Frediano 25 April 1340, and San Frediano 27 August 1348), where we learn that his wife Lore is already dead, and that Bice is to receive a dowry when she is married. At the time of the drafting of the will, there is no sign of an imminent wedding, but we can infer that Bice was a suitable age for marriage, that is around fourteen years old.

which had elected them together as counsels for the Università della Mercanzia on 3 April 1326 (Agostini Muzzi 1978, 634). Also, Gherardo Baroncelli, together with his brother Tano, was a shareholder of the Peruzzi company. Gherardo had two highly ranked wives: first, Gemma di Geri di Simone de' Bardi and, on her death, Laggia di Messer Scolaio de' Pulci. So Boccaccino di Chellino's marriage connected him with magnate families: his new wife was the granddaughter of a member of the Bardi family or of the Pulci family – unfortunately, we do not know who the mother of Lore was. Moreover, one aunt of Bice de' Bostichi, Giovanna di Gherardo Baroncelli, had married Paniccia di Bernardo Frescobaldi (Pampaloni 1964a). Basically, through this second union, Boccaccino demonstrated that he was able to strengthen his alliances with the magnate families of Oltrarno. The couple was blessed soon with the arrival of a newborn, a legitimate heir: Jacopo.

As contemporary readers of the *Decameron*, we wonder if Boccaccio was thinking about his father's marriage when writing the many novellas in which the main character is a young girl married to an old man, those told by Dioneo, for example, the alter ego of the author, about the old judge Riccardo di Chinzica who marries the young Bartolomea (*Dec.* II.10) and the surgeon Mazzeo della Montagna who marries "a young a beautiful girl of his city" (*Dec.* IV.10). Still, certainly, his father would not need him anymore, or not as much as he did when he recalled him from Naples in fall 1340; it is possible, too, that his continued presence in the house would not have been welcome, given the youth of his father's bride.

In any case, Boccaccio left Florence for other places. In fact, we have no documented evidence of his presence in Florence for a five-year period between 1343 and 1348 (Agostini Muzzi 1978; Regnicoli 2013a). We know that he was in Ravenna (Romagna) from 1345 to 1346 with Ostasio da Polenta, and that he was in Forlì from 1347 to 1348 with Francesco Ordelaffi.[55] So, Boccaccio might already have arrived in Romagna in late 1343 or early 1344, or he might have stayed in Naples first before going to Ravenna. Wherever he was, he was no longer in Florence.

55 For recent investigations of Boccaccio's stay in Romagna, see *Boccaccio e la Romagna* 2015. Among the essays, see especially Paolo Pontari's, which reconstructs Boccaccio's movements in Ravenna and Forlì. The exact date of Boccaccio's move to the da Polenta family in Ravenna cannot be confirmed (see Pontari 2015, 129, n. 28). It remains unclear why he relocated to Romagna: It is to be excluded that he is linked to the "Boccaccios from Ravenna," as suggested by Corrado Ricci (1910) and reprised by a number of later scholars, because "Boccaccio" is a patronymic, not a surname. A more promising direction for inquiry would be among Boccaccio's friends in the Anjou court of Naples and the magnate families of Florence. Also, "the novellas of the *Decameron* situated in Romagna are concentrated on the 5th day (4, 5, 8), which is the sunniest and most positive of days" (Branca Delcorno 2015, 49), suggesting that the region made a positive impression on Boccaccio. He often returned to Romagna, at least up until 1362, perhaps for personal reasons: could he have fathered his children with a woman of Romagna? Santagata endorses this conjecture (2019, 125–39, esp. 138).

2 Boccaccio and Politics (1348–1355)

more solito inter publicas privatasque occupationes ultra velle amxior

(as usual, I worry more than I want about my public and private occupations)
– G. Boccaccio, *Epistola* IX.45, 1353

Early in the 1340s, before his departure for Romagna, Boccaccio began creating connections with a group of magnates and neighbours in Oltrarno. When he returned to Florence in 1348, plague was at its peak; his stepmother Bice de' Bostichi had died, and his father was soon to follow her. He inherited property and wealth, and began participating actively in the rapidly changing Florentine political and cultural life, supported by his influential relationships. From 1348 to 1355, Boccaccio was immersed in politics. He discharged several offices, including the prestigious position of communal treasurer (*camerlengo della Camera del Comune*), and served as an ambassador for the city. Many of these activities were related to military campaigns waged by Florence against the Ubaldini and Visconti clans. After 1355, there is another gap in documentation, and we are not able to follow Boccaccio's life until the records resume, in 1359.

The Plague and Its Aftermath

The epidemic of bubonic plague that broke out in March–April 1348 lasted at least until September of the same year. The common people, the small artisans and shopkeepers, and the majority of the representatives of the popular government were hit hard, but wealthier people had greater chances of survival. They fled from the city and found refuge in the countryside and their hilltop villas, breathing in cleaner air and nourished by produce of the land – as exemplified by the narrators of the *Decameron.*[1] Magnates, the wealthier *popolani,* and the old ruling class in Oltrarno who survived the plague regrouped and looked for ways to manage the city. As Gene Brucker states: "While the plague's survivors, particularly among the lower class, were demoralized by the catastrophe, a group of prominent citizens initiated action to revive the machinery of government, which had been literally inoperative since April" (1962, 120–1). Over half the population had died, and the voting bags (*borse*) of 1343, which held the name-slips of those who were eligible for public office, were full of names of people who were deceased. A way had to be found to circumvent the voting process, and it took the form of an electoral college, a special commission known as the *balìa*; this was, effectively, the end of the popular government. John M. Najemy explains the situation:

> What the opponents of the popular regime were unable to accomplish in 1347, however, they achieved in the summer of 1348, taking advantage of the confusion and demoralization caused by the Black Death. Political life came to a halt during the peak months of the plague, but by midsummer it was clear that the high mortality had made the electoral lists of 1343 obsolete and that the *borse* would have to be opened and reviewed in order to eliminate the names of the deceased. This technical problem led to the creation of a *balìa* and to a major reform of the electoral system. The *balìa* of 1348 carried out the first steps in the dismantling of the electoral program of the popular government and signaled the beginning of the gradual return of Florentine electoral politics to conditions that were intended to generate consensus within the upper class rather than provide electoral representation among competing classes in Florentine society. (1982, 158)

The most striking enactment of the *balìa* of 1348 was the reduction of the number of minor guilds from fourteen to seven (Najemy 1982, 159). Furthermore, according to Brucker, only 36 per cent of *gente nuova* (new members) from the major guilds were designated as eligible to serve in public office, the lowest percentage between 1343 and 1363.[2] The *balìa*'s second reform, enacted in August 1348, was to solve the problem of the *borse.* A new *borsa* was created, "de bursa nova" of 1348, to supplement the old, revised bag of 1343, "de bursa veteri." Drawing names from two bags was contrary to the rules set down by the popular

---

1 For the most recent information on the spread of the plague, see Dameron 2015. See also Falsini 1971; Brucker 1977b; Benedictow 2004; Naphy and Spicer 2004; J. Kelly 2005; Little 2011; Green 2015. In addition, the Medieval Academy has sponsored two webinars on the Black Death, which feature the most up-to-date work available on the topic at the time this book went to press: "The Mother of All Pandemics: The State of Black Death Research in the Era of Covid-19," 15 May 2020, https://www.medievalacademy.org/page/webinars; "Disease, Death, and Therapy," 14 January 2021, https://www.medievalacademy.org/page/SpeculumWebinar.

2 See the chart provided in Brucker 1962, 160, n. 47; also Becker and Brucker 1956, 97.

government, but was unavoidable: between 1348 to 1351, "it became necessary to forgo strict observance of the *divieti* in order to fill available spots ... By adopting this procedure, the post-1348 regime departed significantly from the policy of the popular government" (Najemy 1982, 161–2). These changes created a "patrician resurgence," as Najemy calls it (1982, 167), but at the same time, "for the next two decades a tense compromise prevailed in which neither elite nor *popolo* had things exactly to its liking" (2006, 145). In this context, the magnates of Oltrarno and their representatives and affiliates returned to centre stage on the political scene.

Giovanni Boccaccio came back to Florence during this turbulent time. It is not known exactly when in 1348 he arrived from Forlì, but there is no doubt that he was an eye-witness of the terrible effects of the plague.[3] He was in Florence by 10 September 1348, when he took up the position of officer of indirect taxes (*signore delle gabelle*).[4] It's possible that he left the city, like the young nobles of the *Decameron*, for a villa in the nearby hills, avoiding the worst period of plague during the summer – and it's possible that he brought with him his young stepbrother, Jacopo, the only other survivor of the family.[5] Boccaccio became the *pater familias* (a legal status), Jacopo's tutor,[6] and heir to the household; as such, he had to administer the inherited assets, which must have been considerable, even if it is not possible to give a precise assessment of their value. In addition to the liquid assets that a merchant and a banker like Boccaccino di Chellino would have possessed, the inheritance consisted of various properties in Florence (houses in Santa Felicita and Sant'Ambrogio, shops leased to a greengrocer and a shoemaker), his father's home and the other goods in Certaldo, a number of farms in the Val d'Elsa, and all rights and incomes deriving from these (Branca 1976, 83–4, n. 41).[7] An inheritance this substantial would need a careful executor. Boccaccio first appears in the extant tax records on 17 April 1349, after his father's death, when he received all rights to the bank interest certificates that had been in his father's possession (Regnicoli 2013b, 21).

3 Boccaccio: "All this, if it had not been seen by the eyes of many and my own, I would barely dare to believe, let alone to write" ("il che, se dagli occhi di molti e da' i miei non fosse stato veduto, appena che io ardissi di crederlo, non che di scriverlo"; *Dec.* Intr. 16); "my own eyes experienced it" ("di che gli occhi miei ... presero ... esperienza"; *Dec.* Intr. 18).

4 Boccaccio held this position until 10 January 1349, as we know from ASFi, *CR* 28, f. 77r, document retrieved by Luca Azzetta and published by Regnicoli 2013a, 394.

5 According to a new document retrieved by Laura Regnicoli and published in the catalogue *Boccaccio autore e copista* (Regnicoli 2013a), the death of Boccaccio's father, Boccaccino di Chellino, must have occurred between July 1348 and 16 April 1349.

6 He officially appears as Jacopo's tutor in a document dated 26 January 1350 (Manni 1742, 26; Regnicoli 2013a, 394).

7 As Vittore Branca writes (1976, 83–4, n. 41): "We cannot determine with exactness the family hereditament on the death of Boccaccino." In a more recent study on Boccaccio's finances, Laura Regnicoli establishes that "from the extant documents of 1351–1355 it emerges that Boccaccio's economic circumstances were decent" (2013b, 24), or rather, "they were more than modest" (27).

Once he returned to Florence and became *pater familias*, Boccaccio would have reconnected with old friends and with his father's associates, gravitating around the Bardi family and the bankers of the Arte del Cambio who had been in contact with the Anjou court of King Robert. His father was not only an efficient and respected merchant and banker (so much so that he was one of the councillors of the Ufficio di Mercanzia and at least once consul of the Arte del Cambio) but had also served in a number of significant political magistracies within Florence, including the highest office – prior – from 15 December 1322 to 15 February 1323. Indeed, Boccaccino had been particularly active in politics since 1320.[8] Such a political and civic stance surely influenced the young Boccaccio, even if indirectly, and despite the character differences between him and his father.[9] Closely connected to their political and economic interests – which weighed heavily on Boccaccino di Chellino and on Boccaccio – were the links to their neighbourhood, especially that of Oltrarno in Santa Felicita, where they resided. As Emanuela Porta Casucci clarifies (2015–16, 192–3), in the mid-1300s in Florence the *vicinìa* (neighbourhood) represents a practical urban organization regulated by cross-sectional relations of family and cohabitation, of urban and/or district proximity, and of neighbouring origins in the county and surrounding territories, as well as by partnerships in production and investments. She clarifies that, even in the absence of a legal standing, the neighbourhood was recognized in society – for example, in the activities of the town criers who gave public notice "apud domum, ecclesiam et *viciniam* et contratam" ("in the home, church, neighbourhood, and street") – and was identified with the four *gonfaloni* in each of the four quarters that organized the popular armies. From a political point of view, the *vicinìa* did not function only as an enlarged umbrella for electoral candidacies and political clients. This kind of link is described in the introduction to the *Decameron*, in the description of the rituals of funerary remembrance in the magnate families, which observed the hierarchy of relatives, peers, neighbours, and acquaintances (*Dec.* Intr.1.32–3); *vicinìa* further characterizes the seven women narrators, "each related through friendship, neighborhood, or blood to each other" ("tutte l'una e l'altra o per amistà o per vicinanza o per parentado congiunte"; *Dec.*Intr.1.49). This kind of neighbourly relationship in the *Decameron* replicates the structures in the historical reality of Florence. The last chapter of this book analyses how this kind of connection is realized in Boccaccio's work, for example in the novella of Monna Nonna de' Pulci, in which the narrator comments: "[Monna Nonna,] whom you all must know" (*Dec.* VI.3.8). Indeed, Monna Nonna was known by Boccaccio and his neighbours in the Florentine society of the time; she was also

8 For the many offices held by Boccaccino di Chellino, see Zafarana 1968 and Armstrong, Daniels, and Milner 2015, 7–8.

9 On the relationship between father and son, see Chiecchi 1994.

a relative of many of his acquaintances. Boccaccio was writing about people in Oltrarno that he knew, and who were very possibly his first readers.

Boccaccio's Political Years

By virtue of connections through his family, his ties to the neighbourhood, and the friendships he had forged in the early 1340s, Giovanni was intricately connected to Florence. He was Messer Giovanni di Boccaccio da Certaldo of the *popolo* of Santa Felicita, under the *gonfalone del Nicchio*, residing in the quarter of Santo Spirito, and it was this status that enabled him to break into a tight-knit group of merchants and bankers, members of the old urban aristocracy, all living in Oltrarno. The magnate families of the Bardi, Frescobaldi, and Rossi all lived here and were closely connected to one another.[10] The Frescobaldi magnates had their residence in the parish of San Jacopo Oltrarno; the Rossi were neighbours of the da Certaldo family and resided in the parish of Santa Felicita.[11]

On Boccaccio's political activities throughout 1349–51, Vittore Branca writes: "In these years, we see Boccaccio involved in the play of foreign politics … because of the esteem and fame which he had won as an orator and as drafter or official letters, and for his cordial bonds with such personalities who were very influential in the administration of the guilds (Arti) as Pino de' Rossi, Bartolo del Buono, Francesco Benini, Niccolò Frescobaldi, Luca Ugolini, Andrea da Lisca, among others" (1976, 87). Branca notes that the men whose names he lists were influential members of the guilds, but this is not all they have in common: they constituted almost half of the conspirators of 1360. Niccolò di Bartolo del Buono, dedicatee of the *Comedia delle Ninfe fiorentine*, was beheaded; Pino de' Rossi, Niccolo' de' Frescobaldi, Luca di Feo Ugolini, and Andrea di Tello da Lisca were all banned and their properties confiscated. They all were living in Oltrarno, next door to one another, with the same economic and political interests. In the aftermath of the plague, these same people were deeply involved in the politics of the city, gaining significant influence in the field, and, for that reason, they were targeted by opposite factions who wanted to wipe them out later in the 1350s.

---

10 See the map of Oltrarno published by Emanuela Porta Casucci (2015–16, 194), highlighting the residences of Oltrarno inhabitants. Also, see figure 2.1 in the appendix, below.

11 "The links of friendship between the Da Certaldo and the Rossi figure also in the properties belonging to the two families in the town of Certaldo: the house of Fornaino di Andrea di Messer Benghi de' Rossi bordered one of the writer's [Boccaccio's] two homes, in the Borgo of Certaldo. Described in 1374 in his will, drawn up at the church of S. Felicita, this house was to be sold in order to pay the arrears in a maidservant's salary (ASFi, Biblioteca, Miscellanea 360.22). Their consistent physical proximity both in Florence and in Certaldo suggests a connection of blood between the Da Certaldo and the Rossi" (Porta Casucci 2015–16, 196, n. 15).

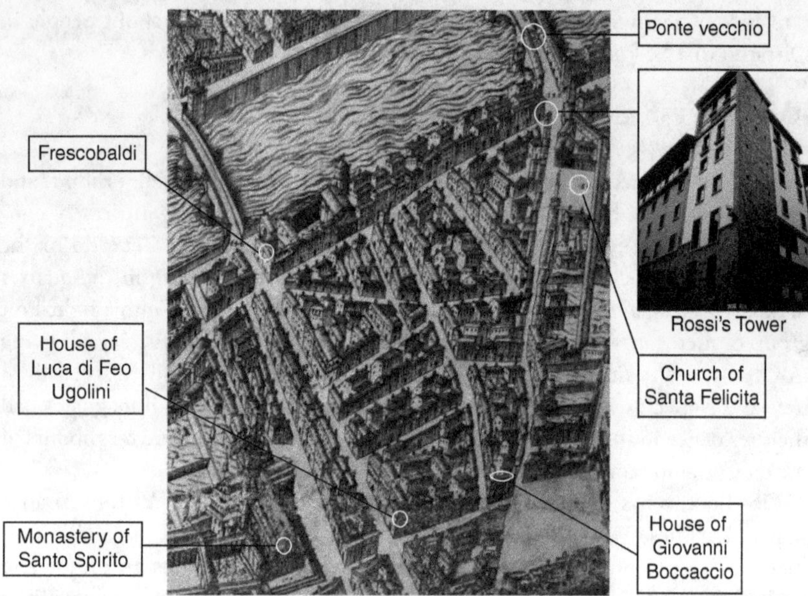

Figure 2.1. The quarter of Santo Spirito

Between 1348 and 1355, Boccaccio reached the apex of his political career, which can be divided into two phases: the first (1348–55) more prestigious, and the second (1364–7) definitely less important. Boccaccio was elected to several offices in the Commune, some of which were particularly eminent and concerned sensitive matters. Thus, he embarked on a political career in Florence in his own right.[12]

- 10 September 1348–19 January 1349: *ufficiale delle gabelle* (supervisor of tax offices) [ASFi, *CR* 28, f. 77r].

12 See the biography by Vittore Branca (1997, 30, 86, 93, 96, 97) and the documents of Giovanni Boccaccio collected by Oretta Agostini Muzzi (1978) and Laura Regnicoli (2013a, 394–6). See also Armstrong, Daniels, and Milner 2015 and Hankins 2019. I list here only the public offices held by Boccaccio, not the embassies and miscellaneous commissions that he undertook. Later in this chapter I give fuller explanation of these offices and more information about sources.

- January–February 1351: *camerlengo della Camera del Comune* (communal treasurer) [ASFi, *Tratte* 890, f. 27v]. In that role, he often spoke in the Council of the Podestà (Azzetta 2001, 33, n. 82) and was among the delegates of the Signoría in the final purchase of Prato [ASFi, *Diplomatico a quaderno*, Certosa, 23 February 1350, Florentine date].
- August–September 1351: *Diciotto di balìa*, an extraordinary office created *ad hoc* in November 1350 to oppose the Visconti's expansionism [ASFi, *balìa* 10, f. 1r; Regnicoli 2021a, 242]
- 3 November 1351–30 April 1352: *difensore del contado* (defender of the Florentine countryside) [ASFi, *Tratte* 891, f. 8r].
- 26 August 1352–26 February 1353: *ufficiale della gabella del pane* (officer of taxes on bread), together with Andrea Lancia [ASFi, *Tratte* 891, f. 22r] (Azzetta 2001, 34).
- January–April 1354: *ufficiale della torre* (officer of the tower) [ASFi, *Tratte* 744, f. 96r].
- May–October 1355: *ufficiale dei difetti* (officer of mercenary troops) [ASFi, *Tratte* 749, f. 57r].
- August 1364–February 1365: *ufficiale delle castella* (officer of castles)[13]
- 30 October 1367–1 March 1368: *ufficiale della condotta* (overseer of the army) [ASFi, *Tratte* 746, f. 86r].

Boccaccio was also able to use his influence to oversee the completion of three crucial cultural projects that were particularly dear to him, indicating that he had achieved some cultural success and prestige within the city. First was the donation in 1350, in the name of the Compagnia di Orsanmichele, of ten gold florins to Suor Beatrice, daughter of Dante Alighieri, in moral compensation for the treatment of the "divine poet" by Florence (Branca 1976, 87; Regnicoli 2013a, 394, doc. 11). The second, in March 1351, was the embassy, in which Boccaccio was a courier of official letters (which he probably drew up himself), addressed to Francesco Petrarch, in which Petrarch's father's conviction and ensuing confiscation of property were repealed and in which Petrarch was offered a chair at the just-created University of Florence (Branca 1976, 90–1). The third achievement, in 1360, was the establishment of the first chair of Greek in Europe, with Leonzio Pilato as professor (Pertusi 1964, 17).[14]

Boccaccio's commissions and cultural successes show that in this period he must have been well regarded for a wide range of skills and experience: he had studied law, he was proficient in Latin and rhetoric, he had grown up among the nobles of

13 The original has been lost, but partially copied by Rostagno 1913, 24; see also Regnicoli 2013a, 398, doc. 109.

14 Boccaccio's involvement at the founding of the University of Florence is highlighted by Paul Grendler (2002, 77–8).

the Court of Anjou and was thus proficient in etiquette at the highest levels of the aristocracy. At the same time, he was accustomed to the markets and banks – his notorious disdain for them notwithstanding – and was thus comfortable in the worlds of the nobles and of the merchants.

At least in these years, despite his constant nostalgia for Naples, he was not lacking in prestige or money. These were secure, productive years, when Boccaccio composed his novellas in vernacular, planned and wrote his Latin works, and made expensive gifts to Petrarch, like the valuable codex of the *Enarrationes in Psalmos* by Saint Augustine. Thanks to the support of his friends and his steady income, he was a free man, politically engaged in a republic in which he could express himself as he saw fit, even mocking openly his "biters" ("morditori"; *Dec.* IV.Intr.42), as noted in the introduction to the fourth day of the *Decameron*, where he evokes the vernacular love poetry so typical of Tuscany, whose exponents included Dante, Guido Cavalcanti, and Cino da Pistoia. Not only was this kind of poetry a great example of how vernacular had the potential to be used as the language for literature, but these authors through their love poems were also promoting the ideal of the nobility of souls against the nobility of blood – an important topic in the contemporary political scene.

His satisfaction with a life of liberty and autonomy comes across in a letter he wrote to his friend Zanobi da Strada in 1353, a day or so after the funeral of Lorenzo, eldest son of Niccolò Acciaiuoli, which took place on 7 April (*Ep.* IX). Boccaccio reproaches the great seneschal Acciaiuoli, who had mocked him with the nickname of "the Giovanni of tranquillity" ("Johannem tranquillitatum"; *Ep.* IX.2), and contrasts himself to Acciaiuoli: "As great as he is, I am small, really insignificant; he is strong, I am impotent; he is full of health, I am sickly" ("ipse magnus, ego parvus, ymmo nullus; ipse potens, ego impotens; ipse validus, ego infirmus sum"; *Ep.* IX.15). He carries on with a celebration of poverty, reminiscent of Seneca, in which he emphasizes his liberty as a life choice, in contrast to those who (like Zanobi) prefer life under a *signore*, that is, a tyrant, and salaried people looking to increase their own wealth (*Ep.* IX.17–19):

> If I will love poverty, it is already with me; and if it should be absent, then I will find it as quickly as possible, wherever it may be. Nor will I serve any king to keep it. If I covet riches, or at least enough money to keep up with my life, I confess that, not having it, there is no lack of places for seeking it out: Padua, Verona, ancient Ravenna, Forlì call me even as I refuse them. If you object about the tyrants, I would say that also desiring money is tyrannical, and having put that forward, another truer response offers itself, even if it is less suitable for the moment. But actually it is suitable: for you are with tyrants now, even if they are adorned with a favourable title. I live for myself as a pauper, as a rich and splendid man I would live for other men; and I take more delight in some of my little books than your kings feel for their grand crowns.
>
> (Si pauperiem amabo, iam mecum est, et si abesset, ubique quam cito comperiam; nec pro habenda ullo regi serviam. Si divitias concupivero aut saltem victui meo

oportunam pecuniam, fateor, cum hec non assit, ad exquirendam tamen non omnino loca deficient: Patavum, Verona, vetus Ravenna, Forlivium me etiam renuentem vocant. Si tyrampnos obicis, dicam et tirampnicum exoptare pecuniam, posito et responsio alia verior, licet ad presens minus congrua, se offerat; ymo congrua: et tu cum tyrampnis es, fausto tamen ornatis titulo … Michi pauper vivo, dives autem et splendidus aliis viverem: et plus cum aliquibus meis libellis parvulis voluptatis sentio quam cum magno diademate sentiant reges tui.)

Boccaccio underscores in this passage how his "poverty" is his own choice.[15] To be clear, this poverty is not real and concrete but is philosophical, as in Seneca, that is, the state in which one is neither wishing nor searching for more than is necessary to live on in dignified fashion. Boccaccio claims that in fact he had a number of other options: if he wished, he could go to the Polenta family in Ravenna or the Ordelaffi in Forlì (where he had already found employment in the past), or to the Carrara in Padua and the Scaligeri in Verona, all places where his presence had been requested.[16] But he had refused. Thanks to his father's inheritance and his new status inside the city, he was in the privileged position of being able to choose for himself, rejecting an employment in a court in favour of living free in a republic. In the quoted passage, he acknowledges that all these *signori* asking for him are tyrants; they also supported the emperor and, as such, were Ghibellines. The Court of Anjou was a tyranny, too, albeit "mantled in a more auspicious title" ("fausto tamen ornatis titulo"), that is, it was Guelf, in favour of the pope.

15 Ginetta Auzzas, who edited his letters for the Mondadori edition, commented: "In this long and beautiful passage we are allowed to perceive clearly a solid and sincere feeling of Boccaccio's now mature dignity as a man and as a poet. These passionate invocations now bear the seal of his new literary and cultural awareness, bearing witness to an aspect of his countenance that would only become clearer as the years went by" (*Ep.* IX, 787, n. 19).

16 Auzzas writes: "In fact, based on the evidence of *Ep.* VI and *Egl.* XVI, his connections with Forlì and Ravenna are well-known, while we are unaware of eventual communications with the Carrara (Padua) and the Scaligeri (Verona)" (*Ep.* IX, 787, n. 19). That Boccaccio might have had such communications is suggested by his friendships in Oltrarno. Besides Petrarch, who would have supported him had he desired to move, the intermediaries among the Carrara could have been Manno and Pazzino di Apardo Donati, who were *condottieri* at the Paduan court in those years. Relations between Petrarch and Manno Donati are well attested (Wilkins 1960; Kohl 1992). Boccaccio was also in close contact with Pazzino (Imbriani 1882, 84; Regnicoli 2013a, 394, doc. 13), who was also a man of letters: he served as tutor to his nephew Manno di Manno Donati, and wrote memoirs, now lost. Costanza da Polenta, sister of Ostasio dal Polenta (Litta 1819–83, vol. 15), for whom Boccaccio had once worked, had married Giacomo II da Carrara sometime after 1340 (Kohl 1977). The Scaligeri connection came through the da Lisca family (Varanini 2002), to whom Andrea di Tello da Lisca was certainly related, as was the wife of Pino de' Rossi, Giovanna di Bandino da Lisca, sister of Giovanni who was *condottiero* for the Scaligeri. Pazzino di Apardo Donati was close to the Scaligeri, too: in April 1354, Pazzino was pardoned for a previous conviction in Florence through the "friendly intercession" of Cangrande II della Scala (ASFi, *PR* 41, f. 9v).

After the brief *signoria* of the Duke of Athens, the dyads *libertas*/*tirannides*, republic/*signoria* had assumed rather specific political connotations, often identified with the opposition between Guelfs and Ghibellines. However, associating specific political styles with particular political groupings is simplistic; there were exceptions to such associations across the Italian peninsula. Matteo Villani cites the Signoria of Volterra, "which was ruled by the tyrant sons of Messer Ottaviano de' Belforti, who despite being declared Guelfs, were inclined by their tyranny to a Ghibelline spirit" ("si reggeva sotto la tirannia de' figliuoli di messer Attaviano de' Belforti, i quali quanto che fossono guelfi di nazione, per la tirannia dichinavano ad animo ghibellino"; M. Villani 1995, 4.63).[17] Some of Boccaccio's peers, like Zanobi di Strada and Petrarch, accepted the patronage of *signori* (and in the case of Petrarch, of Ghibellines, enemies of the Florentine Republic). Boccaccio, on the other hand, understood that although one might profit handsomely under a *signore*, it came at the cost of one's personal liberties. He claims, with some pride, "I live poor, for myself; / I could live wealthy and in splendour, for others" ("Michi pauper vivo, dives autem et splendidus aliis viverem"; *Ep*. IX.19). In other words, he would prefer the modest life of a free man, the kind of liberty usually associated with Republican Guelfs, over a life of wealth and influence under a *signore*, in a tyranny that is always Ghibelline in spirit if not in word.

In the conclusion to *Epistola* IX, Boccaccio writes: "more solito inter publicas privatasque occupationes ultra velle anxior" ("as usual, I worry more than I want about my public and private occupations"). In this "more solito," we see how much Boccaccio's public tasks and concerns have become an integral and essential part in his life in Florence.

Boccaccio's political career in Florence began in a position equivalent to a superintendent of the office of indirect taxes of the Republic, the *ufficiale delle gabelle*.[18] To take on a public office of this kind in Florence, one had to satisfy certain specific prerequisites. One had to be a native of Florence or the *contado*, which meant to reside there (and at this point in history, residence had to go back three generations, as far as the paternal grandfather); be at least thirty years of age; have paid in full all direct taxes on properties, called *estimo*; be a *popolano* enrolled in a guild, major or minor (this determined access to higher or lower offices); be declared and certified as a Guelf, that is, to not be "Ghibelline or not a true Guelf." Those who were Ghibelline, bankrupted, confined, banned, or relegated

---

17 See especially Zorzi (2010, 145–55) and Mazzoni 2010. With the *signoria* of the Belforti in Volterra indirectly involved, so were some members of the magnate families of Oltrarno. Ottaviano Belforti's second wife was Feca di Lippaccio Frescobaldi, and his daughter-in-law – wife of his second son, Bocchino – was Bandecca de' Rossi, sister of Pino di Giovanni de' Rossi.

18 ASFi, *CR* 28, f. 77r: Regnicoli 2013a, 394, doc. 5 (Luca Azzetta brought this information to light).

were ineligible for the magistracies of the Commune, as were all their relatives (Guidi 1981, vol. 2, 99–105).

When Boccaccio took up the office of *ufficiale delle gabelle*, he fulfilled all the requirements: he was born in Florence or in the *contado* (Certaldo); he was thirty-five years of age; he and his family had regularly paid the *estimo*; he was obviously of declared and certified Guelf faith; and he was a *popolano* belonging to a guild. Keeping in mind the higher offices he had held (such as *camerlengo della camera del Comune*), we can infer that Boccaccio must have been enrolled in one of the seven major guilds or *arti*: those of judges and notaries; merchants (Arte di Calimala); the wool guild; bankers; Por Santa Maria, specialized in silk; physicians and pharmacists; and furriers and skinners. But which one? The answer to this question is important. There were different ways to gain access to a guild, some of which were long and difficult, such as years of apprenticeship and professional training in the field. Sometimes, though, enrolment in a guild could take place much faster. In the case of the death ("causa mortis") of a relative or a business associate, the person's heir or partner could replace the deceased in the guild in order to continue the person's work (Guidi 1981, vol. 1, 134). In Boccaccio's case, he was most likely in the bankers' guild, the Arte del Cambio, following his father. Indeed, according to the documents at our disposal today, Boccaccino di Chellino must have died between July 1348, when he added a codicil to his will,[19] and 27 April 1349, when Boccaccio collected the interest on his father's credit.[20] It seems reasonable to believe that, as Domenico Maria Manni speculated, his father died of plague in July or at the latest in August 1348, shortly after making the modification to his testament. If this is the case, we may infer that Boccaccio was enrolled in the bankers' guild *causa mortis patris*, at some point after his father's

19 A manuscript of Carlo Strozzi (BNCF, *Magl.* XXXVII.299) says that Boccaccino di Chellino, "who was living in Florence in the *popolo* of Santa Felicita, on 7 September 1346, drew up a will written by Domenico son of Iacopo Bonaffare di Certaldo, and afterward he added a codicil in July 1348 written by Piero Nelli" ("Dominus Ioannes quondam Boccaccii de Certaldo exponit qualiter Boccaccius eius pater, qui morabatur Florentie in populo Sancte Felicitatis, anno 1346 die 7 settembris fecit testamentum manu ser Dominici filii Iacobi Bonaffaris de Certaldo et postea anno 1348 de mense iulii fecit codicillos manu ser Pieri Nelli"; Manni 1742, 21; Regnicoli 2013a, 385–6, doc. 80). Boccaccino installed a tomb in the Church of Santa Croce, in the crypt underneath Saint Louis Chapel, at the end of the left side of the transept (Bartalini 2005, 180, fig. 212-Q). (The chapel was commissioned by the Bardi family for their burials and to honour Louis of Toulouse, the Franciscan brother of King Robert.) The inscription on Boccaccino's tomb reads "Sepulcrum Boccaccii Chellini et suorum," which implies that he was buried at least with his wife Bice de' Bostichi. Boccaccino's will is preserved in ASFi, *Manoscritti* 619, f. 6r; I thank Anne Leader for sending me a copy of this page. Jacopo di Boccaccio, brother of Giovanni, asked to be buried in the same tomb as his father in his will of 1384 (ASFi, *Diplomatico*, San Miniato al Monte (Olivetani), 19 June 1384; transcribed and published by Latini 1913).

20 Regnicoli 2013a, 385–6, doc. 80; 394, docs. 6–8.

death and before his assumption of the office of *ufficiale delle gabelle* (in all likelihood, in August). This would have been necessary for his political aims and to be able to manage the goods and the businesses his father had left behind. Even if the name Johannes Boccaccii de Certaldo is not recorded as an enrolled member in any of the Arte del Cambio's record books of the period that survive in the Florentine State Archive,[21] the documented facts we do have leave little doubt that Boccaccio was a member of the Arte del Cambio. The books of the guild for this period contain names familiar to any Boccaccio scholar: Niccolò di Bartolo del Buono, dedicatee of the *Comedia delle ninfe fiorentine*, appears frequently for many different reasons;[22] Giovanna, the wife of Pino de' Rossi (ASFi, *Arte del Cambio* 62, np), and their children Stoldo and Francesco, who testified in favour of Niccolò di Bartolo del Buono in a lawsuit (ASFi, *Arte del Cambio* 44, f. 27v); Tommaso di Diodato Baronci – the ugly protagonist of *Decameron* 6.6 – consul of the guild in 1358 and in constant conflict with Uberto degli Infangati, one of the conspirators of 1360;[23] and Boccaccio's correspondent Leonardo del Chiaro, in a case against Andrea di Filippo Balducci (ASFi, *Arte del Cambio* 62, np), the young boy in love with the Florentine "ducks" in the only novella narrated by the author himself in the *Decameron* (IV.Intr.). The records also document a controversy that arose after Boccaccio's death in 1377, between his brother Jacopo di Boccaccio and Friar Martino da Signa of the Augustinian order of the monastery of Santo Spirito, which was connected to the guild, about the possession of the twenty-four notebooks containing the *Expositions on Dante's Comedy*; the fact that this dispute was recorded by the guild is strong evidence that Boccaccio and his brother belonged to the Arte del Cambio.[24] Jacopo di Boccaccio, in fact, appealed to the consuls of the Arte del Cambio. On 10 February 1377, "in front of the consuls of the Arte del Cambio" he presented a petition for the restitution of the notebooks; on 17 March of the same year, Francesco di Lapo di Buonamico, who

---

21 The names of members of the Arte del Cambio are listed in manuscripts produced by the Bakers' Guild and conserved in the Florentine State Archive (ASFi, *Manoscritti* 542 and 545), but Boccaccio's name is not there. I also checked, in the same archive, the nine books covering the Arte del Cambio for the period 1339–80, but he is not listed in any of them: ASFi, *Arte del Cambio* 11, 13, 14, 43, 44, 58, 59, 61, 62. This does not prove that Boccaccio was not enrolled in the guild: the absence of proof in the extant documents does not entail that he was not a member of the guild, since we have only the documents that survived. Boccaccio was almost certainly what is technically called a *scioperato*, someone enrolled in a guild but not practising the profession.

22 ASFi, *Arte del Cambio* 14, ff. 21r, 25v, 28v, 31r, 33v, 38r, 42r; 44, 9v, 21v–22r, 24v, 27v, 38r, 39r–v.

23 ASFi, *Arte del Cambio* 14, ff. 6r, 17v, 18r; 44, 31r–v, 83v.

24 The documents are collected in Agostini Muzzi 1978, 681–2; and by Laura Regnicoli, 2013a, docs. 187–90.

was keeping the notebooks as a guarantor, "in front of the consuls of the Arte del Cambio" said he was unable to give them back until the cause was solved; on 18 April, Jacopo di Boccaccio presented another petition "To the consuls of the Arte del Cambio," after which the notebooks were deposited by "the notary of the Arte del Cambio." The fact that Jacopo, as "father and legitimate administrator of the heirs of dominus Johannes Boccaccii," went to the consuls of the bankers' guild is not casual; he did so again in 28 April 1377, for another reason (ASFi, *Arte del Cambio* 62, ff. 104r–v; Agostini Muzzi 1978, 682; Regnicoli 2013a, 401, doc. 190). None of the records says explicitly that Giovanni Boccaccio was enrolled in the Arte del Cambio, but the circumstantial evidence is overwhelming.

Boccaccio's first office was an important one, and he cannot have been appointed because of his local political experience – he had none. But he was trusted in the world of the higher guilds, and he was healthy and able to serve, when so many were dead. In September 1348, the city's population had been cut by more than half. As Marchionne di Coppo Stefani writes: "This plague began in March … and ended in September 1348, and the people began to trickle back into Florence to see their homes and properties" ("Questa pistolenza cominciò di marzo … e finì di settembre MCCCXLVIII, e le genti cominciarono a tornare a Firenze, ed a rivedersi le case, e le masserizie"; 1910, rubr. 634). In October, it was possible to compile an estimate of the casualties, which ran to at least 96,000, according to Stefani (1910, rubr. 635), or as Boccaccio writes in the *Decameron* (I.Intr.47): "between March and the July following … it is believed that definitely over 100,000 human souls within the walls of the city of Florence lost their lives" ("infra 'l marzo e il prossimo luglio vegnente … oltre centomila creature umane si crede per certo dentro alle mura della città di Firenze essere stati di vita tolti").[25] As Boccaccio writes in the Introduction to the *Decameron*, the ministers and managers of the Commune were either dead or unable to govern the city:

> The venerable authority of the laws, both divine and human, had all but fallen and dissolved because of the death or illness of their ministers and executors, or because their servants and employees were so devastated that they could not hold any office.

25 The actual number of deaths and the time frame cannot be determined with certainty. Boccaccio's figure of "over 100,000" is intended as hyperbole, but it is not far off the number given by Marchionne di Coppo Stefani (1910): 96,000. Giovanni di Paolo Morelli, writing a few decades later and citing Boccaccio, estimates 80,000 (1969, 165); Matteo Villani gives 50,000 (1995, 1.2). The epidemic started in March 1348 – on this the sources are unanimous – but opinions differ regarding its end: Boccaccio calculates the mortality between March and July (unlikely to have been the final month, since the plague thrives in high temperatures); Stefani says the plague was over by September; Matteo Villani writes that mortality rates in November, though decreasing, were still causing concern (1995, 1.8). See also Falsini 1971; Benedictow 2004; Naphy and Spicer 2004; and J. Kelly 2005.

(la reverenda auttorità delle leggi, così divine come umane, quasi caduta e dissoluta tutta per li ministri e essecutori di quelle, li quali, sì come gli altri uomini, erano tutti o morti o infermi o sì di famiglia rimasi stremi, che uficio alcuno non potea fare.) (*Dec.* Intr.1.23)

As Branca writes, citing Carabellese, "We know that 11 Gonfaloniers, 6 Good Men, 4 Treasurers, 2 Officers of Conduct, 9 of the 'twelve of the coin' [*dodici della moneta*] could no longer be found in their offices" (1990, 20).

Boccaccio did not succumb to the plague, and that put him in a good position to move quickly into public service at a high level. He had never served in any public capacity in Florence. Furthermore, he had only just moved back to the city after his years in Romagna, and before leaving he had been particularly close to the magnates in Oltrarno and to the court of the Duke of Athens, neither of these in good standing with the popular government of Florence. Nevertheless, the political regime in Florence had collapsed as a result of the epidemic, the popular government had ended, and the survivors able to govern the city after the plague were very few. "After August 1348 the relationship between the major and minor guilds was once again changed with respect to access to the Priorate: three members of the major, three from the middle, and two from the minor guilds, while the gonfalonier of justice had to come from the major. Shortly afterward, further measures were taken to diminish the influence of the minor guilds" (Guidi 1981, vol. 2, 14). The popular government's institutions were dismantled, and the major guilds were slowly but inexorably taking back control of the city. Whoever survived the plague had the chance to rule Florence.

This extraordinary historical situation in the aftermath of plague no doubt helped Boccaccio to be chosen as one of the eight supervisors of the offices of tax collectors, but there is also no doubt that he possessed the knowledge needed to perform the duties of the office, and the right connections that helped in having his name-slip in the nominating bags. This was one of the highest-ranking offices of the communal tax system: the *ufficiale delle gabelle* oversaw all the other offices on "indirect" taxes – the offices on contract taxes, door taxes, salt taxes, wine taxes, and many others. As the major guilds came back into full power, we can see how well liked, respected, and trusted Boccaccio was by the new ruling class in Florence. As a side note, from 1 July 1347 the salt tax (*gabella del sale*), which was under his direct supervision, was managed by some of his friends: Niccolo' di Bartolo del Buono together with his cousin Francesco di Piero del Buono, and Piero di Lapo da Castiglionchio, the brother of Lapo di Lapo. Although Boccaccio's tasks were probably rather tedious, they were crucial to the Commune, especially at that time. According to David Herlihy (1964), *gabelle* were the fundamental source of urban finance in medieval Italy: in Florence, it is estimated that more than three-quarters of all revenues came from these taxes, especially those on wine (*gabella del vino*), salt (*gabella del sale*), and goods entering and leaving the city (*gabella delle porte*).[26] These kinds of taxes had been dramatically increased during and after the plague, causing great hardship. Stefani writes:

> Anything eaten by those who were ill, sweets and sugar, were exorbitantly priced. A pound of sugar was sold for eight instead of three florins, as was the case with other sweets. Chickens and other poultry became incredibly expensive, and eggs went up from 12 to 24 denari, and it was lucky for anyone to find three per day after searching the entire city.
>
> (Le cose, che mangiavano i malati, confetti, e zucchero smisuratamente valeano. Fu venduta di tre in otto fiorini la libbra del zucchero, ed a simile gli altri confetti. Li pollastri, ed altri pollami a meraviglia carissimi, e lo uovo di prezzo di denari 12 in 24, e beato chi ne trovava tre il dì con cercare tutta la città.) (Stefani 1910, rubr. 364)

On 10 January 1349, Boccaccio left this position at the end of his four-month term and turned to his own family finances. On 17 April of that year he collected the first instalment of interest on his deceased father's holdings, making his debut in the fiscal documents of Florence as *dominus Iohannes eius filius et heres in solidum*; the two remaining payments came on 14 May and 4 August 1349 (Regnicoli 2013a, 385–6, scheda 80, 394, doc. 6-7-8). The phrase *heres in solidum*, "exclusive heir," tells us that Boccaccio inherited everything left by his father.

As the proceeds from his father's estate started to come in, Boccaccio would have needed to make a full assessment of his inheritance. Giovanni di Paolo Morelli instructed his children in the event of his death to "first, make an inventory of what you have" (Morelli 2013, 146). Just so, Boccaccio would have had to inventory and take charge of the family businesses, which demanded much of his attention. He had to guard some of his and Jacopo's farms in Certaldo, for example, from partisan plunderers and ensure that they continued to be worked by the farmers. Lawsuits brought by Boccaccio provide details of the kind of damage and harassment they had sustained.[27] The goods he inherited from his father were only part of what he had to manage, for there were also those inherited from

---

26 On taxes in Florence, see Barbadoro 1929, Sapori 1958, La Roncière 1968, Molho 1971, and Franceschi 2015. Justin Steinberg (2020) connects Boccaccio's experience as a tax collector with the novella of Calandrino and the heliotrope (*Dec.* VIII.3).

27 As Branca notes (1976, 122, n. 4): "On August 18 [1352] in the first suit, before the Giudice dei malefici (judge of torts), Boccaccio speaks through an attorney, Angelo di ser Andrea; in the second, November 19, he personally presents to the same judge an accusation against Francesco and Buccio di Pone of Certaldo, who had abandoned the farm of Santa Maria in Collina, property of his ward Jacopo, but on November 23 he drops the action." Dorini, who transcribed the documents regarding these trials, maintains: "it would appear that we cannot exclude the possibility of a real vendetta against Boccaccio," although we do not know why (Dorini 1914, 74–8).

his stepmother by his young half-brother Jacopo, whose legal guardian he had become by 26 January 1350.[28]

Boccaccio was elected to another position with the city of Florence on 14 December 1350, the prestigious and honorific role of *camerlengo della Camera del Comune* (treasurer of the Commune), for the usual two-month term, January and February 1351, a position he shared with three other people. The Camera del Comune was the main financial office of the city: it collected communal taxes and disbursed money to public officials – for example, the mayor, executors of justice, the chancellor, castellans, policemen, ambassadors, town criers, accountants, bell ringers, and others – and also paid for writing materials, candles, ink, and other incidentals, including public feasts and the city lions, kept in the actual Via dei Leoni, as symbol of Florence. So, it handled incoming and outgoing communal funds, including the salaries and household expenses of the public officials and the indirect tax (*gabelle*) on goods entering Florence (and thus linked with Boccaccio's previous office). In essence, it was the treasury of Florence, or as a modern scholar describes it, "the premier fiscal organ of the Florentine State."[29] Moreover, "in the 14th century, the Camera del Comune wielded considerable autonomy and importance, and contributed in a decisive way in formulating the economic and financial politics of the State" (Guidi 1981, vol. 2, 276). After 1319, the Camera del Comune was located inside the residence of the *podestà*, which is the current Bargello. All the chamberlains lived in this palace during their mandate, so Boccaccio would have stayed in Via del Proconsolo, together with them, the *podestà*, and the *podestà*'s large entourage (Yunn 2015, 180–2; 240, doc. 93). Novella VIII.5 of the *Decameron* may owe something to this experience (Robins and Faibisoff 2020).

Boccaccio was one of four chamberlains,[30] each of whom held a key to the strongbox that stored the communal monies. At least two chamberlains were clerics: they could have come from the Cistercian abbey of San Settimo or from

28 The original document is lost, but a copy survives in BNCF, *Magliabechiano* XXXVII.299, f. 2 (Regnicoli 2013a, 394, doc. 10), reproduced in part by Manni 1742, 26. In 1350, Jacopo must have been between six and nine years old – Jacopo's birth date is still uncertain, but based on archival documents Regnicoli has recently defined his birth some time between 1341 and May 1344 (Regnicoli 2018, 27–8). His mother, Bice de' Bostichi, was daughter of Lore di Gherardo dei Baroncelli and Ubaldino di Nepo dei Bostichi: both parents were magnates and they possessed lands in Certaldo, too. Dorini (1914, 82) notes that extensive documentation proves Jacopo to be the only owner of lands situated in Santa Maria a Colline in the Certaldo commune, inherited from his mother. On Bice di Nepo de' Bostichi, see Regnicoli 2018, 26–7.

29 Guidi calls it the "organo preminente nella politica finanziaria dello Stato" (1981, vol. 2, 277). For the Camera del Comune, see Guidi 1981, vol. 2, 275–9; Gherardi 1885; Davidsohn 1956–68, vol. 4, 200–4; and Caferro 2018a and 2018b.

30 "The sensible Messer Giovanni, one of the chamberlains of the Camera del Comune" ("providus dominus Iohannes Boccaccii, unus ex Camerariis Camere Comunis"; ASFi, *PR* 38, f. 175r, 16 January 1351).

the Umiliati of Ognissanti.[31] When Boccaccio was *camerlengo*, there were two monks from the Dominican monastery of San Marco: Benedetto Caccini and Jacopo Giovanni (Caferro 2018b, 112). The other lay chamberlain with Boccaccio was Paolo di Neri Bordoni. His appointment reveals the political aspect of the job, because he had a long history of political involvement, and served as peacemaker during the *signoria* of the Duke of Athens.[32] The presence of clerics in this role was due to the fact that their loyalty and honesty were assured by their prelate,[33] whereas lay chamberlains had to assure their honesty through bonds, swearing an oath before communal officials, and depositing one thousand florins as surety.[34] This was a significant amount of money. If Boccaccio was able to deposit this sum, we can infer that his financial situation, at least in this specific historical moment, was strong. It is possible that his friends put up the money: in this case, he must have been perceived as a trustworthy, honest person. Indeed, the chamberlains needed to be trustworthy (this was the main qualification for the job) because they held the key to the Commune's strongbox. One thousand florins is a large sum to deposit in comparison to the remuneration earned, which was among the lowest of the official posts in Florence.[35] This was a position of prestige, not income.

The duty of the chamberlains was to supervise more than two hundred employees, overseeing others who actually managed the accounts: "Like the other chamberlain, Boccaccio's role was restricted to participation in decisions involving the disbursement of funds" (Caferro 2018b, 113). The city had two full-time accountants and two notaries, one pair to draw up income and the other to draw up expenditures. In this capacity, Boccaccio "oversaw payments to Antonio Pucci as town crier and Andrea Lancia as ambassador" (Armstrong, Daniels, and Milner

31 See Barbadoro 1929; Marzi 1910; Trexler 1978. The *camerarii camera comunis Florentie* had been clerics since 1289 (Trexler 1978, 320–1), and they were employed because "since the lay bursars of the Camera of the Commune received and disbursed communal money, they had to give surety of their honesty."

32 Paolo di Neri Bordoni had been prior in 1338–9 (Stefani 1910, 188n.); he was active during the period when Walter Brienne briefly governed the city. Bordoni, with Pino de' Rossi, negotiated the peace between Pisa, Lucca, and Florence; Paoli 1862, 17–19); he helped engineer the duke's exile in 1343 and held offices afterward (Paoli 1862, 44); in 1344 he was *gonfaloniere di giustizia*, another very prestigious post (Zafarana 1971). See also Caferro 2018b, 112–13.

33 Clerics swore to execute their duties honestly before the prelate, not the government, as lay chamberlains did. "Thus the Commune relied on the religious person's obedience to his prelate … to guarantee his loyalty and honesty to the Commune" (Trexler 1978, 321–2).

34 See Guidi for documents from 1355 (1981, vol. 2, 275–9), and Gherardi 1885 for those from 1303. See also Caferro 2018b, 112–16.

35 See Caferro 2013, 161, table 3, "Nominal Monthly Salaries of Florentine Government Employees," for the years 1349–50. Caferro points out, "The chamberlains in charge of the *camera* earned less than notaries who worked under them" (2013, 160; also, Caferro 2018b, 130).

2015, 10), intervening several times during the councils of the *podestà*,[36] and he appears as one of the witnesses in the document on the important purchase of Prato by the Commune of Florence.[37]

This purchase marked the definitive victory of Florence over the Angevin claims in Tuscany, and prevented the city falling into the hands of the Visconti with their expansionist ambitions. The seller was the grand seneschal Niccolò Acciaiuoli, in the name of the sovereigns of Naples, Luigi and Joanna, on 23 February 1351; representing him in Florence with full authority were his trusted cousins Jacopo di Donato and Angelo Acciaiuoli. The sale did not go as well as Niccolò Acciaiuoli expected: he had hoped to receive at least 30,000 florins, but he was paid just 17,500, "a ridiculously low price" as Brucker states (1962, 145), paid in three separate instalments and with delays, as well.[38]

The relationship between Boccaccio and Acciaiuoli was of long standing, but strained. Branca writes that the purchase of Prato was "perhaps, in some manner, the moral revenge of Boccaccio upon Acciaiuoli," who had chosen Zanobi rather than Boccaccio as the literary expert at the Angevin court, a choice that wounded Boccaccio deeply (Branca 1976, 90). It is not clear when Zanobi da Strada moved to Naples – Léonard estimates 1352, whereas Paolo Francesco Tocco, with very good documentary proof, believes he was there by 5 August 1350.[39] We cannot know if the purchase of Prato gave Boccaccio an opportunity to take revenge. What we do know is that Boccaccio, in his role as chamberlain of the Camera del Comune, was one of the four people responsible for the disbursement of funds, but according to the new studies presented by Laura Regnicoli (2021, 238), he was not among those who made the decisions about the selling of Prato.

"Petrarch's War" and the War against the Visconti

Nescis posse meum, que sit mea gloria nescis.

(To the Archbishop of Milan on behalf of the Florentine Lion,
"You do not know my power; how great my glory is, you do not know.")

– G. Boccaccio, *Carmina* VI

36 As Azzetta notes (2001, 33–4): 17 January 1351 (ASFi, *LF* 30, f. 97r; ASFi, *PR* 38, ff. 174v–175r); 28 January 1351 (ASFi, *LF* 30, f. 98r; ASFi, *PR* 38, ff. 182r–v); 28 February 1351 (ASFi, *LF* 30, f. 99r; ASFi, *PR* 38, ff. 187v).

37 ASFi, *Diplomatico, Certosa*, 23 February 1350 (Agostini Muzzi 1978, 656; Regnicoli 2013a, 395, doc. 25).

38 For a detailed account of the purchase of Prato from Niccolò Acciaiuoli, see Rao 1995 and F.P. Tocco 2001, 108–22. See also M. Villani 1995, 1.71–3.

39 See Léonard 1932–6, vol. 2, 371–3n; F.P. Tocco 2001, 100–1. For Zanobi da Strada, see Baglio 2013a and 2013b.

Boccaccio was not acting on his own or out of his own interests in his political ventures, for he was a member of a specific group, just as his father had been: the magnates of Oltrarno (especially the Bardi, Rossi, and Frescobaldi) and the *grassi popolani* bound to them, connected by common economic and political interests and marriage alliances, often in close contact with powerful families outside the walls and *contado* of Florence.

Boccaccio and his friends served in high positions of the Commune with the goal of reestablishing the city based on new ideals, like the narrators of the *Decameron* returning to Florence after or during the devastation of the plague. In 1349, for example, important offices were held by some of his friends (men who would be co-conspirators in 1360). Luca di Feo Ugolini was officer of taxes for contracts for the district of Santo Spirito, together with Nicolas Gherardini Jannis; he then became a prior, along with Cione del Buono and Filippo di Recco Capponi (both from Oltrarno); his cousin Piero di Cenni Ugolini was consul of the Wool Guild between January and April 1349. Pino de' Rossi was captain of the Guelf Party between March and April 1340. Niccolò di Bartolo del Buono (with Francesco di Piero del Buono, Maffeo di Lapo di Centellino, and Piero di Lapo da Castiglionchio) collected the duties on salt from 1347 to 1351.[40] In 1349, Uberto di Ubaldini degli Infangati was treasurer for the purchasers of duties on salt, as well as being one of the twelve citizen counsellors (*buoni uomini*) (from 15 September to 14 December).[41] Many of these friends were also involved in the armed attacks against the Ubaldini, which William Caferro called "Petrarch's war" (Caferro 2013 and 2018a).[42]

The war against the Ubaldini, a Florentine Ghibelline faction, was a major preoccupation for the citizens of Florence immediately after the plague, such that Matteo Villani, after chronicling the main features of the kingdoms of Naples, France, and England, devotes almost the entire first book of his *Cronica* to these events. This particular struggle ran from summer 1349 to fall 1350. The Ubaldini family had their possessions in the Mugello, a region north of Florence, through which passed an essential trade route through the Apennines that linked Florence to Bologna and the whole north of Italy. The *casus belli* was the murder of Luca Cristiani and Mainardo Accursio, two of Petrarch's best friends, by the Ubaldini clan in May 1349, when they were travelling in broad daylight from Avignon

40 For the duties on salt, see Guidi 1981, vol. 2, 301–3.

41 For archival documentation on Luca di Feo Ugolini, Piero di Cenni Ugolini, Pino de' Rossi, Niccolò di Bartolo del Buono, and Uberto di Ubaldino degli Infangati, see the prosopographical notes in the appendix.

42 All details of the war against the Ubaldini are from Caferro 2013, 2015, and 2018a. As he notes, the war is well documented in the Florentine State Archive.

to Florence.[43] Petrarch wrote a long letter of protest to the Florentines (*Fam.* 8.10), dated 2 June 1349: "To the Florentines, an expression of indignation and complaint concerning the inhuman crimes perpetrated on their borders, and an exhortation to cultivate justice and to guard their roads." Florence sent out its army soon afterward, in June 1349, after creating an ad hoc committee of eight men called the *balìa*, with full authority in this war (Guidi 1981, vol. 2, 200). Matteo Villani claimed that their attack was brief and successful (1995, 1.48–9), but aggressions by the Ubaldini continued in October and November 1349. Florence finally defeated the clan in September 1350, but fighting broke out again in 1351 between Florence and Milan, when the Ubaldini sided with Milan.

The war is important for our understanding of the contexts in which Boccaccio moved and produced his literary works, because many of Boccaccio's friends and future conspirators were involved. As William Caferro shows (2015, 48), "among the Florentine executives who called for war against the clan were Pino de' Rossi, for whom Boccaccio later wrote the *epistola consolatoria* (1362), and Francesco del Benino ... referenced in the *epistola*. Pino de' Rossi urged Florence to take up arms against the Ubaldini in a 'wise and cautious' manner [ASFi, *Consulte e pratiche*, 1, f. 3r–4v]." Francesco del Benino[44] helped organize supplies for the armies and "served as ambassador in the Mugello at the outset of the war" (Caferro 2018a, 34). Donato Velluti – the author of the famous *Cronica domestica*, neighbour of Pino de' Rossi and related to the Frescobaldi family[45] – "called the Florentine army to proceed against the Ubaldini in a 'manly fashion,' to use 'arson and all means available' to root them out" (Caferro 2018a, 52); he was appointed, in fact, as one of the four consultants for the *balìa*, one for each quarter of the city, together with Jacopo di Donato Acciaiuoli. Velluti was used as ambassador to Bologna as well, asking for help and troops, though the request was denied (Caferro 2018a, 53; 125). Among the priors of 1349, there was also Luca di Feo Ugolini, one of the future conspirators of 1360 and named in the *Consolatoria* as Boccaccio's and Pino's friend.

Other people related to Boccaccio were implicated in this war, too: in the executive branch, along with Pino de' Rossi and Francesco del Benino, there were Jacopo di Donato Acciaiuoli (cousin of Niccolò Acciaiuoli),[46] in charge of military provisions, and Niccolò di Bartolo del Buono (dedicatee of the *Comedia delle ninfe*

---

43 Discussions in the Commune's councils suggest that Florence had already engaged with the Ubaldini in a limited way; Petrarch (*Fam.* 8.9) indicates the same (Caferro 2015, 46). Florence fought against the Ubaldini in 1306, 1342, and again in 1373: for a broader perspective, see Magna 1982, and Mazzoni and Monti 2013, 15–22. On the Ubaldini family in the thirteenth century, see Bellandi 2010.

44 For Francesco del Benino in the *Consolatoria*, see the studies by P.G. Ricci 1959, 29–32.

45 See Velluti 1914; for the family relations, consult the genealogical table in appendix 1.

46 For Jacopo di Donato Acciaiuoli, see F.P. Tocco 2001, 108–9, 286–9.

fiorentine, executed for his role in the failed conspiracy of 1360), who served as ambassador to the war region (Caferro 2018a, 34–5). Caferro adds: "Del Buono had … an important economic role in the war. He is listed on the budgets as a purchaser of the lucrative salt *gabelle*, a major source of city revenue, and served as an associate (*socio*) of the da Uzzano bank, which advanced money to Florentine officials to recruit crossbowmen for the army" (2015, 48–9). Francesco Bruni, Petrarch's and Boccaccio's friend, was the notary in the Ufficio della Condotta, which hired and paid soldiers: "Bruni personally drew up the terms of a 7,000 florins' loan raised by Florence in the early stages of the war to cover expenses" (Caferro 2018a, 35); he also received 7,500 florins from Orsanmichele, designated for the Ubaldini war (Caferro 2018a, 99). Unless there was another person of the same name, Francesco Nelli, the dedicatee of Petrarch's *Seniles*, is listed in the war budget in the role of one of the chamberlains of the Camera del Comune during May–June 1349 (Caferro 2018a, 35). Finally, Andrea Lancia is mentioned in a provision against the Ubaldini clan on 30 July 1349, as notary of the *ufficiali degli stipendiati* (Stipend Office) (Azzetta 2001, 31).

The war against the Ubaldini thus brought together many inhabitants of Oltrarno and many friends of Boccaccio, some of whom – Niccolò di Bartolo del Buono, Pino de' Rossi, Luca di Feo Ugolini, and Uberto di Ubaldino degli Infangati – took part in the failed conspiracy of 1360. Vittore Branca claims: "It is certain that … he and other admirers had successfully interceded with gonfaloniers and the priors of the guilds in support of Petrarch's request that justice be done in the matter of the savage aggression suffered by his friends Luca Cristiano and Mainardo Accursio" (1976, 88). Thanks to Caferro's studies, we know that Boccaccio and his friends not only interceded in favour of Petrarch's quest for justice but also directly and actively intervened in this war in different functions in every way they could.

This is the historical background for the first encounter between the two greatest writers of fourteenth-century Italian literature: Boccaccio and Petrarch. They met for the first time on a cold October evening outside the gates of Florences, when Petrarch was going to Rome for the jubilee. Boccaccio invited Petrarch to be his guest in his house in Oltrarno, and around Petrarch he created a circle of admirers: Zanobi da Strada, Francesco Nelli, and a very young Lapo da Castiglionchio. Together they would listen to Petrarch's declamation of his poems, as Francesco Nelli reminds us in his letter: "I remember you, when that voice of yours worth revering and fearing delivered us some poems for a while, while your most eloquent tongue expressed the stirrings of your soul" ("Memini te … cum dudum carmina nobis vocem illam venerandam atque tremendam, motus animi disertissima lingua interprete, extulisse"; Nelli 1901, ep. XIII, 68). As Giuseppe Billanovich states: "The circle of his friends in Florence was by now established: the affection and attention of the poet [Petrarch] were transferred to it after death and various misfortunes had dispersed the old friends who once had gathered in

Avignon in the circle of Bishop and Cardinal Colonna" (Billanovich 1947a, 94). On 2 November 1350, Boccaccio received the first letter addressed to him from Petrarch: *Familiares* 11.1.

Although the war against the Ubaldini was technically over by September 1350, another, greater interstate war erupted in 1351: the one between Florence and Milan, in which the Ubaldini sided with the Visconti.[47] It was as if the Ubaldini war had converged into the one against the Visconti. The war proper started during the summer of 1351, but Florence had initiated preparations much earlier. As Caferro points out (2018b, 115–16):

> Boccaccio's appointment as chamberlain of the *camera del comune* coincided directly with the enactment of the *balìa* that oversaw preparations for the war with Milan. The *balìa,* consisting in eighteen officials, began in November 1350, in response to the purchase by Milan of Bologna in October – the act that set the military events into motion. Florence did not start fighting Milan until the spring and summer of 1351. Nevertheless, the city had already in winter 1350/51 begun preparing for war, appropriating money for supplies, troops and personnel. Indeed, Boccaccio's first disbursement of funds as chamberlain of the *camera del comune* was on 10 January for 7,820 florins to Gianozzo Lambucci, the chamberlain of the *balìa,* to pay for ambassadors, spies and masons and weapons related to the war. (ASFi, *balie* 7 bis, f. 1r)

Many of Boccaccio's actions as chamberlain had been focused on Florence's defence against the hegemonic politics of expansion pursued by the Visconti. The annexation of Prato in February 1351 required the same action: strengthening the neighbouring cities was vital for Florence's defence. Taking back control of Pistoia in April 1351 on behalf of Florence needs to be seen in this perspective (Prato and Pistoia were the first two cities besieged by Archbishop Giovanni Visconti d'Oleggio in July 1351, at the beginning of the war).[48] At the Florentine State Archive in Florence, Caferro recently discovered a document about an embassy undertaken by Boccaccio in August 1351, listed not on a communal budget but in *balìa* 7 bis, which is the financial account of Gianozzo Lambucci, the chamberlain in charge of the *balìa* that oversaw war. Boccaccio's embassy began on 25 August 1351 and lasted thirty-three days, "ad partes Romandiole et Lombardie," that is,

47 For the war between Florence and Milan, see Baldasseroni 1902 and 1903.

48 "In the period between 1350 and 1352 the *contado* and district were at least partially undergoing reconstruction after the various capitals of the region had proclaimed their independence during the brief *signoría* of the Duke of Athens … In 1349 Colle Val d'Elsa and San Gimignano were reclaimed by Florence; in 1351 Prato was retaken, and in April 1351, arrangements were made for the recovery of control over Pistoia" (Guidi 1981, vol. 1, 150). For the capture of Colle Val d'Elsa and San Gimignano, see M. Villani 1995, 1.43–4; for Prato, M. Villani 1995, 1.71–3; for Pistoia, M. Villani 1995, 1.95–7 and Stefani 1910, rubr. 644.

directly in the war zone: It is likely he went there to negotiate military help from the Romagnol lords.[49] Caferro points out that Boccaccio's friend Francesco Benini was also sent to the Mugello on 19 September 1351 to resupply the Florentine army with infantrymen, and that he arranged the movement of men to the Mugello, particularly to Scarperia, together with other prominent citizens, such as Pazzino di Apardo Donati and Beltramo de' Pazzi (both listed among the conspirators of 1360), and Rosso di Riccardo de' Rossi, a relative of Pino di Giovanni de' Rossi.[50] These men are cited also in the *Cronica domestica* by Donato Velluti, together with two members of the de' Medici family, Giovanni di Conte and Salvestro di Alamanno. As Velluti states: "They made the finest defence ever made" ("fecieno la più bella difesa si facesse mai"; 1914, 210). In addition, Boccaccio was involved in other capacities with preventing Visconti attacks: between August and September 1351, he was one of the eighteen of the *balìa*, the organization created to make decisions on defence against the Visconti; between 3 November 1351 and 30 April 1352, Boccaccio was *difensore del contado* (defender of the territorial state)[51] – a very difficult and delicate military office to hold in this period with the war against Milan. Moreover, at some time between December 1351 and January 1352, the "sensible Messer Giovanni Boccaccio" ("vir prudens dominus Johannes Boccaccij") was sent as "citizen and solemn ambassador" ("cives et ambaxiator solemnis") to Conrad Duke of Teck and to Ludwig Duke of Bavaria, Margrave of Brandeburg and Count of Tyrol, to ask them to assist Florence against the Archbishop of Milan.[52]

Not much is known about fourteenth-century diplomacy and the processes of appointment of ambassadors, but at the beginning of the fifteenth century, ambassadors were appointed by the Priorate and the gonfalonier of justice, together with the guild gonfaloniers and the twelve *buoni uomini*.[53] Sometimes the members of the *balìa* took part, or, when the motivations were strictly military, it fell to the *balìa* of war (i.e., those in charge of the particular ongoing war) to choose the ambassador for the war needs. In this case, the expenses of the embassies were

49 ASFi, *balie*, 7 bis, f. 18r. Caferro treats this embassy at length, clearing up the misinterpretations on the date and the nature of this mission that had been circulating in Boccaccio scholarship (2018b, 116–27).

50 ASFi, *balie*, 7 bis, f. 10r–10v; Caferro 2018b, 172.

51 ASFi, *balia* 10, f. 1r; Regnicoli 2021a, 242; ASFi, *Tratte*, 891, f. 8r (Regnicoli 2013a, 395, doc. 32). The office of *difensore del contado* carried a six-month term. This was the period when war was raging in the *contado* of Florence against Milan, against the Ubaldini and Giovanni Visconti d'Oleggio, who were pushing from the north, and against the pro-imperial allies in Tuscany from the south.

52 The commendatory letters in his record date from 12 December 1351: ASFi, *Miss. I canc.* 10, f. 122v (Regnicoli 2013a, 395, doc. 33). They are published by Attilio Hortis 1875, 45–6. On this embassy, see also Regnicoli 2021a, 245–6 and 2021b, 297–8.

53 For embassies in the following centuries, see Maxson 2014, 116ff.; Pirillo 2018.

administered by the Chamber of Armaments (Camera dell'Arme) (Guidi 1981, vol. 2, 218–19). The structures for appointing and funding ambassadors were probably similar in the mid-fourteenth century. Boccaccio served as ambassador many times during the 1350s, his embassies ranging from the small to the much larger and more difficult:

- September 1350: charged by the Capitani di Orsanmichele to present ten gold florins to Beatrice, Dante's daughter in Ravenna (Branca 1976, 87; Regnicoli 2013a, 394, doc. 11).[54]
- Spring 1351: charged by the *priori delle arti* (priors of the guilds), by the *gonfaloniere di Giustiza del Popolo* (the gonfalonier of justice of the people), and by the Commune of Florence with an embassy to Petrarch to offer him a chair at the new University of Florence and to restitute to Petrarch his father's possessions (Boccaccio, *Ep.* VII).[55]
- August 1351: charged by the ten members of the *balìa* to travel "ad partes Romandiole et Lombardie" (ASFi, *balie* 7 bis, f. 18r; Caferro 2018b).
- December 1351: charged by the *priori delle arti* (priors of the guilds), the *gonfaloniere di Giustiza del Popolo* (the gonfalonier of justice of the people), and the Commune of Florence with an embassy to Corrado, Duke of Teck, and Ludwig of Bavaria, Marquis of Brandenburg and Count of the Tyrol, to discuss intervention against the expansionism of the Archibishop of Milan, in an anti-Viscontean mission (ASFi, *Miss. I canc.* 10, ff. 112v–113r; Hortis 1875, 45–6).
- May–June 1354: with Bernardo di Cambio, charged by the Republic of Florence with an highly sensitive embassy to Pope Innocent VI and the College of Cardinals in Avignon; introduced as "the prudent Messer Giovanni di Certaldo, our dearest citizen" ("providum virum dominum Johannem de Certaldo karissimum nostrum civem," ASFi, *Miss. I canc.* 11, f. 78v–79r; Canestrini 1849, 393–6; Hortis 1875, 48–9).[56]

54 After the plague, the Orsanmichele Company became very wealthy, from bequests left by plague victims. Matteo Villani estimates that they were bequeathed more than 350,000 gold florins (1995, 1.7); for the first three years after the plague, the company was richer than the Florentine Republic itself, so that the extraction of the captains was entrusted to the Commune. For Orsanmichele after the plague, see Henderson 1994.

55 The date of this embassy can be ascertained from *Epistola* X, written to Petrarch on 18 July 1353: "I believe you remember, great teacher, that not even the third year has passed since I came to you in Padua as ambassador of our senate, and having laid out my commission, I drew out my stay with you for many days" ("Credo memineris, preceptor optime, quod nondum tertius annus elapsus sit postquam senatus nostri nuntius Patavum ad te veni, et commissis expositis dies plusculos tecum egerim").

56 For the series of documents, see the proof of payment (ASFi, *CCCU* 101, f. 312r; published in Crescini 1887, 258–9) and letter of instruction (ASFi, *Miss. I canc.* 11, ff. 78v–79r; published in Canestrini 1849, 393–4, although with the wrong year).

- July 1354: embassy to "Valdelsa, and especially to Certaldo" ("ad partes vallis Else, maxime ad partes Certaldi"), to organize the military resistance of his compatriots against the army of the mercenary leader Fra' Moriale (ASFi, *CCCU* 102, f. 339r; Gerola 1898, 356–8).
- June 1359: embassy "ad partes Lombardie" with his brother Jacopo (ASFi, *CCCU* 136, f. 329v; Agostini Muzzi 1978, 662; Regnicoli 2013a, 396, doc. 69).

The first two embassies were more cultural in character and surely dear to Boccaccio; the next three were related to the war against the Visconti. Boccaccio's involvement against the expansionist aims of the Visconti was full and direct, as was that of his friends. Among those friends was Luigi Gianfigliazzi – remembered with great affection in the Latin poem dedicated to Zanobi da Strada (carmen VII 62–5)[57] – who received numerous commissions as representative of Florence in the confederation of communes (Florence, Siena, Arezzo) against the Visconti. Donato Velluti was involved in the creation of this league, as well (Velluti 1914, 210–11).

In this historical context, the language of Boccaccio's epistle X to Francesco Petrarch of 18 July 1353 has even more disruptive force. As we know from a previous letter, written two years earlier (*Ep.* VII), Boccaccio championed a return to Florence of "the venerable Messer Francesco Petrarch, one of the canons in Padua, poet laureate, our dearest fellow-citizen" ("Reverendus vir dominus Franciscus Petrarca, canonicus paduanus, laureatus poeta, concivis nostrus carissimus"; *Ep.* VII).[58] In this letter (*Ep.* VII), written and then handed in person to Petrarch while he was in Padua, the Commune of Florence offered him a chair at the University of Florence, established in 1349, and the restitution of his father's lands; it was addressed to him as "most beloved citizen and auspicious offspring of our country" ("dilectissime civis et fausta patrie nostre proles"; *Ep.* VII.1).[59]

57 In the conclusion of *carmen* VII, addressed to Zanobi da Strada in 1355, Boccaccio writes: "While I wrote this, the most illustrious orator, jurist, and friend Luigi was ever at my side, thinking the same and urging me to write this" ("Hec ego dum scripsi, semper clarissumus ille / affuit orator <michi> legum doctor amicus / Loisius, *sic velle ferens et scribere* mandans"; *Carm.* VII.62–4). Luigi Gianfigliazzi was one of the three representatives for the Commune of Florence at the Congress of Arezzo in 1350 and 1351 for the creation of a confederation of communes against the expansionism of the Visconti (documents published by Canestrini 1849, 374–5; 380–2). One of the other two was Sandro Biliotti (one of the fourteen *buoni uomini*, after the expulsion of the Duke of Athens). On the life of Gianfigliazzi, see Arrighi (2000b), who highlights the cultural profile of the jurist. In this regard, see also Novati 1889.

58 This episode is remembered also in *Ep.* X.24: "nemo me melius novit: medius fui talium atque curator, et muneris oblati portitor" ("nobody knows this better than I do, having been the mediator in these affairs and agent and deliverer of this offer").

59 The offer also had financial advantages for the city of Florence: Petrarch would put the new university on a firm foundation, and it would therefore be able to attract many more students, creating a more secure source of revenue for the city. Caferro also connects the creation of the Florentine university with the Ubaldini war (Caferro 2018a, 31–4; 84–6).

Despite the lavish offers, after a series of vague and indefinite replies, in late spring (certainly after the Peace of Sarzana on 31 March 1353), Petrarch relocated to Milan, guest of the Archbishop Giovanni Visconti, considered by Boccaccio and the Florentines the tyrant par excellence. "With an agitated and disturbed spirit," Boccaccio wrote epistle X to Petrarch; his reaction was at first incredulous, then disgusted by such hypocrisy, and finally he pronounced unequivocal and direct condemnation: "I know that there remains nothing for me but to blush and condemn his [Petrarch's] actions" ("Ego nil aliud nosco quam erubescere et opus suum dampnare"; *Ep*. X.28). Also salient is Petrarch's selfishness – he acts without thinking of his friends and of his circle of admirers who look to him as a teacher and as a model. Referring to him by the pastoral name that Petrarch gave himself, Boccaccio comments: "Silvanus has stained not only himself with this, but you, me and the innocent others left behind that have exalted, loudly and with all our force, his life, his habits, his song and his pen in every wood to every shepherd" ("Non se solum labe hac sua Silvanus infecit, se te me reliquosque, qui vitam, qui mores, qui cantus et calamos eius toto ore, totis viribus, apud quascunque silvas, apud quoscumque pastores efferebamus, fedavit innocuos"; *Ep*. X.21). Indeed, the letter concludes with a series of rhetorical questions, asking how his many friends will react: what will Gherardo, brother of Francesco, say? What of Ludwig von Kempen? And Giovanni Barrilli? And Barbato da Sulmona, and "the many others who honestly from afar regarded him as an almost divine man and singular example among men and admired him and praised his name to the stars? I believe that they will all condemn him, and they will all be in great anguish" ("Aliique plurimi, qui eum a longe tanquam celestem hominem et unicum inter mortales exemplar honesti spectabant mirabantur et laudibus sublimabant? Puto dampnabitis omnes et dolore amxiabimini"; *Ep*. X.30). A series of letters of disappointment and protest were sent to Petrarch in July and August by Zanobi da Strada in Naples; Giovanni Aghinolfi, chancellor of the court of Mantua; Ludovico von Kempen in Avignon; and, more timidly, Francesco Nelli. A fellow citizen of Florence, Gano di Colle Valdelsa, sent a jester named Malice ("Malizia") to sing him a sonnet imploring him to immediately abandon the tyranny of Milan. A detailed analysis of epistle X and of the relationship between Petrarch and Boccaccio would need much more space than is available here.[60]

Boccaccio became very disillusioned in the end stages of the war against the Visconti for what it had done to Florence. From what he wrote to Zanobi da Strada (13 April 1353) a couple of weeks after the Peace of Sarzana (31 March),

60 See the articles by Billanovich (1947a, 178–86); Branca 1997, 93–5; Fenzi 2005 and the response by Ferraro 2015.

it appears that he did not believe that Florence had behaved or was behaving appropriately:

> But I do not know whether I should say that we are led along or drawn along by fate, or rather we are going willingly to meet our ruin. Devouring envy and the fierce desire for possessions have left no good, just, faithful, or wise council to our senate or any others. The Asiatic delights were once a source of destruction for the Greeks, then the Asiatic and Greek were for the Romans. Our pleasures destroy us and from our flowering height they turn us back and will reduce us to a pile of manure. O what shame and idleness of mortals, what absurd scorn of certain men who, by some stupid pretence, want effeminate men who serve most incestuous Venus with all their strength to be born under fierce Mars. Thus God gives peace to my labours, that, since someday I may wander afar, the last name of Certaldo is now dearer to me than that of Florence. (*Ep.* IX.44)

> (Verum nescio utrum dicam ducamur ac trahamur a fatis an potius volentes obviam eamus exitio. Nil boni, nil iusti, nil fidei, nil consilii livor edax atque habendi cupiditas seva nostro liquere senatui reliquisque. Asiatice condam delitie Grecis, asiatice demum greceque Romanis exterminio fuere: nostre non ipsos pessundant et ex florido culmine in sterquilinium redigunt redigentque. Proth mortalium pudor et ignavia, proth ridiculum quorundam fastidium, qui effeminatos homines incestuosissime Veneri totis viribus obsequiosos sub acri Marte insulsa quadam fictione progenitos volunt! Ita Deus pacem meis imponit laboribus, ut michi in posterum forsan peregrinaturo iam carius Certaldi cognomen est quam Florentie.)

Boccaccio refers to the citizens of Florence, who believed themselves directly descended from Mars,[61] but in fact were full of vice, living under the goddess Venus, far from exhibiting the proud behaviour of men of arms. Since he was not naming names, we cannot know exactly who these servants of Venus were. Nevertheless, the evidence of contemporary chronicles suggests that Boccaccio was referring to the Florentine ambassadors at the Peace of Sarzana: "The Commune of Florence in this affair of the exiles was deceived by its own ambassadors" ("Il comune di Firenze in questo fatto degli sbanditi fu ingannato da' suoi medesimi ambasciatori"; M. Villani 1995, 3.60–1). Villani adds: "It was a barter that profited

61 The city of Florentia had its origin in a Roman military base, and thus was under the patronage of Mars. The Baptistery of San Giovanni was built over the remains of a temple to Mars, and a statue of Mars was still standing in Dante's time at the entrance to the Ponte Vecchio before it was washed away by flooding in 1333. Giovanni Villani, in his *Cronica*, writes that the Roman colony of Florentia "arose with Mars in the ascendant," and Dante in his *Inferno* writes: "I was from the city that in the Baptist replaced its first patron" ("I' fui de la città che nel Battista mutò il primo padrone"; *Inf.* 13.143). On the myths recounted by Boccaccio, see Chiecchi 2013.

all those involved, but it caused greater damage and shame to our Commune, and the citizens were greatly distressed. But the authors of this deed, making everyone afraid of disturbing the peace, silenced every tongue, and their pockets were filled" ("Ed era una mercatanzia tra tutti di grande guadagno, ma di maggiore danno e vergogna del nostro comune, e molto se ne dolevano i cittadini. Ma gli autori del fatto, con mettere paura di non conturbare la pace, ogni lingua acchetavano, e le borse si empievano").

Boccaccio's Last Offices and Disappearance

After Boccaccio completed his assignment as defender of the territorial state (*difensore del contado*), on 26 August 1352, he was appointed for six months, until 26 February 1353, as officer of taxes on bread (*gabella del pane*) along with his friend Andrea Lancia (Azzetta 2001, 34). At first sight, this office would appear to involve no more than a routine collection of duties, if it were not for the fact that in the same period, from 1352 through the summer of 1353, also as a consequence of war, Florence was suffering a serious food shortage, as recorded by Marchionne di Coppo Stefani and Matteo Villani.[62] Stefani asserts that the price of grain increased so much that a bushel was selling for a florin (1910, rubr. 658).[63] Food shortages were so widespread that they led to brawls and thefts by "certain corrupt citizens."[64] Some used illegal means, often creative ones, to continue their lifestyles of greed and self-indulgence, illustrating the arrogance of people who feel entitled to break the rules; in one case, a group that stole two hundred salted half-pigs and thought the crime was trivial. As Stefani writes in his *Cronica fiorentina*, perhaps they did it so they could "tell funny stories" ("dire novellette da ridere"; 1910, rubr. 647):

> In the said year [1353], there was famine, but still there were many citizens used to great expenses, and many would routinely enjoy jousts and similar parties who could not do without them, even if there was famine: therefore, every day they would break into a shop by night, and they would not take just a safe with money, but rather they

62 M. Villani records food shortages immediately after the plague, as early as 1348–9. For famine before 1350, see Dameron 2017. For food emergencies, Matteo Villani and Marchionne di Coppo Stefani use the word *carestia* for both food shortage and famine. On the linguistic differences, see Palermo 2013.

63 M. Villani provides more detailed information on the price of food (1995, 3.56).

64 Among these thieves were Michele and Andrea di Alamanno de' Medici, brothers of Salvestro and Bartolomeo di Alamanno de' Medici (who had a great role in the conspiracy of 1360), and Bordone di Michele Bordoni, a relative of Paolo di Neri Bordoni (M. Villani 1995, 3.58), communal treasurer with Boccaccio in 1351. For this information on the Medici family, see Brucker 1957, 13.

would take all they could find. For example, from a *pizzicagnolo* food store they took 200 salted half-pigs. This may sound surprising, that in a crowded city, people would go out to dinner with friends and other dependents and they would never spot any of these things being carried. The reason why they could never catch them was the following: the culprits were all from good families of Florence, who held offices and status, and they would take trumpets and lutes and bagpipes and similar instruments, and they would stay playing in a street, wherever they wanted, and then afterward with iron posts and crowbars and pincers they would break into a shop, and all loaded up they would go to a house, whichever was closest, of one of the gang. And at the entrance and exit to the street two gentlemen from good families would stand guard, and if anyone came by they would tell them: "You, if you please, take another path, as there is someone here in love, and he is making music and singing and does not want to be recognized." The passers-by would then take another path, and these men could do what they wanted. (Stefani 1910, rubr. 659)

(Nel detto anno, essendo carestia, molti erano li cittadini corrotti a grandi spese, ed assai ve n'erano usi di giostrare e di simili feste, che non se ne potieno rimanere, e la carestia era, ed ogni giorno si sconficcava una bottega la notte, e non era portato una cassetta con danari, ma erane tratto ciò che v'era; e ad esempio: e' si trovò una bottega di pizzicagnolo tratti circa 200 mezzi porci salati, … Pare grande meraviglia questo, ch'essendo piena la città, com'era, di cittadini, che pure andando a cena con amici e ad altri servigi, tornando a casa, nulla si trovava mai di queste cose portare. La ragione il perchè non si poteva trovare fu questa: questi erano cittadini di buone famiglie da Firenze e di tali famiglie ch'aveano ufizj e stato, toglieano trombe, liuti, cornemuse e simili stormenti, e poneansi a sonare in una via, ove volessero, e poi tra con pali di ferro e con leve e con tanaglie e' schiavavano una bottega, e con grosse cariche andavano in una casa, la più presso che avea uno della brigata. Da capo e da piè stavano di questa via due di questi di buona famiglia, e se alcuno passava, ed eglino diceano: "Piacciavi di fare altra via, che qui è uno, ch'è innamorato, e fa sonare e cantare, e non vuole essere conosciuto." Lo passante facea altra via; e costoro faceano li fatti loro.)

This "general shortage of bread and a bad year for wine" ("carestia generale di pane e sformata di vino") had been introduced by a comet "judged black" and "Saturnian by nature," entering in the sign of Leo (M. Villani 1995, 2.44). The breakdown in civil order and the famine had depressed the city and the *contado* of Florence to such a degree that all were in "in extreme discomfort" (M. Villani 1995, 2.46). Villani adds:

And even though we have given a full account of Florence, in this year it was thought throughout Italy that Florence still had a thriving trade like in any other place. And it should be noted that such a vast and unusual famine went apparently unheeded by the *popolo minuto* of Florence, and even more so in other lands; and this occurred because they had all become rich from their jobs; they made outlandish profits and they were prepared to buy and live in luxury despite the famine, and they invested even more than the oldest wealthy citizen families – an unsuitable and incredible story to tell, but seen all the time and we can give clear testimony of it. And that which in other times before the plague would have been an intolerable riot of the *popolo*, was this year constant impertinence and trampling by the *popolo minuto* in our city in order to possess more than their superiors and to give more than others. And so, the *popolo minuto* would party and buy clothes and feast as if they had wealth and abundance of everything. (M. Villani 1995, 3.56)

(E benché abbiamo fatto conto di Firenze, in quest'anno fu tenuto che in tutta Italia che Firenze avesse così buono mercato comunalmente come alcuna altra terra. Ed è da notare, che così grande e disusata carestia il minuto popolo di Firenze non parve che se ne curasse, e così di più altre terre; e questo avvenne perché tutti erano ricchi de' loro mestieri: guadagnavano ingordamente, e più erano pronti a comperare e a vivere delle migliori cose, non ostante la carestia, e più ne devano per averle innanzi che i più antichi ricchi cittadini, cosa sconvenevole e maravigliosa a raccontare, di continova veduta ne possiamo fare chiara testimonianza. E quello che a altri tempi innanzi alla generale mortalità sarebbe stato tomulto di popolo incomportabile, in quest'anno continovo improntitudine e calca del minuto popolo fu nella nostra città ad avere le cose innanzi a' maggiori, e di darne più che gli altri. E così festeggiava, e vestiva e convitava il minuto popolo, come se fossono in somma dovizia e abbondanza d'ogni bene.)

After his six months as officer of taxes on bread expired on 26 February 1353, Boccaccio spent some time in Romagna,[65] after which he was again employed by the Commune of Florence in the first four months of 1354, as officer of the tower (*ufficiale della torre*). As Guidi writes, "In the Office of the Tower, all tasks that more or less related to management of immovable goods, public works, and direct taxes were centralized into a single institution. The result was an organ whose aims were certainly not homogenous" (1981, vol. 2, 286). Giulio Rezasco, too, in his still useful *Dizionario del linguaggio italiano storico ed amministrativo*, gives a full but general definition: "The Florentine officers were originally in charge of the fortifications, as well as the economy and buildings of the Commune. Their job was to seek and recover the public accounts of confiscation of goods, censuses, feuds, tributes, subjugations; manage the properties of the Commune; take over those of rebels and other condemned criminals; lease out taxes each year; clean the roads, squares, and bridges; and take care of the fortifications, a task that was

65 As we know from epistle X, addressed to Petrarch on his decision to relocate to the Visconti in Milan; it was written from Ravenna on 18 July 1353.

then given to the *ufficiali delle castella*" (1881, 1196). It is difficult to determine exactly which tasks fell to Boccaccio in this office – whether all or only some of those presented by Rezasco – but we know for certain that originally the officer of the tower was concerned with fortification and defensive towers.

More important than this administrative appointment was Boccaccio's embassy to Pope Innocent VI, in May–June 1354.[66] It was intended as a precautionary measure in a rather complex and often ambiguous historical context. In attempting to stem the expansionism of the Visconti, Florence asked for support from Pope Clement VI, but he and his cardinals had already made a deal with Giovanni Visconti, Archbishop of Milan in 1352 (M. Villani 1995, 3.2). In this paradoxical situation, in which the Ghibelline Milan was striking deals with the Papacy, Guelf Florence was asking for help from the Holy Roman Emperor, Charles IV of Bohemia, in the same year (1352). Among the ambassadors to the emperor were Pino de' Rossi, Uguccione de' Ricci, Filippo Megalotti, and Tommaso Corsini (M. Villani 1995, 3.13; Velluti 1914, 210–11). After the Peace of Sarzana in 1353, the emperor's coming south to Italy was pointless for Florentines and feared by many in Florence. Nevertheless, the emperor came to Italy in the last few months of 1354 and he stayed well into 1355 – in fact, he arrived just after the death of the Archbishop of Milan on 3 October 1354. Once the citizens of Florence were aware that the emperor was on his way, they had to take precautions in applying to the new Pope Innocent VI, pledging their loyalty. For such an important task in this very volatile situation, the priors and the gonfalonier of justice, with the agreement of the twelve *buoni uomini* and the gonfaloniers of the guilds, delegated *dominus Johanni del Boccaccio* as ambassador of the people of Florence on 29 April 1354. The embassy would last fifteen days, and Boccaccio would be paid four lire a day, escorted by three horses, and accompanied by Bernado di Cambio, who was paid only twenty soldi a day and escorted by only one horse.[67] This embassy was a clear sign of the highest respect and confidence the Commune had for Boccaccio. According to his extremely detailed instructions, he was supposed to begin by demonstrating the astonishment of the Signoria at the news of the emperor's march to Italy; if it became clear that the emperor had come to Italy

66 The letter with instructions from the Signoria to Boccaccio regarding the embassy to Pope Innocent VI is in ASFi, *Miss. I canc.* 11, ff. 78v–79r; proof of payment for the embassy led with Bernardo di Cambio is in ASFi, *CCCU* 102, f. 339r. These documents, along with others regarding this embassy, are reproduced in Canestrini 1849, 393–6; Hortis 1875, 48–9; Crescini 1887, 259; Gerola 1898, 358; Agostini Muzzi 1978, 659–60; Regnicoli 2013a, 395, doc. 47–8.

67 On Boccaccio's embassy in Romagna in 1351, Caferro states: "Boccaccio's salary of four lire a day was higher than the going rate, which was four lire a day for a citizen who, like Boccaccio, bore the title of 'dominus.' Ambassadorial wages were connected to status, as were the number of horses provided the ambassador for his entourage. A *dominus* traveled with four horses, each valued at one lire a day, and thus earned four lire a day" (Caferro 2018b, 121).

with the agreement and assent of the pope, Boccaccio was directed to reassure the pope that the Commune of Florence was loyal to the Ecclesia Sancta Dei, and was thus asking to be taken under its wing and protection. If, on the other hand, the pope knew nothing about the emperor's arrival and attempted to find out from the ambassador more about Florence's intentions, Boccaccio was to answer only that "he had no other mandate than to ask the pope's wishes" ("dicat se non habere mandatum, nisi sciscitandi Summi Pontificis voluntatem," Canestrini 1849, 394). The mission to Avignon was a success, for personal reasons as well: Pope Innocent VI would remember Boccaccio well when, on 2 November 1360, he granted him ecclesiastical honours.

As soon as he had returned to Florence, Boccaccio received another mission, caused by an unforeseen emergency created by the Commune's own carelessness.[68] He was asked to travel for six days to the Valdelsa, and especially to Certaldo ("ad partes vallis Else, maxime ad partes Certaldi"; Gerola 1898, 358), to organize military resistance against the army of the Company of Fra' Moriale, a mercenary captain who was wandering through Italy at the time, followed by a large crowd of mercenary soldiers and criminal bandits, both men and women.[69] Naturally, there were personal considerations in this case, as Boccaccio still had lands and properties in and around Certaldo. But he was lucky, for the army marched north, barely grazing Certaldo: the troops of Fra' Moriale set up camp initially in the plains between Siena and Badia Isola above the Elsa, and then they carried on through Staggia, entering the *contado* of Florence in the *borghi* of San Casciano in Val di Pesa, where they stayed at least from 4 through 10 July, burning and plundering the valley. In the end, Florence was rid of them only by handing over 25,000 gold florins. This all took place in July 1354.

For almost a year, Boccaccio was not chosen for any other public commission. His last official appointment in the 1350s was as officer for military infractions (*ufficiale dei difetti*), replacing the deceased Dante di Terio, from the beginning of May until the end of August 1355.[70] The officers of this unit were part of the organization in charge of war and the defence of Florence, and they dealt specifically with mercenary troops: "Their job is to impose fines upon the commanders for any irregularities encountered with the number of men (if they did not correspond to the number contracted); fines for military indiscipline; and expenses for

68 As M. Villani puts it (1995, 4.15), the Florentines did not take the emissaries of Fra' Moriale's army seriously, as they were only asking to travel through their territory on their way to Milan, and they never received a reply from the Commune.

69 For a description of Fra' Moriale, see M. Villani 1995, 3.107; 4.15–16. For documents on Boccaccio, see Gerola 1898, 356–8; Agostini Muzzi 1978, 660; Regnicoli 2013a, 395, doc. 49.

70 ASFi, *Tratte* 749, f. 57r (Gerola 1898, 357, 359; Agostini Muzzi 1978, 660–1; Regnicoli 2013a, 396, doc. 55-57-58).

horses who did not die of natural causes. No installments for the pay of mercenary captains can be disbursed without the signature of these officers."[71]

The year 1355 was interesting for Tuscany, especially for the visit of Emperor Charles IV, who was hosted by Pisa in the first months of the year. It is not known when Boccaccio met Charles IV, but it may well have been during this time. In his letter to Francesco Nelli of 1363, Boccaccio writes that he had been received easily by the two highest powers of his time, pope and emperor: "I remember that I have had access, often and much easier, to the great Pontiff and to Charles Caesar and to many other princes of the world, and the chance to speak as much as I wanted was granted to me."[72] On 22 January 1355, Florence sent an embassy to Pisa of six knights (*milites*) to reach an agreement with Charles IV to ensure the freedom of the Commune: they were Bernardino de' Rossi, Pazzino degli Strozzi, Luigi de' Gianfigliazzi, Luigi de' Mozzi, Uguccione de' Ricci, and Simone dell'Antella.[73] This is how Matteo Villani describes them: "On 22 January, they left Florence with a strict dress code, all with double-layered cloth, one of fine scarlet, the other of fine mixed wool from Brussels, with expensive embellishments, and each with eight personal assistants on horseback all with their own dress code" ("a dì 22 di gennaio si partirono di Firenze vestiti d'un'assisa tutti di doppi vestimenti, l'uno di fine scarlatto, l'altro di fine mescolato di borsella, con ricchi adornamenti, e con otto famigli a cavallo per uno tutti vestiti d'un'assisa"; 1995, 4.49). So, the entire embassy was made up of fifty-four people, six ambassadors and forty-eight assistants. Boccaccio must have been among these assistants, for at least two reasons. First, there was a very practical reason: he might have been useful in this circumstance, since he had already discussed the visit of the emperor with Pope Innocent IV six months earlier. Boccaccio's presence would have served as a kind of record of those talks, which could have helped achieve a broader overview of the relations between pope, emperor, and Florence. The second reason is that among the ambassadors were at least two dear friends of Boccaccio: Luigi de' Gianfigliazzi and Bernardino

71 This citation is drawn from Guidi (1981, vol. 2, 215). For the structural chart of the war and defence of the Commune of Florence, see the picture drawn by Guidi (1981, vol. 2, 201), who refers precisely to 1355. The term of the *ufficiale dei difetti* would last four months.

72 "Io mi ricordo, spesse volte e molto più agevolmente, ed al sommo pontefice ed a Carlo Cesare ed a molti altri principi del mondo avere avuto l'entrata, e copia di parlare essermi conceduta" (*Ep.* XIII.110). Here Boccaccio recalls his embassies, including to Avignon and Pope Innocent IV from 1354. Ginetta Auzzas, in a footnote to her edition of Boccaccio's *Epistole*, writes: "Emperor Charles IV, on the other hand, must have met him in 1355 while he was in Italy, but we do not know in what circumstances and what was his office" (1998, 807, n. 279). My interpretation of the events follows Auzzas.

73 The names are provided in the detailed instructions from the prior of the guilds, the *gonfaloniere di giustizia del popolo*, and the Commune of Florence, dated 21 January 1355, in the document reproduced by Canestrini 1849, 403–4.

de' Rossi, brother of Pino – in fact, it is even possible that Pino was accompanying them, since he had already served as ambassador to Charles IV in 1352, together with Uguccione de' Ricci, who was in the same role in 1355 in Pisa.

The negotiations between Charles of Bohemia and Florence were lengthy and exhausting, often with discussions continuing late into the night (M. Villani 1995, 4.72). The embassy did not return to Florence until two months later, on 20 March 1355. Subsequently, Charles went to Siena and then Rome for his coronation, which took place on Good Friday, 5 April 1355. He returned to Pisa on 6 May, staying until 27 May. Boccaccio could have met with the emperor in this period, but the first meeting more likely took place during the embassy to ask for his assistance to Florence. In Pisa, the emperor was joined by Niccolò Acciaiuoli,[74] who managed to persuade the emperor to crown Zanobi da Strada as the *poeta laureatus* on 15 May – a feat that was met with outrage by Boccaccio and all the intellectuals in Florence.[75] Before Pisa, though, Acciaiuoli passed through Florence, and was criticized by Villani for the "indulgence" ("mollezze") with which he entertained the citizens (M. Villani 1995, 4.91). Nevertheless, while Acciaiuoli and Zanobi da Strada were in Tuscany, Boccaccio envisaged a trip to Naples in the fall of the same year, 1355, to meet up with and perhaps stay with them.[76]

After Boccaccio's last post, as *ufficiale dei difetti*, the only commission he received for the rest of the decade was an embassy of eighteen days "ad partes Lombardie," on 22 June 1359, about which little is known.[77] If we line up all the embassies and the offices Boccaccio discharged, we see that most of them were linked to missions to prosecute or deflect war, or to support the apparatus of war, and the people with whom he was collaborating were often knights. Together with the embassies against the Visconti, many of Boccaccio's offices were related to the defence of the

---

74 For the positive relations between Acciaiuoli and the emperor, see especially F.P. Tocco 2001, 200–8. Acciaiuoli joined Charles in Siena at the end of March, and he accompanied him to Rome for the coronation. He managed to obtain many concessions from Charles, including the troops that he desperately needed, as well as many personal favours, such as the hereditary title of *conte palatino*.

75 On the criticisms, see Guidotti 1930, Léonard 1934, and Branca 1976, 103. A few months after the elevation of Zanobi da Strada to the status of official poet, Petrarch wrote to Boccaccio to comfort him for never having received such recognition (*Fam.* XVIII.15). See also what the contemporary chroniclers wrote: Stefani (1910, rubr. 671) and M. Villani (1995, 5.26). Boccaccio included in his *Zibaldone magliabechiano* (ff. 99v) the speech delivered by Zanobi da Strada on the occasion of his coronation, demonstrating esteem and friendship towards his old schoolmate. Zanobi's speech on the value of poetry was published by Ciampi 1830, 104–30.

76 Very little is known about this journey, though Boccaccio's eighth eclogue gives some indications. See in this regard Branca 1976, 103–8. This 1355 trip to Naples did not go well, and that of 1363 went even worse, as Boccaccio angrily recalls in a letter to Francesco Nelli (*Ep.* XIII). For the relationship between Niccolò Acciaiuoli, Boccaccio, and Zanobi da Strada, see Houston 2018.

77 ASFi, *CCCU* 139, f. 329v; Agostini Muzzi 1978, 662; Regnicoli 2013a, 396, doc. 69.

Commune or the organizational structure of defence and war of the Florentine Republic (see the table in Guidi 1981, vol. 2, 201); he was one of the members of the *balìa* (1351), defending Florence from the Visconti, *difensore del contado* (1351–2), *ufficiale dei difetti* (1355), *ufficiale delle castella* (1364–5), and *ufficiale della condotta* (1367). The roles of the *difensore del contado* and *ufficiale dei difetti* have already been treated in this chapter, but they bear on the other two offices Boccaccio held in the 1360s. The *ufficiali delle castella*, or *castellani* (officers of castles), were chosen from members of the minor and major guilds. The five *ufficiali* from the major guilds had to be *scioperati*, that is, enrolled in a guild but not practising the profession (which was very possibly Boccaccio's own situation), from the Arte del Cambio.[78] As *ufficiali di condotta*, Boccaccio and his colleagues had the task of recruiting mercenary troops for the Commune and following their military exercises and parades. These officers took oaths, in the name of Florence, from mercenary captains and constables, from infantry and cavalry. The officers were chosen by the outgoing officers from among people considered suitable for the position. Clearly, next to the image of the writer and poet Boccaccio, we need to add that of a man who was expert in diplomacy, politics, and military institutions and city defence.[79]

After 1355, we encounter a gap in documentary evidence for 1356, 1357, and 1358: there are no records in the state archives of his having paid taxes or engaged in any public activity in this period.[80] Various suggestions have been offered about what Boccaccio might have been doing during those years, but none are persuasive.[81] The gap, though, tells us something: if he did not pay real estate taxes

78 *Ufficiali delle castella*, together with the priors, took care of towers, fortifications, and defence walls, as well as the restocking of weapons and munitions. Their jurisdiction was over the entire territory of the countryside and district of Florence. These officers, in the company of a religious chamberlain, also directed the Camera delle Armi in the Palazzo dei Priori (Guidi 1981, vol. 2, 213).

79 These military appointments and his expertise in matters of war, together with the title of *dominus*, suggest that Boccaccio might have been honoured with the title of knight at some point in his life. P.G. Ricci (1985, 3–12) argues that the title *dominus* was awarded for his studies in law, and did not constitute knighthood: "Let's reject immediately the knighthood with which Boccaccio never had anything to do" (1985, 5–6). In fact, the title *dominus* was reserved for knights or whoever was affiliated with the guild of judges and notaries or practised law. Knighthood and the practice of law often went together, so much so that it was impossible to make a distinction between the roles, as in the case of the role of *podestá*, for example.

80 The one exception in 1356 occurred on 9 March: Niccolò di Bartolo del Buono repaid sixteen lire and five soldi in Boccaccio's name to the Commune for a loan from April 1355 (Regnicoli 2013a, 396, doc. 60). For the gap in documentation, see Regnicoli (2013a, 396), who has collected documents known to us: note the time gap between docs. 60 and 61.

81 Branca suggests that these years might "represent a period of rigorous concentration and earnest creative activity" (1976, 108). Meloni, on the basis of a document mentioning a *Johannes Boccacii, mercator Montispessulani* (1998, 102), suggests that Boccaccio might have been engaged in trade in Montpellier. Santagata (2019, 199–200) may be the closest to the truth: because Boccaccio's circle was politically ostracized, he could no longer be active in Florentine life.

(*estimo*) and the obligatory loans (*prestanze*) (both of which he had done regularly up until 1355), he was not eligible for any office in Florence. He seems to have withdrawn from the turmoil and disorder of the city: "May God put an end to my toils, so that, if I someday wonder afar, the last name of Certaldo [may] be dearer to me than that of Florence" ("Ita Deus pacem meis imponet laboribus, ut michi in posterum forsan peregrinaturo iam carius Certaldi cognomen est quam Florentie"; *Ep.* IX.45). Given the lack of other evidence, any more substantive hypothesis would be hazardous. The only information we have for this period is from Giovanni Conversini, who states that he met Boccaccio at the new market in Florence during summer 1357 (Gargan 2015, 185–6).

3 The 1360 Conspiracy (1359–1361)

Sempre va lo male per gli meno possenti:
chè li grossi pesci e bestie rompono le reti.

(Things always go badly for the small fry,
because the big fish and wild beasts are able to break through the net.)
– Marchionne di Coppo Stefani, *Cronica fiorentina* (rubr. 685)

After three years with no mention of him in any known document (1356–8), an archival record reports that on 22 June 1359 Boccaccio and his brother went as ambassadors to Lombardy, on a mission whose exact purpose is not known. In the meantime, the political setting of Florence had drastically changed, and not in Boccaccio's favour. With the enforcement of the practice of the *ammonizioni* in 1358, an extremist faction of the Guelf Party aimed to take control over the city.[1] In doing so, it targeted whoever was considered "Ghibelline and not true Guelf," among them several of Boccaccio's friends. They no longer took part in city politics on the official level, often to their economic loss and loss of social standing. Many of them had started plotting a conspiracy to overthrow the faction in power and gain back their privileges. This chapter is focused on the dynamics of this conspiracy, and follows the account in Matteo Villani's *Cronica* as well as the official document of the death sentence. The latter has never been studied by historians and critics, yet it states clearly the reasons behind the failed coup. The names of Boccaccio's close friends – Niccolò di Bartolo del Buono, Pino de' Rossi, Andrea di Tello da Lisca, Luca di Feo Ugolini, Pazzino di Apardo Donati – are stated clearly with all the charges against them: they were traitors to the Republic and conspirators against the tranquil state of the city. When all these events happened, Boccaccio was living again in Florence. Was he also aware of the secret

1 The law is summarized in Mazzoni 2010, 143–6.

treaty they had organized? Maybe. Whatever happened, whether he was aware or not, involved or not, the events had a huge impact on his life.

The Guelf Party and Terror of the *Ammonizioni*

During the 1350s in Florence, particularly in the second half of the decade, an extremist faction of the Guelf Party (Parte Guelfa or Societas Guelforum) was working hard to gain leadership in the Florentine government.[2]

The Guelf Party arose in the second part of the thirteenth century as an association of Guelf nobles contending with the Ghibelline ones for the control of the city. When the Guelf cause finally emerged victorious with the battle of Campaldino in 1289,[3] the party grew in stature, wealth, and power. The Guelf Party was not only the guarantor of Guelfism in Florence, but it also gradually came to represent the bulk of the resistance by the magnates, after the Ordinance of Justice (Ordinamenti di giustizia) promulgated by Giano di Bella in 1293 and reformulated in 1295.[4] This new statutory law had the twin goals of reducing the political power of magnates – identified as nobles or great *popolani*, who were considered bellicose and ungovernable in nature[5] – and ensuring that the guilds of Florence retained control of the city. In the early decades of the fourteenth century, the leadership of the Guelf Party was consistently aligned with the ruling elite of Florence. But with the birth of the popular government in 1343 – which enlarged the governing body to include the lower levels of society, minor guilds, and the "new people" (*gente nuova* or *novi cives*) – the Guelf Party assumed a more partisan character.

During the fourteenth century, to be part of the active political life in Florence, citizens had to fulfil five requirements: be born in Florence or in the Florentine area, be thirty-five or older, have paid real estate taxes, be Guelf, and be a *popolano* enrolled in one of the twenty-one guilds. With the popular government, however, a considerable number of the *gente nuova* – previously excluded from politics – entered government office, upsetting the social balance imposed by the oligarchy.[6]

---

2 The officials of the Guelf Party and their duties are described in a statute of 1335, published by Bonaini (1857). From this statute, we know that another one preceded it, but it has not been traced.

3 For the battle of Campaldino, see Canaccini 2021.

4 A transcription of the Ordinance of Justice is printed in appendix 12 in Salvemini 1899 and in *Ordinamenti di giustizia 1293–1993* (1993).

5 Magnates were associated with arrogance and *grandigia*, and a tendency to oppress others. A list of magnate families was included in the Statuti del Podestà; the earliest surviving list appears in the Ordinance of Justice of 1293, but for our period the later lists, those from 1322–5 and 1355, are more useful. On the creation and revision of the lists, see Klapisch-Zuber 2009, 17–37.

6 For a definition of *novi cives*, see Becker 1967–8, vol. 2, 95; for the role of the minor guilds in this period, see Becker and Brucker 1956, 93–4. Najemy counts 136 new families in the highest Florentine offices in 1343–8; in 1328–43 there were just 38 (1982, 149–50). This is despite

In the fear that through the *gente nuova* old Ghibelline families might have taken positions in the Commune, the Guelf Party promulgated new laws to prevent this possibility – at least, this was the official reason; the unofficial one was to put power back in the hands of a smaller number of families, namely, those who had traditionally held it. The new laws made it possible for the Guelf Party to modify all the offices in the Florentine Commune.[7] This law, promulgated on 26 January 1347, established that no Ghibellines convicted and banished for rebellion between November 1301 and 1347, or any of their descendants, could perform public functions for the Commune. Transgressors should be removed from such offices inappropriately assumed and fined 500 lire. Furthermore, the law decreed the same restrictions to be imposed on men loyal to the emperor who had rebelled against the city after 1347, but it raised the fine to the exorbitant sum of 1,000 gold florins, which could be commuted to a capital sentence if the sum were not paid in full. In addition, it called for the slip inscribed with the name of the convicted Ghibelline to be removed from the electoral bag and destroyed. Finally, all those who had been rightfully elected or drawn for the aforementioned offices were obliged to swear a solemn oath before a judge that they were true Guelfs and loyal to the Papacy.[8] The evidence required to accuse ("admonish") someone of being Ghibelline was the testimony of six men. The denunciation itself could be anonymous and was sufficient to start the judiciary process. There is no doubt that the new law was passed on the wave of emotions created by the coronation in 1346 of Charles IV, the grandson of the great enemy of the Florentine Guelf faction, Henry of Luxemburg, when Charles assumed the titles of King of Bohemia, King of the Romans (Re dei Romani), and Count of Luxemburg.

---

the fact that in 1346 a new law prohibited access to the communal offices to immigrants who were not resident in Florence or in its county for at least three generations (G. Villani 1990–1, 13.79; ASFi, *PR* 34, ff. 93v–94v). An anonymous chronicler wrote: "It seems to the great *popolani* of Florence that the *mediani* and the artisans had too much authority in the government. They procured the passage of a law stating that no citizen who was not born in the city or in the *contado*, and whose father and grandfather were not natives, could accept any position in the government, and the fourteen lower guilds were seriously weakened by this law" (Brucker 1962, 116–17, 117, n. 47).

7 Repression and exclusion of Ghibellines were not new phenomena in Florence; they occurred extensively in the thirteenth century, when the Guelf and Ghibelline conflict was at its peak. See Mazzoni 2010, 143–6: "Pratiche esclusorie e proscrizioni contro i 'ghibellini' nel secondo Trecento." Moreover, the statutory laws of the Florentine Republic of 1322–5 established, if implicitly, the exclusion of Ghibellines, because to be nominated to any office of the Commune, the Florentine citizens had to be true Guelfs ("vere guelfi"), members of the "partis guelfis vere çelotes," or "guelfi fideles et devoti Sancte Romane Ecclesie" (see *Statuti della repubblica fiorentina* 1999).

8 The law is reprinted in ASFi, *PR, Duplicati*, 6, ff. 168r–169r; copy in *CPGNR* 5, ff. 1r–3r; 21, ff. 60r–63v. Also in *Delizie degli eruditi toscani* 1770–89, vol. 7, 314–24; *Il libro del chiodo* 1998, 364–74.

In 1347, there were five trials,[9] two of which were of people in Boccaccio's circle: the banker Uberto di Ubaldino degli Infangati and the cloth manufacturer Andrea di Tello da Lisca – both of them among the conspirators of 1360. Infangati was accused because he accepted membership of a bankruptcy commission "while knowing himself to be Ghibelline and not a true Guelf"; he was admonished and prosecuted for violating the anti-Ghibelline law on 17 April 1347.[10] It was true that the Infangati family was of Ghibelline origin in the thirteenth century (*Delizie* 1770–89, IX, 78). Along with other conspirators of 1360 (Luca di Feo Ugolini and Niccolò di Bartolo del Buono), from 1326 to 1336 Infangati worked for the Bardi Company (Sapori 1955, vol. 2, 753) – the same company for which Boccaccio's father was working. There is no direct proof of a close connection between Infangati and Boccaccio, but they were both part of the same circle of friends and interests. The trial did not materially affect Infangati's role in city office; as Gene Brucker notes: "Although convicted in 1347 of violating the provision barring Ghibellines from office, Infangati nevertheless entered the Signoria in 1348, and was a member of an advisory college in the following year" (1962, 160). In fact, he was elected to several positions: in May 1347, he was consul for the Bankers' Guild (and was again in 1348, 1351, 1354, and 1355); in September 1347, he was gonfalonier of society (*gonfaloniere di società*); and a year later, in November 1348, he was prior and then became *buonuomo*, a member of the Twelve, in September 1349. He was involved in the Salt Tax Office in 1349, along with Niccolò di Bartolo del Buono, and again in 1354. Despite the existence of this new law against Ghibellines, in some ways its provisions were clearly not always enforced.

Another example of this lax application of the laws is Andrea di Tello da Lisca, of a family of Ghibelline tradition (Varanini 2002), indicted in 1347 on the same charge of being "Ghibelline and not true Guelf." He was a rich cloth manufacturer, cousin to Giovanna di Bandino da Lisca, second wife of Pino de' Rossi, with whom Pino went into exile and whom Boccaccio had planned to address in the *Consolatory*. He was convicted on the grounds that his family was of Ghibelline tradition, as we learn from the accusation; this trial, also, seems to have had no consequences at all.[11]

Still, these measures disqualified a substantial number of *gente nuova* (around 135 people) from the Florentine government, who were unable to demonstrate

9 The five people indicted were Uberto di Ubaldino degli Infangati, Andrea di Tello da Lisca, Lorenzo di Bonaccorso, Gallo del fu Rosso da Poggibonsi, and Jacopo di Falco da Poggibonsi. See Mazzoni 2010, 162–4, n. 403.

10 For more information about Uberto di Ubaldini degli Infangati, see appendix.

11 The charge is in ASFi, *ACP* 74, ff. 107r–114r (Mazzoni 2010, 165, n. 404), reproduced in Campanelli 2003, 198: "Item quod in registro seu libro registri partis Guelforum civitatis Florentie, in quo sunt reducti et scripti Ghibellini civitatis Florentie, reperiuntur scripti inter alios Ghibellinos illi de domo de l'Ischia." For more on this trial, see Brucker 1962, 118; Mazzoni 2010, 164–6; Campanelli 2003, 198–9.

exactly who their ancestors were, Ghibelline or Guelf. The mere existence of such a law on the statute books was enough for many "new men" to withdraw from public service (Brucker 1962, 118). Giovanni Villani shows clearly how this provision had a strong impact on the public opinion: "Ubaldino Infangati was condemned because he accepted the Office of the Sixteen over the syndicate of the bankrupts for 500 lire; therefore, some others did not accept or want to take the oath for the same or other offices, because they did not want to be condemned or shamed. For this reason, other Guelfs were placed in the same offices instead" ("funne condannato Ubaldino Infangati, perché accettò l'uficio di XVI sopra i sindacati de' falliti in libre D; e alcuni altri per quello uficio e altri ufici, per non esere condannati né isvergognati, non accettarono né vollono giurare i detti uffici, e altri Guelfi furono messi in quello scambio"; 1990–1, 13.79). Between 1348 and 1357, at least fifty people asked to take the oath to the Guelf Party, which in the meantime tightened its admission requirements by doubling its fees (Brucker 1962, 118–19; Mazzoni 2010, 148). Despite everything, eighty-two "new men" were named eligible to the Signoria for the first time between 1351 and 1354, demonstrating how porous the barriers were (Brucker 1962, 160). With the passage of Charles IV of Bohemia through Italy in 1354–5, however, the legal offensive against Ghibellines was rekindled, and in 1354 the provisions of the 1347 law were reasserted.

According to Marchionne di Coppo Stefani, the anti-Ghibelline movement was created more by city factions than by the historical circumstance in Italy (1910, rubr. 665):

> In the year of the Lord 1354, the evil seed of Guelf and Ghibelline factions, which had already spread in the past, returned … These factions had already caused great damage to the city of Florence, and now they were doing it again. They say that, in this year, because the Albizzi were slanderously accused of being from Arezzo and Ghibelline, the Ricci invented a new way to prevent the Ghibellines from taking offices. Others said that the Albizzi were originally from Alcone, in the countryside of Arezzo, and that they were good citizens of Arezzo, and that they were banished from Arezzo because they were Guelfs. I do not know what is true, because I was not alive when they arrived in Florence, and in any case it is not my duty to find the truth. The Ricci and their sect plotted, and they say: "We will take the offices away from the Albizzi in this manner: we will request a petition to the Guelf Party, so that whoever is Ghibelline and holds an office must pay a fine of 500 lire. The Albizzi will not support this petition, and by doing so they will reveal themselves to be Ghibelline, because we could say that if they were real Guelfs they would be in favour."

> (Negli anni di Cristo 1354 rinovellò lo maladetto seme, che già era stato seminato per adietro … de guelfi e ghibellini. Questi nomi molto feciono di danno alla città di Firenze, e ora nuovamente. In questo anno si dice che perchè gli Albizi erano calunniati essere d'Arezzo e ghibellini, li Ricci prendeano forma nuova di vietare gli

> ufici a' ghibellini. Gli Albizzi si dicea per altri essere d'Alcone del contado d'Arezzo, e poi d'Arezzo buoni cittadini, e cacciati d'Arezzo per guelfi. Quale si fosse la verità io non la determino, perché a mio tempo non era loro venuta, e la verità non istava a me cercare. S'armarono li Ricci e loro setta, dicendo: "Noi torremo gli ufici agli Albizi con modo che noi faremo mettere una petizione alla Parte guelfa, che chi ghibellino sia in uficio, sia in 500 lire condannato. Gli Albizi la contradiranno; allora si vedrà bene loro essere ghibellini, imperocché noi diremo che se fussino guelfi essi la favoreggerebbono.")

The Ricci's initiative was not successful: the Albizzi, in fact, approved the petition, but the Ricci faction was damaged in the effort, which was struck down by its own strategy, as by a boomerang.

Although we do not have the complete list of the members of the Guelf Party,[12] the party was not a single cohesive bloc. On the contrary, inside it there were different currents, but these two factions, the Albizzi and the Ricci, are clearly distinguishable. The Albizzi headed the more oligarchic and conservative group; they had more stability because the family constituted a large portion of its membership and because they were linked more closely to the Guelf Party. They were in favour of the presence of the Church in political affairs and were against the "new men." The opposing clique was much more heterogeneous. It was less a collation of family and more an association of people who, for many reasons, were afraid of the rising power of the oligarchic faction and the Albizzi family. The Ricci followers were liberals, more open to newcomers, and averse to the interference of the Church in Florentine politics.

Although the Albizzi were countered by other factions inside the Guelf Party, they gained the upper hand by enforcing the practice of the *ammonizione* starting in January 1358. This was an effective stratagem to gain full power, "with the criminal purpose of becoming little tyrants" ("a fine reo di divenire tirannelli"; M. Villani 1995, 8.24). The renewed repression was based on the laws promulgated in 1347 and 1354, which, this time, were strictly applied: Vieri Mazzoni counts at least nineteen trials in 1358 alone (2010, 168). For twenty years, from 1358 to 1378 (with the Ciompi Riot), the *ammonizioni* were aimed at everyone charged with "being Ghibelline or not true Guelf." The "Ghibelline question," which had been dead for several decades, reemerged. It was a devious way for the extremist faction of the Guelf Party to seize control of political power in the city. Only those who had a record of being a true Guelf – if they could demonstrate that the whole family had been Guelf from the start of the century – could participate in political life. In practice, that meant that only people from families who had been Florentine citizens for at least two generations could hold office. The "new

12 Stefani (1910, rubr. 775) lists the Guelf Party officials; Mazzoni (2010, app. I) lists the party's captains.

men" would have been unable to pass the test, since they lacked the appropriate documentation. Perhaps to supply this lack, many family memoirs were written in these years, the authors of some of them occasionally inventing historical "facts," as Paolo Morelli did for his ancestor Morello Morelli (Mazzoni and Monti 2013, 30–1).

Until 1358, according to Matteo Villani's *Cronica*, "the city of Florence experienced great peace and quiet at home, while it had no enemies abroad, and enjoyed friendly relations with lords and communes throughout Italy" ("Era la città di Firenze in questi tempi in grande tranquillità e pace dentro, e di fuori non avea nemici, e con tutti i comuni e signori d'Italia era in amicizia"; M. Villani 1995, 8.24). Such an idyllic situation – however superficial[13] – changed drastically. As Matteo Villani writes (8.24), as a consequence, great men and their followers

> gathered together in the seat of their political party, and through their assemblies they created captains, priors, and counsellors who had been in their retinue for years, with distinctly public, shameless, and dishonourable partiality, and – finding ways to destroy and debase under the false name of the Guelf faction its just and holy name – they had the power to do everything in accordance with their disordered appetites. As a result, a great disturbance of the tranquil and good state of the Commune ensued, and any citizens who were disposed to mind their own business, and who did not agree with this obscene sect, were not sure about their status and their dignity: and widespread agitation befell the citizens, and soon afterward obscene injustices and grave dangers ensued for our City, as one can gradually grasp from reading the following pages.
>
> (Si racchiusono insieme nel palagio della parte, e per loro squittini feciono capitani, e priori, e consiglieri di parte loro séguito per molti anni, con assai publica, sfacciata, e disonesta spezialtà, e sotto falso nome di parte guelfa trovando modo di distruggere e bassare il giusto e santo nome di quella, ebbono podere di fare ogni cosa secondo il loro disordinato apetito. Della qual cosa seguitò subitamente grande inquietazione del tranquillo e buono stato del Comune, e tutti i cittadini disposti a volere fare i fatti loro, e non concorrenti alla sconcia setta, stavano sospesi di loro stato e di loro onore: e comune turbazione ne cadde tra' cittadini, e appresso ne seguitarono sconce ingiurie e gravi pericoli alla nostra città, come leggendo innanzi pe' tempi si potrà comprendere.)

The practice of *ammonizione* was exploited for personal gain and revenge by this Guelf faction and the Albizzi family, along with their followers. Villani's

13 Brucker, for example, notes: "The history of the Florentine commune in the 1350's reveals that behind the façade of compromise and conciliation, no real progress had been made toward a permanent settlement of the major controversial issue" (1962, 183).

description is echoed by Boccaccio in his *Consolatoria a Pino de' Rossi* (§§36–7), written between 1361 and 1362:

> These people aim not for the public good but for their own, and they have dragged the city through misery and drag today in slavery that city which today we call our own and, unless circumstances change, we will be sorry to call our own in the future. On top of this we see (I must keep silent out of our sense of shame on the gluttons, the whoremongers, the tavern goers, and others of similar filth) very dishonourable men who with the most serious expression, never saying a word, venerating the frescos by standing at their feet, claiming and showing themselves to be the most tender fathers and protectors of the common good (all people who, if investigated more closely, will be found not to know how many fingers they have on their hands, while – when it is their turn – when it comes to lying and cheating, they are absolute masters), judged to be good men by deceived ones, are placed at the helm of such a mighty boat, labouring amid so many storms.
>
> (Quelli … non l'avere pubblico ma il proprio procurando, hanno in miseria tirata e tirano in servitude la città, la quale ora diciamo nostra e della quale, se modo non si muta, ancora ci dorrà essere chiamati. E oltre a ciò vi veggiamo (acciò ch'io taccia per meno vergogna di noi i ghiottoni, i puttanieri, i tavernieri e gli altri di simili lordure) disonesti uomini assai, i quali, quale con contenenza gravissima, quale con non dire mai parola e chi con l'andare grattando i piedi alle dipinture e molti collo anfanare e mostrarsi tenerissimi padri e protettori del comune bene (i quali tutti, ricercando, non si troverà sappiano annoverare quante dita abbiano nelle mani, come che del rubare, quando fatto loro vegna e del barattare sieno maestri sovrani), essendo buoni uomini riputati dagl'ingannati, al timone di sì gran legno, in tante tempeste faticato, sono posti.)

The Italian historian Nino Valeri writes about a "witch-hunt," for "whoever was Ghibelline, or *thought to be such*, or who had a father or paternal grandfather or son or nephew or uncle or brother among the rebels or who had been confined by the Commune, would never again have the possibility to be raised to any public office," but "nobody was able to prove (to use language reminiscent, both here [in Italy] and in Germany, of the last World War) 100 per cent racial purity."[14] As we find in Stefani's *Cronica* (1910, rubr. 678) and in the *Diario di Anonimo fiorentino*

14 "Chiunque fosse ghibellino, o *reputato tale*, o avesse avuto il padre o l'avo paterno, un figlio o un nipote o uno zio o un fratello, tra i ribelli e confinati del comune, non avrebbe potuto mai più essere elevato ad alcun pubblico ufficio"; "nessuno era in grado di provare (diciamo per adoperare il linguaggio corrente, da noi e in Germania, ai tempi dell'ultima guerra mondiale) la purezza razziale al cento per cento" (Valeri 1965, 657–9). For recent studies of this historical context, see Ricciardelli (2007) and Mazzoni (2010). Still fundamental is Brucker (1962): see the chapter "Precarious Equilibrium 1354–1365" (148–93).

(1876, 293),[15] among the first people to be targeted by this wave of admonitions were Domenico di Donato Bandini (13 April 1358) and Boccaccio's true friend, Niccolò di Bartolo del Buono (20 April 1358), both from San Jacopo Oltrarno and the only two among the twelve conspirators to be caught and executed in December 1360.[16] Other conspirators were admonished; in February 1360, Uberto di Ubaldino degli Infangati was convicted for the second time after 1347 (Stefani 1910, rubr. 681).

Before mentioning Niccolò di Bartolo del Buono, Matteo Villani dejectedly writes (1995, 8.31):[17]

> On the 21st day of this month, having had a new election, and having stuffed into their sacks a huge number of good and dear citizens from the most important families of the *popolari* of Florence from each neighbourhood, so honest that it would be dishonourable to name them all, and since the result of their secret election was already known to everyone, the entire city was grieving, and serious outrage was spreading in all directions, accompanied by scandal, as one denounced while another praised this evil operation, but in general all good Guelfs denounced the law that was passed afterward and the sanctions that ensued … Even though they had taken up public office without fault, and were unable to defend themselves in a court of law, Niccolò di Bartolo del Buono, Simone Bertini, Sandro de' Portinari, and Giovanni Mattei were convicted.

> (E a dì XXI del detto mese, avendo fatto nuovo squittino, e avolti ne' loro sacchi grandissima quantità di buoni e di cari cittadini, e di quelli delle maggiori case di popolari di Firenze di catuno quartiere, ch'a·nnominarle non sarebbe onesto, ed essendo per revelazione del loro segreto squittino già noto a tutti, la città tutta si dolea, e grave infamia si spandea diversamente, non senza scandalo, che l'uno biasimava, e·ll'altro lodava la mala operazione, ma in genero tutti i buoni uomini guelfi biasimavano la legge sopra ciò fatta, e·lla esecnzione che·nne seguiva … essendo senza colpa d'avere preso uficio, e da potersi con giustizia difendere, feciono condannare Niccolò di Bartolo del Buono, Simone Bertini, Sandro de' Portinari, e Giovanni Mattei.)

For Villani, there was no doubt that the conspiracy organized for 31 December 1360 – timed to coincide with the ceremony for the priors' renewal of terms of office – was related to the new proscriptions imposed by the extremist faction of the Guelf Party. In fact, when he concludes the detailed account of the failed coup

15 This anonymous diary starts in 1358, with the new practice of *ammonizione*.

16 Further information on Domenico di Donato Bandini can be found in the appendix. The brother of Domenico di Donato Bandini, Aldobrando di Donato Bandini, was also admonished in 1360 (Stefani 1910, rubr. 686).

17 In 1362, Matteo Villani was *ammonito* as well, probably because of the critical tone he adopted against the Guelf Party in these years (Brucker 1960; Mazzoni 2012, app., 297–8).

in his *Cronica*, he writes the following words: "This law was largely the reason and the occasion of so much evil (and it was promising even worse for the future). This notwithstanding, it was not amended, nor regulated or changed in any part" ("La legge, ch'era stata in gran parte cagione e materia di tanto male, e peggio per l'avenire promettea, per tutto ciò amendata non fu, né regolata né agiustata in niuna sua parte"; 1995, X.25). There is little doubt that one of the major reasons beyond the failed conspiracy of 1360 was the enforcement of the *ammonizioni*. This is why it is important to understand the practice and its causes, implementation, and effects; a full understanding also helps us see the patterns and implications of the historical situation that follows, especially as they impact Boccaccio's friends.

Historians have not been drawn to examine the conspiracy of 1360, because it had very little effect on the big picture of Florentine civic life. The only exception is Gene Brucker, in his book *Florentine Politics and Society (1343–1378)*, which, however, provides only five pages of analysis on these events. This general lack of interest is in spite of the fact that the chronicles of the time recorded the details of the "secret treaty," showing how the conspiracy had a strong impact on the society of the moment. Matteo Villani gives the most accurate report; Marchionne di Coppo Stefani sees this event as a rekindling of the faction's repressive tendencies; Donato di Neri argues that the coup was organized by members of the Wool Guild, who could not trade their product after the embargo on Porto Pisano in 1357. That the people of Florence did not forget the event easily may be inferred from a novella written by Franco Sacchetti more than fifteen years later, in which the author states: "It is true that not long before 1360, there was in Florence a conspiracy made by several citizens, and two of them were beheaded; the goal of that conspiracy was to expel some families from the city" ("Ed è vero che poco tempo innanzi del 1360 era stato un trattato in Firenze di molti cittadini, e furonno due dicapitati; il qual trattato nell'effetto era di cacciare alcune famiglie"; *Trecentonovelle* [1970], 180). We see that the chroniclers of the time have divergent interpretations of the motives of the conspirators, and of the sequence of events – perhaps they did not want or were unable to say openly how matters really went. One thing is certain: for those involved, including Boccaccio's friends, the failed conspiracy was a disaster, and it had repercussions also on the writer's life.

The Ringleaders

Under the double pressure of the Guelf oligarchy and widespread dissatisfaction – personal, political, and economic – among the city's residents, a number of people joined the conspiracy to mount a coup d'état. At first sight, the plotters seem to be a heterogeneous group of people, some well known, some less so; many of them were related by family bonds. They joined the conspiracy for a wide range of reasons. For sure, one-third of the twelve official conspirators had been proscribed as Ghibellines (Domenico di Donato Bandini, Niccolò di Bartolo del Buono,

Table 3.1. Conspirators in the 1360 plot and their involvement with other events of the period.

Conspirators	1340 de' Bardi Conspiracy	1343 The Fall of the Duke of Athens	1349–50 War against Ubaldini and Visconti	Served with *ammonizioni*	1360 plot
Niccolò di Bartolo del Buono			x	x	x
Domenico di Donato Bandini				x	x
Pino di Giovanni de' Rossi	*Also his brothers Salvestrino and Ruberto and other relatives*	x	x		x
Uberto di Ubaldino degli Infangati			x	x	x
Bertramo di Bartolomo de' Pazzi		x	x		x
Andrea di Tello da Lisca				x	x
Niccolò di Guido de' *Frescobaldi*	x				x
Andrea di Pacchio degli *Adimari*					x
Pazzino di Apardo de' Donati		*Also his brother Manno*	x		x
Pelliccia de' Gherardini					x
Luca di Feo Ugolini			x		x
Frate Cristofano di Nuccio					x

Note: The names of Boccaccio's friends are italicized. *Source*: G. Villani 1990–1, 12.118.

Andrea di Tello da Lisca, and Uberto di Ubaldino degli Infangati). Half of them were magnates, who had no intention of being eclipsed by those who held power: the Rossi, Pazzi, Frescobaldi, Adimari, Gherardini, and Donati clans. Their goal, according to the sentencing document issued by the Podestà, was to establish a "new way' ("novi modi") to rule the city by reinstating the twelve-man priorate and eliminating the Ordinance of Justice. It was, actually, the "old way," as it recreates the central features of Angelo Acciauoli's magnate constitution of 1343, written by fourteen "good men," among whom was Pino de' Rossi. Many of the conspirators had tried to regain power before; after the fall of the Duke of Athens and immediately after the plague, they grew in military and political influence during the wars against the Ubaldini and the Visconti (see table 3.1).

Based on a reading of the chronicles from Siena, Gene Brucker suggests that some of the conspirators – Niccolò di Bartolo del Buono, Luca di Feo Ugolini, and Andrea da Lisca (friends named by Boccaccio) – were all cloth manufacturers[18] suffering economically as a result of an embargo started in 1357, which prohibited citizens of Florence from using Pisa's port to trade their goods (Brucker 1962, 187–8). Donato di Neri writes in his chronicle: "In Florence a great *trattato* [the 1360 conspiracy] took place at the beginning of January at the hands of certain business leaders of the Wool Guild, since they were out of business after being deprived of the port of Pisa" ("In Firenze si fe' uno grande trattato a l'entrata di genaio per certi caporali dell'arte de la lana, i quali erano tutti disfatti, perochè l'arte de la lana non lavorava per non avere più el porto di Pisa"; 1931–9, 595). In his book *L'Arte della Lana in Firenze nel basso medioevo*, Hidetoshi Hoshino, analysing the business of the Del Bene Company, acknowledges and agrees with what the chronicler from Siena wrote, which is that the Wool Guild was suffering a great deal after the embargo of Porto Pisano (1980, 164). But this is not all. Because of the closing of Porto Pisano, the Del Bene Company concentrated its activity on Venice, where, already from 1336, other Florentine merchants were running their businesses: they were Albizzi or Alberti, members of the oligarchic factions of the Guelf Party (Hoshino 1980, 164).The closing of Porto Pisano had a negative effect on merchants who traditionally traded in Pisa, but enriched those who traditionally traded in Venice, who were left with less competition. The wool merchants of Florence were indeed suffering. I found evidence of a considerable debt that the wool seller Luca di Feo Ugolini owed to the dyers Giovanni and Bartolomeo Bonaccorsi, who dyed cloth for him between 24 January 1357 and 25 July 1359. Ugolini had been insolvent for a while, starting from 1357, and in 1359 he was forced to suspend his activities. In January 1362, the dyers made a second attempt to recover what was owed to them.[19] This is just one example of a much more widespread situation. When Pisa doubled the taxes on all Florentine goods passing through the port in June 1356, Florence responded quickly, so that by November an agreement with Siena to use the port of Talamone in Maremma was reached.[20] In 1357, the prohibition on using Porto Pisano despite the tariff became real. Brucker identifies 1358–60 as years of economic depression, in which twelve bankruptcies were declared, in comparison with only seven between 1349 and 1357: Brucker reads this as a consequence of the abandonment of the port on the Arno (1962, 15).

From the chronicles of the time and extant documents, it is difficult to determine whether there was a single initiator of the conspiracy, joined afterward by other sympathizers, or whether the attempted coup was brought about by the

18 ASFi, *Lana* 20, ff. 2v, 27r, 80r, 82r (Brucker 1962, 187).

19 ASFi, *Diplomatico*, Santo Spirito, 11 January 1360 (Florentine date).

20 On Porto Pisano and Talamone, see Bowsky 1970, 23–5; and Tangheroni 1973 (esp. chap. 5).

collective effort of a group of people, however diverse – or even, as the sources would suggest, by a number of people agitating for social revolution who had different reasons for impatience with the despotic government of Florence.

Matteo Villani asserts that some bold-spirited citizens had had enough of those who were governing Florence, whom they saw as political rivals who had seized an excessively large slice of power.[21] Other citizens had been offended and humiliated for being admonished as Ghibellines and not true Guelfs, unjustly in their opinion, and they were impatient for revenge and to rescue their name from infamy – among them Domenico di Donato Bandini, Niccolò di Bartolo del Buono, and Andrea di Tello da Lisca. These various motivations provided the impulse to overturn the status quo by means of a conspiracy.

The conspirators elected as their leader Bartolomeo di Alamanno de' Medici, a man well known in Florence for being "intolerant and proud" ("mal sofferente e d'animo grande"; M. Villani 1995, 10.24) – as in fact many of the Medici family were considered throughout the fourteenth century: "The number of criminal cases involving the family suggests that it was one of the most litigious in the entire city. Its record of quarrels, assaults, and homicides was as impressive as that of any of the magnate families, which were notorious for their lawlessness and violence. The extra-legal activities of the Medici ranged from infringement of the city's sumptuary laws to murder" (Brucker 1957, 12–14).

The Medici family in the fourteenth century had been weakened by a political rupture from within: the sons of Alamanno de' Medici (Africhello, Salvestro, Bartolomeo, Andrea, Michele, and others) were all Ricci partisans and opponents of the Guelf Party leadership, that is, the oligarchs. Giovanni di Conte de' Medici and Mari di Talento de' Medici, on the other hand, had joined the Albizzi faction, which controlled the Guelf Party.[22] Indeed, the conspirators were primarily hostile to the oligarchs – the Albizzi and their partisans – who held power and had enforced the practice of admonitions. Therefore, Bartolomeo di Alamanno de' Medici, invited by Niccolò di Bartolo del Buono and Domenico di Donato Bandini (according to Matteo Villani), tried in different ways to organize a conspiracy and seek sympathizers.

They all suspected that Uberto degli Infangati was trying to put something together, so they decided to trust him and "pulled him into their secret plans" ("lo tirarono ne' loro segreti consigli"; M. Villani 1995, 10.24). This was a risky move, because Infangati, confident that his own revolutionary plans were growing in shape and strength (because of the numbers of people involved and the details that were gradually emerging), without saying a word to anybody, appealed to Berarduolo

21 In the following pages, unless stated otherwise, the account of the conspiracy is based on M. Villani 1995, 10.24–5.

22 This is Velluti's account in *Cronica domestica* (Velluti 1914, 241–2). For a Medici family tree of the 1300s, see the very helpful one created by Brucker (1957, 23–5).

Rozzo da Milano,[23] ever on the lookout for outside military aid. Infangati had personal grudges – he had been accused of being Ghibelline twice (in 1347 and in February 1360) – and was defined by Villani as "a covetous man and eager for novelty [i.e., revolution]" ("un uomo cupido e vago di novitadi"; 1995, 10.24). Unfortunately, Infangati gave Rozzo "some writings compiled off the top of his own head, in which written at the bottom there appeared a considerable number of citizens both *grandi* and *popolani*, of high, middling, and low rank, all powerful people in name and deed" ("certe scritture di sua testa compilate, dove soscritto apparea non piccolo numero di cittadini e grandi e popolani, e de' maggiori e de' mezzani e de' minori, tutti persone e da nome e da fatti"; M. Villani 1995, 10.24).

For his own part, Berarduolo Rozzo persevered in his quest for outside allies. Aware that his master, Giovanni d'Oleggio, was no longer interested in his plans, he took the risk of seeking support from the papal legate. Egidio of Albornoz, although a very ambitious man, was not at all desperate, and he was too intelligent to miss the fact that the enterprise was risky and undefined and that there was much to lose in the case of failure (not to mention that he was also engaged militarily elsewhere). Since he also showed no interest, Rozzo went to Albornoz's direct adversary: Bernabò Visconti, tyrant of Milan. Visconti did show considerable interest, but he dithered, playing for time – probably to assess how events were unfolding.

While Rozzo was making these moves, looking for allies indiscriminately, whether papal or pro-imperial, Bartolomeo de' Medici, Niccolò del Buono, and Domenico Bandini could not linger in Florence any longer: each day that passed without action became more dangerous, as their secret plans could always be discovered, with fatal consequences. They had to act, and quickly. As Villani recounts, they pondered "day and night" over how they could fulfil their designs, until finally an idea "fell into their soul" (1995, 10.25): their plan to implement a coup and subvert the power of the Guelf Party and thus regain political power was at last conceived in every detail. They sought, above all, "with inventive means and with subtle and crafty arguments" ("con inventivi modi e argomenti sottili e sagaci"; M. Villani 1995, 10.25) to enlist other domestic allies within the city. In this way, they brought into the conspiracy Pino de' Rossi, Niccolò di Frescobaldi, Pelliccia Gherardini, Beltramo di Bartolomeo de' Pazzi, Pazzino di Apardo Donati, Andrea di Pacchio degli Adimari, Luca di Feo Ugolini, and Andrea di Tello da Lisca. Matteo Villani comments that "according to many, these last two were imagined to have been thrown into the mix blamelessly" ("questi ultimi due per molti si tenne che senza colpa fossono messi in ballo"; 1995, 10.25).[24]

---

23 This is how Matteo Villani identifies him (1995, 10.24); in ASFi, *PR* 48, f. 121v, his name is given as Berarduolus Ruzi.

24 Matteo Villani tries to exonerate Boccaccio's friends in his *Cronica*; they were probably his friends as well: Andrea di Tello da Lisca and Luca di Feo Ugolini.

Archival documents (ASFi, *AP* 1525, ff. 57r–58r) show that each of these conspirators was sentenced to death, but there were many more names on the list compiled by Uberto degli Infangati and given to Berarduolo Rozzo.

The Dynamics of the Conspiracy

The coup was planned for 31 December 1360, on the occasion of the renewal of the priors. It was a particularly delicate moment, because on the one hand the Palace of the Priors (Palazzo Vecchio) remained almost empty during the seating ceremony, and on the other hand, nobody held power during the transition of authority: these six hours could be considered a kind of interregnum in which any subversive action could be undertaken more easily.

The conspirators' plan consisted of two phases: first, occupy the Palace of the Priors by a ploy during the seating ceremony, then assume power by means of an armed intervention implemented with internal (hoping for a popular insurrection) and external forces. Among the apparently many conspirators was a monk destined to play a crucial role during the takeover: Friar Cristofano di Nuccio, from the monks of Settimo, as Matteo Villani notes (1995, 10.25). (The monks of Settimo were Cistercians from the Abbey of Saints Salvatore and Lorenzo in Settimo, today part of the Scandicci neighbourhood of Florence. The abbey was a point of reference for the Florentine church of San Frediano, located in Oltrarno, from where some of the other conspirators came.) In the sentencing document, the monk was named as Friar Cristofano di Nuccio from Florence. This detail confirms that the friar lived at San Frediano, as did one of the primary instigators of the plot, Domenico Bandini. Friar Cristofano had been a long-time guardian of the armoury in the Palace of the Priors and, although he had been relieved of the office, he went in and out often and without difficulty and even kept a copy of the keys.[25] His task was to enter the palace in the evening of 30 December 1360 with four soldiers and hide with them in the palace tower, locking himself in an unused room. This is the version reported by Matteo Villani, who perhaps wanted to avoid mentioning the presence of other clergy members. In fact, in *Atti del Podestà* (1525, 57v; transcription in appendix), it is instead stated that "he would have entered late, to sleep among *other monks* who were living in the said palace" ("ipse adcederet de sero ad iacendum *cum fratribus existentibus* in dicto palatio";

25 Friar Cristofano is also recorded in the archival documents as the helper of the notary Lotto di Puccio, who wrote four lists of the *Prammatica delle vesti fiorentine* (Sznura 2013, 39): "frater Christofanum conversos de Septimo camerarios Camere armorum palatii populi Florentine vel alterum eorum secundum formam ordinamentorum comunis Florentie" (Sznura 2013, 47). From here, we have confirmation that Friar Cristofano was the watchman of the armoury room. On him and his betrayal, see Trexler 1978, who explains that the monks of Settimo were often appointed guardians of the Camera del Comune, because they were deemed trustworthy.

emphasis mine). Afterward, he was supposed to go open the Tramontana door of the Palace of the Priors – the north side door, hardly ever used – and quietly let in eighty soldiers, arranging them in the Chamber of the Officers, which was at that point empty.[26]

The monks of Settimo played several institutional roles in the city of Florence: they functioned in the delicate position of bursars in the Camera del Comune and in the Camera delle Armi, both places where communal monies were locked. Their presence was necessary to guarantee honesty and loyalty in money business, and they were completely trustworthy. The betrayal by Friar Cristofano di Nuccio from the monks of Settimo was a rare or unique case in the history of Florence, and the anguish and disappointment of the Podestà is very well expressed by the sentence: "a person of such a despicable condition and life, forgetful of the given honours and offices by the said *Popolo* and *Comune*, and requested several times to perform the aforementioned [honours and offices]" ("tanquam homo male condictionis et vite, inmemor a dicto Populo et Comune recepti honoris et offitii, per plura tempora ad predicta requisitus"; *Atti del Podestà* 1525, 57v; transcription in appendix).

The morning after, during the ritual procedures for the new priors, the conspirators were supposed to take control of the palace, for the seating ceremony of the priors required all the old priors to exit the building; in the square outside, the old and new priors would be celebrated with words and ceremonies. In the meantime, only a few soldiers remained to guard the Palace of the Priors, and this was therefore the right moment for the conspirators to spring into action. Eighty soldiers were supposed to leap out of their hiding places, kill the gatekeeper, and close all the gates of the palace; the plan was to throw stones at anyone still left on guard on the battlements. The four soldiers hidden in the tower were supposed to leave their hiding place and ring the bells wildly: this would have been the signal for all the conspirators to arrive with their internal and external followers and take possession of the palace and the city. The conspirators hoped that the people would rise up; they hoped all those citizens who had been attacked or put off by the government and all those who lived in fear amid the state of terror brought about by those "little tyrants" in power would join the insurgents, and that the number of rebels would gradually increase. In sum, they were hoping to repeat what had happened with the overthrow of the Duke of Athens on 26 July 1343. In fact, many of the ringleaders of the conspiracy had also participated in the expulsion of Walter of Brienne, among them Pino de' Rossi, the Medici family, Beltramo di Bartolomeo de' Pazzi, the Donati, and the Frescobaldi, who had conspired with the Bardi.

---

26 The Porta di Tramontana derives its name from its position on the north side of the palace. This door provided immediate access to the armoury and was almost never used, to the extent that in 1380 it was closed for good. It was not reopened until 1910; now, it is one of the main entryways to Palazzo Vecchio for temporary exhibits.

The Informants

The plot appeared unlikely to succeed without support from outside Florence: external militias, on hearing the signal of the bells, were supposed to enter the city or arrive shortly afterward to support the coup. So, the conspirators sought the help of armies outside the territory of Florence, approaching without reservation sympathizers of the emperor such as the Visconti of Milan and Giovanni d'Oleggio, Lord of Bologna, but also the legate and general vicar of the Papal States, Cardinal Egidio d'Albornoz of Spain. This appeal to such a wide range of people, both Ghibellines and Guelfs, implies that the conspiracy was not only very disorganized and poorly executed but was also inspired by the bitterness of a disparate group of characters.

The conspiracy was exposed thanks to four different sources, as the sentencing let us understand: "anticipated by public knowledge and secret insinuation, the news caught our attention with increasing frequency" ("fama publica precedente et clamosa insinuatione referente … sepe sepius ad aures et notitiam nostram auditu pervenit," from *Atti del Podestà* 1525, 57v; transcription in appendix), where that "fama publica … sepe sepius" underscores the frequency with which the public news arrived to the ears of the Commune. Cardinal Egidio d'Albornoz of Spain was the first to warn the government of a secret deal hatched in Florence, although he did so informally and without providing names or details. At this point, Berarduolo Rozzo understood that the plot had been discovered and the element of surprise had been lost, but he thought he could still work an angle to his own advantage. He was ready to offer his list with the names of the conspirators to the Commune of Florence for 25,000 florins – an exorbitant price if one considers that Niccolò Acciaiuoli sold Prato in 1351 for 17,500.[27] These negotiations – of which a "mandatory deposition [was] made under oath," as Matteo Villani writes ("scrittura obbligatoria con saramento"; 1995, 10.25) – came to the attention of Bartolomeo de' Medici, who was probably overcome by panic and confided in his brother Salvestro in search of his help.

Salvestro di Alamanno de' Medici was a well-regarded man in the Republic of Florence, and he is the only member of the Medici family to play a significant political role in the fourteenth century.[28] Salvestro and Bartolomeo were hostile to the factional leadership of the Guelf Party, to the practice of admonitions, and

27 Contrary to Matteo Villani's version (1995, 10.25), Stefani mentions 20,000 florins (1910, rubr. 685) – still a huge amount of money.

28 As Brucker notes, Salvestro di Alamanno de' Medici (1331–1388) was regularly called before the Signoria as an influential and esteemed citizen (1957, 16). In 1378, Salvestro was elected *gonfaloniere di giustizia* (one of the highest offices in Florence), when he pursued an anti-Guelf Party policy, reviving laws that placed restrictions on the nobility, reducing the power of the captains of the Guelf Party, and recalling the *ammoniti* (those who had been admonished). He also had a key role in the insurrection of the Ciompi (textile workers not represented by a guild) in 1378.

to the Albizzi.[29] Even so, Salvestro believed that in this situation it would be wiser to collaborate with those in office.[30] Once he realized the plan was destined to fail (since it had been all but exposed), Salvestro informed the priors openly on 30 December 1360, the day before the planned coup. In the death sentence, preserved at the Florentine State Archive in *Atti del Podestà* (1525, ff. 57r–58r), Salvestro de' Medici must be the one addressed as the faithful informant: "veridicis et fide dignis personis."[31] His goals were clear: obtain a pardon for his brother, sparing him from execution or exile, and especially rescue the Medici family from disgrace, guaranteeing its future in the history of Florence (Brucker 1957, 17). According to Matteo Villani, Salvestro led the Commune to believe that his brother Bartolomeo had been drawn into the secret deal somewhat by chance, seduced by the enticements of the other conspirators, but he actually did not know much more about the details and the facts (1995, 10.25). Probably in agreement with his brother Bartolomeo, Salvestro pretended that there were only two people who could reveal everything down to the smallest detail, the two he considered the real ringleaders of the conspiracy: Niccolò di Bartolo del Buono and Domenico di Donato Bandini.

Marchionne di Coppo Stefani gave another version, in which the protagonists are not Salvestro and Bartolomeo di Alamanno de' Medici but a third brother, Andrea di Alamanno de' Medici (who is completely absent in the story told by Matteo Villani):

> Andrea di Alamanno de' Medici, learning that a foreigner was disclosing [the plot] for 20,000 florins, was so wise, that he went to the Signoria, and once he was saved, revealed the conspiracy, and betrayed his fellows, who were caught – and he could have let them know. In this way, everybody came to know about the conspiracy.
>
> (Andrea di messer Alamanno de' Medici, sentendo che uno forestiere per 20000 fiorini lo rivelava, sì fu savio, andonne in palagio, e salvo sé, rivelò il trattato, e ingannò li compagni, che furono presi, che ben lo potea loro fare a sapere, e così fu risaputo lo trattato.) (Stefani 1910, rubr. 685)

Whoever the informer was, the consequences for the conspirators were severe. The only two arrested were Niccolò di Bartolo del Buono and Domenico Bandini,

29 Brucker points out the degree of support among the Medici, and their possible motives, for Salvestro and his brothers' opposition to the Guelf faction. He thinks it is not likely that Salvestro was motivated by sympathy for the lower classes and the *nuova gente*, but rather by political ambition (see Brucker 1957, 18).

30 Scipione Ammirato recounts an apocryphal but nonetheless interesting speech given by Salvestro to Bartolomeo in this situation (1647, 603).

31 "Fama publica precedente et clamosa insinuatione referente, non quidem a malivolis sed a veridicis et fide dingnis personis, sepe sepius ad aures et notitiam nostram auditu pervenit" (ASFi, *AP* 1525, f. 57v; transcription in appendix).

and they became the scapegoats for the whole plot: they were convicted, threatened with torture, and beheaded for having tried to bring down the regime and negotiate the delivery of Florence to the Visconti of Milan. They were the ones who provided the fourth – for the first time official – version of the attempted coup. Under fear of torture, they revealed every detail (*sponte*, of their own accord, as we read in the death sentence) of how it was supposed to proceed, and they revealed the names of those taking part, among whom were Pino de' Rossi, Luca di Feo Ugolini, Andrea di Tello da Lisca, and Pazzino di Apardo Donati, to mention only those close to Giovanni Boccaccio. As I show in the next two chapters, Boccaccio did not forgive his longtime friend Niccolò. He had betrayed his friends, forgetting the sacred name of friendship.

The Death Sentence

The trial was conducted by the Podestà of Florence, Ludovico Giovenale di Cardoli da Narni. Boccaccio writes about him – without actually naming him – in the *Consolatory Letter to Pino de' Rossi*, accusing him as "unjust," "impetous," and "stubborn" (see chapter 6). The death sentence, recorded in the *Atti del Podestà* (1525, ff. 57r–58r; transcription in appendix), was written on two parchment folios that bear the date of 30 December 1360. I transcribed the document and published it in *Studi sul Boccaccio* (Filosa 2016), and reproduce it in the appendix of this book. In previous sections of this chapter, we saw what the chroniclers of the time said about the conspiracy; with the document that reports the tribunal's decision, we have the official version.

After the usual formulaic preamble for a capital sentence, it lists the twelve conspirators to be prosecuted:[32]

1 Niccholaum Bartholi Boni quarterii Sancti Spiritus
2 Dominichum Bandini populi Sancti Fridiani
3 Dominus Pinum domini Iohannis de Rubeis
4 Ubertum Ubaldini Infangati populi Sancte Cicilie
5 Bertramum Bartolomey de Pacçiis
6 Andream Thelli populi Sancti Iacobi
7 Niccholaum Guiddi Samontane de Frescobaldis

32 The same twelve names are given in *Atti del Podestà* 1525 (ff. 57r, 57v, 58r); *Provisioni, Registri*, 48 (f. 125r); *Capitani di Parte Guelfa*, Numeri Rossi, 5 (f. 17r), reproduced by Cortese (1964); and M. Villani (1995, 10.25). In Stefani's version (1910, rubr. 685) and in the *Diario d'Anonimo fiorentino* (1876, 298), Pino de' Rossi and Friar Cristofano di Nuccio are dropped, and Attaviano di Tuccio de' Brunelleschi and Tommaso degli Adimari are listed. Stefani also does not list Uberto di Ubaldino degli Infangati, but includes Bartolomeo di Alamanno de' Medici, who is also named in the *Diario d'Anonimo fiorentino* 1876.

8 Andream Pacchi de Alimariis
9 Paccinum domini Apardi de Donatis
10 Pelliciam Bindi Sassi de Gerardinis
11 Lucham Fey populi Sancti Felicis in Piacça
12 Frater Christofarum Nucii de Florentia

The reasons behind the conspiracy are then listed:

- The conspirators were not happy to live under the pacific and tranquil state of the city ("sub statu pacificho et tranquillo dicte civitatis vivere non contentos").[33]
- They did not have God in front of their eyes, but the human beings' enemy, the devil ("Deum pre oculis non habentes, sed potius humani generis inimicum").
- Some of them were condemned and some "ammoniti" as Ghibellines by the officials of the Commune of Florence and therefore did not have nor could have offices in the said Commune. Because of that they were not happy to live under the said pacific state.[34]
- They were willing to remove, expunge, and erase the law against Ghibellines issued by the Commune of Florence, which was applied to them ("et reformationes dicti Comuni Florentie de gebellinis loquentes et contra eos removendi et cassandi et cancellandi").
- If the conspiracy had been successful, the intention was to govern Florence with a new constitution ("novis modis"), increase the number of priors, and erase the practice of *tamburo* and the Ordinances of Justice against the magnates.[35]

From what we read about the reasons behind the conspiracy, we can assume it was supported by two sets of people: on one hand, a group of *ammoniti* belonging

---

33 This is the typical reason given in court judgments, when a conspiracy is involved: the conspirators are trying to overthrow the "pacific and tranquil state of the city."

34 ASFi, *AP* 1525, f. 57r: transcription in appendix. The reference is to Uberto di Ubaldino degli Infangati, who was condemned as Ghibelline in 1347 (see *Delizie* 1770–89, vol. 13, 327–8) and admonished in February 1360 (Stefani 1910, rubr. 681); Andrea di Tello da Lisca, who defended himself against the same charge (Brucker 1962, 118, n. 54); and Niccolò di Bartolo del Buono and Domenico di Donato Bandini, on 20 April 1358 (Stefani 1910, rubr. 678).

35 ASFi, *AP* 1525, f. 57v: transcription in appendix. The *tamburo* (literally, drum) was a box in which people could leave anonymous denunciations against magnates who perpetrated crimes or offences; the denunciations would be forwarded to the *esecutore di giustizia* (executor of justice). In 1360, the *tamburo* was reinstated after its abolition in 1355. There was a debate about it (ASFi, *PR* 41, ff. 137v–138r). The Ordinance of Justice, created in 1295, with the goal of eliminating magnates from political power, has been transcribed and published by Salvemini (1899, app. 12), and more recently edited by Diacciati and Zorzi (2013). The de' Rossi family had the

to the *popolo grasso* and, on the other hand, a group of magnates who wanted to eliminate the Ordinances of Justice. They wanted to expel the current leaders of the Guelf Party and the "oligarchic" Albizzi clan to create a new government. Or, at least, this is what was reasonably feared by the Podestà.

The charges are very clear: attempting to subvert, disturb, and put an end to the peaceful and tranquil state in the city of Florence ("animo et intentione dictum pacifichum statum subvertendi turbandi et removendi, et ipsum statum in alium commutandi"); creating a secret treaty and conspiring against the Florentine Commune ("tractaverunt conspiraverunt"); and invading, taking, and occupying the Palace of the Priors in the night by force, violence, and arms, with the help of a foreign army ("per vim et violentiam et manu armata cum aliqua forensium peditum comitiva, noctis tempore, invadere capere et occupare palatium Populi et residentie dominorum Priorum Populi dicte civitatis"). In short, the conspirators were accused of high treason.

For these reasons, the judgment called for the condemned men to be banned and put to death, their property to be confiscated by the Commune, and their images painted on the Palace of Podestà for infamy. Ten conspirators condemned *in absentia* were banned in their person and goods from the city of Florence and its district ("in bando poni et exbandiri de civitate comitatu et districtu Florentie per publicum bannitorem Communis predicti in avere et persona"). From a legal point of view, "in bando poni ... in avere et persona" means the deprivation of any kind of juridical protection, that is, the suspension of that person's civil rights along with expulsion from the community. The ban (*bannum*) was not just exile and forfeiture of goods, and being publicly shamed for infamy; among the civil rights lost was the right to defend oneself (both defence against physical aggression and defence in a court of law) against accusations by others or offences committed by others, up to murder, if one reentered the city. No one was permitted to give the banned person aid. Basically, the ban was a kind of capital sentence that affected the social identity of a person, leaving the body intact, but putting him in extreme peril because he was stripped of rights and property: for all these reasons, it was a particularly serious penalty for prominent citizens.[36]

If captured, the conspirators were to be put to death, by decapitation ("capud a spatulis anputetur"),[37] in the usual place of justice outside the wall of Florence, close to the River Arno. Their goods were to be confiscated immediately

---

highest number of denunciations – thirty just from 1345 to 1350; they are followed by the Frescobaldi family with nineteen, and the Adimari with sixteen (see Klapisch-Zuber 2009, 420–1). All of these families took part of the conspiracy. On *tamburagioni*, see Preto 2003.

36 See Maffei 2005, 129. On the ban, see also Ghisalberti 1960 and Milani 2003.

37 The death penalties were carried out in this period mainly in two ways: hanging or beheading. Decapitation was reserved for higher-class people, because it was faster, less painful, and more decent (Massimo Conti 2008, 27).

("ex nunc"). Only the two men in custody, Niccolò di Bartolo del Buono and Domenico di Donato Bandini, were actually executed; the others managed to flee. Among those who witnessed the execution was Marco Bandini, possibly a brother of Domenico. Niccolò and Domenico were given to the "prudent man" Hegideo de Tuderto (the executioner) – "de Tuderto" is simply a descriptive phrase meaning "from Todi," the same city as the notary who wrote the capital sentence, named as Andrea "de Tuderto" – who could perform the execution diligently ("et commictimus prudenti viro ser Hegideo de Tuderto nostro militi et socio, ad hec presenti ac intelligenti, quod contra predictos Niccholaum Bartholi et Dominicum Donati, iuxta formam dicte sententie, executionem faciat et fieri faciat diligenter").[38]

Generally, at executions, the confraternity of Santa Maria della Croce al Tempio,[39] also called Company of the Blacks,[40] had the task of helping the condemned person repent.[41] The goal was reached through a long, nocturnal conversation, in which the condemned was encouraged to identify with Christ or at least with the Good Thief, was helped to make a will, confess sins, and take Holy Communion, so as to arrive prepared at the place where the execution would take place.[42] This procedure must have been skipped in this case, as often happened for political criminals, who were tried and executed quickly (Massimo Conti 2008, 27). Niccolò di Bartolo del Buono and Domenico di Donato Bandini did not go through all these steps: they did not have a full night for repentance, and they could not make wills because they did not possess anything any longer. They may have been allowed to make a quick confession and receive absolution. While they were escorted to the execution ground, outside the gate and wall of the city of Florence next to the River Arno,[43] they were likely assisted by a member of the Company of the Blacks, who would have showed them sacred images of Jesus' crucifixion or (more likely in this case) images of the beheaded

38 In northern Europe, the condemned placed their head on a block; in Florence they were on their knees, as if praying, and the executioner swung a heavy, long sword to do the beheading. This position was significant for the Catholic crowd attending the event.

39 For the foundation of this confraternity (on 25 March 1343), see Cappelli 1927 (esp. chap. 3).

40 The members wore a black gown and hat, completely covering the body and the face. They were, in fact, common people who did this service as an act of mercy, and as such they had to remain anonymous.

41 This was a real act of mercy considering that, at the time, the condemned person was denied every benevolence and any kind of sacrament, not only in life but in death as well: they were denied a decent burial in consecrated ground, and their bodies were dumped in mass graves or in the River Arno. The confraternity's task was to lead the offender to repentance in God's grace while rendering their last hours less harsh. The procedure would have been close to the one described in the handbook of the Consorteria di Bologna (another confraternity in Bologna with the same mission), published in *Misericordie* (2007), pt. 2.

42 For more details, see Niccoli 2011, 50–7.

43 "in loco iustitie consueto extra portam et muros civitatis Florentie et iuxta Arnum" (*Atti del Podestà* 1525, 58r), between Lungarno della Zecca Vecchia and Lungarno del Tempio in front of the Carabinieri headquarters.

John the Baptist.[44] These images were held up in front the condemned, so they could see them and prepare themselves for their end. The image had another role: to shield the criminals from the crowd that was shouting insults and jostling around them, as they passed through the city. The Company of Blacks would be reciting prayers in the ears of the condemned men and expected the men to recite, too, with the double goal of preparing them for death and buffering the screams of the crowd.

At this time Boccaccio was living in Florence, presumably following this affair with some anxiety, since it implicated friends and neighbours. We do not know, but he may have been present at the execution. The entire neighbourhood of Oltrarno was rocked by the news as it spread throughout the city; many more than the twelve officially prosecuted conspirators were holding their breath.

The Other Conspirators

The contemporary chroniclers and commentators indicate that more than twelve conspirators – twelve is a suggestive number for the Catholic faith – were charged and sentenced. Villani states that "people talked about many others" ("di moltri altri si disse"; 1995, 10.25). Stefani, who interpreted the plot as another clash between the two factions of Ricci and Albizzi, wrote that "the most important members of the Ricci faction were involved in the conspiracy" ("de' grandi della setta de' Ricci [erano] impacciati nel trattato") but were not apprehended, since they were "big fish" (1910, rubr. 685):

> In the said year 1360 a secret treaty in Florence was brought to light, which was like this: as has been narrated many times above, the sects of the Albizi and Ricci were so permeated with the citizens that all already knew in a great crowd to which sect each citizen belonged, both of high rank and low. It thus so happened that some men who had greater spirit than others took it in their minds to chase out this and that, and it was said that some high-ranking men of the Ricci were embroiled in the deal. But in such a circumstance it is always the case that things go badly for the small fry, while the big fish are able to break through the net.

> (Nello detto anno 1360 fu in Firenze scoperto uno trattato, lo quale in questo modo era, cioè: che, come è in più luoghi addietro narrato, le sette degli Albizi e Ricci erano sì intrinsicate ne' cittadini, che già tutti i cittadini si conosceano per la moltitudine, grandi e piccoli, di che setta era l'uno e l'altro. Addivenne, come che gli uomini, che hanno maggiore animo uno che un altro, alcuni s'immaginarono di cacciare l'uno e l'altro, e furono, secondo chi disse, de' grandi della setta de' Ricci impacciati nel

44 The bibliography on the topic is extensive, so I limit myself to the following authors: Edgerton 1979, 1985; Weisz 1984; Freedberg 1989, 18–23; Ferretti 2007.

trattato. Ma di queste cose addiviene che sempre va lo male per gli meno possenti: chè li grossi pesci e bestie rompono le reti.)

Both Villani and Stefani assert that the people involved in the "secret treaty" included men who wielded great political and economic influence, to the extent that "perhaps it would have been impossible, or perhaps it would have aroused a great scandal to go after them all" (Stefani 1910, rubr. 685).

The list of conspirators compiled by Uberto degli Infangati was ultimately sold by Berarduolo Rozzo to the Commune of Florence for 570 golden florins. Apparently, after the confessions of Niccolò di Bartolo del Buono and Domenico Bandini, its price dropped considerably – 570 golden florins was still a very sizeable sum. To ratify the disbursement to "Berarduolus Ruzi" and to "Iacobinus Gherardi de Mediolano," the Commune drew up a provision (ASFi, *PR* 48, ff. 121v–122r) on 14–15 January 1361. This document explained that the Signoria had to pay the aforementioned informants because otherwise they would not have given a full version ("integram notitiam") of the plot against Florence; Rozzo did not want to talk without payment ("comoditate pecunie"); and agreements must be kept ("quia fides cuilibet est servanda"). Nevertheless, the full list of the conspirators was destroyed: the Commune, "having assembled the Council, in the presence of all," decided that the list should be burned, "without otherwise putting it on display" (M. Villani 1995, 10.25).

The destruction of Infangati's list was likely motivated by political pragmatism: The individuals on the list must have been important political and economic personages, both outside and inside Florence, too many and too important to be punished. The easiest solution was to make the list disappear, without divulging the names: de facto, an amnesty. The political repercussions of displaying the list in public could have been too serious. The Commune's decision to pin the guilt on a limited number of citizens was certainly more prudent politically.

We can speculate who those unnamed and unindicted co-conspirators might have been. Most prominent was the man who betrayed them all: Bartolomeo di Alamanno de' Medici. According to some chronicles (including that of Villani), he may have been the coup leader.[45] Stefani also named another of Bartolomeo's brothers, Andrea di Alamanno de' Medici. Another source that implies the involvement of Medici family members is Franco Sacchetti's *Three Hundred Novellas,* composed between 1385 and his death in 1400. The main characters of this novella are Giovanni di Conte de' Medici – deceased in 1372, belonging to the

45 In 1364, Bartolomeo di Alamanno de' Medici was convicted and sentenced to death for the murder of his nephew Niccolò, the son of his brother Salvestro. The sentence was later commuted by the judge, with no reason given (Brucker 1957, 14; *Atti esecutore degli Ordinamenti di Giustizia* 424, f. 65v, 18 June 1364). It is sheer speculation, but could Bartolomeo have murdered his nephew in a vendetta against his brother Silvestro, who denounced the conspiracy, destroying the lives of many people? Bartolomeo had to show in some way that he was not the spy and that the betrayer was his brother.

most extremist side of the family and of the Guelf Party – and Ottaviano degli Ubaldini, a Ghibelline. Giovanni di Conte de' Medici and Ottaviano Ubaldini had been on opposite sides in the intrastate war fought in Scarperia between the Commune of Florence and the clan of the Ubaldini in 1349–50 (Velluti 1914, 210). For his prowess on this occasion, Giovanni di Conte de' Medici was assigned the title of knight. Sacchetti's novella reports a witty exchange between the two characters (which took place most likely in the 1360s), each accusing the other in turn and in the process underscoring how the behaviour of the families throughout history had not always aligned with their political sympathies. Medici criticizes Ubaldini for taking part in a ceremony restricted to Florentines and thus to Guelf supporters (the ceremony of the changing of the priors and gonfalons of the city); Ubaldini rebuts this accusation by noting that years before, during that very same ceremony, members of the Medici family had attempted a coup:

> And it is also true that shortly before 1360 there had been a treaty in Florence among many citizens, and two of them were beheaded; this treaty had the effect of forcing some families to leave, and Bartolomeo di Messer Alamanno de' Medici was involved; and still there was neither peace nor goodwill between the Medici and the Ubaldini. Coming now to the point, as Messer Giovanni was seated with the said Ottaviano, he began to speak:
>
> – Look, Ottaviano, who would have ever thought that the Ubaldini would have come in to escort the gonfalons in this city of ours this morning?
>
> And Ottaviano immediately replied:
>
> – Well, in that case, one could have believed this, that the Medici had once desired to overthrow the people of Florence.
>
> Messer Giovanni went silent, and he did not say another word.
>
> (Ed è vero che poco tempo innanzi del MCCCLX era stato uno trattato in Firenze di molti cittadini, e furonne due dicapitati; il qual trattato nell'effetto era di cacciare alcune famiglie; e in questo fu Bartolommeo di messer Alamanno de' Medici; e ancora tra' Medici e gli Ubaldini non fu mai né pace né buona volontà. Ora venendo al fatto, standosi cosí a sedere messer Giovanni col detto Ottaviano, incominciò a dire:
>
> – Deh, Ottaviano, chi averebbe mai creduto che gli Ubaldini fosseno venuti in tal mattina accompagnare i gonfaloni in questa nostra città?
>
> E Ottaviano subito rispose:
>
> – Allora si serebbe creduto questo, che si serebbe creduto che i Medici avesseno voluto sovvertere il popolo di Firenze.
>
> Messer Giovanni ammutolò per forma che non disse piú verbo.)

Messer Giovanni went silent, because Ottaviano spoke the truth. Franco Sacchetti was basing his novella on what was still remembered – and commonly believed – in the city of Florence decades after the event. In fact, only one part of the Medici family had participated in the attempted coup: the sons of Alamanno de' Medici, who sided with the Ricci family. Giovanni di Conte de' Medici sided instead with the faction of the Guelf Party led by the Albizzi.

Two other names can be inferred from the discrepancy between the official list of conspirators and the ones given by Stefani (1910, rubr. 685) and the *Diario di anonimo fiorentino* (1876, 298). These two sources, instead of naming Pino de' Rossi and Frair Cristofano di Nuccio as conspirators, identify two others: Attaviano di Tuccio de' Brunelleschi and Tommaso di Bonaccorso degli Adimari, who was proscribed in Ferbuary 1359, adding another member of the Adimari family to the one already mentioned, Andrea di Pacchio degli Adimari. Not much is known about Attaviano di Tuccio de' Brunelleschi and Tommaso degli Adimari, but the *Dizionario biografico degli italiani* provides a clue: information on another member of the Brunelleschi family, Ottaviano Brunelleschi di Betto di Brunello, who was most likely related to Attaviano di Tuccio Brunelleschi. Names tend to recur in Italian families, usually in memory of the grandparents, so we may speculate a link here. Ottaviano Brunelleschi di Betto Brunelleschi, dead by 1342, had four children: a son named Boccaccio and three daughters, who were all married by the end of that year. Giovanna was married to Albertozzo Alberti; Niccolosa – cousin perhaps of our Attaviano di Tuccio Brunelleschi – had married Bartolomeo di Alamanno de' Medici, the leader of the conspiracy; her sister Tosa was wife of another member of the Adimari family, the same family of Andrea di Pazzino, who had been officially named in the judicial sentence, and to which Tommaso also belonged. This shows how many of the conspirators were related, forming a tight-knit clan, with not only the same political and economic interests but also social connections as neighbours and relatives.

Among the more powerful families, the Ricci family (in constant conflict with the Albizzi) was surely involved, but their name wielded so much influence in the city that it probably counted among the big fish who broke through the nets.

The attempted coup d'état had, as noted earlier, involved military help from outside the city, and although we do not know all the people involved, it is possible to narrow down the likely collaborators. Bernarduolo Rozzo da Milano, chamberlain of Giovanni d'Oleggio di Visconti, was very active in the plot, but, rather than take up the cause of the Florentine liberals, he concentrated on furthering his own economic interests. Bernabò Visconti, ruler of Milan, was an outside "ally," extremely dangerous but at the same time adopting a passive role, waiting for events to unfold in his favour.

To determine who else might have been part of the plan, we can examine the family bonds among the twelve conspirators. For example, Pazzino di Apardo Donati was the brother of the famous and valiant knight and *condottiero* Manno di Apardo Donati. Manno had a strong relationship with the Lord of Padua,

Francesco Carrara the Elder (imperial vicar of Charles IV of Bohemia), and he also was a good friend of Francesco Petrarca (Wilkins 1960; Kohl 1992; Kohl 1998, 187–9). According to *Dizionario biografico degli italiani*, Manno was banished with Pazzino from Florence: "In 1361 Manno and his brother Pazzino were banished again from the Florentine Republic and immediately after they returned at the service of the Lord of Padua" (Kohl 1992). We know why Pazzino was banned, but there is no record of the reason Manno was banned as well. Might he have been involved in the conspiracy in some way? The two brothers were very close and spent most of their time together. Moreover, Matteo Villani recalls how in 1354 Francesco Carrara sent Manno Donati from Florence together with two hundred knights to help Giovanni di Bandino da Lisca, who was fighting traitors of his lord, Cangrande II of Verona (1995, 3.101–2). Giovanni di Bandino da Lisca, who was very dear to Cangrande, was also a relative of other two conspirators: he was cousin to Andrea di Tello da Lisca, the richest wool manufacturer among his family in Florence (Varanini 2002, 21), and the brother-in-law of Pino de' Rossi.[46]

Indeed, Pino de' Rossi had strong and important family ties, not only with the aforementioned *condottiero* Giovanni di Bandino da Lisca – at the service of the powerful Lord of Verona – but he was also related to the Rossi in Parma and, more closely, to Bocchino Belforti, Lord of Volterra: they were brothers-in-law, since Bocchino married Bandecca, Pino's sister (Tripodi 2011, 200).[47] Pino de' Rossi, along with Luca di Feo Ugolini and Andrea di Tello da Lisca, escaped to Volterra after the conspiracy was discovered,[48] and stayed there at least until the Florentine Commune took Volterra on 10 October 1361, when Bocchino was deposed and beheaded. At that point, the government of Volterra was put in the hands of a champion of the Guelf Party, Migliore Guadagni (R. Zaccaria 2003). It is not my intention to investigate if there was a relationship between the conspiracy of 1360 and the taking of Volterra ten months later, but certainly the elimination of strong bonds between Florentine

46 A document I found in the State Archive of Florence identifies the wife of Pino as "Madame Giovanna daughter of the deceased Bandino dell'Ischia and wife of the deceased Pino de' Rossi" ("donna Giovanna figliuola che fue di Bandino dall'Ischia e donna che fue di messere Pino de' Rossi"; ASFi, *Arte del Cambio* 62, np). There is no doubt that she was the sister of Giovanni di Bandino da Lisca – also because names often repeat within households.

47 Bocchino Belforti's stepmother, second wife of his father, Ottaviano Belforti, was Feca de' Frescobaldi, daughter of Lippaccio, another magnate family in Oltrarno (Velluti 1914, 84). Feca married Attaviano after the death of her first husband, Pino de la Tosa, remembered by Boccaccio in the *Trattatello in laude di Dante* (red. 1, §197) as the "valiant and noble Florentine knight" who protected Dante's buried bones from the rage of the Cardinal du Pouget, who wanted to burn them.

48 I found a document proving that Pino de' Rossi and friends escaped to Volterra; see discussion in chapter 6.

magnates in Oltrarno and the "tyrant of Volterra" – as well as other bonds with the powerful *signorie* like the ones in Padua and Verona – was viewed as a reassuring move for the city of Florence. After all, the Belforti of Volterra were also involved in the Bardi Conspiracy of 1340, along with the Tarlati of Arezzo and the Pazzi of Valdarno. For sure, the knights that we have named up to now who were related to some of the conspirators had the military resources to provide the external help the coup needed to be successful. Again, this can only be speculation, because there is no documentary proof, but certainly someone was waiting to hear the bell ring outside the wall of Florence.

In December 1360, the Grand Seneschal Niccolò Acciaiuoli – en route from Bologna to the kingdom of Naples to fight against Hanneken von Baumgarten (known in the Italian chronicles as Anichino) – stopped in Florence to ask for the troops the city promised him the year before (Tocco 2001, 341). Vittore Branca, in his biography of Boccaccio, following Matteo Villani, implies a connection between the conspiracy and the presence of Acciaiuoli in the weeks before the failed coup: "As Villani implies (X, 22–23) even the singularly cautious and courteous visit of Niccolò Acciaiuoli did not appear casual ('setting a fine table most graciously every day and, without the least arrogance, inviting the citizens and the grandees and the commoners to dine, honoring them in turn': among them were probably Nelli and Boccaccio)" (Branca 1976, 121).

Whoever studies the history of Florence of this period sees Acciaiuoli as a cumbersome person to deal with. Acciaiuoli arrived in Florence on 9 December 1360, a few days before the election of the priors, and the slip bearing his name was in the leather bag used for this purpose. As Matteo Villani explains (1995, 10.23):

> Messer Niccola being in Florence or near, there was no doubt that he would have been elected as prior, because in the old bag [containing the names] none was left except his, and it was not possible to pick from the new bag until the old ones were completely empty – generally, his name-slip was picked at every election for prior, but all the time it was put back in the bag because he was absent.
>
> (Fallare non potea che stando messer Niccola a Firenze o vicino non fosse priore, perocchè nelle borse vecchie niuno vi era rimaso se non egli, e delle nuove trarre non si potea se non si votasse le vechie, ed egli a ogni nuovo priorato era tratto, e rimesso per assenza.)

According to Francesco Paolo Tocco (2001), Niccolò Acciaiuoli just happened to be passing by in that moment for the reasons explained above, but Florentines were still afraid of his presence in the city. Thus, a week after, on 16 December, they promulgated an *ad hoc* provision that explicitly prohibited "dominus Nicchola de Acciaiolis" and anyone who possessed lands and castles to be elected to any office of the Commune of Florence.[49] In the meantime, the gossip of a conspiracy started to spread. The official reason for Acciaiuoli's staying in the city was that he was asking the Republic for military aid. Florence quickly gave him the promised people so he could depart, as he did, passing from Siena and Perugia. His real intention will never be known, but the ambiguity of his passage through Florence in this particular moment was noted by the citizens.

49 ASFi, *PR* 48, ff. 111r–112r.

4 Consequences of the Conspiracy (1361–1365)

Et insuper, ad perpetuam memoriam predictorum, exempli gratia, ne alii quilibet presumant de cetero similia attentare vel facere, quod per infamiam predictorum, ipsi inquisiti et quilibet ipsorum superius nominati et ipsorum inmagines omnes simul depengantur et depingii debeant in sala veteri suprascripti palatii dicte nostre residentie in loco patenti, ut ab omnibus videantur.

(And futhermore, in order to remember forever those mentioned above, as an example, so that nobody else may ever presume to attempt or accomplish similar deeds, to the infamy of those mentioned above, all the portraits of those convicted and named above are to be painted and ought to be painted in the old Chamber of the Palace listed above in a visible location of our Residence, so that they may be seen by all.)

– *Atti del Podestà* 1525, f. 58r

The conspiracy was discovered on 30 December 1360, and the fallout from it was severe and extensive. Niccolò di Bartolo del Buono and Domenico Bandini were executed, and the ten surviving indicted conspirators fled the city. Lives and properties were lost, but not only these: the fallout also affected the ways the conspirators would and would not be remembered (a kind of *damnatio memoriae*); it affected their children, their partners in business, and their friends – among them Boccaccio. Through archival documents, literary witnesses, and chronicles of the time, this chapter reconstructs the plot's aftermath in the lives of the some of the conspirators and their heirs, in order to show how powerful, long-lasting, and widespread the punishment was. Boccaccio had already left the city by July 1361 and withdrawn to Certaldo, both because he suddenly found himself in financial difficulties and because the political situation was dire. The years between 1359 and 1364 were difficult for him. Only after 1364 does Boccaccio seem to have found a new balance with the city of Florence and its citizens, but he would never again be in the centre of the political scene. Too much had happened, and his powerful and influential friends had either died or disappeared after the conspiracy.

The Defamatory Portraits

The capital sentence of the conspirators covers three sides of two parchment folios; most of the third side is devoted to explaining the procedure by which the penalty was to be communicated to the citizens: by town crier and defamatory portraits. In the fourteenth century, a defamatory portrait was frequently envisioned as a penalty supplementary to a death sentence, the confiscation of goods, and banishment, particularly in the case of a high treason crime tried *in absentia*.[1] As a penalty, it was felt to be particularly punitive and effective when the defendant had eluded the authorities, so the resulting infamy would follow the guilty person everywhere. Guittone d'Arezzo writes in this regard: "Do not take the loss of one's reputation lightly, for a lesser evil would be to lose one's life!" (Guittone 1923, 145).[2] Ludovico Giovenale di Cardoli da Narni, the judge in the case of the conspirators of 1360, declared that twelve defaming portraits should be displayed in the old chamber ("in sala veteri") of the Palace of the Podestà (known now as the Bargello) as "a perpetual reminder, a warning to the citizens, and an insult to the condemned." Portraits of this kind were typically frescoes on the inside or outside of public buildings, with inscriptions that reported the crimes and punishments of those convicted. A particularly famous example is the portrait of the Duke of Athens, painted on the tower of the Bargello and thus clearly visible to all;[3] it reproduced the vices to which the duke was allegedly addicted, such as luxury, avarice, and corruption: images earnestly requested by Angelo Acciaiuoli, the Bishop of Florence at the time, and by the fourteen eminent men of the city, among whom was Pino de' Rossi (Ortalli 2015, 82)[4] – and now it was Pino's turn to suffer the shame of the defaming portrait. Typically, people who were hanged

1 In Ascoli Piceno, for example, defamatory portraits of those who wanted to disturb the "pacific and tranquil state" were always displayed (Ortalli 2015, 67): this is exactly the accusation made against Pino de' Rossi and the other conspirators. Three fundamental studies have been written on defamatory images: Edgerton 1979, Masi 1931, and Ortalli 2015. For the transcription of this capital sentence, see appendix.

2 "Non leggero stimate perder fama chè menore male saria perder vita" (Guittone d'Arezzo 1923, 132). Nevertheless, there were also those who tolerated this sentence of defamation with a healthy dose of humour and irony (Ortalli 2015, 77). Consider Rodolfo da Varano, *signore* of Camerino, who – as Sacchetti (2014) recalls in novella 41 – "was depicted in Florence, after he incurred the disgrace of the Commune, in order to shame him; as soon as he received the news, he exclaimed: 'Saints receive portraits, hence I have been made a saint there!'" ("Fu dipinto a Firenze, quando venne in disgrazia del comune, per farli vergogna; essendoli detto disse: E' si dipingono li santi: sonci fatto santo!").

3 The defamatory images of the Duke of Athens and his entourage on the Bargello tower were still visible up to the nineteenth century. See Yunn 2015, 484–5 and bibliography.

4 The city of Florence wanted to erase all signs of the presence of the Duke of Athens and his men from the city. Giovanni Villani writes: "A decree was passed that nobody who had been made a prior by this duke would be allowed the privilege of bearing weapons like other priors created by the people; and anyone who had their weapons painted either in their home or outside would

were depicted as hanging; those who had escaped into exile were depicted upside down, hanging from the left foot. Other defaming images did not follow a single style or form, but they were all drawings of those found guilty, especially of high treason – as in this case – and they were placed in particularly visible places in the city: entry and exit gates, the market, and highways. Very few examples of defaming portraits have survived, because of the topical nature of their production and because they were generally out in the open and exposed to the ravages of weather. Among the few extant examples, we find some preparatory drawings for a fresco by Andrea del Sarto, who had been commissioned to represent three captains who had betrayed Florence by defecting to the enemy in 1529. It is likely that the portraits of Niccolò di Bartolo del Buono and Domenico di Donato Bandini showed them as hanged, while the other conspirators, who escaped the city, would have been shown upside down.

This predecessor of the more modern "wanted" poster was also affixed to the home of the condemned person, next to the main entranceway. The infamy thus struck not only the guilty party but also his entire family, and his neighbours, friends, and acquaintances. In the case of this conspiracy specifically, besides the displaying of the paintings inside the Bargello, there was something else marking houses and possessions: To let citizens know that the conspirators' goods and properties had been confiscated, the symbol of *il Popolo di Firenze* – a red cross on a white background – was to be painted in a visible spot ("in signum dicte confiscationis arma Populi dicte civitatis in ipsis bonis et locis apparentibus ponantur et depingantur"). Then the town crier was to spread the news far and wide throughout the city. In this period, the task was fulfilled by Antonio Pucci, a friend of Boccaccio.[5] Pucci held this job from 1349 to 1369, when he became *guardiano degli atti di Mercanzia*.[6] He had a silver trumpet weighing one pound,

have to erase and conceal them" ("Si fece dicreto che niuno priore che fosse stato fatto per lo detto duca non avesse privilegio né potere portare arme come gli altri priori fatti per lo popolo; e chiunque avesse depinta l'arme sua in casa o di fuori, la dovesse ispignere e acecare"), with an added penalty of one thousand florins (1990–1, 13.92).

5 Giovanni Boccaccio and Antonio Pucci (1310–1388) were friends, as testified by their exchange of lyrics. On this friendship, see Ferreri 1970, Quaglio 1976, Bettarini Bruni 1980, and Banella 2015. For Antonio Pucci as a historical and literate person, see Bendinelli Predelli 2006 and Robins 2000.

6 Antonio Pucci tired of being the town crier and asked to become *guardiano degli atti di Mercanzia*: "It pleased God and the good citizens to elevate me and to give me a lighter instrument to play, and more useful, that is a silver trumpet weighing one pound. I fulfilled this office for seventeen years, performing really worse than in my previous one, since the trumpet requires strong lungs and mine are weak, and each day I have less and less breath; therefore I beg you for the sake of God and your own honour, paying attention less to my inability to perform my tasks well and more to the good intentions that I have always had, still have, and always will have toward our Commune and the Guelf Party, as I have indicated in many parts of my book, since

and his commission would take him to more than twenty different areas of the city to cry out decisions from the tribunal and councils, representing in person the authority of the Commune of Florence. He would have made a stop in front of each conspirator's house and the parish church he attended – Santa Felicita for Pino de' Rossi, San Frediano for Domenico Bandini and Luca di Feo Ugolini, Santa Cecilia for Uberto di Ubaldino degli Infangati, Santo Spirito for Niccolò di Bartolo del Buono, and so on.

These announcements would have affected the entire neighbourhood of Oltrarno. We can only imagine their effect: the anxiety and the shame that spread among their homes, all living in uncertainty and in fear that something might happen to them as well – Boccaccio surely was among the inhabitants of the area aware of the implications of the announcements.

Anyone who was in some way connected with these individuals would pay a price, starting with business partners, who would incur financial losses. As I found in archival documents, for example, the Bonaccorsi brothers, who served as dyers for wool merchant Luca di Feo Ugolini, were still waiting for reimbursement for their arrears one year after the conspiracy.[7] Another case involved Ser Betto di Bonavoglia da Prato, a friend of Andrea di Tello da Lisca, who had asked him to stand surety for a financial transaction. Betto had borrowed 1,200 gold florins from Jacopo di Ranieri da Villanova, who asked for a guarantor, so Andrea di Tello da Lisca was called in. In exchange for this service, Betto sold Andrea some of his goods as collateral through a notary act – in reality, a temporary sale, sometimes in name only, which would be voided as soon as the borrowed amount was repaid. Nevertheless, as soon as the goods of the conspirators were confiscated, the property belonging to Betto was also transferred to the Commune. At this point the Commune established that Betto was liable for 1,040 gold florins to the city within fifteen days from the publication of the provision to redeem his goods (22 January 1360, Florentine date); otherwise these would

---

in these affairs I have struggled night and day to honour our Commune with words, insofar as I was unable to do so with deeds" ["Piacque a Dio e a' buoni cittadini di traspormi, e diedermi a sonare uno più leggere stormento, e con più utile, ciò fu una trombetta d'argento che pesa una libra, e questo uficio ò fatto dicesepte anni vie peggio che 'l primaio, però che la trombetta vorrebbe assai alito e io n'ò poco, e ogni dì mi mancha, più l'un dì che l'altro; perchè vi priegho per dio e per onore di voi, che non avendo tanto respecto al mio male adoperare i detti ufici, quanto al buono animo che sempre ò avuto ed ò e intendo d'avere al nostro comune e a parte guelfa, sicome appare in più partiti del libro mio, nelle quali cose mi sono per dì e per notte affaticato per onorare il nostro comune colle parole, poi che co' fatti noll'ò potuto fare"] (Morpurgo 1881, 13–14). The document is ASFi, *PR* 57, ff. 22r–23v.

7 ASFi, *Diplomatico*, 7 January 1361 (Florentine date). Giovanni and Bartolomeo Bonaccorsi were in arrears for a bill incurred by the wool merchant Luca di Feo Ugolini, after they had dyed some clothes for him between 24 January 1357 and 25 July 1359. It would appear that Luca di Feo Ugolini was already insolvent by July 1359.

be considered confiscated.[8] The situation was no different for wives and children. As Varanini pointed out, Andrea di Tello da Lisca's wife and children had serious economic problems: when he died (shortly before 20 February 1365), they inherited a debt of 4,000 florins because his business had been operating at a serious loss. Obviously, on top of the confiscation promulgated by the capital sentence on his goods, goods owned by wife and children were also confiscated because they inherited the debt, and his son, Silvestro di Andrea di Tello da Lisca, faced imprisonment for some time, being unable to pay.[9]

What I examine in the following pages is what happened to the people involved in the conspiracy. When possible, I consider what happened not only to the conspirators themselves but also to their families, friends, and coworkers, and to their reputations. In addition, I reconstruct Boccaccio's life between 1359 and 1363, as far as it can be known. Pino de' Rossi, who played a very important role in this scenario, is discussed in chapter 6.

The Executed: Niccolò di Bartolo del Buono and Domenico Bandini

Niccolò di Bartolo del Buono and Domenico di Donato Bandini became the scapegoats for the plot: they paid with their lives for all the other convicted conspirators who managed to escape from the city. Their infamy did not end with their deaths.

The friendship that linked Boccaccio to Niccolò di Bartolo del Buono was of long standing. In his youth, Giovanni must have met Niccolò in Naples sometime between 1336 and 1339, when the latter was a manager for the Peruzzi Company at the Angevin court.[10] When Boccaccio moved from Naples to Florence during the winter of 1340–1, the sudden change to his circumstances, his activities, and his circle of friends meant that his friendship with Niccolò was invaluable: Niccolò served as the initial mediator between the worlds of Naples and Florence in Oltrarno. The writer thus dedicated the *Comedia delle ninfe fiorentine* to him in sentences full of gratitude and affection (see chapter 1 for the transcription).

As we know from the document of the capital sentence, on 30 December 1360, Niccolò di Bartolo del Buono and Domenico di Donato Bandini named their accomplices and described the dynamics of the plot, apparently without being prompted or forced:

> And it appears to us and to our curia that every aforementioned single detail has been and is authenticated, and that these acts would have been committed and perpetrated

8 ASFi, *PR* 48, ff. 126v–127v.

9 ASFi, *Mercanzia*, 189, ff. 34r–36r, 42v–48r, 50v–54r (Varanini 2002, 21, 39, n. 42).

10 For details on the life of Niccolò di Bartolo del Buono, see Klein 1988; Mazzoni 2010, appendix 180, no. 70; Porta Casucci 2015–16; and also the appendix in this book.

by the aforementioned individuals, who have been investigated and named, each of them, through the lawful confession of the aforementioned Niccolò di Bartolo and Domenico given in front of us in court spontaneously.

(Et costat nobis et nostre curie predicta omnia singula vera fuisse et esse, et fore commissa et perpetrata per predictos superius inquisitos et nominatos et quemlibet ipsorum per legitimam confessionem dictorum Niccholay Bartoli et Dominichi coram nobis in iudicio sponte factam.) (*Atti del Podestà* 1525, ff. 57r–58r)

The speed of the arrest, the confession, the sentencing, and the execution – all within twelve hours – corroborates the claim that this was a voluntary statement. There would have been no time to torture the men to get names; they put up no resistance and made a complete and unconditional confession. Their behaviour is fully understandable – they were aware that nothing and nobody could save them from the hands of the executioner. In the circumstances, the condemned men must have considered it worthwhile to spare themselves the agony of torture. Not everyone agreed that their decision was ethically defensible.

Indeed, if they had kept silent and endured with courage and conviction the painful physical afflictions exacted by their captors until their deaths, then the names of their comrades would have remained hidden. In this way, only Niccolò di Bartolo del Buono and Domenico di Donato Bandini would have been sacrificed, while the others could have carried on with their lives in peace, commemorating the heroic deeds of the two martyrs. But it did not turn out that way, and the other men were forced to flee the city to save their heads, while their property was confiscated and their names were dishonoured.

In his *De mulieribus claris* Boccaccio ridicules men who betray their friends, in comparison with women throughout human history who were able to endure all kinds of torture. An example is Epicharis:

This seems a great thing for a woman to do, but it is even more striking if we consider the weakness of the eminent men who were involved in the same conspiracy. After the revelation of their identities from another source, not one of them was strong enough to endure for his own sake what Epycaris had endured for the sake of others. They could not bear even to hear the description of the tortures without immediately telling their inquisitors what they knew of the conspiracy. Thus, they spared neither themselves nor their friends, whereas that glorious woman had spared everyone but herself.

(Quodquidem, etsi maximum videatur in femina, longe tamen spectabilius est, si spectetur eiusdem coniurationis egregiorum hominum inconstantia, quorum, aliunde quam ab Epycari cognitorum, nemo tam robuste iuventutis fuit qui, nedum pati pro salute propria, quod pro aliena femina passa est, sed nec audire tormentorum nomina pateretur, quin imo percontanti confestim que noverat de conspiratione narraret. Et sic nemo sibi amicisque pepercit, cum cunctis, nisi sibi, femina pepercisset inclita.) (*De mul.* 97.7)

The implication is clear: Niccolò di Bartolo del Buono and Domenico di Donato Bandini did not behave honourably; they neglected the sacred name of friendship at the first opportunity. To ridicule men because they were unable to endure torture was not enough for Boccaccio: he decided to strike out the dedication of the *Comedia delle ninfe fiorentine* to Niccolò di Bartolo del Buono in a second edition subsequent to 1365, as Giorgio Padoan demonstrates (1997, 185–6). Padoan attributes this deletion to the fact that the dedication was obsolete ("Boccaccio had originally hoped for some concrete gratification on the part of the addressee"), and the dedication furthermore "risked reopening, through painful memories, wounds that had only just been healed" (Padoan 1997, 185–6). These suggestions are certainly plausible, but in the light of the events set out above, I would suggest a further and more compelling motivation: in all likelihood, the dedication was suppressed as an act of *damnatio memoriae*. Niccolò di Bartolo del Buono was no longer worthy of the epithet of "friend," he was no longer "the most authentic paradigm of true friendship" ("di vera amistà veracissimo exemplo"). On the contrary, he had not even tried to save his friends – he could have saved them all – and he had neglected the highest value of all, that of friendship. Another reason for Boccaccio's deletion of del Buono's name is that it could have been dangerous for him to be connected with a man who had betrayed the Florentine Republic.

Domenico di Donato Bandini, from the Gonfalon of the Nicchio in the *popolo* di San Jacopo Oltrarno, had behaved no differently from Niccolò di Bartolo del Buono and had given a deposition of his own free will. Therefore, we already know what Boccaccio thought of him. Domenico's defamation had other, serious repercussions: his execution may have put an end to his life, but his deeds affected his family forever.

After the death of his first wife, Filippa, Domenico married Dianora (or Lianora) Gherardini,[11] sister of Pelliccia Gherardini, another of the conspirators.[12] Domenico

11 The first wife appears in the *Prammatica* 2013, no. 3083, under the name of Monna Filippa. We should take 1345 as a date *post quem* for the second marriage.

12 Pelliccia Gherardini is identified by Francesco Datini as the brother of Dianora (Lionora): "This girl's mother is named Mona Lianora, sister of Peliça Gherardini" ("La madre di questa fanciulla à nome mona Lianora, serocha del Peliça Gherardini"); letter, preserved in the State Archive of Prato, ASPo, D. 1114, 6101225, letters Avignon-Prato, Francesco di Marco Datini to Piera Pratese Boschetti, 28 August 1373, transcribed by Houssaye Michienzi 2013, 47, n. 41. According to the detailed study by Klapisch-Zuber (2009, 290), however, "Pelliccia" is the nickname of Cione Gherardini, who would be this Dianora Gherardini's father and Domenico di Donato Bandini's father-in-law. In either case, the family relationship is very close. In this book, I treat Pelliccia as the brother of Dianora, as Datini's letter asserts.

and Dianora had six children (three boys and three girls), including Margherita, well known because at the age of sixteen she became the wife of the famous, wealthy, self-made merchant, forty-one-year-old Francesco Datini from Prato, on 31 March 1376.[13] When Domenico Bandini was beheaded, Margherita had just been born.

Domenico di Donato Bandini, in taking a Gherardini as wife, married a woman of magnate status, but still remained a *popolano*, hence eligible for active participation in public life, where he would no doubt also represent the interests of his new in-laws. This significant marriage certainly indicates that Bandini must have been financially very comfortable. Evidence of this is that when he gave one of his daughters, Francesca, in marriage to Niccolò d'Ammannato Tecchini, he furnished her with a substantial dowry.[14]

Thank to the prosopographical note made by Vieri Mazzoni (2010, app. 199), it is easy to follow Domenico di Donato Bandini's life.[15] After he enrolled in the guild of Por Santa Maria in 1352, he became its consul in 1353; in 1355 he was one of the five board members of the "mercanzia" ("i cinque di mercanzia"); between March and April 1358 he was subject to *ammonizione*. On 13 April, after an investigation instigated by an anonymous accusation, together with Michele di Lapo, apothecary of the *popolo* of S. Frediano, and Cambio di Nuccio, swordmaker of the *popolo* of San Lorenzo, he was fined *in absentia* for having accepted the office of screener for the Commune although he was Ghibelline. This was only the first of the offices that were pried from his grasp because he was anonymously denounced as "Ghibelline or not a true Guelf": on 2 May 1359, he was selected as officer of indirect taxes (*signore delle gabelle*), but the token with his name was defaced for being Ghibelline; on 29 August he was selected as *gonfaloniere di società*, but again his token was defaced after his conviction as Ghibelline. On 21 April 1360, his brother, Aldobrando di Donato di Bandini, was also served an *ammonizione*. We can infer that Domenico Bandini and Niccolò di Bartolo del Buono joined the conspiracy because they were saddled with these anonymous accusations and subsequent *ammonizioni*, which prevented them from participating in public life and thus advancing their interests – in addition to the sense of outrage they must have felt at the injustice of anonymous accusations that could well have been initiated by their business competitors.

After the failure of the coup, and after Domenico had been arrested and executed, Dianora and their six children chose to leave Florence. Pelliccia Gherardini,

---

13 Francesco Datini is well known to scholars because the State Archive of Prato is fortunate to have all the original documents relating to his business enterprise, in addition to his correspondence, including that with his own family. On Francesco Datini, see Melis 1962, and, for an approach to his character, Origo 1957.

14 In this regard, see Bernocchi 1971, 58.

15 See appendix for a prosopographical note on Domenico di Donato Bandini.

Dianora's brother, figured among the conspirators, so he must have already fled the city. We can imagine that Dianora and her children must also have moved shortly afterward, if not immediately. No doubt, living in Florence would have been very difficult for Dianora, not only because she was destitute but also because of the dishonour placed on the whole family by the actions and defamatory portraits of her husband and her brother. Years later, they were all living in Avignon; perhaps the Bandini-Gherardini escaped there right after the coup.

In a letter by Francesco Datini, written in Avignon and addressed to his beloved Piera di Pratese Boschetti (who had brought him up and whom he considered a second mother), in which he reports that he has finally found a wife, the merchant carefully describes the remaining family members of Domenico di Donato Bandini, who at that time were in Avignon. The letter is dated 28 August 1376:[16]

> I think that God ordained at my birth that I should take a Florentine as my wife, therefore I think I found her: a girl whose name is Margherita, who was the daughter of Domenico Bandini, whose head was cut off in Florence some time ago, who had been accused of wishing to hand over Florence to I don't know which lord. This girl's mother is named Mona Lianora, sister of Pelica Gherardini. Of this Domenico three girls and three boys survived. And this girl, of about twenty years old, carries herself in a manner worthy of her name, and I declare her as good a woman as ever existed in Florence. She is considered another goddess Diana. One of her sisters is married in Florence to a man named Niccolò del'Amanato, friend of Messer Pazino. The other two are here [in Avignon], and they are my neighbours, together with their mother and brothers. I am acquainted with them, and they with me. We have been friends for a long time, and I am as familiar with them as nobody else I know; therefore, I got married more surely, because I tried to be as informed about them as I could, from when I lived here. I am telling you this because I know well what I did.
>
> (Io credo che Dio ordinò, quand'io nacqui, ch'io dovese avere moglie e che fose fiorentina, e per tanto io credo averlla tolta: una fanciulla ch'à nome Margherita, la quale fue figliuola di Domenicho Bandini, al quele fue tagliata la testa a Firenze già fa piue tenpo, che fue acholapato che volea dare Firenze a non se singnore.[17] La madre di questa fanciulla à nome mona Lianora, serocha del Pelica Gherardini. Rimase di questo Domenico III fanciulle e III figliuoli. E la donna giovane di venti anni, à fatto si fatta portatura ch'e l'à nome, dicho buona donna chome fose mai in

16 This letter is in the State Archive of Prato, ASPo, D. 1114, 6101225, letters Avignon-Prato, Francesco di Marco Datini to Monna Piera Pratese Boschetti, 28 August 1373, transcribed by Houssaye Michienzi 2013, 47, n. 41.

17 According to chroniclers Stefani and Villani, the conspirators were hoping to hand over the state to the Visconti family in Milan.

Firenze. È tenuta una altra monna Diana. L'una serocha è maritata a Firenze a uno ch'à nome Nicchola del'Amanato conpangno di Messer Pazino; l'altre due sono qua [ad Avignone] mie vicine chon la madre e chon fratelli. Io chonoscho loro ed eglino chonoschono me: è grande tenpo ch'abiamo auta amistà insieme, io gli chonoscho meglio che persona ch'io sapia, e per tanto l'ò fatto pue volentieri ed è pue anni insino ch'io fui costì, che di tutto io era bene informato. Questo vi dicho perch'io soe bene quello ch'io oe fatto.)

Margherita eventually married without a dowry, thus confirming the straits in which the widow and her children found themselves.[18] In exchange, she offered Francesco Datini her youth, her beauty, and especially her Gherardini name, of which she stayed proud and with which she occasionally reproached her husband: "I may well have a little bit of Gherardini blood in me, but I have no idea whose blood yours is" ("i'ò pure un pocho del sanghue de' Gherardini, ma io non so chonoscere il sanghue vostro").[19] Niccolò dell'Ammannato Tecchini, new brother-in-law of Francesco Datini through Margherita's sister Francesca, was well aware of this magnate pride. In a letter dated 28 February 1382,[20] Niccolò d'Ammannato advises Datini on the proper behaviour to adopt towards his wife, using a rather peculiar term, "Gherardiname" ("gherardinaggine"),[21] intended to convey magnate arrogance:

Tell her from me, if she knew how weighty a matter this is for her, she would strive harder, not with *Gherardiname*, but with entreaties and prayers, and if she does this, love will soon turn to affection. They say it is not seemly for a man to praise his wife; I agree, if the man is boasting; but when occasion arises, I think it is well and honest to speak of her virtues, only not in her presence. You praise Margherita for being respectful and obedient and without *Gherardiname*. In good faith, I can say the same

18 For greater clarity on this topic, see Bernocchi 1971.

19 State Archive of Prato, ASPo, D. 1089, 1401887, letters Florence-Pisa, Margherita Datini to Francesco Datini, 23 January 1386. The letter may be consulted online in the Research section of the databank of the State Archive of Prato (http://www.datini.archiviodistato.prato.it), under entry busta 1089.1, inserto 5, codice 1401887.

20 The letter may be consulted online in the Research section of the databank of the State Archive of Prato (http://www.datini.archiviodistato.prato.it), under entry busta 1103, inserto 14, codice 133347.

21 Women's magnate arrogance is exemplified several times in Boccaccio's works, such as in the tirade of Arriguccio's mother-in-law in *Decameron* VII.8.45–8 (Filosa 2007), or in *Corbaccio*: "Therefore threatening, clamouring, and sometimes, beating my family, she ran through my house as if it were her own, becoming a fierce tyrant in it although she had contributed to it but a small dowry. Whether I had or had not done something just the way she wanted it, exaggerating lavishly and profusely, as if I were from Capalle and she of the House of Swabia, she would begin to reproach me with the nobility and magnificence of her family" (*Corbaccio*, 38).

of Francesca; and if any man has good reason to be satisfied with his wife, I have. And since I have always kept the bridle in my hand, I have not needed to jog the bit against her teeth. She is my wife, and as my wife I love her, and this is enough both for her and for me.

(Per mia parte lodi che s'ella sapesse benne qua[n]to 'l fatto le porta ella ne sarebbe più sollicita non usando il *gherardinagio*, ma con preghiere e con invenia, e sacciendolla questo e ll'amore v'è tosto sarà l'afetto; e ssi dicie che il caso mi credo sia bello e onesto a dire delle bontà loro ma non dirle inanzi a lloro, tu lodi la Margherita che'll a te reverente e ubidente e non n'à del *gherardine*, in buona fe' io posso dire con vero di simile della Franciescha, e se niuno à chagione o ragione di contentarsi di sua donna io so' io e come chi abbia tenuto e tengho senpre il freno in mano, no[n] m'è mai bisognato di darle con esso a denti e lla me' donna è chome donna l'amo e questo basta a llei e a me.)

It is clear from all the evidence presented that despite the dishonour derived from the actions of a father "wishing to hand over Florence to I don't know which lord,"[22] past events were unable to damage or dim the prospects of girls of magnate status on their mother's side, through whom different merchants aspired to become nobles. In particular, marrying the daughter of a capable merchant and a noble woman might have benefited the clever Francesco Datini, who could exploit a significant net of business connections already in place and created by the deceased father-in-law.

Margherita's marriage was successful, in the sense that her original family profited from the new alliance, notwithstanding the exile, infamy, and especially loss of property. Her mother was constantly and even petulantly asking her for money, as were her brothers, as illustrated throughout Margherita's correspondence. For her part, Margherita tried in every way to help them and persuade her husband to support his neediest new relatives. As Iris Origo writes in her biography of Francesco Datini, *The Merchant of Prato*: "Relatives were an even greater liability than dependents: their demand never ceased. Margherita's numerous kinsfolk seem to have been unusually rapacious and persistent, and, moreover, they made it clear that whatever they received was rather less than their due: Francesco was so rich, they all agreed, that he could well afford it!" (1957, 180).

---

22 It is interesting how in this phrase Datini conceals the identity of the "signore" to whom Domenico di Donato Bandini wished to give Florence, namely, Bernabò Visconti. Had the mother Dianora Gherardini simply omitted this detail? Or was Datini aware of it but wished to conceal or minimize what had happened? All we know is that the father's past is mentioned almost casually, without giving it any particular importance. Datini is more interested in underscoring the girl's chaste behaviour.

Dianora still kept a house in Florence, which was likely part of her own dowry – wives' dowries could be exempt from confiscation by the Commune insofar as they did not belong to the husband but *ab intestato* to his legitimate descendants.[23] When Francesco Datini decided to relocate from Prato to Florence in 1387, he asked his mother-in-law for the house, and she was willing to give it up, but only for the exorbitant price of 4,000 florins and on one condition: he should give it back to her or to her children, as soon as they had scraped together the same amount. Furthermore, Dianora kept pressuring her daughter to beg her husband to complete the transaction: "I beseech you, my dearest daughter, for the comfort and honor of us all, pray and beseech Francesco to send me the said moneys; he will lose naught by it, and he could do more than that" (Origo 1957, 180). Her plans went up in smoke once Francesco Datini purchased a different house on his own.

Margherita's brother, Bartolomeo di Domenico Bandini, likewise continued to ask his brother-in-law for money, partly to finance ruinous investments, partly because of bad luck, and partly because of his own indigence.[24] These were boys who had grown up without the guidance of their father, who could have introduced them to the commercial world.[25] Not only had Domenico Bandini died without carrying out this duty, he left them with nothing. Here is how Margherita describes Bartolomeo, in terms designed to inspire compassion, to her husband:

> Francesco, when I heard he was here, it did not make me happy, but rather it was more grievous for me than if I had seen him dead before my eyes: I would have not gladly seen him, for he is after all my brother, and I cannot but love him, considering whose son he is, and even if I did not know him, I would not feel half as much pity, since I would imagine that in some way he would be able to recover his fortunes, but I see him old and poor and elderly minded and burdened with children. And I was told that he had a very beautiful wife, who was good and kind to him, and I am as devoted to her as I am to him. I beg you to refrain from other charities and support him in his hour of need, for if I did not think it was in the way it is, I would not say this to you.
>
> (Francescho, quand'i' seppi ch'egn'era costà, non ch'i' me ne alegrassi, ma i' fu' più tristo che s'io l'avessi morto innanzi: non n'è perch'iò l'avessi veduto volentieri, perch'è pure mio fratello e no' posso fare ch'i' no' gn'abia amore, considerando di chi e'

23 In this regard, see Chabot 1998. On dowries, see the Calvi and Chabot 1998.

24 For a description of Bartolomeo di Domenico Bandini, see Origo 1957, 180–2.

25 "To have been left fatherless as very young children" is the first of seven misfortunes, according to Giovanni di Paolo Morelli (2015, 136); the seventh misfortune is the loss of a father's teaching (157–63).

fignuolo e, s'i' 'l cogniosessi da ppiù che nonn è, non mi sarebe la metà pena, perché pensere' che in cualche modo egni si sapessi rifare, ch'io lo vegio veccio e povero e pocho senno e con fignuoli, e dissemi talle l'altro che gn'aveva una bellissima donna e con questo ell'era buona e gentile, e porto io tanta passione di lei com'io faccio a lui ... I' ti prego che tu ne ristringa dell'altre rimosine e sovegna lui nella sua nicistà e, s'i' no' credessi che fusse chosì, non tel dire'.)[26]

One of Domenico Bandini's other daughters, Francesca, initially found a good marriage with the Florentine merchant Niccolò dell'Ammannato Tecchini. At least in the beginning he was condescending towards his future brother-in-law: "It was he who was the established householder, proud of his wife, his home, and his four sons, while Francesco, although rich, was still a homeless and childless exile" (Origo 1957, 182). But his fortunes rapidly changed, so that when Francesco Datini employed Niccolò in the Florence branch of his company, he no longer allowed him to use the informal "tu," for it was now more appropriate that his brother-in-law address him as "voi": "I have become aware," Niccolò replied humbly, "of my fault in not saying *voi* to you in the past; but now I shall amend it, as you see in this letter" (Origo 1957, 183). Still, when Niccolò eventually filed for bankruptcy in 1398, Francesco helped him repay his debts. Furthermore, as we learn from a letter from Margherita to her brother Bartolomeo: "Francesca must earn her living now, with her own hands; Niccolò is old and ill; he has become a broker and makes his livelihood as best he may. I have taken the girl in, and must pay for her keep; and Francesco has sent the boy to Majorca. So, see how many burdens Francesco bears for my sake!" (Origo 1957, 183).

In conclusion, we can say that the surviving family members of Domenico di Donato Bandini were able to maintain a dignified lifestyle after fleeing to Avignon. Without a doubt, two factors worked in their favour: the beauty of their daughters[27] and Dianora's skill in turning this human capital to their advantage. Indeed, it is thanks to these marriages that at least the women of the family found a good placement. Dianora, a Gherardini, must have been taught well the arts of magnate cleverness and strategy. The surviving boys, on the other hand, are an entirely different matter, for without a father to guide them and open doors, they were unable to build up wealth and security.

---

26 State Archive of Prato, ASPo, D. 1089, 1401868, letters Florence-Prato, Margherita Datini to Francesco Datini, 25 April 1399, drawn from the CD-ROM (Margherita Datini 2001) that contains Margherita's letters.

27 Another beautiful woman was later born to this branch of the Gherardini family: Lisa Gherardini del Giocondo, known to the world as Mona Lisa and painted by Leonardo da Vinci (Pallanti 2004).

Dianora never returned to Florence; she spent the rest of her life in Avignon. Her close relative, Pelliccia Gherardini of the *popolo* of San Simone, one of the twelve conspirators, was pardoned by a *provvisione* of 23 February 1369, undoubtedly after much pressure was brought to bear repeatedly on the Commune, and the capital sentence was commuted to exile for a period of five years.[28] A year later, on 17 February 1370, when he was "of weary age" ("decrepite etatis"), he was allowed to return to the Florentine countryside. Only on 25 October 1378, "clearly an old man at the age of eighty" ("homo senex videlicet octuantaginta annorum"), he finally managed to have the ban removed. His descendants, Amedeo and Accerito, who had always lived abroad (maybe in Avignon with the other Gherardini family members), did not return to Florence until 27 February 1405. They settled in Monteficalli, above Greve, where they owned the Vignamaggio estate. In March 1422, Amedeo was forced to sell it to the wealthy Florentine Gherardi family, who were cloth merchants and business partners of the Medici.

The Exiles: The Case of Luca di Feo Ugolini

Particularly informative among the exiles is the case of Luca di Feo Ugolini, because we are able to reconstruct his immediate reactions in the week after his conviction through the documents I uncovered at the State Archive of Florence.[29] The connection between him and Boccaccio is evident in the consolatory letter to Pino de' Rossi, which was addressed indirectly also "to Luca and Andrea, who I understand is there with you" (*Consolatoria* §176).

Luca di Feo Ugolini was the son of Lapa – the daughter of Bartolo de' Bardi and Tedalda di Bartolomeo Acciaiuoli, and thus sister to Ridolfo, Giovanni, and Filippo de' Bardi, important business partners in the Bardi Company – and Feo (deceased before 1341); he resided in Oltrarno in the *popolo* of San Felice in Piazza. Luca di Feo was thus closely related to the powerful de' Bardi family, in whose business at least one other conspirator, Niccolò di Bartolo del Buono, had been employed, as well as Boccaccio's father. Luca di Feo's house was located on the corner of Via di Maggio and the street that led to Pozzo Toscanelli (the current Sdrucciolo de' Pitti); the residence is described "with courtyard, well, vault, and a shop" ("cum curte et puteo et volta et buttega").[30] From the home's position, we know that it was literally just a few steps away from Boccaccio's house in the neighbourhood of Santa Felicita, which was located between Via di Piazza

28 On Pelliccia Gherardini's documentation, see the appendix in this book.

29 Information about Luca di Feo Ugolini's escape from Florence can be found in ASFi, *Diplomatico*, Santo Spirito, 4 January 1360; 6 January 1360; 11 January 1360 (Florentine date). For details, see the proposographical note on Ugolini in the appendix.

30 ASFi, *Diplomatico*, Santo Spirito, 11 January 1360 (Florentine date).

(currently Via Guicciardini) and Via di Mezzo (currently Via Toscanella).[31] The presence of the shop leads us to speculate that Luca di Feo must have had a house with two stories, an apartment on the upper floor and a shop down below. This must have provided access to the Via di Maggio, the street on which the Oltrarno woolsellers traditionally did business (Luca was enrolled in the wool guild). On 23 January 1341, Luca di Feo Ugolini married Monna Nonna, daughter of the late Alessio Rinucci of the neighbourhood of San Jacopo Oltrarno (Alessio is mentioned in the *Decameron* VI.3.8: "Monna de' Pulci, cousin of messer Alessio Rinucci").[32] Monna Nonna, with the permission of her brother Roberto acting as her legal representative (*mondualdo*), brought into the marriage a considerable dowry: 550 florins, from property and money, in which the aforementioned house was included. This is claimed by the notary acts produced immediately after Luca di Feo's conviction. Luca and Nonna had at least three sons: Niccolò, Bartolomeo (known as Meo), and Feo.

Luca was most likely a business partner of his cousin, Piero di Cenni Ugolini of the *popolo* of San Felice in Piazza – about whom we can read in the prosopographical notes listed by Vieri Mazzoni (2010, app. 258) and in the appendix. Cenni was Feo's brother and thus Luca's uncle. Piero was registered in the wool guild as well. Together they conducted business and participated actively in politics. Luca served as prior three times: in 1349, 1355, and 1359; meanwhile Piero di Cenni was consul of the wool guild (1349), prior of the guilds (1352), company gonfalonier (*gonfaloniere di società*, 1353), "good man" (*buonuomo*, 1358), and consul of the wool guild again (1360). Eventually he was targeted with an *ammonizione* for being Ghibelline or not true Guelf in 1363 – perhaps as a result of the conviction of his cousin and business partner. Cenni died in 1365, and his *ammonizione* was removed posthumously in 1378.

Luca di Feo Ugolini's political successes are clear, given that he had achieved the highest magistracy in Florence, that of prior, three times in only ten years, and his last term had taken place exactly one year before the conspiracy, in 1359. In that

---

31 The precise location of Boccaccio's residence can be deduced from the document in which he donates the house situated in the *popolo* di Santa Felicita to his brother, Jacopo, published in Corazzini 1877, cii–cv.

32 In the *Prammatica*, Monna Nonna is named "Nora" (2013, 251 [1655]), but from the *Diplomatico* I consulted in the State Archive of Florence, I have concluded that her name is Nonna, just like her father's cousin, protagonist of a novella in the *Decameron* (VI.3): Monna Nonna de' Pulci. Nonna de' Pulci appears in a notary act from 1340 (BNCF, *Magliabechiano* XXXVII 299, f. 33 – the reference is drawn from the Einaudi edition of the *Decameron* by Vittore Branca, 1992, 728, n. 7): "Monna Lapa known as Monna Nonna, daughter of Uberto de' Pulci, first wife of Passe Passavanti and then wife of Messer Manno de' Donati" ("Domina Lapa vocata Domina Nonna filia Uberti de Pulcis uxor quondam Passe Passavantis et postea uxor Domini Manni de Donatis").

case, why conspire against the government? Why would he want to overthrow the regime? We do not have precise data to answer these questions definitively, but the hypothesis about the economic collapse of the wool manufacturer because of the embargo on the port of Pisa is still plausible, substantiated by Donato di Neri in his chronicle (1931–9, 595). Another hypothesis might be a possible discriminatory taxation, a provision that was often applied by a factional government to bring down political enemies.[33] Whatever the causes are, the wool seller Luca di Feo Ugolini was in financial trouble in 1359 – as his already mentioned debts to the dyers Giovanni and Bartolomeo Bonaccorsi show clearly – and was forced to suspend his activities. The year 1359 was a terrible financial year for Giovanni Boccaccio, too, and the economic distress that followed him to his grave must have started at this time, as we can tell from his tax documents (Regnicoli 2013b). Moreover, it is worth noting that in October 1359, Pino de' Rossi made a suspiciously large donation of properties consisting of houses and lands to his sister Bandecca, wife of Bocchino de Belforti da Volterra (*Lettere ed altre carte* 2010, 48). We may not know for sure why he made this donation, but we may hypothesize that it was to avoid the confiscation of his property. In this context, it is also striking that Luca di Feo Ugolini and Boccaccio himself experienced economic collapse in mid-1359.

In any event, these were hard economic times for everyone. Richard A. Goldthwaite, quoting Charles de la Roncière, writes that the Florentine economy was already bankrupt by 1343–4; "if things thereafter improved somewhat, nevertheless after 1360 there was a general malaise" (2009, 599).

Through the notary documents regarding Luca di Feo Ugolini I found in *Diplomatico*, Santo Spirito, dated 4, 6, and 11 January 1360 (Florentine date) – so written immediately after the attempted coup – we can follow step by step what happened to some of the conspirators. On 30 December 1360, immediately after the arrests of Niccolò di Bartolo del Buono and Domenico di Donato Bandini, a group of people left Florence as quickly and as secretly as they could: Pino de' Rossi, Andrea di Tello da Lisca, and Luca di Feo Ugolini – together with Giovanna di Bandino da Lisca, Pino's wife and Andrea's cousin. They made for Volterra, where they would be welcomed by Pino's sister, Bandecca de' Rossi, wife of Bocchino Belforti, lord of the city. Bandecca set them up in the Abbey of San Giusto e Clemente, of the Camaldolesi Order, near Volterra. It would be a perfect hiding place, situated on holy ground and under the jurisdiction of canon law, off limits to soldiers and outside the city walls. In this way, if asked, Bandecca

33 Discriminatory taxation is the practice of imposing extraordinary tax on the enemies of the regime, generally for military expenses. Examples of this practice can be found in Mazzoni and Monti 2013; also interesting, the case against the famous humanist scholar, politician, and diplomat Giannozzo Manetti (Mazzoni 2015).

would have been able to respond that the fugitives were neither in the city nor in the territory of Volterra,[34] without risking the crime or sin of perjury. Luca di Feo Ugolini made immediate provisions for the protection of himself and his young sons from the confiscation of property and ensuing poverty. The promptness of the legal action can help us picture his anguish, which must have been shared by the other exiles, including Pino de' Rossi, whose cares Boccaccio wrote of, as we read in chapter 6.

Immediately, Luca di Feo Ugolini sent to Florence a short, crucial notary document on parchment drawn up on 6 January 1361 (transcribed in the appendix): he barely had time to finish his journey and arrange for his stay in the monastery in the most critical days after the event. Among the witnesses of the document we find Brother Piero di Fuccio of Florence, from the Order of the Hermits of Saint Augustine, in charge of the church of Santo Spirito in Oltrarno, situated at fewer than sixty paces from the residence of Luca di Feo. The document was in fact "drawn up outside the City of Volterra in the monastery of San Giusto near Volterra in the presence of Brother Piero Fucci of Florence of the Order of Hermits of St. Augustine." It was no doubt this priest who served as intermediary between Volterra and Florence, carrying the indispensable document on his person. The document, in fact, was fundamental to initiate a series of legal counteroffensives to challenge and possibly defeat the expected confiscation of goods by the Florentine Commune. Indeed, Luca di Feo Ugolini of the *popolo* di San Felice in Piazza – as father and legitimate tutor of Meo and Feo, his underage sons – gave up all claims to the inheritance from his former wife (Nonna), who had died in 1357, which thus went directly to Meo and Feo *ab intestato* (that is, without a will), and he renounced all rights and usufruct of these goods and all that belonged to the children's mother in favour of his children. Even so, the first document pertinent to the properties of Luca di Feo is dated just after the conspiracy, on 4 January 1361, only five days after his escape: the lengthy notary act concerns "Niccolò the adult and emancipated son of Luca di Feo" ("Niccolaus adultus filius emancippatus Luce olim Fey"). The terminology is crucial because it indicates that Niccolò could enter into possession of fixed and movable goods. This act carried two important consequences: the first is that Piero di Cenni di Feo, Luca's cousin, became legal counsellor for Niccolò di Luca di Feo, since he was too young and inexperienced to take care of his own affairs ("unde negotia sua propter etatis defectum agere

34 The land on which the Abbey of San Giusto was built was adjacent to a lot with a house owned by Boccaccio's uncle, Vanni di Chellino, according to documents of August 1339 and 1341 (Agostini Muzzi 1978, 644, 651). The same property was already owned by Boccaccio in 1360 (Regnicoli 2013a, 396, doc. 82) and then sold in January 1374 (Agostini Muzzi 1978, 675), probably to pay doctor's bills.

non potest");[35] the second is that all the goods that belonged to his mother, Nonna di Alessio Rinucci, passed directly into the line of inheritance of the sons Niccolò, Meo, and Feo, bypassing their father.[36] Among these goods were a farm with a house, courtyard, farmyard, and arable lands in the *popolo* of Santa Maria del Castagniuolo, in the countryside of Florence; other lands in the same area; and a farm with arable land, woods, and two houses in the *popolo* of San Romolo in Meglari in the countryside of Florence, bordering the property of the heirs of Bernardino de' Bardi. With this notary act, Niccolò di Luca di Feo Ugolini laid claim as legitimate heir of Nonna to his maternal inheritance. The most interesting passage of the document is probably the precautionary legal action to protect himself in court from eventual retaliation from the Commune of Florence. In fact, on 4 January, Niccolò di Luca di Feo and Piero di Cenni di Feo hired three special attorneys, Martino del fu Antonio of the *popolo* di San Felice in Piazza, Ser Bartolo di Signorino, and Ser Niccolò di Ser Serraglio (all notaries from Florence), with full authority to represent them in any private or common claim before all present or future Podestà, captains, executors of the Justice Ordinances, and officers of the "goods belonging to rebels, exiles, and

---

35 "Niccolò the adult and emancipated son of Luca di Feo, of the *popolo* of Santa Felicita, as his emancipation is confirmed to be attested, by the hand of the notary Ser Bartolo ser Chermonteri, together with Piero di Cenni Ugolini of said *popolo* of Santa Felicita, brought together in the presence of the sage and discreet Gentleman Messer Filippo Tommaso Corsini, judge and expert of Florentine law, registered in the guild of judges and notaries of the City of Florence: these men have proposed and set out to said Messer Filippo that the aforementioned Luca is absent from the City of Florence for such a reason that he could not currently be present to take care adequately of said Niccolò, and that the aforementioned Piero comes next to him in degree to all his other agnate and cognate relatives, and that Niccolò himself lacks a counsellor so that he may not look after his business owing to the deficiency of his age and may incur harm, and so that Niccolò himself may not remain unprotected; by Messer Filippo, aforementioned judge, to the extent of his authority discharged through the form of law and statutes and ordinances of the Commune of Florence, and by every way, shape, form, and right by which he may be able to achieve this more effectively, this same Piero, as he is present and willing and requesting it, is allowed, given, established and confirmed in the care and as counsellor for said adult Niccolò, and to this Piero is entrusted the management and administration of the person and goods of said adult Niccolò" (ASFi, *Diplomatico*, Santo Spirito, 4 January 1360, Florentine date). The relevant section of this document is transcribed in the appendix.

36 In the notary act from the *Diplomatico* of the State Archive of Florence, dated 4 January 1360 (Florentine date), we see that Nonna's dowry was published by Ser Albizzo di Maestro Sininbaldo, notary of Florence, from the summary by Ser Marco da Ugnano. It confirms that on 23 January 1341, Luca di Feo (father of Niccolò) and Lapa (wife of Feo, mother of Luca, daughter of Ridolfo de' Bardi) both received from Roberto, son of the deceased Alessio Rinucci of the *popolo* of San Jacopo Oltrarno, the dowry of Nonna (mother of Niccolò, future wife of Luca). Luca di Feo Ugolini and Lapa swore to leave this dowry intact to Nonna or her heirs. In this way, the properties received as dowries by the mother could pass directly to her sons without interference.

convicted criminals." In this context, the reference to the officers of the goods belonging to rebels is particularly meaningful. Also significant: the judge and expert of Florentine law named in the document is Filippo Corsini, the son of Tommaso Corsini, close friend of Forese da Rabatta and Luigi Gianfigliazzi, and several times ambassador for Florence together with Pino de' Rossi as well.

On 11 January 1361, another notary act was drafted to ensure that the residence of Luca di Feo Ugolini and his children would remain in their hands. The act testifies that at the moment of Nonna's death in 1357, the "adult and emancipated son" Niccolò immediately took possession of the house that came from his mother's dowry.[37]

From all that has been said, it is clear that the numerous precautionary legal actions taken by Luca di Feo Ugolini all had the single objective of preserving as much of his real estate, goods, and properties as possible. In fact, his wife's dowry was not subject to the confiscation of property and could be directly transferred to his children – just as we have seen for the house in Florence belonging to Dianora Gherardini.[38]

Boccaccio's Withdrawal to Certaldo

Everyone involved with the twelve conspirators was under suspicion. Boccaccio had personal connections with many of them, and he left the city a few months after the conspiracy; he moved to Certaldo, his village in Valdelsa, in self-exile, in July 1361. Moreover, he did not hold any public office until 1364.

We cannot know what Boccaccio felt, or to what extent he was aware of this plot. What we do know is that out of the twelve defamatory portraits painted on the Palace of the Podestà, five were of men dear to him. Almost half of the

---

37 "As a result on this present day, said Niccolò the adult and emancipated son of Luca and son of monna Nonna has entered into ownership and physical possession of a certain house, with courtyard and well and vault and shop, located in the *popolo* of Santa Felicita, bordered by I. via Maggio, II. dei Boverelli, III. the house of Giovanni of Neri Berti, IIII. via dal Pozzo Toscanelli and dei Biliotti, within these borders or any other if found to be more numerous or more accurate, as legitimate goods of Luca di Feo for his heir, the aforementioned Niccolò" ("Unde hodie hac presenti die dictus Niccholaus adultus filius emancippatus a dicto Luca et filius domine Nonne … intravit et ingressus est in tenuta et corporale possessione cuiusdam domus, cum curte et puteo et volta et buttega, posite in populi Sancti Felicis predicti, cui a I° via Maggio, a II° de Boverellis, a III° Johannis Nerii Berti, a IIII° via dal Pozo Toscanelli et de Bilioctis, infra hos confines vel alios si qui sunt plures vel veriores confines, tanquam bona dicti luce olim Fei obligata eidem Niccholaum heredem predictum"; ASFi, *Diplomatico*, Santo Spirito, 11 January 1360, Florentine date).

38 According to the law titled *Qualiter succedatur in dotem uxoris premortu* (How a dowry is inherited if the wife dies first), if the mother died, her dowry was inherited directly by her legitimate descendants (Chabot 1998). See also note 36 to this chapter.

conspirators were his intimate friends: Niccolò di Bartolo del Buono was the dedicatee of the *Comedy of the Florentine Nymphs*; Pazzino di Apardo Donati was one of Boccaccio's witnesses in the legal document dated 2 November 1351, notifying the payment of the salary for his embassy "in partes Romandiole et Lombardie" (Imbriani 1882, 84), and it is very possible he met him already in Forlì at the court of Francesco Ordelaffi on December 1347; Pino de' Rossi soon became (in spring 1362) the addressee and dedicatee of the famous consolatory letter, indirectly addressed also to Luca di Feo, his close neighbour, and Andrea di Tello da Lisca, who were with him in exile, as Boccaccio states in the conclusion to his introductory letter.

> To Luca and Andrea, who I understand are over there, I offer the kind of compassion that is due to a friend in adversity, and if I had anything to offer to mitigate such woes, I gladly would. Neverthless, when you wish, those comforts I give you, those same comforts – and especially those parts that suit them the best – I intend to be given to them.
>
> And without another word, I pray that God may comfort you and them.
>
> (A Luca e Andrea, li quali intendo che costà sono, quella compassione porto che ad infortunio d'amico si dee portare, e se io avessi che offerire in mitigazione de' loro mali, fare' lo volentieri; nondimeno, quando vi paia, quelli conforti che a voi dono, quelli medesimi e massimamente in quelle parti che loro appartengono, intendo che dati sieno.
>
> E senza più dire, priego Iddio che consoli voi e loro.) (*Consolatoria* §§176–7)

Because most of the conspirators came from the Oltrarno neighbourhoods of Santo Spirito, San Frediano, and Santa Felicita, it is likely that Boccaccio's acquaintances and neighbours included even more of the people involved (Branca 1976, 121). The conspiracy must have had an enormous impact on the writer's life.

Certainly, the friendship binding Boccaccio to these men made him a suspect in Florence, so it is hardly surprising that he was relieved of public offices until August 1364, when we find him listed among the officials of the castles (*ufficiale delle castelle*, a six-month term). Only in 1365 did he resume his function as ambassador for the Signoria to Pope Urban V (Regnicoli 2013a, 398). With great prudence, Boccaccio withdrew to Certaldo, far away from the "ambitions and unpleasantness and annoyances of our fellow citizens" ("ambizioni e le spiacevolezze e' fastidi de' nostri cittadini"; *Consolatoria* §171). Before he left, on 2 July 1361, he transferred to his half-brother Jacopo his house in Santa Felicita;[39] this action may well have

39 The document of the donation is in Corazzini 1877, intro. (cii–cv); Regnicoli 2013a, 393.

been taken because Jacopo had reached the legal age to inherit, but also to ensure that the house would remain in the family. It reminds us of all the legal transfers of properties that Luca di Feo Ugolini made to ensure that his belongings would remain in the family, out of reach of confiscation. This was an important precaution, if we keep in mind that in the following years other citizens of Florence – in particular from the Oltrarno neighbourhood – continued to be convicted as Ghibellines and have their goods confiscated (Stefani 1910, rubr. 686, 688, 692). Other relatives and friends of the conspirators were under attack after December 1360: Aldobrando di Donato Bandini, brother of Domenico, was proscribed on 25 April 1361; Piero di Cenni Ugolini, cousin of Luca di Feo, on 28 April 1363; and even Matteo Villani, the chronicle writer, went on trial in 1363, forced to defend himself, because the Guelf Party accused him of being Ghibelline.[40]

In the period between 1359 and 1364, Boccaccio had to adapt and respond to rapidly changing circumstances, economic, social, and political: his new "poverty" (1359), his taking vows in the religious life (2 November 1360), the transfer to Jacopo of the house in Santa Felicita (2 July 1361), his withdrawal to Certaldo (summer 1361), the message from Beato Petroni (spring 1362), and his search for a new social community outside Florence – which was ultimately unsuccessful, although he did not give up trying until mid-1363.

As Laura Regnicoli demonstrates in her study of Boccaccio's financial documents in the State Archive of Florence, in 1359, for reasons that are still not clear, the writer experienced a financial crisis from which he never recovered (Regnicoli 2013b).[41] Regnicoli's edition of the documents also gives the sense of Boccaccio's civic conscience:

> The corpus of fiscal documents relating to Giovanni Boccaccio restores the image of an intellectual without substantial economic resources, and yet faithful to his duties as a taxpayer, which he fulfilled without becoming mired in speculative games; in fact, he personified the Ciompi motto: "no more financial enterprises, no more forced loans, but just real estate taxes." He was of bourgeois background and "sentimentally attached" to courtly and aristocratic values, but he did not share at all the vision of the ruling class (new money and old nobles) for whom the Treasury was seen as a source of profit.[42]

---

40 For the suit initiated against Matteo Villani, see Brucker 1960.

41 Boccaccio had likely invested in the businesses of his associates and suffered economic collapse along with them (see chapter 3).

42 "Il *corpus* dei documenti fiscali su Giovanni Boccaccio restituisce l'immagine di un intellettuale privo di grandi risorse economiche eppure ligio ai suoi doveri di contribuente, che adempì senza farsi coinvolgere nelle manovre speculative; e che, nella pratica, dette attuazione al motto dei Ciompi, 'non più monti, non più prestanze, ma l'estimo.' Lui borghese 'sentimentalmente partecipe' degli ideali cortesi e aristocratici, non condivise affatto la visione dei ceti dominanti (nuovi ricchi e vecchi nobili) secondo cui l'erario era fonte di guadagno" (Regnicoli 2013b, *I documenti fiscali*, 39–40).

Even before his financial crisis, Boccaccio frequently discusses poverty in his works, using Seneca as a model, whom he annotates in the *Florilegio senecano* in *Zibaldone Magliabechiano* (Costantini 1974), in line with Franciscan directions on poverty: "For Boccaccio, a desire for wealth and honours without any consideration of decorum would exclude the possibility of honouring poetry and of exercising it in public with human dignity" (Veglia 2014, 129).[43] In the *Florilegio senecano*, Boccaccio collects sayings of Seneca under the titles *De paupertate et quis pauper dici possit vel non* (On poverty and who can be said to be poor or not; Costantini 1974, 94–6) and *De divizijs debite appetendis* (On the kind of wealth properly worth pursuing; Costantini 1974, 96–8). Boccaccio is interested in how to define poverty, that is, to define an ideology that can be applied to one's personal life and that has implications for politics and business. It was a theoretical rather than a practical interest. According to his development of Seneca's ethical view, wealth consists of knowing how to enjoy those possessions that are minimal and necessary, such as eating the necessary food and no more, having the necessary clothes and none that are superfluous, owning a house big enough for living with decorum. Poverty, on the other hand, afflicts those who cannot enjoy the simple goods that are needed to survive, coveting instead more and more wealth; no matter how much these people acquire, they will always feel poor. Boccaccio in these writings is not concerned with the kind of poverty in which one is in debt to others, which entails a loss of freedom and control of one's life.

The year 1359, when his economic security crumbled, was a turning point for Boccaccio's discourse on poverty. From this moment, Boccaccio's poverty was no longer that of Seneca's ideals but much more concrete.

Upon his father's death in 1348, Boccaccio had inherited a substantial patrimony, which included real estate in Florence and Certaldo and lands in the Val

43 "Per Boccaccio, una brama di ricchezze e di onori che non si faceva scrupoli di decoro escludeva la possibilità di onorare la poesia e di esercitarla pubblicamente con umana dignità." Veglia discusses Boccaccio's ideas on poverty, emphasizing how already in the *Decameron* the author was devoted to a "poetica facultas" that would enable civilization "to flourish." In his introduction to the Fourth Day, the authorial voice defends himself from accusations of neglecting his self-interest, claiming that many men "in pursuit of their own stories enabled their age to flourish, while others sought only more bread that they did not need, and they died in bitterness" ("dietro alle loro favole andando, fecero le loro età fiorire, dove in contrario molti nel cercare d'aver più pane, che bisogno non era loro, perirono acerbi"; *Dec.* IV.Intr.38); also in the speech of Ghismonda we find "poverty takes away possessions but not nobility from anyone. Many kings, many great princes were once poor, and many of those who work the land and tend flocks once were fabulously rich" ("la povertà non toglie gentilezza a alcuno ma sì avere. Molti re, molti gran prencipi furon già poveri, e molti di quegli che la terra zappano e guardan le pecore già ricchissimi furono e sonne"; *Dec.* IV.1.43). For further analysis of this theme, see the studies by Veglia, especially the first part of the chapter titled "La lettera di Boccaccio al Pizzinga" in Veglia 2014 and the chapter "Fra piacere e povertà" in Veglia 2000. See also Papio 2015–16 and Tufano 2021, 11–44.

d'Elsa, with rights and rents. After 1359, his economic situation must have deteriorated so much that in a letter to Francesco Petrarch (date unknown, original lost, but prior to Petrarch's reply of 28 May 1362), Boccaccio suggested selling his own library to his friend. Petrarch responded:

> If you cling to your resolution to reject these studies we put aside so long ago, and all literature, if you desire to get rid of the very instrument of literature by selling your books and are utterly determined to do so, I am grateful, by heaven, that you have offered them to me before anyone else since, as you say and I do not deny, I am so greedy for books; if I did deny it, my own writings would refute me. Although I seem to be buying what is already mine, I still do not wish such a great man's books scattered here and there or in profane hands, as so often happens. Therefore, just as we have been one in spirit though separated in body, so after we are gone, this paraphernalia of our studies should – if God seconds my vow – come intact and undiminished to some pious, devout place in perpetual memory of us. (Trans. Bernardo, 25)

> (Qui si cepto heres ut studia hec, que pridem post tergum liquimus, literasque omnes – quantum innuis – ac, distractis libris, ipsa etiam velis literarum instrumenta proiecere atque ita undique persuasum tibi est, gratum, hercle, habeo me librorum avidum, ut tu ais (ego non inficior ne, si negem, scriptis ipse meis arguar) in hac emptione omnibus tuo iudicium prelatum. Et quamvis ipse rem meam videar empturus, nolim tamen tanti viri libros huc illuc effundi aut profanis, ut fit, manibus contrectari. Sicut igitur nos, seiuncti licet corporibus, unum animo fuimus, sic studiorum hec supellex nostra post nos, si votum meum Deus adiuverit, ad aliquem nostri perpetuo memorem pium ac devotum locum simul indecerpta perveniat.) (*Sen.* I 5, 63–4)

Petrarch proceeds to request a catalogue of books so he can make a concrete offer; he also offers his friend the opportunity to spend his remaining days in his own home. In fact, neither proposal was realized: Boccaccio never sold his library to Petrarch, nor did he move in with his friend. The letter preserves in its conclusion some important and generally overlooked information: "Finally, for my part, I deny what you say about being in debt to many, me among them" ("Extremum sit ut, quod te multis, inter quos michi, pecunie debitorem facis"; *Sen.* I 5, 66). In this phase of his life, Boccaccio did owe money to many people, among them Petrarch – who generously withdrew his name from the list of creditors.[44] Boccaccio's experience

44 Although Boccaccio did not sell his library to Petrarch, he may have sold individual items from his collection to cover part of his debts. This ties in with the hypothesis formulated by Berté and Cursi on the Capponi codex (Par. Ital. 482), the penultimate version of *Decameron*: "We should suppose that Boccaccio, for reasons unknown to us, decided to give up that codex; though originally destined for his own writing desk, it was probably transferred to Capponi himself. This

with "poverty," therefore, no longer corresponded to that discussed in so many of his works but was something completely different.[45] Whereas Seneca had endorsed poverty as a life choice to avoid enslavement to wealth, Boccaccio found himself for the first time forced into an economic situation that deprived him of freedom and left him in debt to third parties, and thus enslaved to others.

In these years, Boccaccio constantly complained about his constrained circumstances and the effect they had in him: "my low state and my depressed condition" ("la bassezza del mio stato e la depressa mia condizione"), he writes to Pino de' Rossi in spring 1362 (*Consolatoria* §6). On 15 May 1362 (*Epistola* XII), in response to his friend Barbato da Sulmona, he writes that on 16 April of that year Petrarch had been consoling him for certain difficulties of his, "after he had offered some solace from Milan for some of my troubles" ("cum Mediolano quibusdam erumpnis meis solamen placidum porressisset"), and further on in the same letter, he refers to his "poverty and preoccupations for patrimony" ("paupertas et rei familiaris cura"). In *Epistola* XI, written to Petrarch from Ravenna on 2 January 1362, he states: "Since I am living among them because of my *infortunio*" ("quod apud eos infortunio meo morer"). Could this *infortunio* (which can be translated as "misfortune" but also as "punishment") be related to the series of political events leading up to the conspiracy of 1360 and the ensuing economic collapse? It seems unlikely that he was not affected financially, given the circumstantial evidence; his precarious situation and unhappiness were probably compounded also by losses among people he cared deeply for and in his circle, as Branca suggests.[46]

After 1359, as his finances deteriorated, Boccaccio began to search for more stable income and employment. The timing of his taking religious vows might be

---

hypothesis is further corroborated by the recent detection of traces of handwriting in red ink below the *colophon*; although the words were erased and are no longer legible, they may conceal a rough notice of possession bearing the name of the illustrious buyer, Giovanni Boccaccio. This reconstruction, based on circumstantial evidence and difficult to prove, may now be subjected to a compatibility test with the documents published by Regnicoli: precisely in the period in which the codex was planned and composed, Boccaccio's patrimony had begun to seriously decline; may we not suppose that it was economic duress that drove the author to give up by sale his own manuscript?" (2015, 237–8).

45 See note 43 with the examples provided by Veglia.

46 Branca considers several bases for Boccaccio's "misfortune," including a possibility that he was grieving the death of the mother of his children: "It is possible simply to think of the hardship and harm which befell Boccaccio as an aftermath to the conspiracy of Bartolo del Buono and Pino de' Rossi, or to the unpleasant consequences of the death of Bernardino da Polenta (March 9, 1359) which, as Giovanni Conversini writes, 'Boccacii studia magnifice instruxit' (perhaps loss of benefices?), or of sad events (death, misfortunes, dissensions) connected with people who were bound to Boccaccio by affection in the preceding years (Violante's mother for example?). In any case, it is significant that after repeated sojourns over the previous fifteen years, he was in Ravenna for the last time in the winter of 1361 and 1362, and under the shadow of misfortune which is for us mysterious" (Branca 1976, 132).

explained in part by economic necessity. In 1351, he was still defined as a layman, "laicus."[47] After that date, he must have become a cleric: a document in the Vatican Library dated 2 November 1360 mentions ecclesiastical benefits bestowed "upon the beloved son Giovanni born to the late Boccaccio di Certaldo, cleric of Florence" ("dilecto filio Johanni nato quondam Boccacii de Certaldo clerico florentino").[48] This document, a papal bull, elevates him to the rank of "clerico," a status that brought with it pastoral responsibilities and financial prospects. A "trustworthy person" testified on behalf of Boccaccio's character: "The honesty of life and customs, and other distinctions of virtues and integrity, upon which you have been recommended to us through the testimony of a trustworthy person, have secured that we receive your person with the favour of a special grace" ("Vite ac morum honestas et alia virtutum et probitatis merita, super quibus apud nos *fidedignorum commendaris testimonio*, promerentur ut personam tuam favore specialis gratie prosequamur"; Billanovich 1947b, 174). We do not know the identity of the trustworthy person, but Billanovich suggests it might be "the simple Zanobi da Strada, who in the last months of his role as Apostolic Secretary was preparing and dispatching many requests on behalf of relatives and Florentine friends" (Billanovich 1947b, 177, n. 2). This crucial document on Boccaccio's ecclesiastical career suggests that he could be promoted to any order, receive benefits and prebends, and care for souls even in a cathedral church "despite his deficiency" ("non obstante defectu"); the deficiency was his illegitimacy, the fact that his father Boccaccino was not married to his mother ("defectu natalium quem pateris de soluto genitus et solute"). There are four references to his illegitimate birth in this short document, but, as the document states, trustworthy people had guaranteed his virtuous behaviour:

> for we notice that, as we have gathered from the assertion of trustworthy persons, you are able to redeem and compensate for a deficiency of this kind with the fragrance of your virtues in this way, and you thus make yourself a man worthy of higher grace, and we are furthermore willing, so that you may also be constantly encouraged to progress from good to even better, to bestow upon your person even greater grace and favour.
>
> (nos attendentes quod, sicut fidedignorum assertione percepimus, tu defectum huiusmodi sic odore virtutum redimere satagis et supplere quo merito potiori te gratia dignum reddis, volentesque propterrea, et ut ad proficiendum de bono in melius iugiter animeris, personam tuam ampliori prosequi gratia et favore.)

---

47 When Boccaccio was elected *camerlengo della Camera del Comune*, he was defined as "laicus" (Gerola 1898, 358).

48 From the document reproduced by Giuseppe Billanovich (1947b, 174–5): Vatican Archive, *Reg. Aven.*, vol. 144, f. 342v.

From what we read, whoever bestowed the ecclesiastical benefits wanted to closely follow Boccaccio "with more grace and favour, so that you will be constantly encouraged to improve from good to better." It had become imperative for Boccaccio to prove himself worthy of his new status, behave in accordance with his new role, and exhale the "fragrance of virtue," especially to mask the "original sin" of his illegitimate birth. What many critics have historically called the religious conversion of Giovanni Boccaccio could be read in this perspective, as, at least in part, motivated by practicality. Similarly, we might see a practical motive, at least in part, to the moralizing tirades inserted in the second edition of the *De mulieribus claris* and the misogynistic invectives of the *Corbaccio*, which many scholars (and probably many of the readers of the time) interpret as an anti-*Decameron*. Even from a strictly clerical perspective, it was crucial that Boccaccio create a new image for himself, one more closely aligned to the Church's prescriptions for its officials – intellectual and spiritual sobriety, chastity (eventually even with misogynistic attacks), and preferences for Latin over vernacular and for erudite work over entertaining literature.

Despite his distressing economic state, Boccaccio was not impervious to the charms of Greek literature, and in summer 1360 he invited Leonzio Pilato to stay in his house in Santa Felicita: [49]

> Leontius Pilatus, of Thessalonica, is another whom I often mention. By his own statement he was a pupil of the aforesaid Barlaam. He is a man of uncouth appearance, ugly feature, long beard, and black hair, forever lost in thought, rough in manners and behaviour. For all that he is a most learned Hellenist, as any inquirer discovers, and a fairly inexhaustible mine of Greek history and myth. In Latin, he is not as yet so well versed. I have never seen any work from his hand; and all my quotations from him I have made at his oral dictation. For nearly three years I heard him read Homer, and conversed with him on terms of singular friendship; but so immense was the measure of all he had to tell that my memory, quickened though it was by pressure of other care, would not have been good enough to retain it, had I set it down in a notebook.
>
> (Post hos et Lentium Pylatum, thessalonicensem virum et, ut ipse asserit, predicti Barlae auditorem, persepe deduco. Qui quidem aspectu horridus homo est, turpi facie, barba prolixa et capillicio nigro, et meditatione occupatus assidua, moribus incultus, nec satis urbanus homo, verum, uti experientia notum fecit, licterarum grecarum doctissumus, et quodam modo grecarum hystoriarum atque fabularum

49 Information on the life of Leonzio Pilato, and on his relationship with Boccaccio and Petrarch, comes from Agostino Pertusi's *Leonzio Pilato tra Petrarca e Boccaccio* (1964), which includes details of Petrarch and Boccaccio's decision to translate Homer into Latin.

archivum inexhaustum, esto latinarum non satis adhuc instructus sit. Huius ego nullum vidi opus, sane quicquid ex eo recito ab eo viva voce referente percepi; nam eum legentem Homerum et mecum singulari amicitia conversantem fere tribus annis audivi, nec infinitis ab eo recitatis, urgente etiam alia cura animum, acrior suffecisset memoria, in cedulis commendassem.) (*Genealogie* XV.6, 8)

Boccaccio is well aware of being the first to bring Greek poetry back to Tuscany, as he proudly writes in his *Genealogie* (XV.7, 5):

It is my peculiar boast and glory to cultivate Greek poetry among the Tuscans. Was it not I who intercepted Leontius Pilatus on his way from Venice to the western Babylon, and with my advice turned him aside from his long peregrination, and kept him in our city? Did not I receive him into my own house, entertain him for a long time, and make the utmost effort personally that he should be appointed professor in Florence, and his salary paid out of the city's funds? Indeed, I did! And I too was the first who, at my own expense, called back to Tuscany the writings of Homer and of other Greek authors, when they had departed many centuries before, never meanwhile to return.

(Meum est hoc decus mea est gloria, scilicet inter Etruscos grecis uti carminibus. Nonne ego fui qui Leontium Pylatum, a Venetiis occiduam Babilonem querentem, a longa peregrinatione meis flexi consiliis, et in patria tenui, qui illum in propria domum suscepi et diu hospitem habui, et maximo labore meo curavi ut inter doctores florentini Studii susciperetur, ei ex publico mercede apposita? Fui equidem! Ipse insuper fui qui primus meis sumptibus Homeri libros et alios quosdam Grecos in Etruriam revocavi, ex qua multis ante seculis abierant non redituri.)

Boccaccio had managed to secure for Leonzio Pilato the first chair of ancient Greek in the Western world, at the Studium of Florence. Once courses began on 18 October (Billanovich 1947b, 249), Pilato could count on a stipend that would have guaranteed his economic independence. At this time, as we know from the *Genealogie* (XV.6), Boccaccio held many conversations with him, and he took individual tutorials in Greek; Pilato gave public lessons in the Studium over two academic cycles (1360–1 and 1361–2).[50]

---

50 Over the two and a half years of his stay in Florence (from summer 1360 until October–November 1362), Leonzio produced translations of and commentaries on Homer, Euripides, and Aristotle. "It was a pioneering and revealing work for European culture and its future. And not by chance is it due to Boccaccio … to his passion – tenacious and pugnacious – for the Greek world which he had lovingly divined from his Neapolitan youth; to his deeply sensed consciousness of marvelous and uninterrupted continuity of intellectual and cultural life, of poetry and of art, from antiquity to his own days, from Homer to Vergil and to Dante, from

These two years were also when Boccaccio was beset by other, more pressing cares ("urgente etiam alia cura animum"; *Genealogie* XV.8). Besides his personal financial collapse, there was the attempted coup of 31 December 1360.

Only after he had transferred his house in Santa Felicita to his half-brother Jacopo did Boccaccio retire in voluntary exile to Certaldo, where he was hoping to find the solitude that would at least allow him the inner peace he needed to write. His output in these years spiked: the final version of the *De mulieribus claris*, the *Consolatoria a Pino de' Rossi*, the *Vita di San Pier Damiani*, the second edition of the *Trattatello in laude di Dante*, the conclusion of the *De casibus virorum illustrium*, and the ongoing compilation of the *Genealogie deorum gentilium*. In the *Consolatoria*, we have a self-portrait of the author at this time:

> I … have returned to Certaldo and here I have begun, with much less difficulty than I had thought possible, to comfort my life, and the rough clothes and the peasant fare are beginning to please me; and the absence of the ambition and the unpleasantness and annoyances of our town-dwellers is of such great consolation to my heart that, could I remain without hearing anything of them, I do believe that my repose would increase greatly. In exchange for the anxious and continuous intrigues and occupations of the town-dwellers, I see fields, hills, trees, clothed with green leaves and variegated flowers; things produced simply, by nature, whereas in the towns all is artificial. I hear the songs of the nightingales and the other birds with a delight no less great than was the nuisance, formerly, of hearing deceptions and the disloyalty of our citizens all day long; and without any impediment I can commune freely with my dear books whenever I feel like doing so.

> (Io … sono tornato a Certaldo e qui ho cominciato, con troppa meno difficultà che io non estimavo di potere, a confortare la mia vita; e comincianmi già i grossi panni a piacere e le contadine vivande; e il non vedere le ambizioni e le spiacevolezze e i fastidj de' nostri cittadini mi è di tanta consolazione nell'animo, che se io potessi fare senza udirne alcuna cosa, credo che 'l mio riposo crescerebbe assai. In iscambio de' solleciti avvolgimenti e continui de' cittadini veggio campi, colli, arbori, delle verdi fronde e di vari fiori rivestiti; cose semplicemente dalla natura prodotte, dove i cittadini sono tutti atti fittizi. Odo cantare gli usignuoli e gli altri uccelli non con minore diletto che fusse già la noia d'udire tutto il dì gl'inganni e le dislealtà de' cittadini nostri; e con li miei libricciuoli, quante volte voglia me ne viene, senza alcuno impaccio posso liberamente ragionare.) (*Consolatoria* §§171–3)

Apelles to Vitruvius and to Giotto. And whereas Petrarch in the *Secretum* (II) and again in *Seniles* (XII.2), repeating Cicero, affirmed the absolute superiority of Latin literature over Greek, Boccaccio in the *Genealogia* dedicated a whole 'capitolo' to Hellenic culture (XV 7)" (Branca 1976, 118). See Lummus 2012.

The bucolic peace was intermittently broken by news from the city – "if I could carry on without hearing anything, I think my rest would greatly benefit" ("se io potessi fare senza udirne alcuna cosa, credo che 'l mio riposo crescerebbe assai"). Boccaccio was deeply troubled by a message brought him by Gioacchino Ciani, a man he did not know, probably soon after Boccaccio drafted the *Consolatoria* in spring 1362. The message addressed to Boccaccio was from the Cistercian Beato Petroni of Siena (1311–1361) and was delivered after his death by Brother Gioacchino Ciani. All we know of this message is in the letter Petrarch wrote to Boccaccio in response to one from Boccaccio (Petrarch, *Senile* I 5). Thus, we lack Boccaccio's direct account, but Petrarch's letter implies it was both distraught and detailed. The second and lengthier section of Petrarch's *Senile* I 5 aims to relieve Boccaccio of his fear and shock on receiving the news from Ciani. Ciani had arrived bearing a prophecy from Beato Petroni, departed from this world on the path to sainthood – said Ciani – who on his deathbed, directly inspired by Jesus Christ, had foreseen Boccaccio's death. Furthermore, Petroni had warned Boccaccio to change his lifestyle and behaviour, abandoning literature and poetry and devoting himself exclusively to God, given that he had so little time left.

For centuries, "there has been much fabulizing on this warning [from] beyond the grave" (Branca 1976, 130), but it is clear that with this message, meant also for Petrarch's ears, Beato Petroni contributed to the polemic against poetry that was raging at the time; he was vehemently opposed by Boccaccio, as we know from books XV and XVI of the *Genealogie deorum gentilium*. Certainly, Ciani could not have chosen a more appropriate time to deliver this otherworldly message of death and repentance: Boccaccio had retired to Certaldo primarily to distance himself from *ammonizioni*, confiscations, executions, city troubles, and banishments of his friends. The announcement of this warning surely threw him into deepest desperation, perhaps even panic, unable to hide himself and find refuge beyond the borders of Certaldo.

Boccaccio was driven to flee from Florence, but even in Certaldo, in the Florentine county, he most likely still felt that he was in danger. As a result, his literary self-portrait as a man enjoying a bucolic and solitary life in the *Consolatoria* should be seen for what it is: a rhetorical exercise to sweeten an unpleasant reality. The description was completely fictitious, as we shall see in chapter 6. Boccaccio did not want to stay in the small, old village of Certaldo, nor did he enjoy solitary life; he was a social creature, ever in search not only of an audience but also of employment. In Certaldo, he was not – as he claims in the *Consolatoria* – content with a life characterized only by rough clothing ("dei grossi panni") and rural food ("contadine vivande") from the "fields, hills, and green-leaved trees" ("campi, colli, arbori, delle verdi fronde rivestiti"), or by everything "simply produced by nature" ("semplicemente dalla natura prodotte"). He searched for work elsewhere, in places as far afield as Ravenna and Naples. This is why he was in Ravenna over 1361–2 (*Ep.* XI; Foresti 1931; Branca 1976, 131–2). In 1362, he went to

Naples, following up an offer from Niccolò Acciaiuoli, whom he despised. His situation must have been desperate to have accepted the offer to succeed Zanobi da Strada as court scholar. Boccaccio was perfectly aware of the duties that had been expected of Zanobi da Strada, and he knew of the relationship between Zanobi and Acciaiuoli. Francesco Paolo Tocco describes the relationship between Zanobi and his "protector" in these terms:

> If the Seneschal ever had a real friend in the fullest and deepest sense of the term, someone readily available to accept the more unpleasant aspects of his personality, loyally disposed to fulfill his desires scrupulously and to guard his interests profitably, this was definitely Zanobi da Strada ... The specific tasks required of Zanobi in the *Regnum* consisted of assisting, if not actually replacing, Angelo Acciaiuoli in the office of Chancellor, looking after the interests of the *Gran Senechal* in Naples ... while in the meantime serving as his intellectual mentor ... he was also the poet expected to celebrate the achievements of the Great ...
>
> The dependence of Zanobi, a man of modest economic means, upon the Acciaiuoli family was absolute, and despite some complaints by the Grand Seneschal, the scholar did his best in an extremely hostile environment in which he did not have any particular power, and in fact had to endure in silence the abuse eagerly inflicted upon him by all those who had been obliged to lower their heads before his protector. (F.P. Tocco 2001, 302–3)

The work that Zanobi did as court scholar was not at all the kind that Boccaccio could have replicated; he was a "man of glass" ("uomo di vetro"), incapable of hiding his emotions, neither submissive nor malleable, and unwilling to bear others' vexations.[51] The outcome of this brief attempt at collaboration is described in the invective preserved in *Epistola* XIII, written from Venice in July 1363 and addressed to Francesco Nelli.

Boccaccio had reached Naples in mid-October 1362, accompanied by Jacopo and his library. The negotiations for this move must have begun that spring, as we can infer from the letter Boccaccio sent to Barbato da Sulmona on 15 May 1362,

---

51 "Uomo di vetro," "man of glass," is the epithet Francesco Nelli uses to refer to Boccaccio, "and this is not an unfamiliar nickname for me" ("il quale è a me non nuovo soprannome"; *Epistola* XIII 2, p. 596). According to the definition given by Boncompagno da Signa, "The vitreous friend" (*De amico Vitreo*), he is transparent, unable to pretend, "for he cannot conceal the secrets of his soul" ("quia celare non valet cordis archana"); he cannot be moulded, for "he resists the mallet, as he complies with the desires of nobody" ("malleo non obedit, quia nullius voluntati consentit"); and he is even prickly: "this friend of glass is fragile, because for the smallest offence, or even if you are just suspected of it, you lose him" ("amicus vitreus frangibile est, quia pro modica offensa, immo pro suspitione sola, illum amittis"). See the treatise on friendship by Boncompagno da Signa, edited and translated by Dunne (2012, 100).

written from Florence (*Ep.* XII.16). The presence of Boccaccio's library suggests that his relocation was supposed to be long-term, if not permanent. Originally, the occupation had been offered to the only one truly worthy for such a position in the eyes of Acciaiuoli: the other poet laureate, Francesco Petrarch, who declined in the most adamant fashion. Only at this point, with the whole-hearted recommendation from Francesco Nelli, did Acciaiuoli offer the job to Boccaccio. The relationship between Acciaiuoli and Boccaccio went back far; their friendship had endured for decades amid episodes of complicity and great friction, often erupting in open conflicts. Despite these past misunderstandings, Boccaccio agreed to work for him, probably compelled by the unfavourable political conditions in Florence and his own economic duress, but also by constant reassurance from Nelli. To mark the occasion, he donated and dedicated the *De mulieribus claris* – after reorganizing it in a fourth edition – to Andreuola Acciaiuoli, Niccolò's sister, for obvious diplomatic reasons (Filosa 2012, 24–32). He brought his completed *De casibus virorum illustrium*, originally dedicated to King Luigi of Taranto, but now (perhaps) reserved for the Gran Seneschal Acciaiuoli.

Upon his arrival in Naples, however, the reception from Acciaiuoli was extremely discouraging, as Boccaccio recalls in *Epistola* XIII to Nelli: "No differently was I received by your Maecenas than if I were returning from a jaunt to the towns or the countryside near Naples: not with a smiling face nor friendly embrace and gracious words; on the contrary he barely extended his right hand as I entered his house. Surely, no happy augury this!"

Furthermore, the living conditions were much worse than he had expected:

> Amid these glittering things there was, and still is, a small section surrounded and enclosed in a cloud of old spider webs and dry dust, shameful, foul, and stinking; it would be considered vile by any man, however base, and I, quite often to you, referred to it as the "bilge," as though it were the lowest level of a great ship, the receptacle for any filthy thing. In this place, as if it were a great honour, I was consigned, like some noxious person, not like a friend of long standing … A cot, filled with tow folded and sewn in the form of small balls and just then snatched from under a mule driver, half-covered by a stinking little bedspread, without any down filling, and set in a tiny room with gaping holes in its walls; close to midnight it was assigned to me, a tired old man, for my rest together with my half-brother, nearly midnight … This disreputable cot, in this bilge, was set next to the routines of the house: the splendid arrangements for a dinner party … Visible to those entering the royal house, which was constructed with gilded beams, covered with white ivory … to one side was a small pottery lamp, barely alight … Opposite it, was a small table not quite covered by a greasy, filthy, coarse cloth, hanging unevenly down its sides, all gnawed by dogs or simply by old age, with a few cloudy and over-filled drinking cups set out on it; and under the table, instead of a bench, a sort of wooden seat that had lost one of its legs: this I think was intentional, so that, in matching the repose of those seated to

> the joys of the victuals, they would not easily fall asleep ... In convoys, from hither and yon, came rogues: I mean gluttons, devourers, deceivers, mule-drivers and boys, cooks and scullions, and to use a different vocabulary, dogs of the court and domestic rats, excellent gnawers. Running now here, now there, they filled the whole house with the discordant bellowing of oxen, and ... with foul stench they filled the air of the place.
>
> (Intra queste cose così risplendenti era ed è una breve particella attorniata e rinchiusa d'una vecchia nebbia di tele di ragnolo e di secca polvere, disorrevole, fetida e di cattivo odore e da essere tenuta a vile da ogni uomo quantunque disonesto, la quale io spessissime volte teco, quasi d'uno grande navilio la più bassa parte, d'ogni bruttura recettacolo, "sentina" chiamai. In questa io, sì come nella conceduta parte della felicità grandissima, quasi nocivo, non come amico dalla lunga, sono mandato a' confini ... uno letticciolo pieno di capecchio piegato e cucito in forma di piccole spere, ed in quella ora tratto di sotto ad uno mulattiere, e d'uno poco di puzzolente copertoio mezzo coperto, sanza piumaggio, in una cameruzza aperta di buche, quasi a mezzanotte, a me vecchio ed affaticato è assegnato, acciò che insieme col mio fratello mi riposassi ... In questa medesima sentina al disorrevole letticiuolo s'aggiugne l'ordine domestico, de' desinari lo splendido apparecchio ... A quelli che nella casa reale entravano, tessuta di travi orate, coperta di bianco elefante ... si vedeva in un canto una lucernuzza di terra, un solo lume mezzo morto ... Dall'altra parte era una piccola tavoletta, di grasso e spurcido canovaccio, da' cani o vero dalla vecchiaia tutto ròso, non da ogni parte pendente, e non pienamente coperta, e di pochi e di nebbiosi ed aggravati bicchieri fornita; e disotto ala tavola, in luogo di panca, era un legnerello monco d'un piè: credo che questo nondimeno fusse fatto avvedutamente, acciò che, accordantesi il riposo di coloro che che sedevano con la letizia delle vivande, agevolmente non si risolvessono in sonno ... Dopo queste cose, a brigata venieno di quinci e di quindi baroni: dico ghiottoni e manicatori, lusinghieri, mulattieri e ragazzi, cuochi e guatteri, ed usando altro vocabolo, cani della corte e topi dimestichi, ottimi roditori di rilievi. Ora di qua ora di là discorrendo, con discordevole mugliare di buoi riempivano tutta la casa: e ... di fetido odore riempivano l'aria del luogo.) (*Ep.* XIII.12–22)

At the beginning of March 1363, unsurprisingly, Boccaccio left (if not fled) Naples for Padua, intending to visit Petrarch. In Padua, we might suppose he met his friends, the conspirators Pazzino di Apardo Donati and his brother Manno, who were in service at court for Francesco Carrara. Petrarch had in the meantime moved to Venice, into Palazzo Molin delle Due Torri on the Riva degli Schiavoni; Boccaccio found him there, and he was received by his friend with brotherly affection in mid-March 1363. He stayed in Venice for more than three months. The understanding between the friends was so seamless that Petrarch, as Branca remarks, "repeated his insistence that Boccaccio should remain as a permanent and literary counselor. Boccaccio declined the offer once again, for fear of marring a friendship that had become a reason of life for him (*Bucolicum*, XVI 96 ss. and *Sen.*, III 1 and 2)" (Branca 1976, 140).

Boccaccio's return to Florence, or at least to Certaldo, must have happened in summer 1363; by 26 August he was settled, as he and Jacopo paid a *prestanza* (forced loan) in person (Regnicoli 2013a, 397, doc. 93). It may not be a coincidence that in the same year Pino de' Rossi also returned to Florence, where he paid a communal tax to notarize his will.[52] The return of Pino coincides with the return of Boccaccio to the political scene: on 30 January 1364, Boccaccio was nominated by the Guelf Party, captained by Lapo di Fornaino de' Rossi (Regnicoli 2021b), for election to the three highest offices: priors, *gonfalonieri*, and *buonuomini* (Regnicoli 2013a, 398, doc. 100). He did not take on any office, however, until after August 1364, when he was appointed *ufficiale delle castella* for a six-month term (Regnicoli 2013a, 398, doc. 100); this was after the end of the war against Pisa. Victory over Pisa had been achieved at least partly thanks to the intervention of Manno di Apardo Donati, recalled for this purpose from exile as "valorous knight and leader." During the battle of Cascina against Pisa on 28 July 1364, Donati seemed to play a decisive role, at least according to Matteo Villani in his chronicle and Antonio Pucci in his vernacular epic poem (*cantare*), both exalting the actions of the *condottiero*. It may be thanks to his presence and his importance in this historical context that the Commune was more open to negotiating with some of the conspirators. What is certain is that Francesco da Carrara the Elder, for whom Manno and Pazzino worked, interceded in favour of the latter to cancel the death sentence. Thanks to him, Pazzino was pardoned by a *provvisione* of 12 July 1364, sixteen days before the victory against Pisa.[53] On 28 January 1365, a pardon was also issued to Andrea di Pacchio degli Adimari.[54]

Although some of the conspirators were able to return to the city, Boccaccio's life in Florence as he knew it in the 1350s was over: that community of people around him in Oltrarno did not exist any more. Many were still in exile, many others had died, among them Niccolò di Bartolo del Buono (in 1360), Pino de' Rossi (about 1366), and Andrea di Tello da Lisca (in 1365). From this moment on, the writer stayed more and more in Certaldo. He returned to Florence in an official capacity in 1364–5, but not for long. His home was in Certaldo – though he remained to all intents and purposes a citizen of Florence, as he continued to

52 Among the documents transcribed by the seventeenth-century scholar Cosimo della Rena, we find the following: "1363 – m. Pino di m. Giovanni de' Rossi test. C 15–c. 146."

53 ASFi, *PR* 51, f. 171v; Klapisch-Zuber 2009, 227, n. 43.

54 ASFi, *PR* 52, ff. 96r–v.

pay *prestanze* to the city until his death.[55] He no longer had the house in Santa Felicita, after he had given it to Jacopo, who had maybe lost it.[56] When Jacopo remarried around 1365, he no longer had a house to which he could take his new bride, and he was forced to live with his older brother Giovanni in Certaldo, as we know from the letter sent to Donato Albanzani, dated 4 April 1365, and recovered by Augusto Campana:

> More serious news follows. Jacopo has no place to lead his new bride unless I take him into my little hovel, in which, after fleeing the public duties and quarrels of the city (God knows) I had adapted perfectly to my poverty, and I was now living alone in peace and quiet. No doubt, a lot of people have knocked against this quiet as their enemy in the past, but now Jacopo himself, together with other friends both his and mine, begs me to take him in with his wife, as if they were asking for something in my interest rather than theirs.
>
> (Graviora secuntur. Non est Iacobo locus in quem deducat quam sumpsit in coniugem, nisi illum in domunculam meam suscipiam, in qua, postquam officia publica et civium turbellas effugerem [novit Deus], optime cum paupertate conveneram, et iam michi ipsi fere cum quite vivebam. In quam scilicet quieter, tamquam eis adversam, surrexere plurimi; et orat enim ante alios Iacobus ipse, orant et alii amici sui meique ut eum cum sponsa suscipiam, quasi non suum sed meum commodum postulantes.)

The letter goes on at length, describing the expected inconvenience in taking in his future sister-in-law with phrasing that closely recalls the *Corbaccio*.

Boccaccio's final move to Certaldo signalled his effective retirement from Florentine political life, even if not completely: by paying the *prestanze*, he could participate actively inside the Republic, and he did accept some civil offices – *ufficiale delle castella* (August 1364–February 1365), ambassador to Pope Urban V (August 1365), *ufficiale della condotta* (November 1367–February 1368), and again ambassador to Pope Urban V (November 1367).[57] These commitments are few in number, compared with the intense, fully engaged political life he lived in the 1350s. Nevertheless, the respect in which he was held is shown not only by the embassies that he was asked to undertake but also by the request of the Orsanmichele Company for his advice on the building of the tabernacle of the Virgin Mary.

55 This is evident from the fiscal documents collected and published by Regnicoli (2013a).

56 The house at Oltrarno seems to have completely disappeared from Jacopo's assets. After Giovanni's deed of gift to Jacopo, the house appears in no further document; it is not mentioned as part of the inheritance bequeathed by Jacopo to his children. See Tordi 1923.

57 See Regnicoli 2013a, 398–9.

Several other city notables were also asked to give advice, members of Boccaccio's old circle from the early days, and of his father's.[58] The first *Lectura Dantis* ever made was promoted by and commissioned to Boccaccio, who gave his lectures in the Badia starting 23 October 1373. Boccaccio was already severely ill at this point, and he died soon after on 21 December 1375, the shortest day of the year.

58 For example: Luigi Gianfigliazzi, Uguccione di Ricciardo de' Ricci (leader of the Ricci faction, and ambassador with Pino de' Rossi to Charles IV in 1352), Salvestro di Alamanno de' Medici (who reported the conspiracy to the Commune), Alessandro di Riccardo de' Bardi. For this document, see Corazzini 1877, ci.

PART TWO

At the Intersections of Literature and Politics

The second part of this book looks at the works Boccaccio wrote immediately after the attempted coup – *De mulieribus claris*, the consolatory letter to Pino de' Rossi, and the second redaction of the *Trattatello in laude di Dante* – and following those, the *Decameron*, each one through the lens of the historical facts discussed in part 1. This kind of examination has not been possible before, because it is only recently that documents have come to light that show us in much more detail how closely Boccaccio was connected with the politics of Florence in the years preceding his writing of his great works. Boccaccio, we now know, was not simply interested in politics, he was deeply involved with political actors, as friends and as people as passionate as he was to promote republicanism for the city. These friends and their shared causes, we will find, are championed in these works.

5 Antityrannical Motives in *De mulieribus claris*

Ahi serva Italia, di dolore ostello,
nave senza nocchiere in gran tempesta,
non donna di province, ma bordello!

(Ah! servile Italy, grief's hostelry!
A ship without a pilot in great tempest!
No Lady thou of Provinces, but brothel!)

– Dante Alighieri, *Purg.* 6.76–8, trans. Hollander

Boccaccio arrived in Certaldo in self-exile in July 1361, and soon after that date he completed the *De mulieribus claris* (*On Famous Women*), a collection of 106 biographies of women, subdivided into 104 chapters, and bracketed with a dedication, a proem, and a conclusion.[1] This work underwent a series of revisions, but the first draft was finished probably by the second half of 1361.[2] This date is implied by the opening words, in the dedication, to Andreuola Acciaiuoli:

> A short time ago, illustrious lady, at a moment when I was able to isolate myself for a little while from the idle mob and was nearly carefree, I wrote a slim volume in praise of extraordinary women and for my friends' consolation rather than for the great benefit of the republic.
>
> (Pridie, mulierum egregia, paululum ab inerti vulgo semotus et a ceteris fere solutus curis, in eximiam muliebris sexus laudem ac amicorum solatium,

1 All the women are from the pre-Christian or Roman period, except the last six: Popess Johanna; Irene, Empress of Constantinople; Gualdrada of Florence; Constance, mother of Friedrich II; the Sienese widow Camiola; and Queen Johanna.

2 To approach the different stages of composition, see in chronological order: Hortis 1879; P.G. Ricci 1959; V. Zaccaria 1963. For a brief summary in English, see Kolsky 2003, 17–37.

> potius quam in magnum rei publice commodum, libellum scripsi.) (*De mul.* Dedication, 1)[3]

On the assumption that the phrase "at a moment when I was able to isolate myself for a little while from the idle mob" refers to Boccaccio's move to Certaldo, then the first draft of the *De mulieribus claris* was under way after July 1361. The dedication makes his feelings very clear about what he left behind by coming to Certaldo: the ignorant mob (of Florence) and the pressure of every (civic) concern. Moreover, the opening words clarify the goal of the work. The book, he says, was composed to praise women and – as the coordinating conjunction implies – to comfort friends. They are equal goals, of equal value. One might ask who these friends were who were in need of consolation. Given the times in which he was composing, we may suppose they include those who had taken part in the Florentine conspiracy, such as Pino de' Rossi, to whom Boccaccio wrote a consolatory letter in spring 1362.

De mulieribus claris is permeated by a number of republican and antityrannical themes, even if, in the dedication, Boccaccio says it was not his primary aim to provide any substantial benefit to the Republic. The "potius quam" of the original Latin introduces the second and lesser term of the comparison: "more" to praise women and comfort friends "than" to help the Republic. Even so, the republican discourse is never far away from the text.

Friendship in Time of Conspiracy

Boccaccio often speaks of friendship in his works. We need only recall the eighth novella of the tenth day of the *Decameron*, in which the two friends Tito and Gisippo are each prepared to die for the happiness of the other. In the *De mulieribus claris*, Boccaccio dedicates two biographies to the theme of friendship: those of Leaena and Epicharis – *De Leena meretrice* (50) and *De Epycari libertina* (93). From the chapter titles, which identify them as prostitutes, we can infer that these women are linked by their work, and, indeed, their lives are quite similar, almost parallel. Both are ready to take extreme steps rather than betray people they have collaborated with in a conspiracy; in so doing, they exalt the values of liberality and friendship – both classical and humanistic ideals. The most pertinent similarity (given that *De mulieribus claris* was written just after the attempted coup) is that they both conspired against tyrants: Leaena against Hipparchus, and Epicharis against Nero. These biographies clearly exemplify how real friends should behave in the case of a conspiracy and what kind of sacrifices they should be prepared to undertake. Not only this – their lives demonstrate what is expected of a member in a secret plot against the injustice of a tyrannical state.

---

3 For the translation of the *De mulieribus claris* into English, I follow Virginia Brown's edition, often slightly modified or adapted.

The source of the biography *De Epycari libertina* traces back to the *Annales* by Tacitus,[4] one of the most important historians of the Roman Empire, who lived in the first century after Christ. Boccaccio turns to the time of a failed attempt to overthrow Nero in 65 CE, the so-called Pisonian conspiracy, organized by Gaius Calpurnio Piso. While the plot against Nero is fomenting, an informant lands Epicharis in prison, but the interrogators are unable to get a confession. When the conspiracy is exposed, Nero subjects her to torture to get her to reveal the names of those taking part. She manages to endure the agonizing pain and say nothing; the day after, fearing she may no longer be able to hold out, she contrives a clever way to end her own life:

> At last she was called to the next day of torture. Epicharis was unable to walk and fearful that she could not hold out if they called her a third time. She tore off her breast-band, tied it to the arches of the chair in which she was being carried, and made a noose which she put around her neck. Letting all the weight of her body fall, she inflicted a violent death upon herself so as not to bring harm to the conspirators.
>
> (Tandem in diem reservata posterum, cum pedibus ire non posset, timens si tertio vocaretur non posse subsistere, solutam pectori fasciam arcui selle, qua vehebantur, implicuit et facto laqueo gucturi iniecit suo et, cum omnem illi corporis dimisisset molem, ne conspiratis obesset, violentam sibi mortem conscivit.) (*De mul.* 93.6)

Boccaccio compares the glorious woman to the mediocre men:

> This seems a great thing for a woman to do, but it is even more striking if we consider the weakness of the eminent men who were involved in the same conspiracy. After the revelation of their identities from another source, not one of them was strong enough to endure for his own sake what Epicharis had endured for the sake of others. They could not bear even to hear the description of the tortures without immediately telling their inquisitors what they knew of the conspiracy. Thus they spared neither themselves nor their friends, whereas that glorious woman had spared everyone but herself.
>
> (Quodquidem, etsi maximum videatur in femina, longe tamen spectabilius est, si spectetur eiusdem coniurationis egregiorum hominum inconstantia, quorum,

4 In his edition (1967), Zaccaria refers to Tacitus (*Annales* 15.51–3). The story of Epicharis is also recounted by Boccaccio, briefly, in his *Exposition on Dante's Comedy*: "According to Tacitus, after he was arrested and charged with the offence, Lucan saw a woman of ill-repute called Epicharis, who had withstood all their tortures and managed to kill herself before revealing any of the conspirators' names. Unable to wait until they began their torture (indeed, unable even to stand the thought of seeing the torture and the torturers), Lucan confessed his guilt as soon as they asked him if he was involved in the conspiracy. And, as if his confession were not enough, he also implicated his own mother, Atilia" (*Exposition* 194). The analogies between the Pisonian and Florentine conspiracies are unmistakeable.

aliunde quam ab Epycari cognitorum, nemo tam robuste iuventutis fuit qui, nedum pati pro salute propria, quod pro aliena femina passa est, sed nec audire tormentorum nomina pateretur, quin imo percontanti confestim que noverat de conspiratione narraret. Et sic nemo sibi amicisque pepercit, cum cunctis, nisi sibi, femina pepercisset inclita.) (*De mul.* 97.7)

In this biography, Boccaccio instructs his readers on the behaviour required of conspirators against tyranny: secrecy and resistance to torture at any cost. If one's own life is forfeited, one must not jeopardize those of one's friends. The author concludes his story of Epicharis with a rational observation of his own: "Thus they spared neither themselves nor their friends, whereas that glorious woman had spared everyone but herself."

If we place the text in the historical context of Florence in the years the book was written (1361–2), two men immediately come to mind: Niccolò di Bartolo del Buono and Domenico di Donato Bandini. After being arrested by the authorities, these two revealed the plan and the names of all the conspirators without being prompted. In the death sentence, we read that these two men gave a "legitimate confession" *sponte* (spontaneously) in front of the jury ("per legitimam confessionem dictorum Niccholay Bartoli et Dominichi coram nobis in iudicio *sponte* factam"). Were they among those who "could not bear even to hear the description of the tortures without immediately telling their inquisitors what they knew of the conspiracy" (*De mul.* 97.7)? In the end, their cooperation did not win them clemency: they were still executed, and they had also compromised their friends, who suffered banishment and exile, confiscation of their properties, and the threat of a death sentence (as in the case of Pino de' Rossi, Luca di Feo Ugolini, Andrea di Tello da Lisca, and Pazzino di Apardo Donati). Boccaccio's authorial voice is clear, as he ends this chapter:

Shame on these men, I truly think, when they are defeated, not only by a loose female, but also by the most determined endurance of any pain. If, in fact, we are stronger by sex, why is it not fitting for us to be stronger also by perseverance? If this should not be the case, we are effeminate together with the conspirators, and appear with good reason to have deviated from sound morals.

(Erubescendum nempe hominibus reor dum, nedum a lasciva femina, sed etiam a constantissima quacunque laborum tolerantia vincuntur. Nam si prevalemus sexu, cur non ut et fortitudine prevaleamus decens est? Quod si non sit, cum ipsis effeminati, iure de moribus transegisse videmur.) (*De mul.* 93.9–10)

The phrase "shame on these men" comes at the beginning of that final paragraph, emphasizing Boccaccio's strong criticism of the men who were bested by Epicharis; their counterparts in Boccaccio's time would include Niccolò di Bartolo del Buono and Domenico di Donato Bandini: soft, "effeminate" deviants from natural law, unable to withstand torture.

The other biography that takes up issues uncannily like those in the Florence of December 1360 is *De Leena meretrice*. Leaena, like Epicharis the "libertina," is a prostitute, "meretrix." She likewise conspires against a tyrant, Hipparchus; her co-conspirators are Harmodius and Aristogeiton, two celebrated tyrannicides (there is a statue of them from the Roman period in the Archaeological Museum of Naples).[5] She is no less prepared than Epicharis was to undergo horrifying torture rather than reveal the other conspirators. In the end, to maintain her own silence with confidence, she bites off her own tongue, as she recalls the sacred and venerable name of friendship:

> During the cruel torture to which she was subjected in an effort to make her reveal the conspirators, this dissolute woman reflected with gratitude on *the value of the holy and venerable name of friendship*. At first she steeled herself for a long time with marvellous constancy and did not answer any questions lest she save herself by harming others. Finally, as the torture increased and the strength ebbed from her body, this manly woman feared that her resolve would weaken along with her physical strength. Leaena then rose to an even greater resolve and acted so that her ability to speak was lost together with her strength. She bit down sharply on her tongue, severed it, and spat it out. Thus, by a single but most noble act, she deprived her tormentors of all hope of getting information from her.
>
> (cum ad prodendos coniurationis conscios diris cogeretur suppliciis, secum lubrica mulier, *quantum esset sanctum atque venerabile nomen amicitie*, pia volvens consideratione, ne illi, ut sibi parceret, in aliquo violentiam inferret, primo diu, ne diceret quod querebatur, mira constantia animo imperavit suo; tandem, convalescentibus cruciatibus et corporeis deficientibus viribus, timens, virilis femina, ne, debilitata virtute corporea, etiam enervaretur propositum, in robur maius excessit egitque ut eque cum viribus et dicendi potestas auferretur; et acri morsu linguam precidit suam et expuit; et sic actu unico, sed clarissimo, spem omnem a se noscendi quod exquirebatur tortoribus abstulit.) (*De mul.* 50.4; emphasis added)

5 As Zaccaria shows (*De mul.* 518, n. 3), the episode occurred in the reign of Amyntas, following the *Chronicon* by Saint Jerome: "Harmodius et Aristogiton Hipparchum Atheniensium tyrannum interfecerunt: et Leaena meretrix amica eorum, cum tormentis cogeretur ut socios proderet, linguam suam mordicitus amputavit" ("Harmodius and Aristogiton killed the Athenian tyrant Hipparchus: and their friend the prostitute Leaena, while she was being tortured to betray her associates, cut off her own tongue with her teeth"; *Eusebii Chronicorum Liber II*, in *Patrologia Latina*, vol. 17, coll. 379–80). Delcorno cites a new literary source that Boccaccio might have known for the character of Leaena: a manual titled *De informatione virginum et defectu virginitatis* in the *Communiloquium* by John of Wales (Delcorno 2015). The *Communiloquium* was widely circulating throughout Europe (Swanson 1989, app. 2, 232–56).

Leaena's biography is in a central position – the fiftieth in the *De mulieribus claris* – and it begins with an unusually long preamble about virtue, written with elaborate style:

> Moreover, such is our devotion to virtue that we cannot only glorify merits found in high places but we are also bound to bring to light merit that lies hidden under a shameful exterior. Virtue is precious everywhere; it is not stained from contact with vice any more than the rays of the sun are sullied when they touch mud. If at times we see virtue implanted in the breast of someone given to detestable practices, we must condemn those practices but in such a manner that we do not lessen the praise of virtue. In such instances, virtue is more worthy of admiration since the person in question was thought incapable of it.
>
> (Insuper, adeo virtuti obnoxii sumus ut, non solum quam insigni loco consitam cernimus, elevemus, sed et obrutam tegmine turpi in lucem meritam conari debemus educere; est enim ubique preciosa, nec aliter fedatur, scelerum contagione, quam solaris radius ceno inficiatur immixtus. Si ergo aliquando pectori, detestabili offitio dedito, eam infixam viderimus, ita detestari debemus offitium, ut sue laudes non minuantur virtuti, cum tanto mirabilior digniorque in tali sit, quanto ab eadem putabatur remotior.) (*De mul.* 50.1–2)[6]

Two important concepts are here clearly expressed: on one hand, sometimes virtue is hidden under a disgraceful exterior; on the other, there is a discrepancy between the nobility of soul and that of caste. The noble soul can be found everywhere, and we must acknowledge it wherever it is. This preamble recalls the last novella of the *Decameron*, where Boccaccio states in the conclusion: "Even into the huts of the poor the heavens let fall at times spirits divine, as into the palaces of kings souls that are fitter to tend hogs than to exercise lordship over men" ("anche nelle povere case piovono dal cielo de' divini spiriti, come nelle reali di quegli che sarien piú degni di guardar porci che d'avere sopra uomini signoria"; *Dec.* X.10.68).[7] The biographies of Epicharis and Leaena can be read on many different levels: beside the exaltation of friendship, beside the topic of hiding virtue under a filthy practice (which is another way of demonstrating the distinction between nobility of soul and nobility of caste), and beside the denunciation of a social situation in which young girls are forced into prostitution, we see political intention, whether or not it is pointing directly to events in Florence.

---

6 The simile of the rays of the sun that are not sullied when they touch mud is taken from Guido Guinizzelli, as Zaccaria notes in his edition (*De mul.* 518, n. 2). For a more specific analysis, see Delcorno 2015.

7 For a more detailed analysis about intertextualities between *Decameron* and *De mulieribus claris*, see Filosa 2012, 127–35.

At this point the questions and the answers are clear. Niccolò di Bartolo del Buono and Domenico di Donato Bandini behaved like "effeminates" (*De mul.* 93.9), like deviants ("deviated from sound morals"; 93.9), like those who forget "the value of the holy and venerable name of friendship" (50.4), like those women who keep silent only about what they do not know. Epicharis and Leaena belie several common notions about women, among them that women talk too much ("Certainly, whoever says that women keep silence when they are ignorant was not acquainted with Leaena"; *De mul.* 50.5; "Thus [Epicharis] proved false the old proverb that teaches us that women keep silent only about what they do not know"; *De mul.* 93.6). In short, Niccolò di Bartolo del Buono and Domenico di Donato Bandini behaved worse than two prostitutes. For Boccaccio, praising these two particular women seems like a pretext for criticizing this kind of behaviour in men.

Florence: The Prostitutes Venus and Flora and the Seduced Hercules

The comparison between cities, countries, and institutions, on the one hand, and prostitutes and brothels, on the other, has a long literary tradition; there is Dante's criticism of Italy (see the epigraph to this chapter), or the numerous invectives of Petrarch against Avignon, the papal court in France during the western schism, addressed as "the new Babylon," as a "slave to wine, delicacies and good living, / where Luxury performs her worst" ("de vin serva, di lecti et di vivande, / in cui Luxuria fa l'ultima prova"; *RVF* 136.7–8).[8]

Boccaccio injects the brothel theme into two more biographies in the *De mulieribus claris*, which, in the context of Florence in the mid-1300s, have interesting implications, particularly regarding references to the goddesses Venus and Flora. It is worth underscoring here the intimate relationship between Florence and these divinities. Many Florentines believed in the fables that trace the origins of Florence back to Rome; the more notable among them are told in the *Cronica* by Giovanni Villani (1990–1), the chronicle by Marchionne di Coppo Stefani (1910), and the anonymous *Chronica de origine civitate Florentie* (2009), which Boccaccio knew well.[9] In addition, Virgil's *Aeneid* connects the foundation of Rome with the descendants of Aeneas, a son of Venus. Boccaccio knew these stories from his youth, and he proposes his own versions in different works: in *Filocolo* (III.33.5; V.39.7); through the voice of Lia in the *Comedia delle ninfe fiorentine*; at the end of the *Ninfale fiesolano*, where, according to the editor

8 Invectives against Avignon, "new Babylon," can be found in *RVF* 114, 136, 137, 138, 259, 305; *Sine Nomine* 18 (Piur 1925, 232–3). On this topic, see Falkeid 2017.

9 Traces of the *Cronica* by Giovanni Villani are in many works by Boccaccio, such as the *Ninfale Fiesolano* (see notes to octave 455 by the editor Armando Balduino), whereas the anonymous *Chronica de origine civitate Florentie* was transcribed in the *Zibaldone Laurenziano* (ff. 36v–39r, in Hortis 1879), as Petoletti shows in his description of the *Zibaldoni* (2013, 305).

Armando Balduino, he closely follows the chronicle by Giovanni Villani; and in the first version of the *Trattatello in laude di Dante*: "Florence, more noble than all other cities, according to the ancient histories and current popular opinion, began with the Romans" ("Fiorenza, intra l'altre città più nobile, secondo che l'antiche istorie e la comune oppinione de' presenti pare che vogliano, ebbe inizio da' Romani"; red. 1, §11).[10] The intimate relationship between Flora and Florence is already implied in the assonance with Florentia – an old legend says that the village Florentia was founded in spring during the *ludi Florales* (games in honour of Flora) by Roman soldiers.[11] The mythological figures of Venus and Flora were so important in the Florentine tradition that, a century later, the Medici dynasty commissioned two works to Sandro Botticelli: his masterpieces *The Birth of Venus* and *The Allegory of Spring*, where Venus and Flora represent Florence's greatness and prosperity. We do not know whether Boccaccio believed in these legends, but he certainly intended to ridicule both of them and whoever thought they were trustworthy.

In his *Genealogie deorum gentilium*, Boccaccio identifies no fewer than three different Venuses, who in the classical tradition blend together and are often mistaken for one another.[12] For my purposes, I set aside the better-known Great Venus (or the Roman *Venus Verticordia*), sixth daughter of Celus, who is present at a legitimate wedding (*Gen.* 3.22), as well as the second Venus, seventh daughter of Celus, born from the foam of the ocean (*Gen.* 3.23). Of the three mentioned by Boccaccio, the one that interests us most is the daughter of Jupiter and Dione, who is the mother of Love and Aeneas: *De Venere, Iovis XI filia, que peperit Amorem* (*Gen.* 11.4). In this chapter of the *Genealogie*, Boccaccio tells us that this third Venus founded the first brothel. In the *De mulieribus claris*, Boccaccio chooses to discuss this last Venus as the inventor of public prostitution:

> Finally, so that she might seem to have wiped a bit of her blush from her unchaste face and given herself greater scope of wantonness, Venus devised something that was abominably foul. She was the first, so they say, to establish public prostitution by setting up brothels and forcing married women to enter them.

---

10 For a more detailed analysis of the fable of the foundation of Florence, see Benvenuti 1995; and specifically in Boccaccio's work, see Bruni 1990, 279–88, and Chiecchi 2013, 2014.

11 Another legend is reported by the Anonimo fiorentino: "And in that place and the surrounding lands where the city was founded, flowers and lilies were always growing. Therefore, most of the inhabitants agreed to call the city Flora, so that it was built amongst flowers, that is among many delights" ("Et in quello luogo e campi intorno ove fu la città edificata, sempre nascea fiori et gigli; et però la maggior parte degli abitatori furono consenzienti di chiamarla Flora, e sì che fosse in fiori edificata, cioè con molte delizie"; *Commento alla Divina Commedia* 1866, 356). Another possibility, according to the *Chronica de origine civitate Florentie* (2009), is that "Florence" derives from the name of the Roman consul Fiorinus, who founded the city.

12 For a specific analysis of these three Venuses, see Lummus 2011.

(Postremo autem, ut ab impudica fronte paululum ruboris abstersisse videretur et lasciviendi sibi ampliorem concessisse licentiam, infanda turpitudine excogitata, prima – ut aiunt – meretricia publica adinvenit et fornices instituit et matronas inire conpulit.) (*De mul.* 7.9)

Flora's case is not very different from that of Venus.[13] Already in the title of her biography, we learn that she is a *meretrix* like Leaena: *De Flora meretrice dea florum et Zephiri coniuge* (*De mul.* 64). Within the *De mulieribus claris*, the biography of Flora is undoubtedly unique because it perfectly exemplifies the process of deification – a kind of feminine version of Ser Cepperello/San Ciappelletto:[14] Boccaccio sets out in detail all that transforms a woman into a goddess. Originally Flora was a prostitute who had made a considerable fortune. On her death-bed she decided to leave all her possessions to the people of Rome, on condition that she be commemorated every year with games in her honour. For this reason, during the *Floralia*, naked prostitutes would act out mimes accompanied by "obscene gestures" ("gesticulationibus impudicis"; *De mul.* 64.8). After a while, the Senate grew uncomfortable with the spread of such a ritual and reinvented the "fable" of Flora: the local nymph, beautiful and eagerly desired by the god Zephyr, allegedly received divine powers as her wedding gift, as well as the task of adorning with flowers all plants, hills, and fields every spring. Since the flowers are followed by crops, ancient Romans offered her sacrifice in exchange for a bountiful harvest. Boccaccio enhances and emphasizes how Flora was reinvented first as a nymph and then as a "new" goddess. The chapter concludes as follows:

The general public was misled by this deception. Flora, who during her lifetime had lived in brothels and had debased herself with any and everyone for even the smallest fee, was now thought to sit with Queen Juno and the other goddesses, as if Zephyr had borne her on his wings to heaven. And so, through her shrewdness and the gift of her ill-gotten fortune, Flora was transformed from a prostitute into a nymph. Profiting from her marriage to Zephyr and her divinity, she dwelt in temples and received divine honours from mortal beings. Thus not only did she become Flora instead of Clora, but from a notorious prostitute of her own day she was made into a world-famous celebrity.

(Qua seducti fallacia, eam, que vivens in fornices coluerat, a quisbuscunque etiam pro minima stipe prostrata, quasi suis alis zephyrus illam in celum detulerit, cum Iunone regina deabusque aliis sedere arbitrati sunt. Et sic ingenio suo Flora et fortune munere

13 Kolsky (2003, 112–13) noted the association between Flora and Florence. For a study on Flora and her worship in Rome, see Fabbri 2019.

14 Guido Guarini, in the introduction to his English translation of the *De mulieribus claris* (*Concerning Famous Women*, 1963, 23–4), suggests an interesting parallel between the "creation" of the goddess Flora and that of "San Ciappelletto": both, he claims, are inspired by a parody of the *Vitae Sanctorum*.

ex male quesita pecunia, ex meretrice nynpha facta est zephyrique lucrata coniugium et deitatis numen, apud mortales, in templis residens, divinis honoribus celebrata, adeo ut, non solum ex Clora Flora, sed clara ubique locorum, ex insigni sui temporis scorto, facta sit.) (*De mul.* 64.12)

Flora's tale reappears in the *Genealogie deorum gentilium* (IV.61), where Boccaccio references the *Divininae Institutiones* of Lactantius (I.20.6–17) and the *Fasti* of Ovid (5195–5212). Clearly, Boccaccio retells the legends of these two founder-goddesses not only to ridicule the myth itself but also to testify how Florence is a brothel, a city whose citizens are ready to do anything for money, a point he makes in epistle IX 44.

Two further biographies within the *De mulieribus claris*, those of Iole (*De Yole Etholarum regis filia*) and Deianira (*De Deyanira Herculis coniuge*), touch on another myth closely connected to the foundation of Florence – that of Hercules. No one knows exactly when and in what form the myth of the hero-founder began, but the official seal of the city-state of Florence certainly included the image of Hercules.[15] The seal was used to stamp and thus authenticate letters dispatched within and outside the borders of the Republic of Florence: it stood for the entire city. Proofs of the existence of this seal go back at least to 6 July 1277.[16] The original seal, probably made out of bronze, has been lost, but Armando Nuzzo recently found two wax seals stamped by this *sigillum Erculis*, one in the State Archives of Siena and the other in the State Archives of Modena,[17] dating back to

15 As Dante reports, the first master ("il primo padrone") of Florence was Mars, the god of war (*Inf.* 13.144) – after all, the city was originally founded by soldiers. We can thus hypothesize a line of descent from Mars to Hercules – along the lines of *Mars Gradivus* in Rimini (Centanni 2008) – and from Hercules to Saint John the Baptist, as suggested by Panofski (1939), during the process of Christianizing the pagan protectors of Italian cities. The totemic animal of Florence is the lion, whose hide is a distinctive characteristic of Hercules. The "Marzocco," which is the lion peacefully resting with its right paw on the lilied shield, allegedly derives from "Martocus," "little Mars" – another link between Hercules and Mars through the lion. Throughout the fourteenth century, next to Palazzo Vecchio, the Republic maintained a lion cage, as the animals were used after military victories for the ritual of the "baciaculo del leone," as Morelli reports in his chronicle: after the defeat of Pisa in 1364, the prisoners had to kiss the posterior of a lion cub, symbol of Florence, as a sign of submission (Morelli 2015, 171–3).

16 Canaccini (2012, 646, n. 31) writes: "The first testimony of the seal 'in quo … erat figura sive ymago Erculis' is dated 6 July 1277, in Arch. M. Pist., Lib. Censuum, f. 285." Demetrio Marzi, in his monograph on the Chancellery of Florence, asserts that despite the lack of hard evidence, he is assured by documentary notices that "from 21 July 1184 onward there is a record of letters stamped with the seal of the Commune of Florence, and that already on 13 September 1282, Florence had the so-called seal of Hercules, that is, engraved with the figure of Hercules and his club, with the inscription 'Seal of the Florentines' all around it" (1910, 277).

17 For an overview of studies and other details on the Florentine seal depicting Hercules, see Nuzzo 2010.

1404 and 1497, respectively. These are the only two known examples, for when a sealed letter was opened, the seal would normally be broken. In both examples, an oval-shaped mandorla is fashioned out of green wax, and the letters SYGILLUM FLORENTINUM are clearly visible, surrounding the figure of Hercules displayed in frontal view with his head turned to the right; behind his neck, the tail of the lion hide is recognizable. The myth of Hercules as founder of the city had not taken form in Boccaccio's times. It was eventually canonized in literature by the *De laboribus Herculis* of Coluccio Salutati, written in the early fifteenth century, and was subsequently embellished and developed in greater detail in Florentine art with the Medici: in the painting of *Hercules and the Hydra* and the bronze statuette *Hercules and Antaeus*, both by Pollaiuolo; *Hercule e Cacus* by Baccio Bandinelli; and *Hercules and the Centaur* by Giambologna.[18]

The Florentines were very interested in the labours of Hercules, and in his *Genealogie deorum gentilium*, Boccaccio does not stop at numbering the usual seven or twelve, but counts as many as thirty. The thirty-first, though, was fatal to the legendary hero: it involved his love for women. Having fallen in love with Omphale (known also as Iole), Hercules obeys her command to put down his club, take off his lion hide, and devote himself to domestic works, including spinning wool, using perfume, and wearing delicate clothes. In the meantime, his wife, Deianira, overcome with jealousy, sends Hercules a cloak dipped in the blood of the centaur Nessus, who had given it to her with the promise that the cloak would make whoever wore it fall in love with her. Nessus's promise was a lie; in fact, the cloak had been dipped in poisonous blood from the Hydra killed by Hercules himself, which, on contact with skin, would penetrate the pores and kill the unfortunate wearer; thus, we encounter the rather unheroic death of the strong and crafty Hercules.

In his *De mulieribus claris*, in contrast to his *Genealogie*, Boccaccio decides to focus in detail only on this last "labour," writing that Hercules has become "effeminate" – the same word he had used for the traitors in the biography of Leaena:

> She began by instructing Hercules to adorn his fingers with rings, anoint his rough scalp with Cyprian unguents, comb his shaggy hair, smear his prickly beard with nard, and adorn himself with girlish garlands and a Maeonian headdress; next she had him wear purple cloaks and dainty garments. The sweet young thing was naturally given to trickery, and so thought there was more glory in making a strong man *effeminate* using seduction than there was in killing him by poison or the sword.
>
> But even all this Iole deemed insufficient to satisfy her anger. Finally, she forced Hercules – by this time totally *effeminate* – to sit in the midst of her servant girls and tell the story of his labours. Taking the distaff, he would spin wool, and though now

18 See Canaccini 2012, 646 and notes.

an adult – indeed a man of advanced years – he softened to stretch threads the very fingers he had hardened to kill serpents while still a baby. (Emphasis added.)

(et primo digitos anulis et hyrsutos pectine discriminari crines ac hyspidam ungi nardo barbam et puellaribus corollis et meonia etiam insigniri mitra; inde purpureos amictus mollesque vestes precepit indueret, extimans iuvencula, fraudibus erenata, longe plus decoris tam robustum hominem *effeminasse* lascivis quam gladio vel aconithis occidisse.

Porro cum nec his satis sue indignationi satisfactum arbitraretur, in id egit mollitiei deditum, ut etiam inter mulierculas, femineo ritu sedens, fabellas laborum suorum narraret et, pensis a se susceptis, lanam colo neret digitos, quos ad extinguendos in cunis, adhuc infans, angues duraverat, in valida iam, imo provecta etate, ad extenuanda fila molliret.) (*De mul.* 23.4–5)

We are a long way from the familiar image of Hercules as the killer of monsters, triumphing in his twelve labours. Boccaccio takes care to narrate every single detail of his gradual but inexorable transformation from warrior to a "common female": first, the setting aside of his weapons and lion hide; then adopting female clothing, cosmetics, and hairstyle; and finally the company of handmaidens as he spins wool, accustoming his fingers to distinctly female labours, while ironically speaking of "masculine" ones. We find before us a man with no spine, enslaved to luxury, and thus deprived of free will.

In this context, it is worth recalling the figure of Hercules in Petrarch, who recounts the hero's life in his *De viris illustribus*. Petrarch evaluates his Hercules positively, and the episode involving Iole is no more than a moment of weakness in the hero, who is able to make the right choice, leave luxury, and continue his extraordinary life. Petrarch presents the myth of Hercules once again in his *De vita solitaria*, where he attributes the divine reputation of the hero to his valiant journey along the steep path of virtue and his related disavowal of the path of pleasure. Hence, against the image of the legendary hero who at the crossroads chooses the narrow path of virtue, Boccaccio juxtaposes the opposite: his Hercules chooses not *virtus* but *voluptas*. Worse, impelled by erotic desire, he becomes weak, effeminate, and mortal; in Boccaccio's version, the hero dies precisely because of his weakness and lust.[19]

Flora, Venus, and Hercules, the three mythical founders of Florence, in Boccaccio's accounts are all deviants, devoted to vice and subjugated by eros. The city

19 For a detailed analysis of Petrarch's biography of Hercules, see Mommsen 1953, Rombach 1977, and Rossi 2010. Mommsen points out that Petrarch is the father of the proverbial phrase "Hercules at the crossroad" ("Hercules in bivio"; 188) that he uses for the first time in *De vita solitaria*. Besides lashing out at Florence, the contrast between Petrarch's heroic, divine character, who chooses *virtus*, and Boccaccio's gutless Hercules, who chooses *voluptas*, could also constitute veiled criticism of the solitary life proposed by Petrarch.

likewise is corrupted by the same evils. We have clearly come a long way from assertions like those found, for example, in his earlier *De montibus*, written during the 1350s:[20] "Florence, peerless honour of all of Italy" ("Florentiam, totius Ytalie singulare decus"). The icons of decency in this city have become unrecognizable, and Boccaccio suggests they no longer exist.

Boccaccio could hardly have inserted casually and without ulterior motive these revisionary stories into *De mulieribus*, given the time period in which he was composing this collection. In the same years that he was purging anti-Florentine invective from his *Life of Dante*, because it was too blunt, he was taking indirect aim at the city and its inhabitants by ridiculing grandiose myths from which they claimed their origin.

Antityrannical Motives

At the same time that Boccaccio points his finger at the moral decadence of Florence, he also indicates a path to correct behaviour, both moral and civic – in his treatment of women characters and expressions of republican ideals and antityrannical sentiment within the *De mulieribus claris*. Many of his biographies of exemplary women may be considered examples of zeal for a just state, which often correspond to models that are typical of medieval Christian moralism. In the hands of Boccaccio, they contain nuances that distinctly recall civic humanism.[21]

For example, we have Boccaccio's biographies of Lucretia and Virginia, which constitute an abrupt contrast to the mythical founders of Florence, whose reckless and vicious behaviour damaged the community. With the biographies of these women, Boccaccio provides models of chastity and virginity that become ethical and civic ideals. The concepts of chastity and virginity in the *De mulieribus claris* are praised no longer in accordance with medieval precepts – as absolute self-standing values – but in relation to the state and the freedom it provides. In the biographies of Lucretia (*De Lucretia Collatini coniuge, De mul.* 48) and Virginia, daughter of Virginius (*De Virginia virgine Virginii filia, De mul.* 58), chastity and virginity are no longer connected only to purity of mind and body (which is the goal of medieval Christian moralism) but are especially ethical and civic values connected to the morality of the state. The idea is well represented in the biography of Cloelia (*De Cloelia romana virgine, De mul.* 52), who, along with other virgins, is given as hostage to the

---

20 The *De montibus, silvis, fontibus, lacubus, fluminibus, stagnis seu paludibus et de diversis nominibus maris* was composed in about 1355 for his own amusement – at least that's what Boccaccio implies in the introduction to his work (*De mont.* I.2) – and it is a toponomastic catalogue of the Greco-Roman world, arranged into seven categories of locations: mountains, forests, springs, lakes, rivers, marshes, and seas. The work reflects the author's erudition, an inventory of his most diverse readings. On the seriousness of the *De montibus* and its connection with the *Genealogia*, see Cachey 2013 and Monti 2016.

21 On civic humanism, see Hankins 2000 and 2019.

Etruscan king Porsenna as a guarantee of peace. Under the cover of nightfall, Cloelia manages to escape the enemy camp; then, on horseback (even though she has never ridden a horse in her life), she liberates the other young women to return them to their families. To explain the motivations behind this heroic gesture, Boccaccio asserts (*De mul.* 52.3): "Perhaps she did not deem it honourable for the Republic that so many young females were in the control of a foreign king" ("Cui cum forsan videretur minus de republica apud exterum regem tot detineri virgines"). This passage thus associates virginity and chastity with the dignity of the state, as Boccaccio supposes that the girl considered it "minus de republica" that Roman virgins would be in enemy hands: for these young virgins, being held hostage is considered not so much a personal disgrace as a social one, involving the citizen body.

In his biography of Lucretia, Boccaccio presents the woman who prefers suicide to the disgrace of rape and who became the paradigm of chastity in the medieval period and for centuries afterward. As Boccaccio concludes his account of this heroine's life, he not only pays tribute to her purity ("pudicitia") but also explicitly underscores how her extreme actions restore both the matron's reputation and Rome's freedom ("decus … romana libertas"):

> Hers was an unfortunate beauty. Her purity, which can never be sufficiently commended, should be extolled all the more highly as she expiated with such severity the ignominy thrust violently upon her. Her action not only restored the reputation that a dissolute young man had destroyed with his filthy crime, but led ultimately to freedom for Rome.
>
> (Infelix quidem pulcritudo eius et tanto clarius, nunquam satis laudata, pudicitia sua dignis preconiis extollenda est, quanto acrius ingesta vi ignominia expiata; cum ex eadem non solum reintegratum sit decus, quod feditate facinoris iuvenis labefactarat ineptus, sed consecuta sit romana libertas.) (*De mul.* 48.9)

The biography of Virginia draws attention to her virginity, starting with the alliterative tricolon of the title: *De Virginea virgine Virginii filia* (*De mul.* 58). But this is not the detail that Boccaccio exalts: instead, he celebrates the way her death restores liberty and the republic to Rome against the despotic power of the decemvirate. His emphasis on Rome's liberty is evident from the opening of the biography:

> Virginia, a Roman, was a virgin in name and in fact, and she should be remembered with reverence. Notable for her remarkable virtue, she was the daughter of Aulus Virginius, a plebeian but an honourable man. Although Virginia had an excellent character, she became famous not so much for her constancy as for the wickedness of her ill-starred lover, the extraordinary severity of her father, and the liberty of the Romans that resulted from it.

(Virginea nomine et facto romana virgo pia est recolenda memoria: fuit enim insignis decoris conspicua et Auli Virginii, plebei hominis sed honesti, filia. Que esto optime esset indolis, non tantum tamen sua constantia clara quantum scelere amantis infausti et severi nimium patris facinore, ac ex illo Romanorum libertate secuta, facta est.) (*De mul.* 58.1)

In these few lines the narrator emphasizes several key elements; the one he leaves for last, for greatest emphasis, is that from the sacrifice of her person the highest of ideals sprang forth – Roman freedom. This is no small detail, yet the possible sources for this biography (Valerius Maximus and Livy) scarcely mention it. In fact, Valerius ignores it altogether, and Livy applauds the actions of the father, thanks to whom the Roman people rose up against tyranny: "The masses were stirred in part by the atrocity of the crime, and in part by the opportunity to recover their freedom" ("Concitatur multitudo partim atrocitate sceleris, partim spe per occasionem repetendae libertatis"; *Ab urbe condita* 3.49.1).

These two biographical narratives well reflect how, in the *De mulieribus*, chastity is redefined as ethical behaviour that reflects civic values. In this context, the biographies of Lucretia and Virginia become profound expressions of civic humanism. The women are no longer merely medieval examples of simple *pudicitia*; rather, because of their upright conduct and their tragic and unjust deaths, Romans are driven to rebel against tyranny and reclaim their freedom. From this perspective, Lucretia and Virginia become examples of righteousness against the immorality that corrupted the *Res Publica*. If Lucretia had accepted her fate with resignation after the outrage of Sextus Tarquinius and had carried on living with her disgrace in silence, and if Virginia had yielded to the lust of the decemvir, the Roman people would never have begun their insurrection against tyranny and corruption. In this new view of chastity, private life mirrors public life, private virtue and vice reflect the characteristics of the state: if one's private life is corrupt, then so is the state. Women must strive to be chaste for the sake of the republic. Honourable behaviour must be aligned with the public health of the state, and this is one of the cardinal principles of civic humanism. With their chastity, Lucretia and Virginia refuse to submit to the corruption of tyrants, and thus drive the Roman people to rebellion and liberty. In effect, Boccaccio reapplies the principles of the Roman Republic.[22]

---

22 In *Women in the History of Political Thought*, Arlene W. Saxonhouse analyses female figures in Livy's history of Rome, and she thus writes on the Roman period: "Historical causation and political transformation are understood as the result of private virtues and vices. The life of the ruler is not abstracted from his private passions, and often these passions are directed against the chastity of women. The chaste women of olden times, so unlike the women Livy sees in Rome at the end of the first century BC, preserve public morality by attending to their private morality. Virginia's preserving her chaste nature has an effect on Roman political history that would have been impossible had she yielded to the lustful decemvir. As Livy presents it, the decline in

It is no coincidence that Virginia and Lucretia become symbols of resistance to tyrants, starting with Coluccio Salutati. In the second chapter of Coluccio's treatise *De tyranno*, on "whether it is permissible to kill a tyrant" ("An liceat tyrannum occidere"), we read:

> Thus under the leadership of Lucius Brutus, because of the crimes of Tarquinius Superbus and of his children, the Roman people overthrew the lordship of kings. And so thanks to Virginia who, because of the wickedness of Claudius, under the pretext of slanderous servility, was being taken away to be raped, the authority of the decemvirs was removed.
>
> (Sic autore Lucio Bruto Romanus populus ob Tarquini Superbi filiorumque facinora regium depluit dominatum. Sic propter Virginiam, que Claudii nequitia, sub calumniose servitutis obtentu, rapiebatur ad stuprum, ablata fuit autoritas decemvirorum.) (2014, 2.15)

In the late medieval period, Lucretia and Virginia had become associated with chastity and virginity for both married and unmarried women, but in Florence, in the dawning of a new age of civic humanism, these women assumed an entirely different significance. Lucretia opposes the tyranny of a single person (Tarquinius Superbus) with a single decisive action; Virginia is sacrificed in a stand against the oligarchic domination of corrupt decemvirs, including Claudius. Indeed, this pairing, with these connotations – against individual tyranny (Lucretia) and a corrupt ruling class (Virginia) – could evoke in a contemporary reader's mind the most recent political events in Florence: on one hand, the tyranny of Walter of Brienne, Duke of Athens, which lasted eleven months before ending in 1343, and on the other, the corrupt government who gained power with the practice of the *ammonizioni* in January 1358.

Starting with Boccaccio, who drew these biographies from the classical era, and with Salutati, who linked these two women as paradigms, Lucretia and Virginia were recognized figures in the Republic of Florence. We see them in two paintings by Botticelli, in compositions centred on insurrections of the Roman people against tyrants.[23]

---

the moral life of Roman women serves well to mark the decline in the moral life of the men who rule the state. Lucretia and Virginia are the *exempla*, 'the fine things to take as model', for those, male or female, who care about welfare of the political unit" (1985, 109–10).

23 For further information on these two works (*The Story of Lucretia* and *The Story of Virginia*), see Nelson (2010, 196), who sees in the *De mulieribus* a possible source of inspiration for the iconography of Virginia: "While Livy had described the girl as dazed and disoriented, Boccaccio writes that Virginia had put up resistance to the rape. This detail may have inspired Botticelli, who represents Virginia as looking for shelter in the arms of an older woman." Following this idea, I investigated further in Filosa 2019.

With these examples, Boccaccio demonstrates that even matrons and virgins can contribute to the state and be vehicles of liberty against tyranny, maintaining honourable conduct and resisting the corruption that is contrary to the very essence of a righteous state.

In Roman times, the absolute importance of the well-being of the state and the sacrifice required to preserve it reflected the ethical hierarchy of the *mos maiorum*, the way of the ancestors, which ranked the state first in order of importance, then the family, and last the individual. Each person had to act above all in the interests of the state, then for that of the family, and only last for his or her personal needs. This lowest priority, on the other hand, is exactly what drives a tyrant to commit evil deeds – his own self-interest guided by excessive and uncontrollable passions. The hierarchy of a tyrant's values is the inversion of the ancient and honourable *mos maiorum*.

We find in the *De mulieribus claris* a biography that exemplifies this paradigm, that of the Roman matron Veturia (*De mul.* 55), mother of Coriolanus, who acts in conformity with ancient Roman principles: Rome and its freedom come before family. Veturia is one of those many heroines commemorated for the good she brought to the state, even when it ran against her personal interests. The lengthy chapter *De Veturia romana matrona* deals initially with her son Gaius Marcius, named Coriolanus for his victories against the city of Corioli. In the midst of a famine, by order of the senators, he proposes to withhold from the people the meagre amount of grain left in the city, and this provokes a popular uprising. To avoid riots, the tribune of the plebs sets a day on which Coriolanus is expected to present himself to explain his antidemocratic stance. He refuses and is thus exiled from Rome. Outraged, he joins the neighbouring Volsci to attack the city and set up camp four miles away, precipitating a crisis. The Roman Senate repeatedly send envoys to obtain peace with reasonable conditions, but they are in vain. At this point his mother is persuaded by the other matrons to talk to her son. She says to him:

> Stop right there, you troublesome young man! Before I embrace you, I want to know whether you have come to receive me as your mother or as an enemy prisoner. The latter, I think. O wretched woman that I am! Must my longevity – the very longevity for which mortals yearn – bring me to this, that I see you condemned to exile and become an adversary of the Republic? I ask you: do you know on what soil you stand, armed as an enemy? Do you recognize the country you see before you? Indeed you do. But in case you do not, this is the land where you were conceived, where you were born, where you were raised through my efforts.
>
> What is going on in your spirit, your mind, your passions, that you have been able to bear arms against it like an enemy? The respect owed your mother, love for your sweet wife, compassion for your children, reverence for your fatherland – did not these feelings come to meet you as you entered your country? … Wretched woman that I am, I see well enough that my fertility has become a curse directed against my

country and against me. I thought that I had given birth to a son and a citizen, but now I realize that I have produced a dangerous and implacable enemy.

Better, truly, not to have conceived! By my sterility Rome could have remained free from siege, and I, a poor old woman, could have died in a free country.

(Siste gradum, infeste iuvinis; scire velim, antequam in amplexus veniam tuos, an matrem an captivam hostem suscepturus advenias; hostem puto. Me miseram! In hoc exoptata mortalibus evi longitudo deduxisse me debuit ut te damnatum exilio et inde rei publice hostem cernerem? Cognoscis queso quo armatus hostis consistas in solo? Cognoscis quam habeas in conspectu patriam? Cognoscis equidem, et si nescis, hec est in quo genitus, in quo natus, in quo labore meo educatus es.

Quo igitur animo, qua mente, quo inpulsu, hostilia potuisti inferre arma? Non intranti tibi parenti debitus honos, dulcis uxoris amor, filiorum pietas et native patrie reverentia obvii facti sunt? … Satis, me miseram, adverto fecunditatem meam patrie michique fuisse adversam; ubi filium et civem peperisse arbitrabar, hostem et infestissimum atque inflexibilem peperisse me video.

Satius quippe non concepisse fuerat: potuerat sterilitate mea Roma absque oppugnatione consistere et ego misella anus in libera mori patria.) (*De mul.* 55.5–9)

In sum, Veturia would give up her status as a mother for the good of Rome, of the Republic, of liberty. She acts precisely according to the ethical hierarchy of the *mos maiorum*, claiming that first comes the state, then the family, then the individual: before her role of mother and before her family come Rome and its freedom.

The Stoic Suicide: Escape towards Freedom

Epicharis kills herself to save her friends, conspirators against tyranny; Lucretia prefers suicide to living with disgrace; Virginia is sacrificed by her father with the words: "Qua possum via, dilecta filia, libertatem tuam vendico" ("Dear daughter, I restore your liberty in the only way I can"; *De mul.* 58.9); Veturia values her life and status less than her duty to Rome. In the *De mulieribus claris*, a number of women face death with great courage. Rather than collaborate with the enemy, or even worse, a tyrant, they prefer a distinctly stoic suicide. Choosing death, especially when this is the only escape route or the only way to preserve one's personal freedom, is another classical value (or, more accurately, a republican value) that Boccaccio uses within this work. In this sense, Boccaccio parts ways with Christian-medieval thought, for the conventional view was that suicide transgresses divine commandments.[24]

24 Among the Ten Commandments, the sixth, "You shall not kill," implies also "You shall not kill yourself." For suicide in the Middle Ages, see the extensive studies by Murray 1998. In Christianity, suicide can be legitimated only and exclusively by divine command; in his index, Murray lists different theologians who discussed this situation (1998, 608).

In canto 13 of the *Inferno*, Dante condemns suicides to eternal damnation in the Forest of the Suicides. The presence of Cato of Utica at the threshold of Antepurgatory seems to contradict this principle. Cato is the "honourable guardian" ("veglio onesto") in charge of the mountain of Purgatory because he committed suicide out of love of liberty ("libertà va cercando").[25] Cato has an entirely positive value in Dante's work, not just in the *Commedia* but also in his *Convivio* and *Monarchia*. In the *Commedia* and the *Convivio* Dante does not speak directly of Cato's suicide, though he certainly does in the *Monarchia*:

> Now add to their number those most holy victims, the Decii, who laid down their lives dedicated to the salvation of the community ... and the sacrifice (words cannot express it) of the most stern guardian of true liberty, Marcus Cato. The former for the deliverance of their fatherland did not recoil from the shadows of death; the latter, in order to set the world afire with love of freedom, showed the value of freedom when he preferred to die a free man rather than remain alive without freedom.
>
> (Accedunt nunc illae sacratissimae victimae Deciorum, qui pro salute publica devotas animas posuerunt ... accedit et illud inenarrabile sacrifitium severissimi verae libertatis tutoris Marci Catonis. Quorum alteri pro salute patriae mortis tenebras non horruerunt; alter, ut mundum libertatis amore accenderet, quanti libertas esset ostendit dum e vita liber decedere maluit quam sine libertate manere in illa.) (*Monarchy*, ed. Shaw, 1996, II.5.15)

Dante thus goes against Saint Augustine's declaration in the *De Civitate Dei* (I 22–4) that suicide is a sin under every circumstance. As Alexander Murray notes, "From time to time in this volume [*Suicide in the Middle Ages*], a medieval suicide problem has opened up an identical distant landscape, a landscape marked out by the long, irregular, twin lines of the classical and Christian traditions" (1998, 310). The case of Dante, Murray explains, could involve only a citizen of Florence: the city had a strong classical tradition, and the Christian Florence of Saint John the Baptist existed alongside the classical Florence with origins in Rome. But which Rome was the model of Florence – imperial or republican? The Republican Florentines with oligarchic sympathies – those who in Boccaccio's time defined themselves as "very Guelf" or "true Guelf" – claimed descent from imperial Rome, conqueror of the world, to which Florence was the legitimate heir. However, there is also Republican Rome, in which each citizen is loyal to the authority of the community of equals, obeying only the government that acts in the name of the equality of citizens, of which Cato is the most celebrated hero. Boccaccio chooses

25 *Purg.* 1.31–108, 2.118–33. For greater detail see the entry "Catone" by Mario Fubini (1970–8) and his bibliography; "Cato of Utica" by Martinez (2000); "Opus restaurationis" by Mazzotta (1979, 14–65).

Republican Rome, embracing Dante's views in the *Monarchia* and extolling stoic suicide in his biographies of women when this is the only way to freedom.

The number of women's suicides within the *De mulieribus claris* is surprisingly high: we find fourteen cases,[26] plus one attempted suicide – Pompeia Paolina, wife of Seneca. Of course, not all of these protagonists kill themselves in embrace of stoic morality – they have a variety of motivations[27] – but I focus here on those for whom stoic morality was paramount.

An eloquent example is Theoxena (*De mul.* 71), a noblewoman of Thessaly, whose father, husband, and brother-in-law are all killed by Philip, the evil king of Macedonia. When her sister also dies, the woman raises her nephews as if they were her own children. After Philip delivers an edict that calls for the death even of the children of those he had already killed, Theoxena realizes that her son and nephews are in mortal danger. She steels her heart to kill her children with her own hands, rather than give Philip this power over them. For "if they fell into the king's hands, they would not only become an object of sport for the king's cruelty but would also be subjected necessarily to the scorn and the lust of the prison guards" ("si in regis devenirent manus, non solum sevities eius eos ludibrio futuros, sed etiam custodum, necessitate cogente, libidinem et fastidia subituros"; *De mul.* 71.5). In these circumstances, she first attempts escape by sea, but adverse winds drive her back to shore, cutting off escape. Without a moment to lose, she prepares poison in a cup, unsheathes some swords, and addresses these words to her son and nephews:

> Only death can bring protection and safety to us all. The cup and dagger are our means of death; we must flee the king's arrogance in whatever way each of us chooses. Therefore, my children, rouse your noble spirit, and let the eldest among you act in manly fashion. Take the sword, or drink from the cup if you prefer a crueller death; find refuge in an end that is freely chosen, since the force of the raging sea does not allow us to set course toward life.
>
> (Mors sola vindictam salutemque nobis omnibus prestare potest. Ad mortem poculum gladiusque sunt vie; qua quenque delectat, regia superbia fugienda est. Mei ergo

26 The fourteen biographies, with their chapter numbers, are *De Tisbe Babilonia virgine* (13), *De Aragne colophonia muliere* (18), *De Yocasta Thebarum regina* (25), *De Didone seu Elissa Cartaginensium regina* (42), *De Lucretia Collatini coniuge* (48), *De Hyppone greca muliere* (53), *De Armonia Gelonis syculi filia* (68), *De Sophonisba regina Numidie* (70), *De Theosena Herodici principis filia* (71), *De coniugibus Cymbrorum* (80), *De Portia Catonis Uticensis filia* (82), *De Cleopatra regina Egyptiorum* (88), *De Agrippina Germanici coniuge* (90), and *De Epycari libertina* (93).

27 Thisbe (*De mul.* 13) kills herself for love on the lifeless body of Pyramus; Arachne (*De mul.* 18) hangs herself because she cannot bear the disgrace of being defeated at the loom by Minerva; Jocasta (*De mul.* 25) stabs herself in the chest, in her old age tired of so many misfortunes; Harmonia (*De mul.* 68) voluntarily gives up her body to the assassins, overcome by pity for the faithful maidservant who had taken her place and was killed.

iuvenes generosos excitate animos et qui maiores estis viriliter agite: capite ferrum, aut poculum haurite, si mors sevior fortasse delectat, et in eam liberam confugite, postquam in vitam tendere estuosi maris impetus prohibet.) (*De mul.* 71.10)

The youths thus perish by a "free death," by poison, sword, or throwing themselves into the waves. Theoxena, too, "when for the sake of liberty she had driven to their deaths the children she had so devotedly reared" ("quos pie educaverat ob libertatem egisset in mortem"; *De mul.* 71.12), throws herself into the stormy sea, along with her second husband, in a fatal embrace. Boccaccio concludes the chapter by affirming:

> She thought it better to die in freedom than live to languish in vile slavery. Thus the enemy found an empty ship, Philip was deprived of the solace of his cruelty, and the austere Theoxena acquired for herself a memorable place in history.
>
> (Satius libere mori rata quam vivens feda servitute tabescere; et sic, hostibus nave relicta vacua, solatium sevitie sue Phylippo abstulit et sibi dignum memoria mulier austera monimentum peperit.) (*De mul.* 71.12)

In praising Theoxena, who kills herself, her children, and her husband as the *ultima ratio* to preserve their freedom, Boccaccio embraces stoic Roman values, rejecting the medieval Christian dictates of the Catholic Church. Note also that Livy – the source for this chapter – calls Theoxena "cruel" ("ferox"; *Ab Urbe condita* 40.4.13), whereas Boccaccio prefers and uses the adjective "austere" ("austera"; *De mul.* 70.12). In Roman stoic thought, the foundations of which were intensely political, suicide was a valid alternative to the disgrace of slavery – in case one fell into enemy hands – or otherwise a way to escape tyranny. Among the Roman stoics who committed suicide can be found Cato of Utica, who protested against the tyranny of Julius Caesar; his son-in-law, Marcus Junius Brutus, one of the conspirators who killed Ceasar; and Seneca, who preferred to cut his veins rather than be condemned to death by Nero. Among the suicides in *De mulieribus* we find Portia (*De mul.* 82), daughter of Cato and wife of Brutus, as well as Pompea Paolina (*De mul.* 94), Seneca's wife – even though her plan failed when she was saved by order of the emperor. Among the most important Roman theorists are Cicero, with the *De officiis*, the *De finibus*, and the *Tusculanae Disputationes*, and Lucius Anneus Seneca with his *Letters to Lucilius*, of which Boccaccio included a selection in his notebook, the *Zibaldone Magliabechiano* (Costantini 1974). In the *Florilegio senecano*, Boccaccio transcribes a list of sayings drawn from Seneca's *Epistles*, organizing them by topics, of which three are particularly interesting in this context: "De morte non timenda et quid sit mors" ("On death that should not be feared, and what death is"; Costantini 1974, 99–101); "De his qui mori cupiunt et se ipsos occidunt" ("On those who wish to die and who actually kill themselves"; Costantini 1974, 114–15); and "De libertate et servitute" ("On freedom and slavery"; Costantini 1974, 105). The first, as the heading indicates, concerns the strictly ontological aspect of death, giving reasons a human being should not dread it. The other two collections deal with suicide, but in a starkly different fashion. More specifically, those who wish to die for tedium or fear (of none other than death!) are condemned by Seneca,[28] who cites Epicurus – and since Boccaccio includes these texts, he clearly agrees. But a different kind of suicide is celebrated: death as flight to freedom, rather than wallowing in slavery. Here are two samples that dovetail nicely with the biographies of Theoxena and Epicharis:

> He who has learned how to die has unlearned how to be slave: he transcends all power of others, or at least is outside it. What does he care for prison and guards and shackles? His door lies open. There is only one chain that keeps us bound, and that is love of life, which just as it should not be entirely rejected, likewise it must be so diminished that if circumstances ever demand it, nothing will detain or prevent us from being prepared to do immediately that which at some point must be done anyway.
>
> (Qui mori didicit servire dedidicit; supra omnem potentiam est, certe extra omnem. Quid ad illud carcer et custodia et claustra? Liberum hostium habet una est catena que nos alligatos tenet, amor vite, qui ut non est abiciendus, ita minuendus est, ut si quando res exiget, nicil nos detineat nec impediat quominus parati simus quod quandoque faciendum est statim facere.) (Costantini 1974, 105)

See also:

> You ask me what freedom is? It means being a slave to nothing, to no necessity, to no accidents; it means to challenge Fortune on an equal footing. On whichever day I come to accept that I am more powerful, She will have no power over me; and so will I really put up with Her when I have death at my disposal?
>
> (Que sit libertas queris? Nulli rei servire, nulli necessitati, nullis casibus, fortunam in equum deducere. Quo die intellexero plus posse, nicil poterit: ergo illam feram cum in manu mors sit?) (Costantini 1974, 105)

---

28 "Ridiculum est currere ad mortem tedio vite, cum genere vite ut currendum esset ad mortem effeceris" ("It is ridiculous to run toward death out of weariness for life, since with your way of living you have already forced yourself to run toward death"); "Quid tamen ridiculum quam appetere mortem, cum vitam inquietam tibi feceris metu mortis" ("What on the other hand is so ridiculous than to desire death, since you have made your own life stressful because of your fear of death?"); and finally, "licet, tantam hominum imprudentiam esse, ymo dementiam, ut quidam timore mortis ducantur ad mortem" ("such is the short-sightedness, or even the madness of people that some are actually driven to death by their fear of death").

From these extracts, it is clear that Boccaccio was well acquainted with Seneca's version of stoic philosophy, and that the biography of Theoxena, just like that of many other heroines of the *De mulieribus claris*, corresponds perfectly with these ideas.

Theoxena's biography is preceded by that of the Numidian queen Sophonisba (*De mul.* 70). Petrarch had already immortalized this historical figure in books 5 and 6 of his *Africa*, but Boccaccio provides a much more positive version. Whereas Petrarch portrays her negatively as a manipulator of men (at least in his *De viris illustribus* and *Africa*),[29] Boccaccio sees her as a pawn in the political games of her father, Hasdrubal: he gives her in marriage to the Numidian king Syphax, in the hope of breaking Syphax's alliance with Rome (*De mul.* 70.2); he also prompts her ("Hasdrubalis monitu") to draw Syphax into an alliance with Carthage (*De mul.* 70.3). Subsequently, Scipio defeats Syphax, who was chained and exposed to his people. As a prisoner, he lost everything, including his wife. When Massinissa, the victorious Numidian king allied with the Romans, enters the royal palace in triumph, Sophonisba – "while still preserving the spirit of her prior regal fortune" ("pristine fortune animum retinens") – throws herself as a suppliant at his knees and implores:

> I humbly implore you to do to me ... whatever in your eyes seems right and good, as long as I am not handed over alive to the Romans ... And if there is for me no other way of escape, I beseech you to let me die at your hands rather than let me fall alive into the power of the enemy.

---

29 Simone Marchesi, on Petrarch's Sophonisba in the *Africa*, writes: "The combined import of the two episodes redefines Sophonisba as an eloquent and conniving schemer who has already taken advantage of her seductive power with her first husband and who is now ready to maneuver the enamored Massinissa to her political advantage. The *Africa* dispels any potential sympathy its readers might have entertained for this new character Sophonisba" (2009, 122). In this work and in the *De viris illustribus*, this character is profoundly influenced by Livy's treatment (*Ab Urbe condita*, 30), in which the Numidian queen is presented by Syphax's words as a woman interested in power who achieves it through her talents of seduction. Bartuschat (2010) offers a detailed analysis of the relationship between Sophonisba and Massinissa in Petrarch's works – *Africa, De viris illustribus, Trionfi* – highlighting the differences on the basis of each context. There is no doubt that the true protagonist of the lovers is always Massinissa, while Boccaccio focuses his attention on Sophonisba, reevaluating her in a positive light. In the *De mulieribus claris*, he presents her as a heroine who makes the stoic choice of liberty through death against imprisonment, and he adopts an elegiac tone in the *Fiammetta* (VIII.11). While Petrarch pays tribute to the masculine Massinissa confronted with the dilemma between passion and duty and ultimately choosing Roman virtue, Boccaccio makes this Numidian hero a rather wretched character. First he is predisposed to lust; furthermore, after being rebuked by Scipio for marrying Sophonisba, he withdraws to his tent and weeps at length, and his sobs and sighs reverberate throughout the camp. The differences between the authors are notable; I am not aware of a published close comparison between these characters, but it would be desirable.

(deiecta precor … in me … agas quod in oculis tuis pium bonumque visum sit … Romanorum arbitrio viva non tradar … Et, si omnis in hoc alius tollitur modus, ut tua manu potius moriar facito, quam hostium in potestatem viva deveniam, precor et obsecro.) (*De mul.* 70.6–7)

With this desperate speech, Sophonisba begs for mercy, and as soon as he sees her Massinissa is overcome with erotic frenzy. He is the one tainted with the "guilt" of passion, and as a Numidian, says Boccaccio, he is susceptible to lust: "Massinissa qui et ipse numida erat et, uti omnes sunt, in libidinem pronus" ("Himself a Numidian, Massinissa was, like all his countrymen, inclined to lust"; *De mul.* 70.8).[30] Blinded by the beauty of the young queen, he celebrates his wedding soon afterward with the dual goals of satisfying his erotic impulses and granting the woman's wish of not being handed over to the Romans.

In the *De mulieribus claris*, Sophonisba is a tragic heroine in the grip of fate, but she is also the victim of an excessively ambitious father and weak husbands. Indeed, when Massinissa realizes that he cannot fulfil his marital pledges, he withdraws into his tent and cries ("Suspiriis lacrimisque oppletus diu ingemuisset"; *De mul.* 70.9). Only afterward does he send a cup of poison to his new bride, in this way discharging his promise. Sophonisba, unwavering in her intentions, takes the poison with an impassive and resolute expression – but not before making a brief but incisive speech:[31]

"I willingly accept this wedding gift and, if my husband can give no other, I am grateful for it. But tell him that I would have had a better death had I not married on the very day I was to die." Taking the cup with a sharpness equal to that of her words, she quickly drained it without trace of fear. Not long after she swelled up and fell piteously to the ground in the death she had sought.

("Accipio nuptiale munus et, si nil aliud a viro coniugi dari poterat, gratum habeo; sed refer satius me morituram fuisse si non in funere meo nupsissem." Nec acrius dicta dedit quam poculum sumpserit et, nullo signo trepidationis ostenso, confestim hauxit omne; nec diu tumescens in mortem, quam petierat, miserabunda collapsa est.) (*De mul.* 70.10)

30 Here Boccaccio borrows from both Livy and Petrarch: "ut est genus Numidarum in Venerem praeceps" (*Ab Urbe condita,* 30.12.18); in the *De viris illustribus*, Massinissa acts out of "libidine" (*De mul.* 6.69), the same word used by Boccaccio.

31 Note also the close analogies here with the figure of Ghismonda in the *Decameron* (V.1): both protagonists show a unique combination of seriousness and resolution in the face of death, which they choose deliberately and achieve through poison. Both accept with gratitude a cup given by men who collapse in tears. Finally, both are given extraordinary last words, despite the extreme circumstances of their deaths. See Velli 2019, 196–7.

Boccaccio's praise for Sophonisba and Theoxena is unreserved, demonstrating the value of choosing death:

> By heaven! To have faced certain death so boldly would have been a great and admirable deed worthy of notice even in the case of an old man, tired of life and with nothing to hope for except his demise. It was far more so for a young queen who, so far as knowledge of the world is concerned, was just entering upon life and beginning to see what joys it held.
>
> (Edepol annoso homini, cui iam vita tedium, nec spes alia preter mortem, nedum puellule regie, tunc, habito ad notitiam rerum respectu, vitam intranti et quid in ea dulcedinis sit percipere incipienti, magnum et admirabile fuisset, et nota dignum, morti certe adeo impavide occurrisse.) (*De mul.* 70.11)

In sum, these heroines prefer suicide to falling enslaved into enemy hands.

Another example is provided by the wives of the Cimbrians (*De mul.* 80), who first kill their children and then hang themselves so as to not become "toys of the victors" ("victorum ludibrium"; *De mul.* 80.10). Here is Boccaccio's comment:

> But the Cimbrian women resolutely kept themselves for a better destiny and did not allow the glorious dignity of their race to be stained with ignominy. Their resolution in escaping slavery and shame by means of the rope showed that their people had been overcome not by might, but by fault of fortune.
>
> (Ast Cymbre constanti pectore meliori fortune servavere animos nec ulla passe sunt ignominia maiestatis gentis sue gloriam fedare; dumque servitutem et turpitudinem laqueo obstinate fugerent, non viribus, sed fortune crimine suos homines superatos ostendunt.) (*De mul.* 80.12)

The Cimbrian wives earn a better fate through their deaths, but above all they rescue and preserve the glory of the reputation of their people. Ensuring freedom and avoiding the enemy's hands are again described as heroic gestures. It is worth noticing that Theoxena and these women are celebrated not only for their own suicides but also for killing their children. Clearly Boccaccio's reasoning here is not Christian but stoic, exalting death as an escape from enslavement and disgrace.[32]

The biography of Zenobia, the 100th of the 106 in the work, illustrates the fate the other women escaped. Zenobia, the defeated queen of Palmyra, is in many

---

32 Contempt for death is thoroughly a stoic value. Examples of courage in death include the biographies of Polyxena (*De mul.* 33), who despite her tender age is celebrated for having offered her neck to the executioner with resolute spirit and expression; Olympias (*De mul.* 61); and Marianna (*De mul.* 87).

ways a positive role model for readers, but here she offers a cautionary tale. After many victorious wars with Rome, she is finally captured by Aurelian's soldiers. The emperor brings her and her children back to Rome to expose her to public abuse as a slave during the triumphal procession into the city. She is bound hand and foot with chains of gold, and the parody extends to a crown and royal dress covered with pearls and precious stones: the weight of all the gold is so great that she often stops walking from exhaustion. Behind her and her children comes the chariot she had commissioned for her victorious entrance into Rome had she overcome her powerful enemy. It is a humiliating scene that the other women who behaved as stoics managed to avoid, as they found in death a more dignified escape.

With these stories, the *De mulieribus claris* transmits expressions of republican antityrannical ideals, especially pertinent given that the first edition of the work was composed in an extraordinary political period. Some of these ideals also anticipate traces of civic humanism. In this sense, the *De casibus virorum illustrium* and the *De mulieribus claris* should not be viewed exclusively as paired texts devoted to men and women as a kind of study of gender but also as denunciations of tyranny, a study of political activism. While the *De casibus* is informed by events that took place after the tyranny of the Duke of Athens and warns against the overbearing power given to a person, the *De mulieribus* even more directly addresses the corruption of oligarchic power and celebrates freedom from the enemies of the homeland – especially when such freedom is achieved through personal sacrifice.

6 The *Consolatoria a Pino de' Rossi*: A Manifesto on Innocence

Treason is a matter of dates.

– Charles Maurice de Talleyrand-Périgord

The consolatory letter written to Messer Pino di Giovanni de' Rossi on his exile after the failed coup of 31 December 1360 is the literary work that shows most clearly Boccaccio's involvement with the conspirators.[1] We saw, in part 1, the dynamics of the conspiracy and the political context in which Boccaccio lived and worked; with this context in mind, we are in a better position to understand many passages of the letter that have till now been overlooked or underestimated. The piece is indubitably a consolatory letter, but it also makes a strong case for the innocence of Pino de' Rossi, and if it had been circulated widely, as a pamphlet, it would have functioned as an argument for his pardon.

Who Was Pino de' Rossi?

Pino de' Rossi is perhaps best known as the addressee of this letter from Boccaccio. Rossi belonged to the Iacoppi branch of the Rossi of Oltrarno, and he lived among the *popolo* of Santa Felicita in the *gonfalone* del Nicchio, in the Santo Spirito quarter – exactly where Boccaccio lived during his time in Florence. He was born around the turn of the century; in the *Consolatoria*, which was most likely concluded in spring 1362,[2] Boccaccio describes him as "close to old age, portly and heavy" (§57), a man who had to struggle against his declining years (§92).

The Rossi of Oltrarno, devoted Guelfs, were a large clan (*consorteria*) of patrician extraction, and many of their members had been invested with knighthood

1 A summary of the letter may be found at the end of this chapter.

2 For the date of the *Consolatoria*, see P.G. Ricci 1959.

(*cavalierato*).[3] From 1176 the family wielded considerable influence among the ruling class that governed Florence. The family possessed lands and castles in the territories of Siena and Volterra (Ciabani 1998, 244), as well as towers and houses in Florence situated near the church of Santa Felicita or massed near the Ponte Vecchio, which the strategic location of their properties allowed the family to control. The importance of the Rossi holdings in the city can be inferred from their surroundings.[4]

Stoldo de' Beringhieri di Iacopo de' Rossi was the glorious progenitor of the family lineage to which Pino belonged: Friar Pietro da Verona (later called Saint Peter Martyr) gave him command of the Catholic contingent in the struggle against the Cathar heretics in Florence, a struggle in which the Catholics emerged as victors in 1244. This event brought the Rossi enormous prestige, and to commemorate it, they erected a column in front of the church of Santa Felicita. Within the church, the family had its own chapel to the right of the altar – the most prominent position – dedicated to Saint Catherine of Alexandria, later sold to the Barducci family in 1376.[5] When Boccaccio was alive, the abbess of Santa Felicita was Costanza de' Rossi, the daughter of Fornaino, whose family were Boccaccio's neighbours in Certaldo, as we know from his testament. Also, according to the chronicler Giovanni Villani, Stoldo de' Rossi made a name for himself fighting next to Charles of Anjou, future king of Sicily, against Manfred in the battle of Benevento in 1266 – he was the bearer of the pope's banner, which he placed in the highest part of the conquered castle. For his service in this battle he was awarded the right to include symbols of the Anjou court (the so-called *cap d'Anjou*) in his family coat of arms, which were an indisputable marker of Guelf faith. When Pino's son Giovanni become *popolano* in 1378, he chose to change his last name to de' Stoldi, thus claiming a direct link back to the illustrious Stoldo.[6]

The family was honoured by the Florentine Commune at various times. For services rendered to the Commune of Florence by Pino di Stoldo de' Rossi (our Pino's grandfather) and his brothers Coppo and Liscio, on 2 April 1311, the city councils decided to make their children, Giovanni di Pino, Stoldo di Coppo, and Bandino di Liscio, *cavalieri del Popolo* (knights of the people). The ceremony was led by Messer Diego della Ratta (*marescalco* of King Robert Angiou), one of the protagonists in *Decameron* VI.3 – the tale of Monna Nonna, cousin of Alessio Rinucci.[7]

---

3 For a short version of the life of Pino de' Rossi, see Filosa 2017; a more detailed one is in Filosa 2018; see also the prosopographic table in the appendix.

4 See chapter 1, n. 3.

5 See Fiorelli Malesci 1986, esp. 159–62, 294, doc. 35; Richa 1972, vol. 9, 322–35.

6 On 10 November 1378, just before the Ciompi Riot, Giovanni changed his last name from de' Rossi to de' Stoldi (*Delizie* 1770–89, vol. 14, 266).

7 For the knighthood ceremony, see Salvemini 1896, 102–3, doc. 5.

These honours increased the house's fame and were considered an indisputable sign of "greatness" (*grandigia*). This and the reputation of their power – and violent behaviour – led to their inclusion in the catalogue of *magnati*. In fact, the de' Rossi family was among the most denounced family in Florence. Because of their *grandigia*, they were excluded from Florentine political offices after the Ordinances of Justice of 1295, which aimed to eliminate magnates from political power; everyone considered a magnate was excluded from government offices and could not even enter the Palace of the Priors (Palazzo Vecchio). Nonetheless, magnates still covered other important roles as representatives of the Florentine Republic, such as ambassadors, and *podestà* in other cities, and took on critical military responsibilities. The Rossi family, for example, served as *podestà* in other communes several times; between 1250 and 1350, "the house that far surpassed the others was that of the Rossi d'Oltrarno, who, with 109 elections won, covered on its own more than 7% of the total posts recorded (as well as 8.6% of those beyond the borders of the State of Florence)" (Raveggi 2000, 623–4).

Pino de' Rossi epitomized the knights of Oltrarno. He married twice: Monna Lisa,[8] still alive in 1345 but probably dead of the plague in 1348; and Monna Giovanna di Bandino da Lisca, who is recorded as his wife at least before 1351.[9] Monna Giovanna was sister to the *condottiero* Giovanni di Bandino da Lisca, at the service of Cangrande II della Scala, Lord of Verona, and was related to Andrea di Tello da Lisca, who eventually joined Pino in exile.[10] With these women he had several children, of whom we know Giovanni,[11] Agnolo,[12] Betto, Maddalena,[13] and Lisa, who in 1363 was married to one of the Rossi of Pistoia, and then afterward to Jacopo de' Pulci.[14]

On 23 September 1325,[15] Pino de' Rossi was included among the front-line horsemen (*feditori a cavallo*) in the war of Altopascio against Castruccio Castracani, along with many other members of his family and of the Bardi, Frescobaldi, and Gianfigliazzi families, and Boccaccio's consolatory letter may be referring to this

8 Monna Lisa, whose lineage is unknown, is recorded as "wife of Messer Pino de' Rossi of the people of Santa Felicita" in the *Prammatica* 2013, 272, no. 1828.

9 BNCF, *Magl.* XXVI 142, f. 288; ASFi, *Spogli Ancisa*, LL 284 and 566; P.G. Ricci 1959, 32, n. 4.

10 On the da Lisca family, see Varanini 2002. On Giovanna di Bandino da Lisca, see ASFi, *Arte del Cambio* 62, np, and M. Villani 1995, 3.101–2.

11 This is the Giovanni de' Rossi who changed his last name to de' Stoldi in 1378.

12 In ASFi, *Notarile Antecosimiano* S. 212 (Agostini Muzzi 1978, 679), Agnolo di ser Pino is mentioned as the owner of some land bordering land owned by Boccaccio: it's possible that this Agnolo is Pino de' Rossi's son.

13 Maddalena is registered after her mother, Lisa, as "daughter of Messer Pino de' Rossi of the aforementioned people" in the *Prammatica* 2013, 273, no. 1829.

14 ASFi, *Spogli Ancisa*, NN 180; P.G. Ricci 1985, 139, n. 3. On the second marriage, see Tripodi 2011, 197, n. 30.

15 For references to archival documents and sources on Pino de' Rossi's life, see appendix.

event when he writes: "on behalf of whom [Florence] you and your ancestors have engaged not only your money but also your persons in order to save Her" ("per la quale [Firenze] li vostri maggiori e voi, acciò che salva fosse, non solamente l'avere, ma ancora le persone avete poste"; *Consolatoria* §9). The first evidence of Pino's political career is his appointment as *podestà* in Faenza in 1337 and in Volterra in 1341. It is likely that when he was in Volterra he arranged the marriage of his sister Bandecca with Paolo Belforti, known as Bocchino, eldest son and heir of Ottaviano Belforti, who became the "tyrant of Volterra" and was also among the councillors of Walter of Brienne during his *signoria* over Florence (G. Villani 1990–1, 13.8). The *signoria* of the Belforti family in Volterra lasted from 1340 to 1361, alongside Ottaviano and then Bocchino, who was deposed and executed in piazza dei Priori in Volterra on 31 October 1361, with the support of the Florentine government ten months after the failed coup of December 1360.[16]

Under Walter of Brienne on 6 March 1343, Pino – along with the jurist Paolo di Neri Bordoni – performed the function of peacemaker in the pacts drawn up between Florence, Lucca, and Pisa. On 8 September, Walter of Brienne, invoked by the Commune of Florence in May–June 1342 and supported by the patriciate class, assumed the title of *signore di Firenze* with an appointment for life and absolute power, thus establishing what has gone down in history as "the tyranny of the Duke of Athens." As soon as he failed to meet the expectations of the magnates who had called and supported him, they felt betrayed and "used as whores," as Giovanni Villani phrased it ("puttaneggiava"; 1990–1, 13.8). The discontent was widespread, and all Florence conspired against him and expelled him on the feast of Saint Anne, 26 July 1343. This final conspiracy against the duke was preceded by three failed conspiracies, the first of which was organized by Angelo Acciaiuoli with other members of the Bardi and Frescobaldi families, and also with Pino de' Rossi and his brother Salvestrino. As soon as the Duke of Athens was banished from the city for good, a committee of fourteen men was created, led by Bishop Angelo Acciaiuoli, the cousin of the future *gran seneschal* of the Kingdom of Naples, Niccolo' Acciaiuoli. One of the fourteen was Pino de' Rossi; others included Ridolfo de' Bardi, uncle of Luca di Feo Ugolini; and Simone Peruzzi, the husband of the Lisa Buondelmonti who appears in Boccaccio's *Contento quasi ne' pensier d'amore*. The drafter of the deed that created the committee was the jurist Forese Rabatta, who is recalled in the *Decameron* (*Dec.* VI.5).[17] This administration was

16 On his lordship in Volterra and on Bandecca de' Rossi – a woman defined by a contemporary (Raimondo Tabonati) as "not a woman but a pillar of strength in every adversity" – see Tripodi 2011. As well as his brother Pino de' Rossi, Bandecca also had a notable correspondent; in her case, Saint Catherine of Siena, who wrote to her after her exile and the death of her sixteen-year-old son (see Caterina da Siena 1939, letter 68: "A Madonna Benedetta, donna che fu di misser Bocchino de' Belforti," "To the Blessed Lady who was wife of Messer Bocchino de' Belforti").

17 For the names of the fourteen men, see chapter 1, n. 50.

superseded in turn by the "popular government," which lasted from 1343 to 1348. The Rossi requested "as a bloc" to be admitted to the *popolani*[18] in this new political arrangement, but their request was denied. Pino de' Rossi therefore no longer had a say in running the city affairs; he was even targeted by the popular government, along with other magnates of Oltrarno. In December 1343, two Rossi were exiled (with members of other families such as Bardi, Frescobaldi, Donati, Pazzi, and Cavicciuli [G. Villani 1990–1, 13.44]), and in May 1345 Pino's properties, previously given to his father for merit by the Commune, were confiscated "against all appropriate reasoning" ("contro ogni debita ragione"; G. Villani 1990–1, 13.44).

After the plague, in 1349, Pino de' Rossi returned to the political stage: in March and April 1349 he held the position of captain of the Guelf Party – "an association with institutional functions recognized by the statutes of the Commune, in which many prominent houses of the city were included, even though none of them managed to emerge as a consistent leader" (Mazzoni 2010, 9). In the same year, he served as ambassador to King Charles IV of Bohemia, as *podestà* of Faenza, and as a member of the executive board that began the war against the Ubaldini clan (1349–50). In this last function, Pino de' Rossi urged the Commune of Florence to take up arms against the Ubaldini in a "wise and cautious" manner.[19] There were others involved in this war who were related to Pino de' Rossi and Giovanni Boccaccio: Francesco Benini (recalled in the *Consolatoria*) was on the same executive board;[20] Jacopo di Donato Acciaiuoli (another cousin of Niccolò Acciaiuoli) and Niccolò di Bartolo del Buono (dedicatee of the *Comedia delle ninfe fiorentine*, executed for his role in the plot of 1360) were involved with military provisions; Francesco Bruni, the well-known correspondent of Petrarch and friend to Boccaccio, was notary of the Chamber of the Commune and drew up acts related to war financing; and Francesco Nelli was chamberlain of the Chamber of the Commune in the same period.[21] Velluti recorded that Giovanni di Conte and Salvestro di Alamanno, both of the Medici family (Velluti 1914, 210), were involved in the Ubaldini war in Scarperia; for their military valour they were knighted by the Florentine Commune (Salvemini 1896, 112, doc. 32).

---

18 Klapisch-Zuber (1988, 1214) writes: "While the Rossi who had requested their admission as a bloc obtained nothing for their cause, many other 'houses and offshoots of magnati' were welcomed on two conditions, that they withhold aid and solidarity, in particular in vendettas, from relatives who had stayed magnates." From this we can infer the desire to keep the Rossi away from political power and marginalize them as much as possible.

19 ASFi, *CP* 1, f. 4; see Caferro 2015, 48, n. 38.

20 Caferro writes: "Francesco del Benino likewise demanded an attack and played a leading role in the actual prosecution of the war. According to balie 6 [fol. 9r], Francesco organized supplies for the army in the field, a task that involved making the actual purchases for the city" (2015, 48). On Francesco del Benino in the *Consolatoria a Pino de' Rossi*, see P.G. Ricci 1959, esp. 29–32.

21 There was another Francesco Nelli, and it is not clear which one might have been involved. For all these details, see Caferro 2015, esp. 48–9.

In November 1350, Pino was elected among the eighteen of the *balìa*, an office created to oppose the Visconti's expansionism (ASFi, *balie* 10, f. 1r; Regnicoli 2021a, 243). In 1351, he was a member of the committee in charge of overturning the convictions of Florentine citizens who had been banished and were currently residing in Pistoia and who had courageously favoured reconquering Pistoia on behalf of Florence; among these, Francesco Benini's name stands out. In May 1352, Pino was ambassador to King Charles IV of Bohemia for a second time, along with the jurist Tommaso Corsini, Gherardo Buondelmonti, Filippo Megalotti, and Uguccione Ricci, the leader of the liberal Ricci faction. Matteo Villani states:

> Because the ambassadors included the most prominent leaders of a city faction, once they left, many citizens feared that they posed a danger for the commune and the public freedom of the Florentines, being ambassadors in contact with the emperor for a long period and under his advice. For this reason, in the commune there was much debate about limiting their time with the emperor and constraining them with specific rules.
>
> (E partiti loro, molti cittadini … perocchè tra gli ambasciatori erano i più reputati caporali di cittadina setta, temettono, che essendo costoro al continuo con l'imperadore, e di suo consiglio, che pericolo si commettesse contro al comune e pubblica libertà de' cittadini, e però si mosse questione di limitare il loro tempo, e strignerli con certe leggi, e di questo fu gara e lunga tira nel nostro comune.) (1995, 3.13)

The language Villani uses implies that Pino de' Rossi belonged to the Ricci faction, which is extremely important information: the Florentine citizens were suspicious of a possible alliance between this faction and the emperor (implying that the Ricci group were suspected of being Ghibellines).

Not much evidence survives on the life of Pino de' Rossi in the 1350s, except that he held the office of *podestà* in Perugia in 1357. The next time he appears in documents it is as one of the conspirators of 1360. After the plot, we know that Pino was in exile with his wife, Giovanna di Bandino da Lisca (described by Boccaccio as "another Hypsicratea"; *Consolatoria* §114), his relative Andrea di Tello da Lisca, and Luca di Feo Ugolini. For the first ten months, they stayed in Volterra,[22]

22 Pino had been *podestà* of Volterra in 1341, and his sister was married to Bocchino Belforti, lord of the city. In the *duomo* of Volterra, there is a funerary inscription addressed to Giovanni di Pino de' Rossi (father of Pino and Bandecca), who had been captain in Volterra in 1309 – "in eternal peace lies … Iannes d. Pini de Rubeis" – bearing the date 1331 (Leoncini 1869, 34). Giovanni Villani tells us that Giovanni di Pino de' Rossi "died at Avignon in Provence, serving as ambassador of the Commune to Pope John on important affairs" ("morì apo Vignone in Proenza, essendo ambasciadore del comune al papa Giovanni per gran cose"; 1990–1, 13.44), so apparently his descendants transported his body to Volterra.

but when Bocchino Belforti was deposed and beheaded on 10 October 1361,[23] the city was not a secure place anymore: the Commune of Volterra had "entered the league of the lofty signoria of Florence" ("intrò in lega con l'excelsa signoria di Firenze"), as we know from the *Cronichetta* of Volterra (Tabarrini 1846, 317). The conspirators were forced to flee again, possibly to Padua.[24] In some sense, the exile of Pino de' Rossi began at the moment of his flight from Volterra. This had been a city where he could still feel at home, surrounded by friends, relatives, and properties. Only after abandoning this refuge in late 1361 could he feel truly "exiled." If the date of Boccaccio's consolatory letter is spring 1362, as seems likely, it is not that distant from the moment in which Pino de' Rossi "left home," as opposed to the year and a half from his leaving of Florence that has been commonly considered up to now.

Boccaccio's Letter: A Manifesto on Innocence

The *Consolatoria a Pino de' Rossi* has been mostly analysed as literature; specifically, as a consolatory text – indeed, one of the earliest examples of this genre in Italian literature (Chiecchi 2005). But if we take into consideration the historical context in which it was written, and the parties involved, the letter can clearly also be studied as a historical document. There are many questions that literary critics and biographers of Boccaccio have not raised, such as why Boccaccio felt a need to console Pino de' Rossi if he did not at least sympathize with the motivations behind the coup. Given that Boccaccio wrote this letter to Pino de' Rossi, and by extension to Andrea di Tello da Lisca and Luca di Feo Ugolini, we can presume that he knew where to send the letter and how to address it. In other words, Boccaccio very likely knew exactly where his friends were in exile. Boccaccio was clear in the letter that he wanted to help them in some way: if he was unable to help his companions in any concrete manner, he could at least try to comfort them with words – "you know the limits of what I can do, nevertheless I support you as much as I am able" (*Consolatoria* §169). The need to be discreet about the historical context is evident in every page of the letter, from the opening sentence onward. Boccaccio often used periphrasis and circumlocution when referring to individuals and circumstances; for example, often avoiding naming names, such as that of Francesco Benini.

---

23 The capital sentence for Bocchino Belforti was issued by Migliore Guadagni, one of the champions of the Guelf Party. For details on the *signoria* of Volterra as a "tyranny," see the first part of the article by Fabbri (2011). For Migliore Guadagni, see R. Zaccaria 2003.

24 Padua was the refuge of other conspirators: Pazzino di Apardo Donati and his brother, Manno, who were at the court of Francesco Carrara the Elder. Bandecca de' Rossi, Pino's sister, moved to Padua as well for a period: see Tripodi 2011, 200; and doc. 29 in *Lettere e altre carte* 2010, 76–7, for Bandecca's memories of her stay.

The opening sentences of the *Consolatoria* read as follows:

> [1] Messer Pino, waiting for the right moment to do anything is, I think, not only useful but also necessary. [2] Who is so out of his mind that he would consider useful consoling a miserable mother who sees her son's corpse in front of her? [3] The physician is hardly wise who prescribes a purgative, medicine before the disease has fully developed, even less so, he who in harvesting seeks the fruit, before the plant is just starting to produce flowers. [4] That is why, although I reflected a lot until today, I did not write to you: it would have been useless, because the recency of your misfortune closed the ears of your mind not only to my consolations but also to everyone else's.
>
> ([1] Io stimo, messer Pino, che non sia solamente utile ma necessario l'aspettare tempo debito ad ogni cosa. [2] Chi è sì fuori di sé, che non conosca invano darsi conforti alla misera madre, mentre ella davanti da sé il corpo vede del morto figliuolo? [3] E quello medico è poco savio, che, innanzi che 'l malore sia maturo, si affatica di porvi la medicina che 'l purghi; e vie meno è quegli che delle biade cerca di prendere frutto, allora che la materia a producere i fiori è disposta. [4] Le quali cose mentre meco medesimo ho ragguardate, insino a questo dì, sì come da cosa ancora non fruttuosa, di scrivervi mi sono astenuto, avvisando nella novità del vostro infortunio, non che a' miei conforti, ma a quelli di qualunque altro voi avere chiusi gli orecchi dell'intelletto.)

The first words Boccaccio writes concern the timing of the composition: "waiting for the right moment to do anything is, I think, not only useful but also necessary." Boccaccio proceeds to give examples to illustrate and amplify his point: one cannot console anyone before they are ready to be consoled; a consolation has a defined time frame; a certain amount of time must pass between the traumatic event and the opportunity for a *consolatio*. This argument corresponds exactly, from a rhetorical and literary point of view, to the time to be silent (*tempus tacendi*) and the time to speak (*tempus loquendi*) tropes of the consolatory genre: "The *tempus tacendi* of the writing in turn corresponds to an established if not unambiguous consolatory strategy, which prescribes prudent procrastination for the therapeutic intervention" (Chiecchi 2005, 267).[25] Rhetorically, it is an

---

25 Ecclesiastes 3:7 speaks of "a time to keep silence, and a time to speak," a phrase echoed and amplified by Dante in his *Convivio*, which Chiecchi believes Boccaccio must have read: a *tempus tacendi* and a *tempus dicendi* (*Conv.* IV 2, 5). Chiecchi argues (2005, 277–8) that the entire rhetorical structure of the consolatory letter would appear indebted to Dante: "Drawing from the *Convivio*, Boccaccio could reproduce Dante's considerations on the driving need for a man stained with infamy to restore his own honor (*Conv.* I 4, 10), on wealth and poverty (*Conv.* I

appropriate beginning, one that reflects the contemporary discursive techniques of the genre, and introduces what will turn out to be specific topic of the letter: the consoling of Pino de' Rossi. We can read the opening sentences also in terms of their material, contingent status as a text. A *consolatoria* is above all a letter and thus in need of being sent. The recipient in this case is a real person who was prosecuted for trying to overturn the regime in late 1360. If we resituate the letter in its historical context, it seems obvious that Boccaccio had to wait "for the right moment" to send it: it was not only useful but also necessary, otherwise the risks would have been enormous. It was necessary to let some time pass after those notorious events, because if Boccaccio had sent the letter too soon, he could have jeopardized his friend's hiding place and life if the letter had been intercepted by the wrong hands. Some time had to pass until tensions had been dispelled, not only for Pino but also and especially for the outside world.

It is no accident that just over a year had passed since the tragic events that had driven the addressee into exile; the letter has been dated by Pier Giorgio Ricci to some time between July 1361 and October 1362 – but this could be narrowed down to spring/summer 1362 (Chiecchi 2005, 265–7; P.G. Ricci 1959, 21–6). In the spring of 1362 Pino would truly be feeling that he was in exile, far from his own lands in the Volterra area, where other relatives also held property. In Volterra, he could still feel as if he was "with his family."[26] Boccaccio's reasons for not writing immediately after Pino's conviction in December 1360 were rhetorical, historical, and practical; but after Bocchino Belforti's execution and after Pino's flight from Volterra, these considerations were not so compelling. For these reasons, we may shift the letter's date post quem up to 10 October 1361, the day of Bocchino Belforti's execution. In that case, the interval of a few months between Pino's exile from Volterra and Boccaccio's beginning of the consolatory letter would respect the rhetorical requirement of the *tempus tacendi*, and the execution would provide Boccaccio the occasion to break his year-long silence towards his friend.

As Giorgio Padoan correctly notes, at the same time that Boccaccio was composing this work, Pino de' Rossi continued to apply political pressure wherever he could and reorganize those who had stayed loyal to him and his house, hoping to obtain the repeal of his sentence and his return to Florence; he was eventually successful, returning in 1363. Padoan suggests that Boccaccio wrote the *Consolatoria* to secure some benefits for himself, should Pino in fact return, and

---

11–13), on old age in need of rest (*Conv.* IV 23–28); he furthermore found a repository of illustrious examples of moral integrity and victims of injustice (*Conv.* IV 5), which he expands in his letter by using further erudite sources at his disposal." For further influences of Dante, see again Chiecchi 2005, 284.

26 San Giusto monastery in Volterra, where Pino and other conspirators found refuge, lies next to Boccaccio's property in Pulicciano (Agostini Muzzi 1978, 675).

was using this letter to demonstrate that he had remained "faithful" to him (Padoan 1998, 273–4). Although the suggestion is certainly provocative and interesting – tailored to the practical needs of Boccaccio, who had sentenced himself to exile in Certaldo – it is nonetheless true that Pino de' Rossi too could have benefited from the circulation of the letter.

It is worth recalling that this letter, which has gone down in history as the *Consolatoria a Pino de' Rossi*, analysed and transmitted as a literary text, was first and foremost an actual letter, addressed to a real person and written by a real person, despite its undoubtedly formal rhetorical character. It was generated as a response, as we can infer from the fact that the text seems to respond to complaints from a letter by Pino de' Rossi, no longer extant: the suddenness of the exile decree; his grief at losing his birth city and being far from his friends and family; the humiliation of living in poverty after his estate had been confiscated, combined with his advanced age; his inability to take care of his family, especially his wife and children; and the disgrace that accompanies the title of "infamous." Boccaccio's topics, however much enriched by the philosophy of Seneca and an ample supply of examples, are based on specific historical circumstances. Indeed, the letter did not bear the title commonly known to us, *Consolatoria*, but simply named an addressee: "To Pino de' Rossi." Of course the first and immediately evident intention of the letter is to console: "Now, forced by necessity, your shoulders bent, I believe you are ready to receive any suggestion and any comfort that would help you in tolerating the labour" ("Ora, costringendovi la forza della necessità, chinati gli omeri, disposto credo vi siate a sostenere e a ricevere ogni consiglio e ogni conforto che sostegno vi possa dare alla fatica"; §5). But soon another intention emerges: to proclaim not once but repeatedly the innocence of his friend. In this sense, the letter can also be read as an argument, meant for public view, for the innocence of Pino de' Rossi. In fact, it would have made no sense for Boccaccio to convince Pino of his own innocence. Furthermore, the letter was written in the vernacular, which would enable a wider circulation among those who could not read Latin. This would not have been necessary for Pino de' Rossi, who was surely versatile in Latin and knowledgable in jurisprudence, as his repeated positions as *podestà* must have required.[27] Unfortunately, the whereabouts of Boccaccio's autograph of the letter is unknown, but this letter was copied an enormous number of times – well over one hundred.[28] Although only three copies go back to the

27 Raveggi (2000, 623–4) records that the Rossi were among the families with the greatest number of posts as *podestà* outside Florence; their children were surely educated well. The Rossi women were instructed in Latin; Bandecca owned two books of "grammar" (that is, Latin grammar) (Tripodi 2011, 191).

28 See the list of manuscripts compiled in the "nota al testo" in Chiecchi's 1998 edition of the *Consolatoria* in the Mondadori collection of Boccaccio's works (655–63), which is based on Vittore Branca's survey (1958, 47–51; 1991, 32). Finally, Tanturli 2013.

fourteenth century,[29] and most were penned during the fifteenth, it remains undeniable that the circulation of this letter – which was presumably private – has been remarkable. The modality of transmission is unknown to us, but I believe we may assume that Pino de' Rossi himself had every interest in publicizing Boccaccio's text, advertising his own innocence to Florentines and non-Florentines alike. If Boccaccio through this letter demonstrated his "faithfulness" to Pino's cause, Pino, for his part, could use it to demonstrate his innocence – an authoritative document of more than 8,200 words, embellished with every rhetorical figure to promote his own appeal for clemency, to be disseminated among the right circles. Another end, too, would be achieved if Boccaccio could succeed in demonstrating Pino de' Rossi's innocence – the letter would also show that Boccaccio had always stood on the right side.

The argument for Pino's innocence begins immediately after the introductory paragraphs, where Fortune is blamed for the dramatic events: "the onslaught of Fortune" (§8), "hostile Fortune" (§10), and "adverse Fortune" (§167). Fortune alone is responsible for the unhappy events that Pino de' Rossi is now suffering. The Fortune to which Boccaccio refers is the one he describes in his *De casibus virorum illustrium* (*The Downfall of Illustrious Men*), which he had just finished writing. The author Boccaccio, a character in the *De casibus*, comes face to face with this "minister of human affairs" ("rerum ministra mortalium Fortuna") at the beginning of book 6 in a chapter titled "Dialogue between Fortune and the author" ("Collocutio Fortune et auctoris"). He is frightened but also fascinated by this horrifying monster ("horridum monstrum"), and he addresses her with the following words: "I know well, distinguished spinner of events, that it is because of your tireless initiative that nothing in the world is stable" ("Novi equidem, rerum revolutrix egregia, indefessa molitione tua nil stabile esse sub sole"). Now, in this different context, it is Pino de' Rossi whose life has been turned upside down by Fortune. The question follows, what can be done? How does one confront adverse fortune? This is exactly what Boccaccio wishes to explain to Pino – and, in turn, to the other conspirators in exile, Andrea di Tello da Lisca and Luca di Feo Ugolini. The only weapon at his disposal against this "minister" of human affairs, who has the power to bring down those high up and elevate those down below (according to the characteristic medieval figure of Fortune's wheel) is virtue: "where there is virtue, Fortune has no part" ("Ubi virtus est, ibi nulla partes esse Fortuna"; *De cas.* V.iv.1).[30]

29 The three copies are the Strozzi codex 180 (fragmentary) in the Biblioteca Medicea Laurenziana, and two in the Bodleian Library, Codex Canoniciano it. 87 and it. 89.

30 "Boccaccio's *De casibus virorum illustrium* (The Downfall of Illustrious Men) is a nine-book encyclopedic history devoted to a review in a moralizing vein of Fortune's impact on both individual and collective destinies" (Marchesi 2013, 245).

To achieve virtuous behaviour against the adversity in which hostile Fortune has placed Pino and the other conspirators (and Giovanni himself), Boccaccio proposes practical strategies rooted in the stoic philosophy adapted by Seneca. Naturally, bad luck consists not only in exile but also in poverty, old age, shame, isolation, and concern for one's family. Boccaccio suggests philosophical remedies to deal with these problems, illustrating his argument with multiple examples of illustrious men and women from past and present, who bore exile and adverse conditions with austerity: these are examples from which to derive inspiration and emulation. In this way, Boccaccio tries to create an image of de' Rossi (and himself) as sage, virtuous, and still able to improve and confront the trials and tribulations of life stoically. This is Boccaccio's intention as a friend to Pino: to provide tools for facing the difficulties of his misfortune and to suggest solutions. Boccaccio's comfort is constructive, entirely designed to outline a *forma mentis*, a state of mind, capable of looking at the real world with wisdom. We thus have a kind of portrait: a sage who finds both inspiration and strength in ancient philosophy.

Against Judges: Milex Ludovicus Juvenalis Cardolis de Narnia

Pino de' Rossi had more difficulties than just exile and poverty to contend with; he had an implacable enemy in Ludovico Giovenale di Cardoli from Narni – "Milex Ludovicus Juvenal Cardolis de Narnia." It was Cardoli, the *podestà* who issued the capital sentence, who had bestowed "such an abominable title" ("titolo così abbominevole"; §115) on Pino, as most egregious traitor of the Republic of Florence. According to the sentence, Pino de' Rossi and his comrades were convicted of high treason and sentenced to death and to the further disgrace of permanent defamatory pictures, painted in the Bargello as a warning to the citizens of Florence. Hence Pino de' Rossi's desperation, represented by Boccaccio in the form of direct speech, the only occurrence in the letter:

> Perhaps you may say: "This is not enough for me: the nearby nations are falling into the same mistake as the citizens, and popular opinion, however false, takes the place of truth; that is how I who am blameless, in addition to injury do bear disgrace as well."
>
> (Direte forse: "Questo non basta a me: le nazioni circumvicine in uno medesimo errore co' cittadini sono e la generale oppinione, quantunque falsa sia, in luogo di verità è avuta; e così adiviene che io senza colpa, oltre al danno ho la vergogna.") (§136)

Disgrace and dishonour were intolerable for Pino de' Rossi. Or at least that is how Boccaccio posits it. Pino was certainly devastated by the fact that the city for which he and his forefathers had fought – "on behalf of which you and your ancestors have engaged not only your money but your persons in order to save her" ("per la quale il vostri maggiori e voi, acciò che salva fosse, non solamente l'avere, ma ancora le persone avete poste"; §9) – had absolutely no desire to listen to his declarations of innocence. His fellow-citizens were the epitome of ingratitude:

> It has then been said to me by some friend that whatever burden the present adversity could have inflicted or is inflicting on you, it would have been easy for you to bear it, if your own fellow-citizens, whom you consider ungrateful in refusing to listen to any explanation of yours, however true and legitimate, had not expelled you with such an abominable title as they did, taking it into consideration.
>
> (Èmmi adunque per alcuno amico stato detto che ogni gravezza, che la presente avversità avesse potuto porgere o porgesse, vi sarebbe leggera a comportare, dove i vostri cittadini, li quali in non avere voluto alcuna vostra scusa, quantunque vera e legittima stata sia, ricevere, ingrati reputate, non v'avessono, considerandolo, con titolo così abbominevole cacciato, come fatto hanno.) (§115)

It seems that some of Pino's friends confided to Boccaccio that this "abominable title" – not just the label but the material and permanent form of it in the defamatory paintings – was the hardest penalty for Pino to accept. Boccaccio tried to demonstrate Pino's innocence, but he was not the only person in Pino's circle to do so. The chroniclers Matteo Villani and Marchionne di Coppo Stefani tried the same, altering facts to bolster their cases. For example, Matteo Villani writes explicitly that the conspirators, except those executed, "were condemned in the person by the *podestà* without vituperative title" ("furono per lo potestà senza vituperevole titolo condannati nella persona"; M. Villani 1995, 10.25); we know this is not true from the capital sentence extant in the State Archive of Florence.[31] Stefani omitted Pino's name from the list of conspirators, together with that of Friar Cristofano di Nuccio, inserting instead those of Attaviano di Tuccio Brunelleschi and Tommaso degli Adimari.

From the moment he was exiled, Pino de' Rossi tried in every way to prove his own "true and legitimate" innocence, but – thus far – Florentines had refused to listen to his explanations. Boccaccio writes in this regard:

> You have written not just once but many times both to private citizens and to your magistrates, and with as much gravity as you were able, you tried to demonstrate your own innocence; not only that, but also you offered up your own head, as long as you come to stand trial for this accusation before a just judge, not an impetuous one.

31 Matteo Villani leaves the names of Luca di Feo Ugolini and Andrea di Tello da Lisca at the end of his list of the conspirators, adding the following sentence: "People thought these last two guiltless but dragged into the investigation" ("questi ultimi due per molti si tenne che senza colpa fossono messi nel ballo"; 1995, 10.25).

(Scritto avete non una volta, ma molte e a private persone e a' vostri maestrati e con quella gravità che per voi s'è potuta la maggiore, ingegnato vi siete di mostrare la vostra innocenzia; e oltra a ciò avete la vostra testa offerta, dove del fallo appostovi dinanzi a giusto giudice, non ad impetuoso, siate convenuto.) (§134)

Rossi had written to the highest offices of Florentine government: priors, captains of the Guelf Party, the gonfalonier of justice[32] – actions that certainly would reap benefits as time went by, seeing that his conviction was eventually overturned in 1363. Not only that, he accepts the risk of a new trial by a judge who acts with more deliberation than Ludovico Giovenale di Cardoli. The swiftness of the conviction is mentioned at the beginning of the letter: "Although you are both strong and wise amid such a great onslaught of Fortune, like that which all of a sudden hit you" ("Quantunque voi e forte e savio siate, in sì grande impeto della Fortuna, come quello è quasi in un momento vi giunse addosso"; §8). The "impetuous" judge, the "onslaught of Fortune," the event that "suddenly" befell Pino de' Rossi without a doubt correspond to what actually happened: the conviction took place in a summary trial on the same day the plot was discovered, 30 December 1360. The only two executions, of Niccolò di Bartolo del Buono and Domenico di Donato Bandini, also took place that day.[33] Exile and confiscation of goods were included in the same sentencing, further specified on 22 January 1361.[34] The *podestà* did not waste any time.

Boccaccio ends the letter with a concluding and summarizing clause: "I believe that in this we can hear: the judges were stubborn and the defendant is innocent" ("in questo credo si possa sentire: i giudici essere ostinati e l'accusato innocente"; §135).

Boccaccio's opinion of judges is generally not positive. Already in the *Decameron*, there are several judges to criticize. A typical example comes in *Decameron* VIII.5, in which a trick is played on a magistrate from the Marches, which, the narrator declares, is known for "mean-spirited men who lead such wretched, beggarly lives that everything they do looks like chicanery" ("li quali generalmente sono uomini di povero cuore e di via tanto strema e tanto misera, che altro non pare ogni lor

32 In the State Archive of Florence, I was able to consult the inventories of letters and responses of the Republic, but those written between 26 June 1359 and 3 September 1364 have been lost.

33 In ASFi, *AP* 1525, ff. 57–58r, f. 58r, blank spaces indicate breaks in the day between the salient points of the capital sentence: one comes after the deposition of Niccolò di Bartolo del Buono and Domenico di Donato Bandini and the measures taken by the *podestà*, and the second, after the execution of the prisoners.

34 The exile from Florence and the confiscation of goods are stated clearly in ASFi, *AP* 1525, ff. 57r–58r. On 22 January 1361, the Commune of Florence decided that the confiscated goods of the conspirators had to be transferred to the Guelf Party, which was creditor of the Florentine Republic. See ASFi, *PR* 48, ff. 125r–126v, copied from the Guelf side in *CPGNR* 5, ff. 17r–19r, and published in Cortese 1964, 16.

fatto che una pidocchieria"; *Dec.* VIII.5.4).[35] Another example is in *Decameron* III.7, Tedaldo's tale:

> What he had heard set Tedaldo musing on the number and variety of the errors to which men are liable: as, first, how his brothers had mourned and interred a stranger in his stead, and then charged an innocent man upon false suspicion, and by false witness brought him into imminent peril of death: from which he passed to ponder the blind severity of laws and magistrates, who from misguided zeal to elicit the truth not unfrequently become ruthless, and, adjudging that which is false, forfeit the title which they claim of ministers of God and justice, and do but execute the mandates of iniquity and the Evil One.
>
> (Tedaldo, udito questo, cominciò a riguardare quanti e quali fossero gli errori che potevano cadere nelle menti degli uomini, prima pensando a' fratelli che uno strano avevano pianto e sepellito in luogo di lui, e appresso lo innocente per falsa suspizione accusato, e con testimoni non veri averlo condotto a dover morire, e oltre a ciò la cieca severità delle leggi e de' rettori, li quali assai volte, quasi solliciti investigatori del vero, incrudelendo fanno il falso provare, e sé ministri dicono della giustizia e di Dio, dove sono della iniquità e del diavolo esecutori.) (*Dec.* III.7.16)

If the considerations delivered by Tedaldo are specific to this novella, the opinion expressed by the authorial voice in the *De mulieribus claris*, composed just after the plot, could be applied without modification to the case of the twelve conspirators.

> There is nothing more dangerous than a corrupt judge. Whenever he follows the dictates of his wicked mind, every due procedure of justice is necessarily perverted, the power of the laws is broken, virtuous activity is weakened, curbs on crime are loosened: in short, the public welfare as a whole is dragged down to ruin …
>
> Alas! How often are we mortals endangered by a plague like this! How often are we brought undeservedly to ruin and held in dishonourable restraint, persecuted, robbed, and killed at the bidding of such wickedness!
>
> (Nil pernitiosius iniquo iudice. Hic quotiens sceleste mentis imperium sequitur, omnis iuris ordo pervertatur necesse est, legum potestas solvatur, virtutis enervetur opus, sceleri laxentur habene et breviter omne bonum publicum in ruinam trahatur …
>
> Hei michi! Quotiens hac periclitamur peste mortales, quotiens in exitium immeriti trahimur et turpi premimur iugo, agimur spoliamur et occidimur, urgente nequitia!) (*De mul.* 58.12–14)

35 For this novella, see Robins and Faibisoff 2020, which puts Boccaccio's relationship with the judges in historical context.

A judge who drags innocent people into ruin, disgraces and persecutes them, confiscates their goods, and kills them – this is precisely what Ludovico Giovenale Cardoli had done to the conspirators. This invective against the judges, emitted by the authorial voice of the *De mulieribus*, uses repeated first-person plural verb endings: "periclitamur," "trahimur," "premimur," "agimur spoliamur et occidimur." It is an inclusive verb form, ambiguous in its reach. Certainly, it refers to all people engaged in the legal process. It would also include Boccaccio, forced into self-exile in Certaldo. At the very least, it implies his empathy towards those who suffer the strong hand of injustice.

But in fact, who was the *podestà* Ludovico Giovenale Cardoli from Narni? What was his self-interest in "persecuting" Giovanni's friends? Was he truly corrupt? We cannot know with certainty, but we can make some preliminary judgments, based on two historical facts.

Since the thirteenth century, the *podestà* of the city-state had wielded significant executive power, as they combined various public offices: "command of the army, presidency of the Councils, political representation, judicial functions, oversight of public works, etc." (Zorzi 2000, 641–2). Over time and especially halfway through the fourteenth century, however, their functions had been reduced to those of a judiciary nature (Zorzi 2000, 640–1): justice, both civil and penal, was administered by the *podestà*. The office of *podestà* in Florence was assigned exclusively to "foreign" officers, especially from Milan, Rome, Gubbio, and other urban centres from the Apennine strip through Tuscany, Umbria, and the Marches (in other words the Papal State). The term of office was six months; an outgoing *podestà* could be reelected to a following second term, but after this he was barred from the office for the next ten years. Among his powers was the right to detain in his palace, for a day or longer, those accused of capital crimes; the practice of torture was permitted to obtain a confession, but only in the case of particularly heinous crimes where suspicions were well founded. The *podestà* would move to Florence with his "comitiva et familia" – "comitiva" here refers to the group of people who help the *podestà* in military or civic matters, and "familia" indicates the group of judiciary officers consisting of at least eight judges and eight notaries, two for each quarter of Florence.

In our case, Pino de' Rossi and his co-conspirators had been convicted by the *podestà* along with a panel of judges, as confirmed by the document of the capital sentence – as was common for judiciary cases that were more serious or involved residents of different quarters.[36] Nevertheless, as emerges from the act and the

36 "The convictions and sentences were delivered, given, and legally promulgated by the aforementioned lord *podestà* as he sat before the tribunal at the seat of justice in said room and in said council, and in the same place in accordance with his mandate to the cry of a herald and the sound of a bell before those who had been duly assembled, in accordance with the agreement, presence, and desire of those said to be his judges" (ASFi, *AP* 1525, ff. 57–58r; transcription of the original in the appendix).

inventories of the *Atti del Podestà del Comune di Firenze* (vol. 1, 1343–65), among the measures that the Commune issued during the *podestà* term of Ludovico di Cardoli da Narni, crucial to this case, is the one issued on December 1360: due to a severe illness, the judges Giovanni di Pietro da Amelia (deputy to the quarters of Santo Spirito and Santa Croce) and Niccolò da Montone (deputy to the quarter of San Giovanni) were absent; standing in for them were the *podestà* and other judges for the entire month of December. Note that all the conspirators were originally from these quarters, Santo Spirito, Santa Croce, and San Giovanni. Everything was thus in order on paper, but the fact remains that the judge assigned to Santo Spirito, Pino de' Rossi's quarter, was absent: "Giovanni da Amelia, his judge and assistant, was absent because of the impediment of his illness" ("absente ... domino Iohanne de Amelia ipsius iudice et collaterale propter impedimentum sue infermitatis"). This is the first crucial point about the trial. Would Pino de' Rossi have been judged more fairly by Giovanni di Pietro da Amelia? Perhaps. In any event, it seems he would have done better not to have Ludovico di Cardoli da Narni, a judge who Boccaccio implies in his letter is "impetuous" and unjust.

A second significant point is that in three years (between November 1359 and May 1362), during the spring semester, no fewer than three *podestà* came from Narni, and two were from the same family:

- 8 November 1359–8 May 1360: Ciappus Tanti de Ciappis de Narnia
- 21 November 1360–21 May 1361: Ludovicus Juvenalis Cardoli de Narnia
- 16 November 1361–16 May 1362: Clericus sive Quiricus Cardoli de Narnia

The *podestà*'s term of office was six months, so that the elected *podestà* would not have time to join a faction and thus would provide a more reliable guarantee of neutrality in public affairs. Furthermore, the *podestà* were chosen from different cities, in the hope that this would bolster their neutrality. The fact that three *podestà* came from the same city, and two from the same family within such a brief time span, is very rare, and it certainly transgressed the axiom of absolute neutrality for which the legislation regarding this office strove.

The Corruption of the Florentines

According to Boccaccio, writing in the *Consolataria*, Pino de' Rossi was "blameless" ("senza colpa"; §136), yet prosecuted, exiled, and disgraced. The guilty ones are "hostile Fortune," the "corrupt judges," and especially the ungrateful citizens of Florence. People have forgotten that Pino de' Rossi was "greatly prized by the citizens" ("in grandissimo pregio appo i cittadini"; §24); that on behalf of the city he and his ancestors risked their wealth and their lives ("l'avere, ma ancora le persone"; §9) – an idea repeated twice more in the letter. The city should be more lenient towards him, argues Boccaccio. Pino de' Rossi fought at the battle of

Altopascio (1325). He hunted down the "tyrant of Florence," the Duke of Athens (1343). His ancestors fought against the heretics and in the battle of Benevento next to King Charles I of Anjou (1266).

> Now, although any good citizen puts not only his possessions but also his blood and his life in the service of the common good in order to lift up his city, he still expects that, in any situation in which he is at fault (since even the most virtuous men can sin), he should find more mercy and leniency than others because of his past services; if he does not obtain it, the punishment is much more severe than if his past services had not deserved this benefit. And if there are any such citizens in our city, who thanks to their own deeds or those of their ancestors deserved pardon, I think that you are one of those; therefore, since you have not found it, as I see that you have not found it, I am hardly surprised that you grieve.
>
> (Per ciò che, quantunque ciascuno buono cittadino non solamente le sue cose, ma ancora il suo sangue e la vita per lo comune bene, per la esaltazione della sua città, disponga, ha ancora rispetto che, dove in alcuna cosa gli venisse fallito (per ciò che eziandio i più virtuosi peccano), egli per lo suo bene adoperare passato debba trovare alcuna misericordia e remissione innanzi agli altri; la quale non trovando, gli è molto più grave la pena che se meritato il beneficio non avesse. E se alcuni cittadini nella nostra città sono, che per sua opera o de' suoi passati grazia meritasse, voi estimo che siate di quelli; per che, non trovandola come veggio che trovata non l'avete, meno mi meraviglio che vi dolete.) (§117–18)

Nevertheless, according to Boccaccio, Pino de' Rossi should not be surprised that he obtained no mercy from his fellow citizens, because Florence is a circle of Hell, where appreciation and justice do not exist. Florentines are described as belonging to one of two categories: on one side are those who are fickle and ungrateful, namely, those who hold "the governing reins of our Republic" (§34); on the other stands the mob deceived by the former (in which we can make out the common people). Boccaccio's lengthy description of Florence is rhetorically and lexically close to Dante's description of Hell in the *Inferno*, starting with the image of the city as a melting pot for multiple deadly sins (envy, pride, anger, avarice, luxury). The sin he singles out as the worst, one he would like to attack (like a predatory animal), is avarice:[37] "with a fierce bite I will pierce the

37 Boccaccio on wealth: "This is that for which miserable mortals struggle more than they need to; for this they squabble, they fight, and they eternally taint their reputation" ("Queste sono quelle per le quali i miseri mortali più che loro non bisogna s'affaticano, per queste s'azzuffano, per queste combattono, per queste la loro fama in eterno vituperano"; *Consolatoria* §65).

abominable avarice of Florence" ("con agro morso trafiggerò l'abominevole avarizia de' Fiorentini"; §70).

> [34] Moreover, if to someone whose spirit is not at all fastidious a place is unpleasant to see or live in, one of those places is our town, if we consider the people and the habits to whom, as a consequence of stupidity or evil, have been given the governing reins of our Republic. [35] I will not blame those who came to this from Capalle, Ciliciaule, Sugame, and Viminiccio, who gave up the trowel and the plough and were raised to our highest magistracy. This because the farmer Serranus became a Roman consul, whose hands accustomed to breaking up tough clumps of dirt could sustain the consular spear; Gaius Marius, who was raised by his father in the army, responsible for making stakes for erecting tents, conquered Africa and brought Jugurtha to Rome in chains. [36] In order not to talk any longer about these men (and I am not surprised, given that God rains upon mortals different souls no less than different fortunes), and even coming to talk about anyone considered the most ancient citizen, those [who hold the governing reins of our Republic], occupied by insatiable envy or inflated by intolerable pride or enflamed by inappropriate anger, mind not the common good but their own, and by doing so have placed and still place our town in misery and in slavery, which now we call ours and of which we will be sorry to be named, if the way of governing does not change. [37] Furthermore, there we see (and, because it would be embarrassing, I do not want to talk about the gluttons, the whoremongers, the drunkards, and others affected by similar vices) many dishonest men, some with the most solemn behaviour, some by saying no words, some scratching with their feet the floor mosaics as they walk, and many more pretending to be worried or to be the sweetest and most caring fathers and protectors of the common good (yet, if you look more carefully, they would not even know how many fingers they have on their hands, even though they are masters in stealing, when they have the occasion, and they are great masters of haggling), these are the people who are considered good by those deceived. These are the people who, at the helm of such a great ship, steer our Republic that labours in such a difficult storm.
>
> ([34] Senza che, se alcuno luogo a spirito punto schivo fu noioso a vedere o ad abitarvi, la nostra città mi pare uno di quelli, se a coloro riguarderemo e a' loro costumi, nelle mani de' quali, per la sciocchezza o malvagità di coloro che avuto l'hanno a fare, le redine del governo della nostra repubblica date sono. [35] Io non biasimerò l'essere a ciò venuto chi da Capalle e quale da Ciliciaule e alcuni da Sugame o da Viminiccio, tolti dalla cazzuola e dall'aratro e sublimati al nostro maestrato maggiore, per ciò che Serano, dal seminare menato al consolato di Roma, ottimamente colle mani use a rompere le dure zolle della terra, Caio Mario, col padre cresciuto dietro agli eserciti faccendo i piuoli a' quali si legano le tende, soggiogata, l'Africa, catenato ne menò a Roma Iugurta. [36] E acciò che io più di questi non conti (per ciò che non me ne meraviglio, pensando che simili alle fortune piovano da Dio gli animi ne' mortali),

> eziandio a quali noi vogliamo più originali cittadini divegnendo, quelli o per avere d'insaziabile invidia gli animi occupati o di superbia intollerabile enfiati o d'ira non convenevole accesi, non l'avere pubblico ma il proprio procurando, hanno in miseria tirata e tirano in servitudine la città, la quale ora diciamo nostra e della quale, se modo non si muta, ancora ci dorrà essere chiamati. [37] E oltre a ciò vi veggiamo (acciò ch'io taccia per meno vergogna di noi i ghiottoni, i puttanieri, i tavernieri e gli altri di simili lordure) disonesti uomini assai, i quali, quale con contenenza gravissima, quale con non dire mai parole e chi con l'andare grattando i piedi sulle dipinture e molti colo anfanare e mostrarsi tenerissimi padri e protettori del comune bene (i quali tutti, ricercando, non si troverà sappiano annoverare quante dita abbiano nelle mani, come che del rubare, quando gatto loro vegna e del barattare sieno maestri sovrani), essendo buoni uomini riputati dagl'ingannati, al timone di sì gran legno, in tante tempeste faticato, sono posti.)

The gluttons and whoremongers and others and the great ship that labours in a storm are images derived from Dante (see *Inf.* 11.58–60 and *Purg.* 6.67–8). Boccaccio sees this rabble of greedy and hypocritical rulers at the helm of the Republic, reducing it to misery and slavery. In using the word "slavery" he implies that the rulers are "tyrants," and that Pino de' Rossi is one of their victims.

> You have heard and seen and experienced the words, deeds, methods, and unpleasantries of these men, however great and numerous and nauseating they are; therefore I will omit them, grieving if, having seen so much violence, injustice, dishonesty and trouble there, you still grieve at your own expulsion.
>
> (Le parole, le opere, i modi, le spiacevolezze di questi cotali, quante e quali elle sieno e come stomachevoli, e udite e vedute e provate l'avete; e perciò lascerò di narrarle, dolendomi se d'avere tante violenze, tante ingiurie, tante disonestà, tanto fastidio veduto, vi dolete di essere stato cacciato.) (§38)

But whom does Boccaccio blame? The "new people" who have migrated into the city and prospered there? Or others? Many scholars have drawn attention to this as an attack on the newcomers, but a more careful reading points to a different target. The "new people," coming from rural and barely urbanized places (Sugame, Viminiccio, Capalle, Ciliciaule, today in the province of Florence) and only recently elevated to the priorate (that is, eligible for the highest offices of the city), are not the target of his invective ("I will not blame those who came to this from …"). Boccaccio cites people from Roman history who had similarly humble origins. Furthermore, the next paragraph begins: "In order not to talk any longer about these men," as Boccaccio ends discussion of the "new people" – although without missing the opportunity to insert a comment on the nobility of the spirit: "I am not surprised given that God rains upon mortals different souls no less than different fortunes." This passage closely recalls the conclusion of the last novella of the *Decameron*, whose protagonist, Griselda, says: "Even in poor homes divine spirits rain down from the sky" (*Dec.* X.10.68).[38] Although this section of the letter is among those most compromised in the manuscript tradition and has been much discussed,[39] I remain certain that Boccaccio wanted to exempt the new people from the charge of misrule, redirecting it towards those who actually wielded power.[40] After all, accusing the new people would have been highly counterproductive: he was new himself. His father, Boccaccio di Chellino da Certaldo, had moved to Florence in 1313–14; he had lived for a long time in Naples, working for the Florentine Bardi Company, returning to Oltrarno only around 1339 (Zafarana 1968).

With his defence of those who migrate from country to city, Boccaccio enters a thorny discussion in an intelligent and innovative manner. The topic was salient after the plague of 1348, with the mass immigration from the countryside to replenish the population of Florence, and after 1358, with the souring of anti-Ghibelline legislation that created a climate of fear in the city. For example, as Vieri Mazzoni (2010, 104) points out, an anonymous writer of the period found that the increased presence of recruits – immigrants as well as city residents – in the medium-ranked and minor corporations and in the Commune offices, together with the temporary eclipse of the oligarchs, was causally connected to the strengthening of anti-Ghibelline legislation. Another anonymous fourteenth-century writer, source of the chronicle of Domenico di Leonardo Buoninsegni, had likewise noted the link between the phenomena.[41] Boccaccio is not swayed by the anti-immigrant political rhetoric, but like Matteo Villani he points a finger at "certain great and powerful men" who

> with solemn and cunning malice and with the criminal intention of becoming little tyrants, deliberated together on what they should and could arrange through a just and honest law in order to make a new election; they overturned it, in the name of the Guelf Party, claiming that the Ghibellines were in control of the magistracies,

38 Velli (1991) traces the interrogation of Dioneo at *Dec.* X.10.68 to Seneca: "Potest ex casa vir magnus exire" ("A great man can come from a humble hut"; *Ep. ad Luc.* 66).

39 A survey of the manuscript copies of the *Consolatoria* is in Branca 1958 and 1991. On the manuscript tradition, see Nicola Bruscoli (in the *nota al testo* in G. Boccaccio, *L'Ameto–Le lettere–Il Corbaccio*, 283–9); P.G. Ricci 1959; Giuseppe Chiecchi, in the *nota al testo* to the Mondadori edition, followed here (655–63); Padoan 2002, 153–60; and Tanturli 2013.

40 The same reading has been offered recently by James Hankins (2019, 11): "In the letter to Pino de' Rossi he explicitly refused to blame *gente nuova* exclusively for the political corruption of Florence (as one might have expected a member of the Rossi family to do), finding plenty to blame among the *originali cittadini.*"

41 For the sources, see Mazzoni 2010, app. 4, n. 3, f. 95v, 311–12, and 316–17, available from http://www.pacinieditore.it.

and that if the Guelfs did not react, they would soon lose their communal status and power … These men in agreement with one another did not serve the needs or the benefits of the Commune or of the party, but rather that goal I have already mentioned, so, they drew up a petition that basically contended that anyone from the city or countryside who was Ghibelline or not a true Guelf and who had held in the past or currently held any office of the Commune of Florence could be accused both openly and in secret, even concealing the name of the accuser.

(certi uomini grandi e potenti … con grave e sagace malizia, affine reo di venire tirannelli, s'avisarono insieme, e quello che·ssi dovea, e potea aconciare con ordine di buona legge e onesta al fare delli squittini, convertirono sotto il titolo della parte guelfa, dicendo che' Ghibellini occupavano li ufici, e che se i Guelfi no· riparassono a·cquesto, poteno pensare di perdere tosto stato e·lla franchigia del Comune … costoro tutti in concordia traendo non al bisogno, o al beneficio del Comune o della parte, ma a·cquello fine che già è detto, ordinarono una petizione, che in sustanza contenne che quale cittadino o contadino di Firenze, ghibellino o non vero guelfo, avesse avuto per adietro, o avesse per inanzi alcuno uficio del Comune di Firenze, potesse essere accusato palesemente e ocultamente, no·nominando eziandio l'acusatore.) (M. Villani 1995, 8.24)

For Boccaccio, the responsibility for the disarray of Florence does not rest on the newcomers but on those who have strengthened their own power. The latter had pointed their fingers at the men who had recently moved to the city and at some imaginary Ghibelline counteroffensive. From the 1350s onward, two family-led factions competed for political supremacy. On one side were the "Albizzeschi," also called "ducklings" ("paperini") for the kind of cap they wore, led by Piero di Filippo Albizzi, members and/or supporters of the old patricians, Guelf activists eager for the proscription of Ghibellines, hostile to the newcomers, and in favour of the pope since they had received benefits from the Church. On the other side were the "Ricciardi," led by Uguccione de' Ricci,[42] open to the *novi homines* who had moved to the city, opponents and victims of Guelf extremism, hostile to the privileges of the clergy, and fearful of the growing power of the state and Church.[43] Very possibly, Pino de' Rossi supported the latter side: in 1352, Uguccione, Pino, and others had travelled as ambassadors to the court of King (and future Emperor) Charles IV; Matteo Villani reports that "the ambassadors included the most prominent leaders of a city faction" ("tra gli ambasciatori erano i più reputati caporali di cittadina setta"; 1995, 3.13), implying the Ricci. Boccaccio's target is thus the faction of the oligarchic patriciate, who had taken control of the Guelf Party and

42 For Uguccione de' Ricci, see the entry by Mazzoni 2016.

43 Mazzoni 2010; Brucker 1962, esp. 159–93.

made it the stronghold of oligarchic Florentine ideas, after it had been the citadel of the magnates for half a century. Boccaccio in denouncing the oligarchs was supporting his friends in the Ricci faction, men such as Andrea di Tello da Lisca – wool seller from Via di Maggio, related by marriage to Pino de' Rossi and with him in exile – who had been subject to *ammonizione* as a Ghibelline or not a true Guelf, as had other members of the same conspiracy: Niccolò di Bartolo del Buono in 1358, Domenico Bandini in 1358, Umberto di Ubaldino degli Infangati in 1347.

At the time, only people who were Florentine citizens going back at least three generations, and who therefore had city documentation of being from a long-standing Guelf family, were able to defend themselves against the accusation of being "Ghibelline or not true Guelf"; newcomers, by contrast, could not produce this kind of proof. Boccaccio's appreciation of the nobility of soul over the nobility of blood in this context can be read as an ideological plea in support of the *novi homines*, among whom many of Boccaccio's friends and he himself belonged.[44]

Pino de' Rossi and Friends

Friendships, clans, and factions: in a context like that of the second half of the fourteenth century, these are the centre of political life. Boccaccio emphasizes the absolute value of friendship, of the "joining of souls," in the consolatory letter. According to him, these forces have the greatest power to defeat bad Fortune. References to friends recur throughout the letter. For example, in dealing with exile, the first and most poignant of Pino's misfortunes, Boccaccio affirms:

> And if we really want to call yours not a move, but exile, you should bear in mind that you are neither the first nor the only one, and that having companions in misery usually helps to lighten it ... [29] However, so that you may not believe that you alone have been injured by Fortune, and you may feast your eyes on something when the tedium of exile pricks you, I think it will be profitable to remind you of some others.
>
> (E se pure vogliamo il vostro non permutazione, ma esilio chiamare, vi dovete ricordare non essere primo né solo, e l'avere nelle miserie compagni suole essere grande alleggieramento di quelle ... [29] E però, acciò che solo non crediate nello esilio essere dalla Fortuna ingiuriato e abbiate in cui ficcare gli occhi quando la noia dello esilio vi pugne, estimo non senza frutto ricordarvene alquanti.) [30]

In the misery of exile, having some companions and friends at your side alleviates the sorrow. Indeed, we know that Luca di Feo Ugolini and Andrea di Tello da

---

44 On the topic of noble spirit versus noble blood, see chapter 7.

Lisca shared exile with Pino – Boccaccio himself writes at the end of his letter: "To Luca and Andrea, who I understand are there" ("A Luca e Andrea, li quali intendo che costà sono"; §176). The writer continues to comfort his reader, adding ten examples of great figures from the past who were sent into exile: Cadmus, King of Thebes; Sarca, King of the Molossians; Dionysius, tyrant of Syracuse; Syphax, the greatest king of Numidia; Perseus, King of Macedonia; Vitellius Caesar; Darius the Great; Olympias; Nero; and Marcus Aurelius. These examples are drawn from ancient history, but ten was also the number of conspirators still alive and in exile after the failed coup of 1360. It may be a coincidence, but it is a remarkable one.

An entire section focuses on the topic of friendship (§42–56). It starts:

> But it is time to move on: some may say that while in every part of the world the Sun rises, not everywhere are there dear friends, relatives, neighbours, with whom men are used to rejoicing amid prosperity and taking comfort amid misfortunes. I say that paying attention to friends is difficult, worrying about any other is a childish concern. However, since friendships are rarer than many may think, it should be valuable to have in a man's entire life at least one accident that enables him to distinguish true friends from the false ones … Therefore just like a touchstone shows true gold, an adversity shows a true friend. Fortune has thus in part shown you a way to discern that which you were never able to see beforehand: who was a friend to you, and who to your state.
>
> (Ma tempo è omai di procedere alquanto più oltre: diranno alcuni che, perché in ogni parte della terra si levi il sole, non in ogni parte i cari amici, i parenti, i vicini, coi quali e rallegrarsi nelle prosperità e nelle avversità condolersi gli uomini sogliono, trovarsi. Dico che degli amici è difficile cosa, degli altri è fanciullesca cosa il curarsi; ma per ciò che molto sono più rade l'amistà che molti non credono, non è da avere discaro avere almeno in tutta la vita dell'uomo uno accidente per lo quale li veri da' fittizi si conoscono … Adunque, come il paragone l'oro, così l'avversità mostra chi è amico. Havvi adunque la Fortuna in parte posto che discernere potete quello che ancora non poteste giammai vedere: chi era amico di voi e chi del vostro stato.) (§42–6)

Boccaccio cites "dear friends, relatives, neighbours." In this context, the reference to neighbours is particularly interesting. In fourteenth-century Florence, neighbourly connections were very strong. Although nonexistent in the eyes of law, neighbourliness was socially recognized by the town criers, who were obliged to give notice of their announcements "at the home, church, neighbourhood, and street" of those concerned; the neighbourhood "politically … functioned as an enlarged pool of electoral candidates and political clients both within and outside the individual parish and its patrons, identifying – in the case of Florence – with the gonfaloni of each quarter who organize the popular *militia*" (Porta Casucci 2015–16, 193). Pino de' Rossi, Luca di Feo Ugolini, Andrea di Tello da Lisca, and

Boccaccio were all neighbours. Boccaccio and de' Rossi both lived in the *gonfalone* del Nicchio in Florence, and in Certaldo the Boccaccio and de' Rossi families lived side by side.[45] Some neighbours were also related by marriage: for example, Andrea di Tello da Lisca and Pino de' Rossi were connected through Pino's wife, Giovanna, who belonged to the same family as da Lisca.

Boccaccio follows Seneca in his claims about the value of friendship,[46] when he says that a disaster such as exile and an unjust conviction may be welcome because in these moments one can discern true friends from false. In Pino de' Rossi's case, those who were truly friends are distinguished form those who were friendly only to his social status as a powerful magnate of Florence. Not incidentally, Boccaccio proves with this letter that he is a genuine friend: he does not hold back in the face of adversity, and he tries as much as he can to be close to his friend by comforting him and pleading his innocence.

A passage in praise of friendship appears towards the end of the letter:

> And in order to bring my words, reasoning, and consolations to a conclusion, at some point, I say that you must convince yourself that you are at home, for the world is everyone's universal city; and however many times you find what you need from Nature, then you should consider yourself rich, not poor, according to Nature; and you should value old age, as experienced in troubles and full of useful advice, as more precious than the excesses of youth; and especially in this case, without complaining about being overweight, consider its addition to venerable *gravitas*. And so, prepare your children to be your aides, once old age diminishes your strength; and think of your wife as your companion in all your tribulations, neither superfluous nor tedious, but instead useful. Be satisfied that your misfortune has equally enabled you to distinguish true friends from false, and to recognize how great is the ingratitude of your fellow-citizens [of Florence]; in which, not knowing it well, and maybe expecting too much from it, you might afterward have fallen into a more abominable peril than this one.
>
> (E acciò che ad una conclusione, quando che sia, vegnano le mie parole, gli argomenti e' conforti, dico che persuadere vi dovete voi essere in casa vostra, poiché universale città di tutti è il mondo; e quante volte l'opportune cose alla natura avere vi trovate, non povero, ma secondo natura ricco stimate; e la vecchiezza, sì come sperimentata

45 Boccaccio's will lists the house in Certaldo as adjacent to that of Fornaino d'Andrea di messere Benghi (de' Rossi), related by marriage to Pino. On the will, see Regnicoli 2014, as well as Porta Casucci 2015–16.

46 In the *Florilegio senecano*, a collection of excerpts mainly from the *Epistolae ad Lucilium* by Seneca, collected in his Zibaldone Magliabechiano, Boccaccio transcribes: "illa [paupertas] verso certosque amicos retinebit, discedet quisquis non te sed aliud sequebatur. Non est autem vel ob hoc unum amanda paupertas, quod a quibus ameris ostendet? O quando ille veniet dies quo nemo in honorem tuum mentiatur!" (Costantini 1974, 94).

negli affanni e piena d'utili consigli, avere più che la strabocchevole giovanezza cara; e massimamente in questo caso, senza rammaricarsi della corpulenzia, aggiungitrice a quella di gravità veneranda. E così i figliuoli apparecchiatevi per bastone, dove forze mancassero alla vecchiezza; e come compagno di tutte le fatiche la moglie, non superflua né noiosa, ma utile giudicate, contento che l'infortunio v'abbia parimente fatto conoscere i falsi amici da' veri e quanta sia la 'ngratitudine de' vostri cittadini; nella quale non conoscendola e forse troppo sperando, potreste per l'avvenire essere caduto in più abbominevole pericolo che questo.) (§152–3)

At the end, Boccaccio adds that he could "in all honesty put an end to his words now" ("assai onestamente far qui fine alle parole"; §154), but he wants to arm his friend with one more weapon: "good hope," one of the three theological virtues, especially the hope in God, whose mercy is limitless. After listing some examples drawn from history (Camillus, Alcibiades, Massinissa, Scipio), Boccaccio reports the adventures of an unnamed fellow citizen (§162–6). He is talking about Francesco di Benino of San Felice in Piazza, and thus of Oltrarno (as Pier Giorgio Ricci has identified). Benino was exiled from Florence for the assassination of Banchello di Ser Belcaro of San Frediano; his conviction was overturned when Pino de' Rossi was on the committee for his acquittal;[47] on 22 November 1351, he obtained reinstatement of his rights, once again belonging to the *popolani*, and in March and April 1352, he is among the priors, the highest magistracy in Florence.[48]

The Consolations of Giovanni Boccaccio

Boccaccio, in writing his consolatory letter, expresses an extraordinary empathy towards his friend. He tries in every way possible to underscore common traits between himself and his friend: starting from physical features (they are both old and overweight) and continuing with financial circumstances (both have become poor) and sociopolitical status (both are in exile after a political disappointment, even if Pino's exile is coerced and Giovanni's is voluntary). From a strictly rhetorical point of view, of course, the sharing of suffering is a necessary prerequisite for the efficacy of a letter of consolation, which may explain why Boccaccio portrays

47 P.G. Ricci 1959, 30; ASFi, *PR* 38, f. 206.

48 Boccaccio gives another contemporary example of success outside Florence, drawn from contemporary life: "Many of our citizens have received great fame among foreign nations rather than here among us" ("assai nostri cittadini sono già di troppo più splendida fama stati appo le nazioni strane che appo noi"; §28). He may have in mind men like Niccolò Acciaiuoli (a friend of both Pino and Boccaccio) – as Chiecchi suggests in a footnote to his edition – who then became grand seneschal of the kingdom of Naples.

his own condition in such detail.[49] In the letter's conclusion, Boccaccio describes his solitary life in almost bucolic terms, recalling to some extent Petrarch's *De vita solitaria*, possibly to encourage his friend to do the same:

> I ... returned to Certaldo and here I began to console my life with much less difficulty than I thought; I have already begun to enjoy the rough clothes and peasant's food ... In exchange for the sudden and continuous twists and turns of the citizens, I see fields, hills, trees, clothed in green leaves and different flowers; all produced by Nature with simplicity, while those produced by the citizens are all artificial acts. I hear the nightingales singing as well as the other birds with no less joy than the annoyance with which I would listen all day to the deceits and treachery of our fellow-citizens; and I can freely discuss with my little books in complete freedom, however many times I wish, with no distraction.
>
> (Io ... sono tornato a Certaldo e qui ho cominciato, con troppa meno difficultà che io non estimavo di potere, a confortare la mia vita; e comincianmi già i grossi panni a piacere e le contadine vivande ... In iscambio de' solleciti avvolgimenti e continui de' cittadini veggio campi, colli, arbori, delle verdi fronde e di vari fiori rivestiti; cose semplicemente dalla natura prodotte, dove i cittadini sono tutti atti fittizi. Odo cantare gli usignuoli e gli altri uccelli non con minore diletto che fusse già la noia d'udire tutto il dì gl'inganni e le dislealtà de' cittadini nostri; e con li miei libricciuoli, quante volte voglia me ne viene, senza alcuno impaccio posso liberamente ragionare.) (§171–3)

At the end, we may ask: in reality, what kind of friend was Boccaccio? Of course, he wants to be considered among the true friends. After the plot, he fulfilled the role of comforter; *De mulieribus claris* was composed for the purpose of "solatium amicorum," no less than the consolatory letter. When writing to Pino de' Rossi, he

49 In his *Morals* (*Expositio in beatum Iob seu Moralium libri*), Gregory the Great discusses the right times for consolation. The work was translated into the vernacular by Zanobi da Strada, a schoolmate of Boccaccio, who was a student of Giovanni da Strada, father of Zanobi; in his rendering, Gregory advises: "This is the right order for consolation; if we want to relieve someone afflicted with suffering, first we study how to tune our tears to his crying, for he who does not tune to another's suffering cannot console him from it[;] as soon as he detaches himself from the suffering of the afflicted, immediately he is less accepted; this is because he has separated himself from the other's mental condition. But first one must soften one's spirit so that it may reflect that of the afflicted and in corresponding sentiments come closer, and in this closeness draw the afflicted to oneself: for one cannot join iron with iron before both have become molten in fire: something hard can never draw alongside something soft unless it tempers its own hardness. And thus we cannot raise those who lie on the ground if we do not draw alongside them, for if we do not stoop to their level, we cannot otherwise lift them up" (Gregorio Magno 1877, vol. 1, 76).

states that he does all he can to console his friend: "You know the limits of what I can do, nevertheless I support you as much as I am able" (§169). He asks Pino de' Rossi, along with his two friends in exile, not to reject his efforts at comfort with the retort "A consoler has no headache":

> … nor do I want you to mention our own city's proverb:
> *A consoler has no headache*
> I am well aware that there is a great difference between comfort and action, and that one is very easy, the other is very difficult, but he who gives whatever he has cannot be accountable for more.
>
> (… né voglio che voi diciate il nostro cittadinesco proverbio:
> *A confortatore non duole capo.*
> Bene so che dal confortare all'operare ha grande distanza; e dove l'uno è molto agevole, l'altro è malagevole sommamente, ma chi dà quello ch'egli ha non è tenuto a più.) (§§167–8)

The ten conspirators who survived (including Pino de' Rossi, Luca di Feo Ugolini, and Andrea di Tello da Lisca) were condemned to exile and endured the confiscation of their property (30 December 1360). Their portraits were put on display along with those of the two who lost their heads as a warning to the people. If Pino de' Rossi and his comrades had been caught attempting to cross the borders of the city of Florence, they would have been beheaded. Therefore, the urban proverb that the exiles might cite against Boccaccio acquires further significance, more literal and painfully sarcastic. The "headache" he describes not only derives from the preoccupations of Pino's exile – and he still tries to comfort him as he identifies with his struggles – it also would entail a stronger, literal ache, entirely physical, if his head were to be cut off.

Even though Boccaccio repeatedly identifies with Pino de' Rossi in his consolatory letter, the fact remains that for the sender, exile is voluntary, but for the recipient, it is compulsory. It is easy to provide comfort, but any more direct action would have life-threatening consequences. In that case, why would Boccaccio want to retire to Certaldo in voluntary exile? Above all, why does he identify with Pino de' Rossi? I believe that his motivations are more than merely rhetorical. We can never know whether and to what extent Boccaccio was aware of the conspiracy, but there is no doubt that these events coincide, as Chiecchi (1979) writes, "with one of the darkest seasons of Boccaccio's biography."

Boccaccio also paid a price: suspension from public posts in Florence, self-exile and withdrawal to Certaldo, and perhaps the loss of independence and freedom of speech due to fear, caused by what happened to his own circle of friends. In consoling Pino de' Rossi, Boccaccio also consoles himself, trying to keep calm in adversity and portraying the choice as voluntary when in fact it was imposed by unhappy events. The rhetoric applied to the *Consolatoria* is the means by which he dignifies and sheds light on a dark reality. Boccaccio writes this letter to Rossi from the "lowness" of his circumstances, and from a "depressed" condition.[50]

The Questionable Innocence of Pino de' Rossi

Perhaps it was the surely considerable pressure that Pino de' Rossi put on the ruling class in Florence, perhaps it was the changed political climate (the tyrant of Volterra had been finally defeated, and the city had been fully annexed by Florence, since it posed no further danger) because the borders of Florence were more secure, and perhaps it was the dissemination of Boccaccio's *Consolatoria* that raised awareness among circles close to de' Rossi, but the fact is that Pino finally returned to Florence in 1363, according to the Florentine calendar (that is, some time between 25 March 1363 and 25 March 1364); there is documentation proving that he drew up a will there at that time. Among the seventeenth-century examinations (*spogli*) of Cosimo della Rena we find the following note: "1363 – m. Pino di m. Giovanni de' Rossi test. C 15–c. 146."[51] Pino's exile was over at this point, and, all things considered, his difficulties had not lasted very long. As Pier Giorgio Ricci writes: "The atmosphere in the Rossi house in 1363 had certainly changed since the period of conviction, flight, and exile," emphasizing how Pino's daughter, Lisa, was getting married to Matteo dei Rossi di Pistoia, from a rich family living in

50 Boccaccio twice mentions in the *Consolatoria* his "depressed state": "However much the lowness of my state and the depression of my condition may impair the trustworthiness and authority of my words" ("Quantunque la bassezza del mio stato e la depressa mia condizione tolgano molto di fede e di autorità alle mie parole"; §6); "And if my lowly and depressed name deserved a place among the excellent men mentioned above and others similar, I would say that it is for that reason that I left Florence and now stay in Certaldo, adding that if my poverty allowed it, I would go even further away, so that I would not be forced to hear about their evils, just as now I do not have to see them" ("E se 'l mio piccolo e depresso nome meritasse di essere tra gli eccellenti uomini detti di sopra e tra molti altri che feciono il simigliante nomato, io direi per quello medesimo avere Fiorenza lasciata e dimorare a Certaldo; aggiungendovi che, dove la mia povertà il patisse, tanto lontano me n'andrei, che come la loro iniquità non veggio, così udirle non potessi giammai"; §41).

51 The first reference to Pino de' Rossi's will (*testamento*) is in P.G. Ricci 1959, 32, n. 4; Ricci cites "Biblioteca Nazionale di Firenze, Spogli della Rena C 15 c 146." Cosimo della Rena's collections were subsequently merged in the *Magliabechiano* XXVI, so the reference in question is in BNCF, *Magl.* XXVI 230, f. 197v, which reads: "1363 – m. Pino di m. Giovanni de' Rossi test. C 15 c 146." Della Rena was most likely drawing his information from the archive of registers of contract duties (*registro delle gabelle*), which is the office that received tax on notarized documents. This archive was afterward destroyed, during one of the devastating "purges" of archives taking place throughout the eighteenth century. Cosimo della Rena was simply recording that Pino de' Rossi had written his will in 1363 ("test. C 15 c 146"), and that this notice had appeared on folio 146 of the register, bookmark C15.

the *gonfalone* of the Lion d'oro (San Giovanni quarter), and who had been raised to the priorate.[52] Pino died by 1366, when his heirs Betto and Angelo appear as "filii *olim* d. Pini d. Johannis de Rubeis (sons of the deceased Pino de' Rossi)."[53]

One final question: was Pino de' Rossi truly innocent? Was it really bad fortune that toppled him? Was he prosecuted unjustly by corrupt judges? There is no way we can know. From contemporary chronicles and documents at our disposal, Pino de' Rossi clearly did not have an entirely clean record (to put it in modern terms): he was a hothead. As a matter of fact, he took part in numerous conspiracies, as did the other co-conspirators: the Rossi family joined the Bardi conspiracy of 1340 and they assisted in the installation and coup of Walter of Brienne – Pino to some extent collaborated with him; but afterward, Pino also conspired against the same Walter of Brienne, once he realized that the latter was not acting in the interests of the magnates. Pino was one of the "fourteen good men" hoping to revive his political career in the city, and he managed to install some benefits (such as the remarkable shift in Florence from *sestieri* to *quartieri*). Last, there was the attempted coup of 1360, which targeted above all the despised Ordinances of Justice. These activities had a clear goal: returning power to the magnate class, more specifically to the Rossi and the magnates of Oltrarno. Thus, we can affirm that Pino de' Rossi was guilty of having conspired against the state of Florence, a state that was unstable, in constant change, where treason was only a matter of dates. Boccaccio stood with an "outlaw," whom he defended with paper, ink, and rhetorical expertise. He wrote his letter perhaps because he realized that the winds were changing and that by writing it he was catering to his own interests, perhaps out of sincere friendship, perhaps because he belonged to the same faction, or perhaps because, deep inside, Boccaccio approved of the same ideas as Pino de' Rossi.

Appendix: Summary of Boccaccio's *Consolatoria a Pino de' Rossi*

1–6[54]	*Incipit*: the date of composition. *Tempus tacendi* as opposed to *tempus loquendi*.
7–11	Purpose of the letter: strategies for dealing with adversity.
12–23	The true home for all human beings is the entire world; therefore "we must call that which we are doing not exile but rather exchange of one land for another, whether forced or voluntary."

52 See in this regard P.G. Ricci 1959, 24, referring to the Spogli dell'Ancisa NN 180 in the State Archive of Florence – available on request with the shelf mark *Manoscritti* 316.

53 This reference is also in Rena's collections: BNCF, *Magliabechiano* 133, f. 12.

54 The numbering of paragraphs here follows the edition of Giuseppe Chiecchi (1998), in *Tutte le opere di Giovanni Boccaccio*, gen. ed. Vittore Branca (Mondadori, 1964–98), published under the auspices of the Ente Nazionale Giovanni Boccaccio.

24–30 Virtue and virtuous people are welcome everywhere. In fact, virtuous people are often better appreciated outside their own land (examples: Coriolanus, Alcibiades, Hannibal, and even some Florentines).

31–3 Examples of illustrious men and women sent into exile: Cadmus, King of Thebes; Sarca, King of the Molossians; Dionysius, tyrant of Syracuse; Syphax, the great king of Numidia; Perseus, King of Macedonia; Vitellius Caesar; Darius and his golden chains; Olympias and her imprisonment; Nero and his flight; Marcus Aurelius and his hardship.

34–7 Invective against those holding the reins of government.

38–41 It is better to stand apart from their "unpleasantness." Examples of some who chose to leave their own city: Democritus, Scipio Africanus, Scipio Nasica, Boccaccio himself.

42–56 Friendship: the pain of being separated from friends, relatives, and neighbours. Examples of those who nevertheless used their misfortunes to distinguish true friends from false: Orestes, Pirithous, Euryalus. True friends are not to be found in physical company but rather in the soul. Thanks to the medium of letters, one can never be truly separated from one's friends.

57–78 Poverty: poverty takes little to appease, and it "trains our more sensitive virtues and makes light of our cunning." Examples: Scipio in Miturna, Cato in Spain, Aldobrandini d'Ottobuono. The Roman Empire was founded upon poverty: Quinctius Cincinnatus, Marcus Curtius, Fabricius Licinius.

79–91 How to resolve practical concerns for one's family.
Praise for the Golden Age.
Hardships build character in one's children. Examples: David, Mithridates.

92–102 Old age: "No tribulation can last long in old age," for desires are mitigated, spirits are tougher, adversity is more easily endured. Overweight? No need to run!
The joys of having a large number of sons, for they can avenge offences done to their fathers.

103–15 Marriage: a good, modest, and strong wife provides the highest form of comfort. Negative examples: Cleopatra, the rage of Jezebel, the fury of Tullia Servilia, the profligacy of Messalina, the arrogance of Cassandra, of Olympias, and of Agrippina. Positive examples: Hypsicratea, Sulpicia, the wives of Meni, Porcia, Julia wife of Pompey. And then Giovanna, the wife of Pino de' Rossi, a modern Hypsicratea.

115–29 The ingratitude of fellow-citizens. Examples: Theseus, Miltiades, Lycurgus, Scipio Africanus, Scipio Asiaticus.

130–51 The natural desire for fame, and the disgrace of infamy. Examples: Socrates, Scipio Africanus, Julius Caesar, Christ.

152–3	Summary of the letter.
154–66	One final weapon: hope in God, who is merciful. Example: Francesco del Benino.
167–77	Conclusion: discussion of the proverb *A confortatore non duole capo.* Description of Boccaccio in retirement in Certaldo.

7 The *Lives of Dante*

Finchè lo vollero i fati ho cantato i diritti della *Monarchia.*

(As long as the fates allowed, I sang the rights of *Monarchia.*)

– Bernardo di Canaccio Scannabecchi

Omnia nobis mala solitudo persuadet.

(Solitude prompts us to all kinds of evil.)

– Seneca, *Ad Luc.* 25.5

In *De mulieribus claris*, Boccaccio demonstrated how friends should behave in cases of conspiracy, and in his consolatory letter to Pino de' Rossi, he showed something of his views on political issues, including his openness towards the *gente nuova* of Florence. Boccaccio's political views are evident also in his *Life of Dante*, along with an important, correlated notion: the nobility of soul. Because Boccaccio produced three versions of *The Life*, we have an extraordinary opportunity to analyse how he tries to align himself not only with Petrarch's thoughts on Dante – a subject that has been well studied – but also with the faction of the Guelf Party that was the new political power in the city of Florence. The first version, written in the early 1350s, was designed as a monument to Dante; absent a monument of stone, he made one with words.[1] In the second version, written in the 1360, Boccaccio made some significant changes, in order to please his new readership in a changed city. A third version, with few differences, was drafted in the early 1370s.[2]

1 See especially Jason Houston, *Building a Monument to Dante* (2010); also, Eisner 2013.

2 For the dating of the three versions, see P.G. Ricci 1974 and Paolazzi 1983. The first version is an autograph, Toledo, Biblioteca Capitolar de Toledo, MS 104.6; the second, also an autograph,

The Life of Dante: First Version

In late March 1351, Giovanni Boccaccio made his way to Petrarch in Padua as an ambassador of Florence; his purpose was to announce the repeal of Petrarch's father's conviction and of the confiscation of his property and to offer Petrarch a chair at the University of Florence.[3] This was the second meeting between the two writers – the first encounter was in 1350 in Florence, when Petrarch was travelling for his jubilee voyage – and it sealed their friendship. It was the beginning of a warm relationship that lasted until their deaths; Petrarch was to write later of this friendship: "We may be separated in body but we are joined in spirit" ("seiuncti licet corpori, unum animo"; *Sen.* I 5). Boccaccio too wrote of this bond between the two men. In a letter of 1353 to "the most illustrious laureate Francesco Petrarca" he recollects their days together:[4]

> I think you remember, my excellent teacher, that three years have not yet passed since I came to you in Padua as the ambassador of our senate, and after I had completed my task, I stayed with you for a number of days, all of which we passed more or less in the same way. You found time for your studies and I, eager for your compositions, as you wrote them down I made copies. As the day dwindled into evening we would rise together and we would go into your garden, which was already adorned with flowers and foliage from the new spring. A third man would join us, a man of distinguished virtue, your friend Silvano, and as we sat and told stories together in turn, we would draw on into the night as much as was left of the day, in peaceful and praiseworthy leisure.
>
> (Credo memineris, preceptor optime, quod nondum tertius annus elapsus sit posquam senatus nostri nuntius Patavum ad te veni, et commissis expositis dies plusculos tecum egerim, quos fere omnes uno eodemque duximus modo. Tu sacris vacabas studiis, ego compositionum tuarum avidus ex illis scribens summebam copiam. Die autem in vesperam declinante a laboribus surgebamus unanimes, et in ortulum ibamus tuum iam ob novum ver frondibus atque floribus ornatum. Accedebat tertius vir

---

Vatican City, Biblioteca Apostolica Vaticana, Chigi MS L.V. 176; for the third, no autograph survives, but there are a number of Florentine copies (see P.G. Ricci's "Nota al testo," in *Tutte le opere*, vol. 3, 848–56). For the text of all three versions, see Boccaccio, *Trattatello in laude di Dante*, ed. P.G. Ricci, in *Tutte le opere*, vol. 3 (1974). For an English translation of the first version, see Boccaccio, *The Life of Dante*, trans. Vincenzo Zin Bollettino (1990), from which I quote. Unless otherwise indicated, all references are to section numbers, not page numbers. There are no English translations of the second and third versions of the *Trattatello*; translations of these are my own.

3 For the meeting in Milan between Boccaccio and Petrarch, see Branca 1976, 88–95; Velli 2005; for the historical context, Caferro 2013, 2015, and 2018a.

4 In this memory, Petrarch is doubled and is identified with a third person, Silvanus, Petrarch's pastoral nickname.

virtutis esimie, Silvanus, amicus tuus, et invicem sedentes atque confabulantes quantum diei supererat placido otio atque laudabili trahebamus in noctem.) (*Ep.* X.4–6)

At this meeting, one of the most significant in the history of Italian literature, amid so much "story-telling together," the friends initiated a discussion on the value of poetry and probably began a debate about Dante and his work. From an early age Boccaccio was an enthusiastic admirer of Dante, who in his eyes was "first guide and first light of [his] studies" ("primus studiorum dux et prima fax"), as we learn from Petrarch (*Fam.* 21.15), writing a few years later in 1359.[5] Boccaccio could not believe that the library of the "excellent teacher" Petrarch did not contain the works of Dante. For Petrarch – always worried about influences from other poets in that "anxiety of influence" so aptly described by Harold Bloom (1997) – Dante represented a danger, for he too, willingly or otherwise, could have become Dante's imitator ("vel invitus ac nesciens imitator"; *Fam.* 21.15, 11) – an imitator, that is, of a poet considered too "popular" in style ("popularis quidem quod ad stilum attinet"; *Fam.* 21.15, 1) for an "aristocratic" soul like Petrarch. Petrarch had never sought or wanted the *Divine Comedy* in his classical collection.[6]

To remedy this absence, probably between 1351 and 1352 Boccaccio put together as a gift to Petrarch a manuscript (the current Vatican Latino 3199) that contained the *Divine Comedy* and a poem of dedication, *Ytalie iam certus honos.*[7] In this poem, we first find an impetuous and assertive outburst on the greatness of Dante and his poetry. Boccaccio wants Petrarch to agree with his judgment: "That Dante – whom you praise and justly worship; whom Florence, mother of great poets, produced and honours with applause – will be the second after the other [Claudiano]" ("Erit alter ab illo / quem laudas meritoque colis, per secula, Dantes, / quem genuit grandis vatum Florentia mater / atque veretur ovans"; *Carmina*, V, 29–32). He concludes with a peroration that consists of five hortatory imperatives (*suscipe*, *perlege*, *iunge tuis*, *cole*, *comprova*: "take it up, read through it, join it to your own, worship it, approve it"). As Giuseppe Velli says:

It is definitely at first sight surprising to find such force and urgency in his message. But I believe that an explanation is close at hand. The force and urgency both

5 For this and other citations of *Familiares*, I follow the English translation by Aldo S. Bernardo; for the text in Latin, I follow *Le familiari*, ed. Vittorio Rossi and Umberto Bosco (1933–42). For Boccaccio's passion for Dante, see *Dante e Boccaccio: Lectura Dantis Scaligera, 2004–2005* (2006).

6 The absence of the *Divine Comedy* in Petrarch's library did not prevent Dante's words from entering Petrarch's works; moreover, as Marco Santagata says (in his 2001 edition of the *Canzoniere*), Dante "has been one of the teachers, to not say *the* teacher, of the vulgar Petrarch" ("è stato uno dei maestri, per non dire *il* maestro, del Petrarca volgare"; lxiv). On the influence of Dante on Petrarch, see also Santagata 1990, 79–91; Velli 1995, 60–73; Velli 2002 and 2007; and Barański and Cachey 2009.

7 For the occasion and the dating of *Ytalie iam certus honos*, see Massera 1927; Paparelli 1979; and the introduction to the *Carmina* by Velli (1998), Mondadori edition (386–91).

> reflect the stakes in question, which are undoubtedly high, namely the very career of Boccaccio, an ostentatiously "vernacular" writer from his *Filocolo* to his *Decameron.* His defence of Dante is a self-defence, even before the overbearing assertiveness of Petrarch. (*Carmina,* ed. Velli [1998], 390)

It is in this context that we must place the origin and composition of *The Life of Dante* by Boccaccio – commonly known in Italian as the *Trattatello in laude di Dante* ("Little Treatise in Praise of Dante"), as Boccaccio himself defines it in his *Expositions on Dante's Comedy.*[8]

The *Trattatello in laude di Dante* is the first extensive biography of a "modern" poet in the vernacular, one that would have a lasting influence in Italy on the genre of the literary *vita.*[9] It is also one of Boccaccio's first efforts in a form he came to master, especially through his Latin works *De casibus virorum illustrium* (*The Downfall of Illustrious Men*) and *De mulieribus claris* (*Famous Women*). Boccaccio wrote out the first two versions by hand (1351–5 and early 1360s); the third survives only in copies (probably early 1370s).

The first and longest version had a Latin title: *De origine, vita, studiis et moribus viri clarissimi Dantis Aligerii florentini, poete illustris, et de operibus compositis ab eodem* (*The origins, life, habits, and studies of the most illustrious poet Dante Alighieri of Florence, and the works he composed*). Boccaccio originally planned Dante's *vita* as an *accessus ad auctorem*[10] of a *liber Dantis* (Dante book) that would include the *Vita nuova*, the *Commedia* (including *argomenti*, or canto summaries in tercets, by Boccaccio), and fifteen canzoni.[11]

The Life of Dante reflects Boccaccio's intention to build a verbal monument to Dante, given that Florence – contrary to ancient custom – had not done anything for its extraordinary son, after sending him into exile:

> Although I, with my paltry powers, am not fully fitted for the task I am undertaking, I will try to do what the city, with its magnificent resources, has not done. I shall not express his honour with a statue or with splendid rites (a custom that is no longer among us, and for which my strength would not be sufficient), but with words – even though they may not be equal to this enormous task. I do have

8 "Because I have already written a brief treatise in praise of him, however, I shall refrain here from elaborating"; in the *Expositions on Dante's Comedy* (2009), ed. and trans. Papio, 44. In the *accessus* (introduction) to the *Expositions*, Boccaccio includes a brief life of Dante, recalling the *The Life of Dante* with this passage.

9 On this topic, see Bartuschat 2010.

10 For more details on the medieval form of *accessus ad auctorem*, "introductions to the author," see Minnis 1988.

11 Toledo, Biblioteca Capitolar, Toledo, Spain, MS 104.6, autograph.

plenty of these, and I shall use them so that other nations, whether in whole or in part, may not claim that his native land was totally ungrateful to a poet of his great stature.

(Come che io a tanta cosa non sia sufficiente, nondimeno secondo la mia picciola facoltà, quello che essa [città] dovea verso lui magnificamente fare, non avendolo fatto, m'ingegnerò di far io; non con istatua o con egregia sepoltura, delle quali è oggi appo noi spenta l'usanza, nè basterebbono a ciò le mie forze, ma con lettere povere a tanta impresa. Di questo ho, e di questo darò, acciò che igualmente, e in tutto e in parte, non si possa dire, fra le nazioni strane, verso contanto poeta la sua patria essere stata ingrata.) (*Trattatello*, red. 1, §8)

This monument consisted not only of *The Life of Dante* but also the whole Dante book, which created a canon in the manuscript tradition and rescued the fifteen songs for posterity.

The first version of *The Life of Dante* begins in a polemic vein against Florence, opening with a maxim from Solon (a recognized font of wisdom), that every republic needs to walk on two feet:

The right foot had to see that no act of wrongdoing would go unpunished, while the left foot had to reward every good deed. He added that, if either of these operations was hindered by vice or negligence or was less than well carried out, a republic that functioned in this manner would go lame; and if, through some catastrophe, it should be deficient in both operations, Solon would have to consider it in all certainty to be unable to stand on its feet.

([Solone] … affermava essere il destro [piede] il non lasciare alcuno difetto commesso impunito, e il sinistro ogni ben fatto remunerare; aggiugnendo che, qualunque delle due cose già dette per vizio o per negligenza si sottraeva, o meno che bene si servava, senza niuno dubbio quella repubblica, che 'l faceva, convenire andare sciancata: e se per isciagura si peccasse in ambedue, quasi certissimo avea, quella non potere stare in alcun modo.) (*Trattatello*, red. 1, §1)

With this opening, Boccaccio begins a vehement attack on Florence, not only for having exiled Dante but also for being a culturally insensitive city. As the son of a merchant enlightened and driven to poetry by the *Divine Comedy*, he gives due tribute to the poet who was his inspiration through this work on Dante's life. By rehabilitating Dante, in effect Boccaccio returns the Muses to Florence. He defends literary culture itself and, by extolling Dante's vernacular poetry, affirms the status of Italian as a literary language. Indeed, the first version of *The Life of Dante* includes two great digressions: one is the invective against Florence, which gives the work a political dimension;

the other is his statement on the nature and origins of poetry. These sections may appear at first sight unconnected, but they share a single objective: the defence and glorification of vernacular poetry and the character of the poet, Dante specifically.

After its polemical opening, the work largely follows the life of Dante: his ancestors and parents (red. 1, §§11–16); his birth (accompanied by a premonitory dream of his mother) and childhood devoted to studies (red. 1, §§17–27); his love for Beatrice (red. 1, §§28–38); his grief upon Beatrice's death, and his ensuing marriage – accompanied by an invective against marriage (red. 1, §§39–59);[12] his political career and exile (red. 1, §§60–85); his last years in Ravenna, his death and funeral, and the epitaph by Giovanni del Virgilio (red. 1, §§86–91); a second invective against Florence (red. 1, §§92–110); Dante's physical appearance, habits, and character (red. 1, §§111–26); the digression on poetry (red. 1, §§127–62); the qualities and flaws of Dante (red. 1, §§163–74); his literary works (red. 1, §§175–204); an interpretation of his mother's premonitory dream, and an epilogue (red. 1, §§205–28).[13]

Self-Censorship in the Second Version

After sending Petrarch the first version of *The Life of Dante*, Boccaccio revised the text in the 1360s, making several cuts. The reason he created this second version might be inferred from a letter written by Petrarch. In 1359, a few months after his third meeting with Boccaccio (this time in Milan), Petrarch wrote *Familiares* 21.15. It was a response to what Petrarch calls his friend's "apologetic epistle" ("Excusatoria … epystola"; *Fam.* 21.15.4), no longer extant and written after the latter's return to Florence. In the lost letter, Boccaccio apparently apologized to Petrarch for having excessively extolled Dante, as we know from the beginning of *Familiares* 21.15. As Carlo Paolazzi writes (1983, 183):

> Petrarch's letter refers to a clearly defined "corpus" of praise, equally available for the two epistolary interlocutors [very likely the *Trattatello*], whose author Boccaccio, fearful of having praised Dante at the indirect expense of Petrarch, submits to the latter's judgment, begging him to examine and to evaluate the work, while Petrarch

12 Antimarriage invectives such as the *Adversus Jovinianum* by Saint Jerome and the *Dissuasio Valerii ad Rufinum* by Walter Map, copied into the *Zibaldone Laurenziano*, try to establish the incompatibility between marriage and intellectual life, a topic further developed in the *Corbaccio*.

13 *The Life of Dante* contains scant personal data. In his *Expositions on Dante's Comedy*, Boccaccio makes it clear that his aim is principally to magnify the character of the poet and of poetry, even at the expense of truth. Modern biographies of Dante show Boccaccio's chronology to be dubious; see Mazzotta 1979; and more recently Santagata 2016.

deflects any suspicion of jealousy by approving the praise of Dante, encouraging Boccaccio to polish and to publish it.[14]

Familiares 21.15 is crucial to the history of *The Life of Dante* because of its connection with cuts and corrections made to the second version of the work. This time the title is vernacular: *La origine, vita, costumi e studii del chiarissimo poeta Dante Alighieri di Firenze, e dell'opere composte da lui* (*On the origin, life, habits, and studies of the most famous poet Dante Alighieri of Florence, and the works composed by him*). This second redaction is commonly called the *Compendio*, as it is shorter than the previous one, but it is a definite rewriting, with greater sobriety.

The main differences are as follows: much of the invective against Florence has been deleted, along with the tone of resentment; Boccaccio also dramatically reduces his praise of Dante, and the narrative is tighter, free of digressions; even the theme of poetry has been retouched – in the first version, poetry is identified with theology; in the second it is only "similar" ("simigliante di quella"; red. 2, §91). Overall, there is no doubt that many cuts were aimed at tempering enthusiasm for Dante to please Petrarch – and probably to placate others, as we will see.[15]

Boccaccio, indisputably, made these cuts and changes in response to Petrarch's *Familiares* letter 21.15, but I would like to underscore how some of these changes might also be motivated by the political issues I described earlier in this book. In Boccaccio's work of revision, "we cannot guess everything" ("tutto non si può indovinare"), as Michele Barbi states (1913, 419), but there are still leads that can be traced and followed. For example, the fact that the first of two invectives against Florence is gone,[16] and the second has been abbreviated, might be explained by

14 Paolazzi shows how, conversely, the *Trattatello* influences some passages of *Familiares* 21.15. Scholars, from Ugo Foscolo on, have written extensively on *Familiares* 21.15. Foscolo defined it as "extended by contradictions, ambiguities, and indirect apologies" (1953, 111); Gianfranco Contini talks about its "psychological ambiguity" (1970, 663); Gioacchino Paparelli remarks, "Frankly, to me it looks like a masterpiece of hypocrisy!" ("a me francamente pare un capolavoro d'ipocrisia!" 1979, 77). On *Familiares* 21.15, see Feo 1943; for a more exhaustive bibliography, Vecchi Galli 2009. On Petrarch's relationship to Dante, see Barański 2009 and the bibliography cited there (93–4), and Barański 2020.

15 A detailed analysis of the differences between the two versions can be found in Pier Giorgio Ricci's edition of *Trattatello* in *Tutte le opere di Giovanni Boccaccio* (1974). See also, in particular, Billanovich 1947a, Paparelli 1979, and Paolazzi 1983.

16 A representative passage from the first invective: "But, o wicked thought! O shameful deed! O miserable example, notorious proof of ruin to come! Instead of giving him these rewards, his fellow citizens handed him an unfair and violent condemnation: perpetual exile with loss of his family goods and, if it had been possible, the sullying of his illustrious name by false accusations. Witness to these deeds is partly borne out by the footprints of his recent flight, his bones, which are buried in an alien place, and his children, who are scattered in the houses of others. Even if all the other sins of Florence could be hidden from the eyes of God, who sees all, would this one not bring down His wrath upon her? Indeed it would. I consider it proper to pass over in silence the

the political events that took place there between 1358 (with the enforcement of the new practice against Ghibellines that lasted until the Ciompi Riot in 1378) and 1360 (when many of Boccaccio's friends and neighbours were involved in the failed coup). On 30 December 1360, Domenico di Donato Bandini and Niccolò di Bartolo del Buono were hanged; the others took flight and were banished. Moderating the harsh invective against Florence was probably a wise precaution for Boccaccio to take, along with his move to Certaldo in 1361.

Much more interesting in this historical context, however, are other changes and deletions, which P.G. Ricci notes in his introduction to Boccaccio's *Trattatello* (1974): "And finally we must not ignore that other details were suppressed by Boccaccio and yet we cannot determine why, as we cannot hypothesize mere distractions: he did not keep the title of the *Monarchia*, he did not specify the number of eclogues, he did not mention the epistles" (433).

The *Monarchia* is a controversial treatise by Dante on secular and religious power; as we learn from Boccaccio's *The Life of Dante* (red. 1), the work had initially "hardly been known," but then "became very famous" (§53), owing to the use made of it by Holy Roman Emperor. In the first version, Boccaccio writes:

> In addition to the Comedy, at the coming of the Emperor Henry VII into Italy, this magnificent writer composed another book, in Latin prose, which was titled *De Monarchia* [On Monarchy] … Ludwig, the Duke of Bavaria, who had been chosen by the German electors to be the king of the Romans, went to Rome for his coronation against the wishes of Pope John. While he was in Rome, he made a minor friar, called Pietro della Corvara, pope, contrary to the ordinances of the Church, and he also created many other cardinals and bishops; and he had himself crowned by this new pope of his there. When his authority was challenged in many cases, he and his followers, having discovered this book by Dante [*Monarchia*], began to employ several of its arguments in defence of themselves and their power.
>
> (Questo egregio auttore nella venuta d'Arrigo VII imperadore fece uno libro in latina prosa, il cui titolo è *Monarcia* … E la cagione fu perciò che Lodovico duca di Baviera, dagli elettori della Magna eletto in re de' Romani, e venendo per la sua coronazione a Roma, contra il piacere del detto Giovanni papa essendo in Roma, fece, contra

reverse case of those who have been strongly exalted" ("Oh scellerato pensiero, oh disonesta opera, oh miserabile esemplo e di futura ruina manifesto argomento! In luogo di quegli, ingiusta e furiosa dannazione, perpetuo sbandimento, alienazione dei paterni beni, e, se fare si fosse potuto, maculazione della gloriosissima fama, con false colpe gli fur donate. Delle quali cose le recenti orme della sua fuga e l'ossa nelle altrui terre sepulte e la sparta prole per l'altrui case, alquante ancora ne fanno chiare. Se a tutte l'altre iniquità fiorentine fosse possibile il nascondersi agli occhi di Dio, che veggono tutto, non dovrebbe questa una bastare a provocare sopra sé la sua ira? Certo sì. Chi in contrario sia esultato, giudico che sia onesto il tacere"; *Trattatello*, red. 1, §§5–7).

gli ordinamenti ecclesiastici, uno frate minore, chiamato frate Pietro della Corvara, papa, e molti cardinali e vescovi; e quivi a questo papa si fece coronare. E, nata poi in molti casi della sua auttorità quistione, egli e' suoi seguaci, trovato questo libro, a difensione di quella e di sé molti degli argomenti in esso posti cominciarono ad usare; per la qual cosa il libro, il quale infino allora appena era saputo, divenne molto famoso.) (*Trattatello*, red. 1, §196)

Nevertheless, after this favourable first dissemination in a Ghibelline environment, once Ludwig and his followers had returned to Germany, the *Monarchia* was defenceless against the attack of clergy:

> This book was condemned by Messer Beltrando, the cardinal of Poggetto, who was the papal legate in the region of Lombardy during the papacy of John XXII … The already mentioned cardinal, lacking any meaningful opposition, seized this book and condemned it to public burning for having contained heretical reasoning.
>
> (Questo libro più anni dopo la morte dell'auttore fu dannato da messer Beltrando cardinale del Poggetto e legato di papa nelle parti di Lombardia, sedente Giovanni papa XXII … il detto cardinale, non essendo chi a ciò s'opponesse, avuto il soprascritto libro, quello in publico, sì come cose eretiche contenente, dannò al fuoco.) (*Trattatello,* red. 1, §§196–7)

Hence, already in 1329, the book was condemned as heretical and persecuted by the papal legate, Bertrand du Pouget; copies were destroyed, banned, burned in the square, and hunted down (*Monarchia*, ed. Ricci 1965a, *Introduzione*, 3–4). In fact, Boccaccio writes that the book was burned in the main square in Bologna and that Cardinal du Pouget would have burned Dante's buried bones if the Florentine knight Pino della Tosa and the Lord of Ravenna, Ostasio da Polenta, had not stopped him. The book was also attacked in writing by the Dominican Guido Vernani in *De reprobatione Monarchie composite a Dante Aligherio florentino*, penned between 1327 and 1334 and dedicated to the commentator of the *Comedy* Graziolo de' Bambagioli.[17] Despite these offensives, the *Monarchia* circulated in contemporary juridical, scientific, and cultural circles: Bartolo di Sassoferrato draws on it, as Diego Quaglioni shows in his edition of the *Monarchia* (2014c, ix–xvii) and in his *Politica e diritto nel Trecento italiano* (1983); allusions can also be found in the work of the jurist Alberico da Rosciate,

17 *De reprobatione Monarchie* by Guido Vernani is published in Matteini 1958. The comment on Dante's *Inferno* by Graziolo de' Bambagioli was brought to light by Luca Carlo Rossi and published in the *Dartmouth Dante Project* at http://dante.dartmouth.edu. On Guido Vernani, see also Pérez Carrasco 2016.

in the glosses to the text attributed to Cola da Rienzo, and in traces detected in some of Petrarch's works.[18]

How was the *Monarchia* received, though, in the Guelf-dominated Florence of 1360? Was it still considered heretical? How much power might the Inquisition and the Church still have in Florence? The answer to this last question is, on the face of it, not much. As Maria Picchio Simonelli points out, the "golden period" of the medieval Inquisition (created to stop the heresies spreading particularly in Italy and in southern France) lasted more than a century: from the papacy of Innocent IV until the death of Benedict XII in 1343, when the Church was facing internal problems that led to the Great Western Schism. Hence, midway through the fourteenth century, the Inquisition courts continued, but their action was milder (Picchio Simonelli [1979] 2000, 307). Also in 1343, the popular government was taking control of Florence: the new regime was very intolerant and hostile towards the clergy. This new political class, formed by shopkeepers, small artisans, and lower guildsmen, saw the highest ranks of the Florentine clergy as delegates of the magnates because an ecclesiastical career was pursued mostly by the highest echelons of society. At the same time, Pope Clement VI persisted in supporting Walter of Brienne after Florence had rebelled against him and expelled him as a tyrant (Leoni 1875). Also, the inquisitor of the time, Piero dell'Aquila, was "filling the ecclesiastical courts with citizens of every rank" (Brucker 1962, 133), collecting more than 7,000 florins in two years (G. Villani 1990–1, 12.58) – a truly unbearable situation for the Florentine citizens. In April 1345, a new provision was promulgated to strike at ecclesiastical privileges. Brucker writes:[19]

> Anyone accused of injuring a Florentine citizen in his person or property was subject to the jurisdiction of the communal courts, and could not claim immunity or demand trial before any other tribunal. Violators were subject to severe penalties. Although the provision made no specific reference to the Church or its judicial system, its intent was clear, as Giovanni Villani noted [1990–1, 12.43]. It placed all clerics accused of crimes against Florentine citizens under the exclusive jurisdiction of the secular courts, and it prohibited any appeals by either layman or cleric to an ecclesiastical tribunal …
>
> The commune also took the offensive in the legislative sphere. It passed a provision that prohibited the institution of a judicial process against any citizen in a court not

18 For Alberico da Rosciate, see Prosdocimi 1960; Petoletti 1998; Quaglioni 1979–80. For the comments by Cola di Rienzo, see P.G. Ricci 1965; the *Monarchia*, edited by Furlan (2004); and more recently Furlan 2015. For *Monarchia* in Petrarch, see Billanovich 1947a, 239–40; and Quaglioni, who quotes Petrarch's *Sine Nomine* 4 (intr. *Monarchia*, 2014c, xi). On the reception of the *Monarchia* in the thirteenth century, see Cheneval 1995, ch. 4.

19 The provision can be read in Panella 1913, 327–65. For the Inquisition in Florence in these years, see also Felice Tocco 1909, esp. 524–46; and Becker 1959 and 1962.

> under communal control (that is, a Church court) without the express authorization of the Signoria, the colleges, and the *capitudini* of the guilds … The measure substantially curtailed the authority of the inquisitor, whose jurisdiction was restricted to serious cases of heresy. (Brucker 1962, 134)

It is clear at this point that in Florence the Inquisition had almost no power. Furthermore, the "anticlerical legislation remained in force and was incorporated in the statute of the captain of the *popolo* compiled in 1355" (Brucker 1962, 140). For several reasons, "The various priorates that ruled the city from the Black Death until the aftermath of the Ciompi permitted that statute against heretics to fall into abeyance and it became 'a historic memory' ["un ricordo storico," F. Tocco 1909, 414]" (Becker 1959, 70). In conclusion, at least in this period, which ranges from 1345 to 1378, the *Monarchia* could have circulated more or less freely in the city.[20] Precisely in this window, sometime between 1351 and 1353, Boccaccio wrote the first version of *The Life of Dante*, in which he described all the works he knew by Dante: *Comedy*, *Vita Nuova*, *Monarchia*, two beautiful *Eclogues*, *Convivio*, *De vulgari eloquentia*, *Epistles*, and songs and sonnets.[21]

Given all the conditions and contexts just explained, deleting any direct mention of the *Monarchia* by title from the second edition of *The Life of Dante* cannot be ascribed to the Inquisition or to the ecclesiastical court, because nothing changed in this respect from 1351–3 to 1363–6, when the second version was put together. So what happened in that decade? Why was Boccaccio "tactfully or perhaps fearfully omitting the title given in the first version ('Monarcia')," as Anthony Cassell writes (2004, 37)? If there was no fear of the Inquisition, what might have changed about *Monarchia*?

The Deletion of *Monarchia*

For twenty years, from 1358 until 1378 (with the Ciompi Revolt), *ammonizioni* were applied to everyone charged with being "Ghibelline or not true Guelf," according to a standard set by a law of 1347 that was enforced only after 1358. This was how an extremist faction of the Guelf Party, let by the Albizzi family, wrested control of political power in the city. After 1358, prosecution and suppression were rampant; throughout Florence, including Oltrarno, many were convicted as Ghibellines. We can imagine that, in this context, Boccaccio felt that

20 On the early circulation of Dante's *Monarchia*, see Cheneval 1995, Bologna 2006, Belloni and Quaglioni 2014, and Pistolesi 2014.

21 When Boccaccio wrote the first version of *The Life of Dante*, Piero d'Aquila had already been removed from the office of inquisitor. This happened in 1346; he was replaced by Fra Michele di Lapo Arnolfi, a Florentine citizen (Becker 1959, 69).

he, too, was in danger. His finances collapsed in 1359, and he became a priest in November 1360.[22] People in his circle fled the city, as did he.

It does not seem much of a stretch to conclude that Boccaccio, in drafting his revision in the early 1360s, omitted the direct reference to Dante's work not so much because the *Monarchia* was condemned as heretical as because of its evident Ghibelline content. The *Monarchia* was dangerous for the most conservative faction of the Guelf Party in power after 1358 and was therefore unacceptable to them.

The passage referring to the *Monarchia* (without naming it) in the second version of *The Life of Dante* reads as follows:

> This distinguished author moreover composed a work in Latin prose upon the arrival of the Emperor Henry VII, in which over three different books he proves that for the good of the world there should be an emperor, and that Rome deserves to hold the imperial power, and that lastly the authority of the Empire derives directly from God, without any intermediary. Since its arguments were used in favour of Ludwig Duke of Bavaria against the Roman Church, this book, under Pope John XXII, was condemned for heretical content by Messer Bertrand Cardinal du Pouget, who was at the time legate of the Roman Church in Lombardy, and he ensured that the study of this book would be prohibited. And if a courageous knight of Florence named Messer Pino della Tosa, and Messer Ostasio da Polenta, who were both recognized as great by the legate, had not challenged the legate's frenzy, he would have had burned in the city of Bologna not only the book but also the bones of Dante.
>
> (Compose ancora questo egregio auttore ne la venuta d'Arrigo VII imperadore un libro in latina prosa, nel quale, in tre libri distinto, prova a bene esser del mondo dovere essere imperadore, e che Roma di ragione il titolo dello imperio possiede, e ultimamente che l'auttorità dello 'mperio procede da Dio senza alcun mezzo. Gli argomenti del quale perciò che usati furono in favore di Lodovico duca di Baviera contro alla Chiesa di Roma, fu il detto libro, sedente Iovanni papa XXII, da messer Beltrando cardinal dal Poggetto, allora per la Chiesa di Roma legato in Lombardia, dannato sì come contenente cose eretiche, e per lui proibito fu che studiare alcun nol dovesse. E se un valoroso cavaliere fiorentino, chiamato messer Pino della Tosa, e messere Ostagio da Polenta, li quali amenduni appresso del legato eran grandi, non avessero al furor del legato ovviato, egli avrebbe nella città di Bologna insieme col libro fatte ardere l'ossa di Dante.) (*Trattatello*, red. 2, §§133–4)

In comparison with the first version of the text, we notice, first, that there is no mention of the book by its title, and second, that Boccaccio has cut more

22 For his financial problems, see Regnicoli 2013a; for Boccaccio as priest, see Billanovich 1947b, 167–80.

than half of the content of his discussion of this "work in Latin prose." In the first redaction, a whole paragraph was dedicated to explaining the subdivision of the work into three books, each of which was carefully constructed around three arguments (*questioni*). Boccaccio pays attention, in the earlier version, to describing the method Dante used to discuss the three arguments: through logic, Dante proves that the empire is necessary for the welfare of the world; with history, he proves that Rome quite justly ruled over the world; through theology, he proves that the authority of the empire descends directly from God. In this way, Boccaccio certainly demonstrates in this first version that he has read the book and studied it in some detail. The second redaction does not imply such a close knowledge; moreover, one suggestive clause has been added: "He [Cardinal Bertrand du Pouget] ensured that the study of this book would be prohibited." By not quoting the title and shortening the content, Boccaccio could claim not to have studied or read Dante's book; he is simply telling the reader about its existence, just as a historical fact. In this way, Boccaccio aligns *The Life of Dante* not only to the dictate of Bernard du Poujet (the Church) but also to the political view of the Guelf Party.

Another important deletion that can be attributed to the same political motives is the absence of any mention of Dante's letters, the *Epistles*. The cut sentence is: "This excellent poet also wrote many *Epistles* in Latin prose, of which quite a few survive." As we know, Boccaccio copied in his *Zibaldone Laurenziano* three of Dante's *Epistles* (III, XI, and XII), and he was acquainted with a letter addressed to Moroello Malaspina (Billanovich 1947b, 53–5); hence we have a total of four letters known to Boccaccio. Thirteen letters by Dante survive, five of them on political topics, the so-called political epistles: I, V, VI, VII, and XI. Epistles V, VI, and VII were written between September 1310 and April 1311, and they represent a unique block for chronology and for their topic, focused on the arrival of Emperor Henry VII in Italy. We cannot assume that Boccaccio knew all or even some of these three letters, but we cannot exclude it. What we can infer is that Boccaccio was aware of the political content of at least some of Dante's letters and knew their content was "pro-Ghibelline," and as such knew that it would be wise to avoid mentioning them, just as it was wise to cut back his detailed exposition of *Monarchia*.

A Change of Audience

There are several other small changes in the second version of *The Life of Dante* that make it more suitable for a new audience. The first comes at the beginning of the work, and suggests an attempt to bestow a status on Dante that could have pleased the Guelf Party. In the first version, after a long preamble, Boccaccio finally names Dante for the first time and states: "I am going to review the exile of that most famous of men Dante Alighieri." In the next sentence, he adds: "who was born of parents who were by no means obscure." In the second version, we meet the name of Dante for the first time much earlier because Boccaccio removed the long invective against Florence, introducing him with the following words: "the most illustrious man Dante Alighieri, man of noble blood" ("chiarissimo uomo Dante Alighieri, uomo di sangue nobile"; *Trattatello*, red. 2, §3). The reference to Dante's "noble blood" would have resonated well among the oligarchs of the Guelf Party: it was a way to make Dante appealing to a new, and powerful, readership in Florence.

Another change in the second version that may be attributed to a desire to fit the new version to his new audience is a deletion of critical remarks about nobility. It comes in the passage in which Boccaccio praises Dante's conduct as a child. In *Trattatello*, red. 1, §§ 21–2, the passage reads:

> I will say, however, that from the beginning of his childhood, having already the rudiments of literary education, he did not abandon himself to childish pleasures and laziness, dawdling in his mother's lap (according to the customs of the nobles of today), but he gave himself and all his time in his native city to an uninterrupted study of the liberal arts, and became remarkably expert in them. As his mind and genius matured over the years, he did not pass on to lucrative studies, which almost everyone is seeking today, but his admirable aspiration for perpetual glory made him scorn ephemeral wealth.

> (Dico che dal principio della sua puerizia, avendo già li primi elementi delle lettere impresi, non, secondo il costume de' nobili odierni, si diede alle fanciullesche lascivie e agli ozii, nel grembo della madre impigrendo, ma nella propia patria tutta la sua puerizia con istudio continuo diede alle liberali arti, e in quelle mirabilmente divenne esperto. E crescendo insieme con gli anni l'animo e lo 'ngegno, non a' lucrativi studii, alli quali generalmente oggi corre ciascuno, si dispose, ma da una laudevole vaghezza di perpetua fama [tratto], sprezzando le transitorie ricchezze.)

This is the passage in *Trattatello*, red. 2, §17:

> And during his childhood he began to manifest signs, to any who would pay attention to them, of what his maturity would one day become, since he left behind any childish idleness, and in his native city he devoted himself entirely and with uninterrupted study to the liberal arts; and once he became an expert in those, he devoted himself not to those lucrative studies prematurely pursued today by everyone eager to make a profit, but rather to speculative arts, drawn by admirable aspiration for perpetual fame.

> (E nella sua puerizia cominciò a dare, a chi avesse acciò riguardato, manifesti segni qual dovea la sua matura età divenire, però che, lasciata ogni pueril mollizie, nella propria patria con istudio continuo tutto si diede alle liberali arti, e, in quelle già divenuto esperto, non alle lucrative facultadi, alle quali oggi ciascun cupido di guadagnare

s'avventa innanzi tempo, ma da ludevole vaghezza di perpetua fama tratto, alle speculative si diede.)

In the first passage, Boccaccio contrasts Dante's good conduct with the "childish pleasures and laziness" and "dawdling" in their mother's laps indulged in by nobles. In the second version, the attack on nobility is deleted and Dante is contrasted only with those "eager to make a profit"; this time, the *popolo grasso* and the "new people," merchants and craftsmen newly arrived in the city from the countryside, are the example not to follow.

If the second version of *The Life of Dante* has been changed to defer more to Petrarch (in response to Petrarch's complaints in *Familiares* 21.15), and to be more congenial politically to a different audience, the question arises: Who was the target audience of the first version of *The Life of Dante*? Petrarch's *Familiares* give us an indication.

In *Familiares* 21.15, Petrarch complains that Dante's readership is the *vulgus* (rabble), which overturns, confuses, and cheapens the reading of poetry; for the same reason, he prefers Latin over the "vulgar" language.

> On the other hand, there are none by whom he [Dante][23] would have been disliked [more] than these silly admirers who never know why they praise or censure, who so mispronounce and mangle his verses that they could do no greater injury to a poet; and if my many concerns were not so pressing, I might even strive to the best of my powers to rescue him. As it is, I can only express my reprehension and disgust at hearing them befouling with their stupid mouths the noble beauty of his lines. Here may be the proper place to mention that this was not the least of my reasons for abandoning his style of composition to which I devoted myself as a young man, for I feared for my writings what I saw happening to the writings of others, and especially of this poet about whom we speak; I had no hope, then, that the tongues or minds of the rabble would be any more flexible or kind to my works than they were to those whom long habit and favor had made popular in the theater and public squares. Events have proved my fears well founded since a few pieces that I slipped from my youthful pen are constantly being mangled by the multitude's recitation, something that is so vexing as to make me hate what I once loved.
>
> (Sicut ex diverso nullos quibus esset infestior, quam ineptissimos laudatores, qui omnino quid laudent quid ve improbent ex equo nesciunt, et qua nulla poete presertim gravior iniuria, scripta eius pronuntiando lacerant atque corrumpunt; que ego

23 Petrarch never mentions Dante by name in the letter, even though Dante is the subject of *Familiares* 21.15. Translation here and elsewhere of Petrarch's *Familiares* and *Seniles* is by Aldo S. Bernardo.

forsitan, nisi me meorum cura vocaret alio, pro virili parte ab hoc ludibrio vendicarem. Nunc quod unum restat, queror et stomacor illius egregiam stili frontem inertibus horum linguis conspui fedarique; ubi unum, quod locus exigit, non silebo, fuisse michi non ultimam causam hanc stili eius deserendi, cui adolescens incubueram; timui enim in meis quod in aliorum scriptis, precipueque huius de quo loquimur, videbam, neque volubiliores vulgi linguas aut spiritus molliores meis in rebus speravi, quam in illorum essent, quos vetustas et prescriptus favor theatris ac compitis urbium celebrassent. Meque non frustra timuisse res indicat, quando in his ipsis paucis que michi iuveniliter per id tempus elapsa sunt, vulgi linguis assidue laceror, indignans quodque olim amaveram perosus.) (*Fam.* 21.15)

Who exactly are these people who make up the *vulgus*, the *ydiotas* (as Petrarch calls them a few lines before the quoted passage), who exalt Dante in the taverns and squares? Petrarch gives the answer shortly afterward: "the fullers or tavern keepers or woolworkers who offend the ones whom they wish to praise, whom I, like Virgil or Homer, delight in doing without" ("fullonem et cauponem et lanistratum … qui quos volunt laudare vituperant … quibus cum ipso Virgilio cumque Homero carere me gratulor"). These are the eulogists, the readers, the fans of Dante, who recite him in the squares and streets where they work. They are, however, also the readers of Boccaccio's *Decameron*, so Boccaccio has reason to want to appeal to them and to praise Dante, who was beloved by the same common people. He focuses the sixth through ninth days of storytelling on characters in such as these in Florence and Tuscany.[24]

With *Familiares* 21.15, Petrarch cautions Boccaccio to tone down his enthusiasm for Dante, and in the second revision of *The Life of Dante*, Boccaccio does so, no doubt under the influence of Petrarch. Boccaccio, however, had other reasons to moderate his praise for Dante, not just because Dante was perceived as the Ghibelline author of the *Monarchia* but also because he was loved by a certain stratum of the population of Florence – merchants, wool sellers, fullers – the people most despised by the zealots of the Guelf Party.

Lapo da Castiglionchio

One of the champions of the extremist faction of the Guelf Party was Lapo da Castiglionchio:[25] "This man was made 'Sage of the Party' for life by order of the Fifty-six [counsellors], since, while a member of the Fifty-six, he did much good

24 Padoan (1978, 108–9) demonstrates how Days Six through Nine are situated in Florence or Tuscany, unlike other days of the *Decameron*.

25 Mazzoni (2005) shows Lapo da Castiglionchio's importance in the Guelf Party; see especially 96–100 and the prosopographic chart (110–13). Stefani describes him as a "champion" of the party (1910, rubr. 775).

but for an evil purpose" ("Questi era fatto per l'ordine de' Cinquantasei savio di Parte a vita, perocchè nell'ordine dei Cinquantasei molto adoperò bene, ma a male fine lo fece"), as the fourteenth-century chronicler Stefani (1910, rubr. 778) wrote. Stefani noted that these men "called themselves champions of the Guelf Party, and were actually those who with their boundless appetites ruined Florence" ("Si chiamavano campioni della Parte Guelfa, ed in effetto furono quelli che con appetito smisurato, si potè dire, [ebbero] guastato Firenze"; 1910, rubr. 775). "Whoever was Lord of the Party was also Lord of Florence," commented Stefani, and Lapo kept "full powers for life" ("la balìa a sè a vita"; Stefani 1910, rubr. 778). Stefani's words convey both the influence and the power of Lapo, "the jurist produced by a line of *domini loci*, devoted to the noble virtues, and zealous partisan of the Guelf cause" (Mazzoni 2005, 97), who "joined *toto corde* the oligarchic side."

The importance assumed by Lapo da Castiglionchio, as promoter and upholder of exclusionary practices through *ammonizioni* and as expert in recognizing who was a true Guelf, is highlighted in the contemporary book of recollections by Giovanni di Paolo Morelli (2015). In a crucial passage, Morelli underscores how it was thanks to Lapo da Castiglionchio that his ancestors' qualifications as true Guelfs had been "renewed" and "reaffirmed" (Morelli 2015, 115); it would appear that Lapo had the power to grant the "licence" of being a true Guelf.[26]

At this point, it is worth recalling Lapo's views on the aristocracy, and thus on the "new people," as well as his literary inclinations. Claudio Donati (2005) provides a broad discussion of Lapo's view of social rank, with which da Castiglionchio deals extensively in the letter to his son Bernardo. According to Lapo, anyone can be "noble" who chooses "the path of virtue," and "can thus make an ignoble status noble, and a noble ignoble" – the reference is clearly to the anti-magnate legislation. Lapo appears to embrace the theory of nobility ascribed to Bartolo da Sassoferrato, of whom he transcribes word for word a few passages of the *De Dignitatibus* (I of Book XII of the *Digesta*). But an intriguing episode that occurred in 1353, while Lapo was still a law student in Bologna, reproduces in full his views on nobility in the midst of an argument with a fellow student. The following is drawn from the essay by Donati (2005, 35–6):

> This man [the fellow student], "puffed up" because "his father and grandfather, through craft and merchandise, had been made citizens of Florence and had become

---

26 See Morelli 2015, 114–15; Mazzoni (2005, 98–9) transcribes the passage in full. See also Mazzoni and Monti (2013, esp. 30–1): "Evidently still in his times [i.e., those of Paolo Morelli], ancient activism among the losing faction could pose problems, and not only in politics. And so Pagolo Morelli decided to distort historical facts in order to construct a blameless past for himself and for his family" (Mazzoni and Monti 2013, 31). Indeed, as the authors note, Morelli's ancestor, Morello Morelli, was not the Guelf champion outlined in his great-grandson's work.

rich," had claimed equal nobility and antiquity for his own ancestors, adding that they had lived in Castiglionchio before Lapo's ancestors. Immediately the latter, "stung by youthful disturbance," had mockingly replied: "You speak the truth, that you were indeed in that place first, but, when my forefathers purchased that place, they also purchased your ancestors and fathers as loyal subjects, as I can prove to you with a public document. You should thus learn – I said to him – that not every ancient family is noble, and that even a vassal can be as ancient as his master, since there is no master without his servant, and no servant without his master. It is thus one thing to be an ancient in servitude and another to be ancient in lordship." Once his interlocutor had confirmed through personal reading of the thirteenth-century document that this was indeed the case – Lapo writes – he "from that point on lived in more humble and reverent fashion, and he always respected me as his superior, as if this seemed appropriate, given his ancient servile status, and we always remained friends." Even the conclusion to the anecdote deserves to be reported: "turning to his son, Lapo urged him not to be surprised "that this young man descended from one of those said to be such ancient loyal subjects of ours, as even today in the area of that castle of Castiglionchio there are many of the successors of those families, our ancient loyal subjects, and many of these in the city of Florence have become citizens and artisans and wealthy, even in the magistracies of the city of Florence all the way up to that of the Lord Priors.

(Costui [il compagno di studi], "superbetto" perché "l padre e l'avolo, per artificio e mercantia, erano fatti cittadini di Firenze, e divenuti ricchi", aveva rivendicato la pari nobiltà e antichità dei propri avi, aggiungendo che loro avevano vissuto a Castiglionchio prima degli avi di Lapo. Subito quest'ultimo, "punto da iovanile turbatione", gli aveva replicato beffardamente: "Tu di' vero, che prima fosti di quello luogo, però che quando i miei progenitori comperarono quello luogho, con esso comperarono i tuoi antichi e progenitori per fedeli e vaxalli, come mostrare ti posso per publico instrumento. Appara, adumque – dissi io a llui – a saper che non ogni anticho è nobile, però che tanto può essere anticho il vaxallo, quanto il signore, però che non è signore sanza servo, né servo sanza signore. Altro è adunque essere anticho nella servitù, altro è essere anticho nella signoria." Accertatosi attraverso la diretta visione del documento ducentesco che le cose stavano proprio così, il compagno – scrive Lapo – "sempre poi vivette umile e riverente, e sempre onorò me come suo maggiore, quasi ciò gli paresse convenevole, considerata l'anticha e servile sua conditione, e fumo poi sempre amici." Anche la conclusione dell'aneddoto merita di essere riportata alla lettera: rivolgendosi al figlio, Lapo lo invitava a non meravigliarsi "che 'l detto giovane fosse de' descendenti d'uno de' detti nostri fedeli e vaxalli così antichi, però che anchora al dì d'hoggi sono nella contrada del detto castello di Castiglionchio molti de' successori delle dette famigle, nostri antichi fedeli e vaxalli, e molti ne sono nella città di Firenze fatti cittadini e artefici e ricchi, e negli uffici della città di Firenze infino all'uficio de' Signori Priori.)

As Donati emphasizes, the conclusion conveys the epic and speedy transition from a feudal society to a new system in which the status of "citizen" is born. Even though within the new city there were binary oppositions and hierarchies, "a nostalgic longing for a mythical age that was actually not that distant, in which masters were sharply distinguished from servants, had not entirely disappeared; and on certain occasions it would burst the banks of self-censorship, as in the case of the Lapo's response to his fellow student, evident in all its sarcastic bitterness" (Donati 2005, 37).[27] There is no doubt that Lapo, together with the other ultra-Guelfs in Florence, embraced the oligarchic ideals of caste nobility. To bolster Dante's *bonas fides*, therefore, it was crucial for Boccaccio, in the second *Life of Dante*, to emphasize that Dante was of noble blood.

Another factor in play was the relationship between Lapo da Castiglionchio and Petrarch. Their close relations are well known: in 1350, when Petrarch was passing through Florence for his jubilee voyage, Lapo had met the poet laureate and sought his friendship, sharing with him various speeches by Cicero and the *Institutio oratoria* by Quintilian, and he kept up a correspondence through letters. Unlike his contemporaries among *populares*, Lapo da Castiglionchio preferred the authority of Petrarch to that of Dante, as he made his son Bernardo memorize a few letters received from him (Fubini 2005, 19), and he grew up surrounded by the myth of Petrarch's greatness. Under his father's influence, Bernardo writes to his father: "two most excellent Florentine poets, that is Alighieri and the other no less than he – and if I were to call him superior, you, Dante, would perhaps not be angry – namely Francesco Petrarch" ("due excellentissimi poeti fiorentini, cioè Dante Alleghieri e l'altro non minore di lui e s'io dicessi maggiore forse tu Dante non isdegneresti, cioè Francesco Petrarca") (da Castiglionchio 2005, 434). Also among the admirers of Petrarch were Francesco Nelli, Zanobi da Strada, Niccolò Acciaiuoli, and Boccaccio himself – even though Boccaccio acknowledged Dante as his "first guide and light of [his] studies."[28]

Boccaccio's support of Petrarch and the positions he takes regarding *Familiares* 21.15, so well analysed by distinguished scholars, may also be contingent on the specific historical context and the controversial "new culture" that favoured vernacular literature. At the time of Boccaccio's *Lectura Dantis*, there was "opposition – often harsh and violent – from several factions. Some came from Guelph extremists, who – like Lapo da Castiglionchio – were then dominant in Florentine politics … Also, the new culture was opposed by those who entertained a jealously aristocratic conception of literature, too often bound exclusively to Latin tradition" (Branca 1976, 185). In this context, Boccaccio was accused, either by those traditionalists

27 For a more in-depth study on nobility, see Donati 1988. See also Robiglio 2006; Castelnuovo 2014; Borsa 2014 and 2017.

28 Boccaccio called Dante "primus studiorum dux et prima fax" (*Fam.* 21.15 [1359]).

or by his own circles, now turned against him, of "prostituting" the Muses to the "ungrateful masses," and he felt he had to defend himself in four sonnets (CXXII–CXXV). "Probably this person [accusing Boccaccio] belonged either to the class ruling Florentine politics, or to one of those circles to which we have seen Boccaccio bound with affection" (Branca 1976, 185). One can still perceive beyond this accusation the mind-set and power of Lapo da Castiglionchio.

We may, in fact, read the entire revision of *The Life of Dante* as compelled by immediate historical circumstances. Boccaccio excluded even sections of the text that "had come straight from the heart" (as Ricci states, citing the laudatory paragraph 19)[29] in order to tone down his enthusiasm for Dante. A significant factor in his decision must have been Petrarch's positions on these issues. I have already noted this elsewhere (Filosa 2013, 219–20), following the extensive demonstration provided by Giuseppe Velli (2005, 149). The fact remains that Petrarch was perceived as an authority in literary and in political circles, and it was thus wise to indulge him. Yet, despite the fact that Boccaccio felt he had to make these changes and placate the current thinking, there is a moment in the second version in which he comes out with an attack on the studied pastoralism of the kind championed by Petrarch.

Tensions with Petrarch: On the Solitary Life

As Giuseppe Velli (2005) shows clearly, the shorter, second version of *The Life of Dante* amplifies the narrative considerably on at least one point, when Boccaccio, after recounting obstacles overcome by Dante in his dedication to study, contrasts him with those who allow themselves to be disturbed by what Petrarch called a "slight murmur" ("leve murmur") (*Familiares* 21.15.8):

> What will those say now whose houses are not sufficient for their studies and who thus seek solitude in the forests? Or those who have complete repose, and whose ample faculties without any anxiety provide them with every necessity? Or those who, free from wife and children, have as much leisure as they desire? Many of those are such that, if they were not sitting in comfort, or if they were to hear a murmur, they would not be able to read, much less reflect or write, if their elbow were not at rest.
>
> (Che diranno qui coloro, a gli studi de' quali non bastando della loro casa, cercano le solitudini delle selve? Che coloro, a' quali è riposo continuo, e a' quali l'ampie facoltà senza alcun pensiero ogni cosa oportuna ministrano? Che coloro che, soluti da moglie e da figliuoli posson vacare a lor piacere? De' quali assai sono che, se ad agio non

29 Ricci, introduction to Boccaccio's *Trattatello* (1974), 431: "veramente gli era uscito dal cuore."

> sedessero, o udissero un mormorio, non potrebbon, non che meditare, ma leggere, né scrivere, se non stesse il gomito riposato.) (*Trattatello*, red. 2, §61)

The difference between Dante and more fortunate men is couched in an "ironic gibe against excessively delicate minds," Velli notes, as Boccaccio expands Petrarch's reference to a "slight murmur" into the common disturbances of everyday life. Velli continues, "Even apart from the 'solitude of the forest,' and from 'the continuous repose,' was it not Petrarch who had 'ample faculties,' and who was 'free from wife and children'? This is not a malicious question on our part: the ambiguity is in the text itself. The least that can be said is that it escapes the absolute control of its author" (2005, 149). In this irony, whether deliberate or unintentional (and in any case instinctual), we perceive Boccaccio's autonomy as a writer and thinker, despite the adverse historical context he found himself in.

Giorgio Padoan writes a chapter entitled "Il Boccaccio 'fedele' di Dante" ("Boccaccio faithful to Dante"; 1978, 229), and, as he puts it: "Rather than admiration, it would be more appropriate to speak of a revelation, that lasted all his life" ("Piuttosto che di ammirazione converrà parlare di folgorazione, durata tutta la vita"; 1978, 230). Indeed, starting with his earliest works, which are full of references to Dante, right up until his commentary on the *Divine Comedy* shortly before his death, Boccaccio spent his life preserving Dante as his model in literature, politics, and life. His deep and declared admiration for Dante remained constant for the duration of his long friendship with Petrarch, and it was a major source of tension between the two writers.

Throughout the twentieth century, Boccaccio was called "the great disciple" of Petrarch, following Giuseppe Billanovich's characterization of him, but this image of master and disciple was undercut in 1990 with the publication of *Per moderne carte* by Marco Santagata, who demonstrated how in his "accounting book" ("libro del dare e dell'avere") Petrarch repeatedly borrowed from Boccaccio. Their relationship was far more equal and reciprocal than their own statements would indicate. The notion that Boccaccio was the dutiful disciple is further eroded by Boccaccio's evident independence of thought and opinion. Giuseppe Velli points to the evidence in "their respective texts" (that is, those of Boccaccio and Petrarch) and "the peculiarity of their relationship, which was not at all unanimous, rather it was tense and contentious" ("[i] rispettivi testi ... [il] carattere nient'affatto concorde, anzi teso, contrastato"):

> We should redefine the relationship as contentious, the opposite of our contemporary view of it as "quietistic," so to speak (too much credit has been given to the writer's own professions), which constantly places Boccaccio in the role of "disciple," and which effectively accepts without question the dependence and even subordination of Boccaccio toward the man he declared explicitly and repeatedly would become his "teacher" and *preceptor*.

In fact, when we consider the human and cultural parabola of Boccaccio's life and the sum of his literary output, we cannot miss how absolutely original they are, their distinctive character marked by an openness, even adventurousness, a constant amenability, the exceptional interest in experiment. It is worth recalling that we owe to Boccaccio the exploration, and even in certain cases the creation, of new genres in the vernacular (the pastoral novel, the epic, the "psychological" novel) and new metrical forms for "high" literature (the octaves of the *Teseida*). Boccaccio's otherness with respect to Petrarch needs no further proof.

(e questo rapporto contrastato, di contro alla visione, oggi corrente, per così dire "quietistica" (troppo credito è stato concesso alle ammissioni dello scrittore stesso) che trova Boccaccio costantemente nel ruolo di "discepolo", che insomma dà per scontata la dipendenza se non sudditanza del Certaldese nei confronti di colui che, per esplicite dichiarazioni, variamente ripetute, doveva diventare il "maestro", il *preceptor* suo.

In verità, per poco che si guardi alla parabola umana e culturale del Boccaccio, alla totalità della sua produzione, non si può non coglierne la cifra assolutamente originale, il cui carattere distintivo è dato dalla grande apertura, perfino avventurosa, l'irrequieta disponibilità, l'eccezionale sperimentalismo. A lui è dovuta – è bene ricordarlo – l'esplorazione, e perfino, in alcuni casi, la creazione di generi nuovi in volgare (il romanzo pastorale; l'epos; il romanzo "psicologico") e di forme metriche inedite per la letteratura "alta" (l'ottava del *Teseida*). L'alterità della posizione del Boccaccio [rispetto al Petrarca] non avrebbe bisogno di altre prove.) (2004, 215)

A further difference between Boccaccio and Petrarch, which added to the tension between the two, is Petrarch's consistently sought and defended solitary life, in contrast to the urban and political life pursued and experienced by Boccaccio – and by Dante, as well. So, while Petrarch repeatedly praised the solitary life in his writings, Boccaccio pursued an active and social life, at least in the 1350s.

This brings us to an important and rather delicate episode that took place in the beginning of their friendship, when Petrarch rejected the offer of a chair at the newly established Studium of Florence in 1351. The offer had been forwarded by none other than Boccaccio and supported by his circle of friends in Florence (Francesco Nelli, Lapo da Castiglionchio, Zanobi da Strada); Petrarch subsequently decided to take up residence, in 1353, under the aegis of the tyrant of Milan.

Boccaccio learned the news while he was in Forlì, and received confirmation from Francesco Nelli a few days later in Ravenna (around 12 July 1353) through the *Dispersa* 19 (according to the Pancheri edition). Evidently shocked and embittered by Petrarch's decision, after that first refusal, Boccaccio wrote his famous *Epistola* X, on 18 July 1353, in which, speaking to Petrarch about Silvanus (i.e., Petrarch in bucolic disguise), he rails against him:

> What will this distinguished sustainer and worshiper of solitude do when surrounded by the masses? This man who is accustomed to celebrate with highest praise a life of freedom and an honourable poverty, what will he do when he is subjected to a foreign yoke, adorned with dishonourable wealth? What will this most illustrious exhorter of virtue extol when he has become a follower of vice?
>
> (Hic solitudinum commendator egregius atque cultor, quid multitudine circumseptus aget? Quid tam sublimi preconio liberam vitam atque paupertatem honestam extollere consuetus, iugo alieno subditus et inhonesti ornatus divitiis faciet? Quid virtutum exortator clarissimus, vitiorum sectatur effectus, dacantabit ulterius?)

In the irony of the initial question, we can detect Boccaccio's contempt for those who love solitude. This contempt recurs throughout his works – solitude always bears negative connotations. An example is Madonna Beritola, "poor and alone and forlorn" ("povera e sola e abbandonata"; *Dec.* II.6.11), who gradually changed into a wild beast. Life in the country, away from the culture and company of town, can be brutish and squalid, as is illustrated by the example of the "almost crazy" Cimone, the "human beast" of the *Decameron* (V.1), who was ordered by his father "to go out to the country farm and live with the labourers there; and this was greatly appreciated by Cimone, as the customs and habits of the gross men there were more agreeable to him than those of the city" ("comandò che alla villa n'andasse e quivi co' suoi lavoratori i dimorasse; la qual cosa a Cimone fu carissima, per ciò che i costumi e l'usanza degli uomini grossi gli eran più a grado che le cittadine"; *Dec.* V.1.5).

In the *Corbaccio* and in the *Esposizioni*, solitude is linked to thoughts of despair. At the start of his story, the narrator of the *Corbaccio* recalls:

> Finding myself alone not long ago in my chamber ... I suffered so much, first bemoaning my stupidity, then the insolent cruelty of that woman, that by adding one grief to another in my thoughts, I decided that Death must be far easier to bear than such a life; and I began to cry out to him with the greatest longing. (Trans. Cassell)
>
> (Non è ancora molto tempo passato, che ritrovandom'io solo nella mia camera ... in tanta d'afflizione trascorsi, ora della mia bestialità dolendomi, e ora della crudeltà trascutata di colei, che un dolore sopra un altro col pensiero aggiungendo, estimai che molto men grave dovesse essere la morte che cotal vita, e quella con sommo desidero cominciai a chiamare.)

As soon as the protagonist mends his ways, his first resolution is "to leave behind his solitary existence" ("la solitaria dimoranza lasciare"; V.1.48) and rejoin his friends.

A lack of interest in the company of others is targeted in *Esposizioni sopra la Comedia*, where Boccaccio provides a commentary on canto 7 of the *Inferno*, in which he describes the slothful:

> He would not aspire to rise to public office and, even if he did so because of the merits of one of his relatives, he would behave like a man who is sound asleep. He considers his bed, interminable nights, and naps (the latter no shorter than the former) to be quite appealing and desirable things. He prefers solitude, darkness, and silence even to the most amiable company. (Trans. Papio, 381)

> (Alle publiche cose non ardirebbe di salire, alle quali se pur sospinto fosse per li meriti d'alcun suo, come uno adormentato si starebbe in quelle; il letto, le notti lunghissime e i sonni, non più corti che quelle, gli sono graziosissimo e disiderabile bene: la solitudine, le tenebre e il silenzio prepone ad ogni dilettevole compagnia.) (*Esp.* 7.2, 150)

Boccaccio copied maxims on the theme of solitude from the *florilegium* of Seneca, collected in the Zibaldone Magliabechiano. Examples are grouped under the title "On shunning solitude" ("de solitudine fugienda"):

- No thoughtless person ought to be left alone; in such cases, he only plans folly, and heaps up future dangers for himself and for others; he brings into play his base desires; the mind displays what fear or shame used to repress; it whets his boldness, stirs his passions, and goads his anger. And, finally, the only benefit that solitude confers – the habit of trusting no man, and of fearing no witnesses – is lost to the fool; for he betrays himself. (Nemo est ex prudentibus qui relinqui sibi debeat; tunc mala consilia agitant, tunc aut alijs aut ipsis futura pericula struunt, tunc cupiditates improbas ordinant; tun quicquid aut metu aut pudore celabat animus exponit, tunc audaciam acuit, libidinem irritat, iracundiam instigat. Denique quod unum solitudo habet commodum, nicil ulli committere, non habere indicem, perit stulto; ipse se prodit.) (*Ad Luc.* 10.2)
- Solitude prompts us to all kinds of evil. (Omnia nobis mala solitudo persuadet.) (*Ad Luc.* 25.5)
- What profits it, however, to hide ourselves away, and to avoid the eyes and ears of men? A good conscience welcomes the crowd, but a bad conscience, even in solitude, is disturbed and troubled. If your deeds are honourable, let everybody know them; if base, what matters it that no one knows them, as long as you yourself know them? How wretched you are if you despise such a witness! (Quid autem prodest recondere se et oculos omnium auresque vitare? Bona conscentia turbam advocat, mala etiam in solitudine amsia atque sollicita est. Si honesta sunt que facis, omnes sciant; si turpia, quid refert neminem scire cum tu scias? O te miserum si contempnis hunc testem!) (*Ad Luc.* 43.4–5)

- For the mass of mankind consider that a person is at leisure who has withdrawn from society, is free from care, self-sufficient, and lives for himself; but these privileges can be the reward only of the wise man. Does he who is a victim of anxiety know how to live for himself? What? Does he even know (and this is of first importance) how to live at all? For the man who has fled from affairs and from men, who has been banished to seclusion by the unhappiness which his own desires have brought upon him, who cannot see his neighbour happier than himself, who through fear has taken to concealment, like a frightened and sluggish animal – this person is not living for himself; he is living for his belly, his sleep, and his lust – and that is the most shameful thing in the world. He who lives for no one does not necessarily live for himself. (Otiosum enim hominem seductum existimat vulgus et securum et se contemptum, sibi vivere, quorum nicil ulli contingere nisi sapienti potest. Ille qui nulla re sollicitus scit vivere sibi; ille enim, quidem primum, scit vivere. Nam qui res et homines fugit, quem cupiditatum suarum infelicitas religavit, qui alios feliciores videre non potuit, qui velud timidum atque iners animal metu oblituit, ille sibi non vivit, sed, quod est turpissimum, ventri, sompno, libidini; non continuo sibi vivit qui nemini.) (*Ad Luc.* 55.4–5)

The evidence from his life and writings makes it clear that Boccaccio's understanding of solitude is diametrically opposed to that of Petrarch, who celebrates solitude in his *De vita solitaria*. For Boccaccio, solitude should be shunned and avoided, as it leads to all kinds of vices, to despair, and especially to closing oneself off – only a sage (perhaps) knows how to live well on his own, but a true sage knows how to live everywhere (even surrounded by a multitude of people). The "political animal" Boccaccio, unlike Petrarch, prefers life in the company of friends, an urban life, and especially a republican life, in which, to manage the common good, people need to live together, organize together, work together. This is public and political life, of which Dante is an example, if not *the* example, for Boccaccio.

On the other hand, solitude had also been associated by tradition and necessity with speculative studies in particular, as Boccaccio tells us in his *Life of Dante*:

> Generally, studies depend on solitude and removal of all cares, and in particular the speculative ones, to which – as we showed – our Dante gave himself, as much as circumstances allowed. Instead of removal of cares and quiet, from the beginning of his childhood until the end of his life, Dante bore a powerful and unbearable passionate love. Besides, he had a wife; and whoever has one, knows how they are the greatest enemy of the study of philosophy. Likewise, he had family cares and those of the Republic; and above all, he endured long exile and poverty.
>
> (Gli studii generalmente sogliono solitudine e rimozione di sollecitudine disiderare e tranquillità d'animo, e massimamente gli speculativi, a' quali, sì come mostrato è, il

> nostro Dante, in quanto la possibilità permetteva, s'era donato. In luogo della quale rimozione e quiete, quasi dallo inizio della sua puerizia infino allo stremo della sua vita, Dante ebbe fierissima e importabile passione d'amore. Ebbe oltre ciò moglie; le quali chi 'l pruova sa come capitali nemiche sieno dello studio della filosofia. Similmente ebbe ad aver cura della re familiare e oltre a ciò della re publica; e, sopr'a tutte queste, lungamente sostenne esilio e povertà.) (*Trattatello*, red. 2, §24)

In this description, Boccaccio outlines his image of the poet-hero, who, despite circumstances that make it difficult to study, nevertheless devotes himself to literature and philosophy with the greatest success – the true sage knows how to live in any situation (as Seneca said: "That man indeed, and this is of first importance, knows how to live" ["ille enim, quidem primum; scit vivere"]). Dante's life and biography serve as proof that an intellectual can thrive in an active life, not only in the literary kind of seclusion promoted by Petrarch. In the second redaction of *The Life of Dante*, Boccaccio's mockery of those intellectuals who need forest and solitude to think is among the rare passages added to the first version. The comparison between Dante, beset by the issues and challenges of the world, and those "lucky" men who have the opportunity for isolation and absolute dedication to their studies is cloaked in "an ironic jab at excessively delicate minds" ("frecciata ironica contro gli ingegni troppo delicati"; Paolazzi 1983, 204). In this light, it is worth noting how often Boccaccio depicts Petrarch as a lover of solitude in his biography (*De vita et moribus Francisci Petracchi*), in *De casibus virorum illustrium*, and in *Genealogie deorum gentilium*.

There is one moment in Boccaccio's work in which he perhaps not praises but at least appears to embrace the solitary life: his self-portrait in the conclusion to the *Consolatoria a Pino de' Rossi*. Critics have perhaps taken this self-portrait too literally, when they claim that these words show Boccaccio embracing Petrarch's philosophy of solitude. In this passage, the release from all urban activities gives the writer the opportunity to "discuss freely" and "without any distraction" his own "little books." We have here the same literary topos as in Petrarch, for whom the intellectual can freely pursue his own creative occupations, far from the city and its nuisances and obligations. But note that this passage was composed in the same years as Boccaccio's second redaction of the *Life of Dante*. After all that Boccaccio has written on solitude, this description may best be read as a response to his unfavourable historical, political, and personal circumstances at the time. Indeed, after the failed coup by many of his friends, Boccaccio moved back to the country in a kind of self-exile, where he was able to write and live undisturbed.

Boccaccio's Enduring Fidelity to Dante

By viewing Boccaccio's changes to his second version of the *Life of Dante* in their historical context, we see more fully how Dante and his works were received and perceived in Florence when it was under the control of the Guelf Party from 1358 to 1378. Dante's *Monarchia*, his political epistles, and his eclogues could all have been read as "Ghibelline," and thus dangerous to the dominant political class. Dante was not favoured because of his choice of language – the vernacular – readable by everybody, including the "new people" just arrived from outside the city and the illiterates (those who could not read Latin). Dante became "the Author" for the major part of Florence, opposed by a minor, more elitist one that preferred the Latin works by Petrarch. We have seen how the city was divided politically; the same division ran along cultural lines: the liberal side (led by the Ricci family) was more open to different strata of the population, including merchants, bankers, wool traders, and rich new arrivals, enrolled in their respective guilds, and people who did not know Latin. On the other side, the oligarchic faction (led by the Albizzi family) was more inclined to the city aristocracy, those who were well educated and literate, many of whom were in the Judges and Notary Guild, and had university educations. After the economic collapse at the end of the 1330s and beginning of the 1340s, power passed from the great companies – run by the Bardi, Peruzzi, Frescobaldi, and Acciaiuoli families – to a new ruling class whose bastion was the Guelf Party; their power came from their sophisticated knowledge of jurisprudence, as they manipulated Florentine laws to their own interests. The new ruling class consisted of members of the old aristocracy, often proud of their noble origin, well educated, closely allied with the clergy and the dominant academic culture: for them, Latin was the language of culture. From their perspective, Dante was an author to shun: he wrote mostly in the vernacular, even exalting this language as dignified (*De vulgari eloquentia*); he was a Ghibelline (*Monarchia*); in favour of "nobility of spirit" (*Convivio*), against the nobility of caste; and he was the writer of the heretical *Comedy*. He was, in sum, "the Author" of the political opposition. It became natural that the officially crowned poet laureate, Petrarch, who wrote consistently in Latin and had a very distinct taste for *auctoritas*, became "the Author" for this new ruling class. Petrarch even had family ties with the Albizzis, the family of the leader of the extremist oligarchic party.[30]

By viewing Boccaccio's writings in their historical context, we see Boccaccio more fully, too. We see that he is not, as commonly thought, a humble disciple of Petrarch, accepting Petrarch's valuation of such things as solitude and language; we detect the autonomy of a writer and thinker whose intellectual identity rebels against the legislation and interferences of Petrarch and the Guelf Party. His celebration of Dante and his own active life, fully immersed in the real world, is also a celebration of his *modus vivendi*, of a Boccaccio who served as politician, ambassador, and cultural promoter within the citizen and republican environment in Florence, alien and antithetical to the *modus vivendi* desired and pursued by his

30 Petrarch was related to Franceschino degli Albizzi, a mediocre poet whom Petrarch had on occasion praised. See Piccini 2002.

friend Petrarch with his solitary life. Boccaccio's friends who collaborated in the plot had taken this *modus vivendi* to its extreme, jeopardizing their property, their families, and their own lives – had not Dante done the same, repaid with exile, banished from the lilied city?

In this context, Dante emerges once more as Boccaccio's model and inspiration, not only for literature but for life: he was a writer who lived in a republic, pursuing a political life of activism, unlike the one who *chooses* to live as a subject at the court of a tyrant (unlike Dante, who *was forced* to taste the "salty" and bitter bread of others); he was a writer who aimed for *urbanitas*, not the solitary life. Boccaccio's defence of Dante is a defence of himself in respect to literature and specific life choices.

Boccaccio's second redaction of *The Life of Dante* tells us a lot about the changes in the life and outlook of its author. His ordination in November 1360, the conspiracy of December 1360, his flight to Certaldo, and above all the political changes that occurred in Florence with the eventual domination of a faction of the Guelf Party: these factors caused Boccaccio to change his method of approaching reality through his writings. He was obliged to adjust to the rule of a new political class, and the second redaction of the *Trattatello* reflects that new ideological leadership. The envisioned readers of the *Life of Dante* were no longer just his neighbours, magnates open to Florentine outsiders, and wool-workers, but also the new political class, with whom it was wise to make compromises. The loss of financial independence, the loss of a circle of friends who had supported him, and the rise of a new ruling class also imposed a loss of intellectual freedom: Boccaccio was compelled by daily necessity and by the political realities to construct an image of himself more aligned to the new perspective promoted by the Guelf Party and the Church.

8 Conspirators in the *Decameron*

Nobility cannot be handed down
except as are things as virtue, knowledge, and holiness;
everyone must seek it,
and, whoever would like to have it, let him acquire it for himself.

– Boccaccio, *The Corbaccio*, trans. Cassell (1975, 70)

La gentilezza non si può lasciare in eredità,
se non come le virtù, le scienze, la santità e così fatte cose;
ciascun conviene che la si procacci,
e acquistila chi aver la vuole.

– Boccaccio, *Corbaccio*, ed. G. Natali (1992, §508)

Boccaccio wrote the *Decameron* well before the attempted coup of 1360, so it cannot tell us anything directly about the political moment of the early 1360s. But we can note that some of the conspirators' relatives are highlighted in stories narrated on the sixth day. Their presence in this work is further confirmation of Boccaccio's deep connections with these families, and explains why his destiny was so closely entwined with theirs. The *Decameron* provides not only indications of Boccaccio's political and social life but also the ideological positions that inform political discussions in the work, such as those to do with nobility of caste and nobility of soul.

What's in a Name? Donati and Monna Nonna

In Italian families, traditionally, first names tend to pass from grandparent to grandchild, from uncle to nephew, from aunt to niece, or from some other important or beloved member of the family. Thus, for example, Pino di Giovanni de' Rossi takes the name of his grandfather, Pino di Stoldo de' Rossi; Boccaccio di Michelino di Bonaiuto da Certaldo, father of the writer, had three brothers, named Giovanni, Francesco, and Jacopo, and he gave the same names to his own sons, probably preserving the order of seniority; Corso di Simone Donati, a leader of the Black Guelf faction in thirteenth- and early fourteenth-century Florence, had a grandchild named Corso di Amerigo Donati. Because of this naming tradition, it can be difficult to identify a historical character if one does not have the full name or a specific time reference.

Sometimes, in the *Decameron*, Boccaccio wants to identify his characters precisely. He finds ways to give his readers the exact time and space in which his characters move. For example, in *Decameron* IX.8, we know that the character "Corso Donati" is Corso di Simone Donati because of the presence of his antagonist, Vieri de' Cerchi. To us today, such a signal might not suggest much, but in his time, it would have confirmed that the story takes place around the thirteenth and fourteenth centuries. For a reader of the 1350s, when the novella was composed, the name Corso Donati would immediately recall one of his grandsons, Corso di Amerigo Donati, one of the promoters of the expulsion of the Duke of Athens in 1343 (along with his cousins, Manno and Pazzino di Apardo Donati), who was condemned to death *in contumacia* in 1344 for having plotted with Luchino Visconti to take control of the city during the popular government (G. Villani 1990–1, 13.32). Furthermore, the fourteenth-century reader of *Decameron* IX.8 would have recalled the Donati family as a whole – one of the most ancient patrician families in Florence, standing together with other magnates. In other words, behind the name of a specific historical character there is also, hidden, the name of the descendants and the whole family, of which that one person becomes the representative.

The rubrica to *Decameron* IX.8 states: "Biondello gulls Ciacco in the matter of a breakfast; for which prank Ciacco is cunningly avenged on Biondello, causing him to be shamefully beaten" ("Biondello fa una beffa a Ciacco d'un desinare, della quale Ciacco cautamente si vendica faccendo lui sconciamente battere"). Biondello and Ciacco are the two hungry and thirsty main characters of the novella, who gravitate around the tables of Vieri de' Cerchi and Corso di Simone Donati, hoping to snag some delicacies during the forty days of fasting for Lent. Kristina Olson points out in her reading of this novella: "It is noteworthy ... that the only character portrayed in an arguably benevolent light within this story is Corso Donati; not only Dante, but also Villani and Compagni, criticize the historical Corso Donati for his conspiracies and violence" (Olson 2014, 71). Olson also provides an interesting analysis of Boccaccio's comments on the *Inferno* 6 in his *Exposition on Dante's Comedy*, in which he glosses Ciacco's discussion of Florence, drawing the conclusion that "Boccaccio openly favors the Blacks over the Whites in *Esposizione* 6 not because he agreed with their political agenda but because he favored the Donati family over the Cerchi family" (Olson 2014, 84). Boccaccio certainly favoured the Black Guelfs, as did (officially) everybody else in Florence, at least after 1347. In that year, the Guelf Party decided that to participate actively in public life one had to be a "true Guelf" and demonstrate that the whole family had been Guelf starting from when the Blacks had taken power. Saying that one was a true Guelf was equivalent to claiming descent from Black Guelf families going back to at least 1301. How far people would go to furnish such genealogies is illustrated by the case of Paolo Morelli, inventing proof that his ancestor Morello Morelli had been a true Black Guelf (Mazzoni and Monti 2013, 31): "And because we always sided with the Blacks, we called ourselves Morelli – indeed, Giraldo, out of respect for the Black party, to which he was greatly devoted, named his son Morello" (2013, 115). (In Italian, "Morello" is a cute diminutive of "Moro," black.)

Boccaccio understood the ephemeral power of great families, the inexorable passing of time that erases names and deeds, the arbitrary nature of a bitter fortune that decides the life of people. In his *Esposizioni sopra la Comedìa*, he claims: "In our time [1372–3], the Cerchi, the Donati, the Tosinghi, and others were once of such pre-eminence in our city that they controlled small and great affairs alike according to their whims. Nowadays, however, there remains hardly any memory of them" (*Esp.* 7.63, lit., trans. Papio, 342). But Boccaccio had not forgotten the Donati family, and there is clear proof that "he favored the Donati family over the Cerchi family" (Olson 2014, 84). Boccaccio treated the Donatis favourably in his works, as Olson demonstrates. The third wife of Boccaccio's brother, Jacopo, was Bianca di Geri di Simone Donati (Tordi 1923, 81 n. 33; Piattoli 1970); and Pazzino di Apardo Donati, one of the conspirators of 1360, was witness for a notarized document, dated 2 November 1351, certifying the payment to Boccaccio of the salary for his embassy "in partes Romandiole et Lombardie" (Imbriani 1882, 84). This document shows the trust and the friendship existing between the two men.

Mention of Corso di Simone Donati in *Decameron* IX.8 evokes the memory of Corso di Amerigo Donati, who led the revolution against the Duke of Athens in 1343, together with his clan, among whom were his cousins Pazzino di Apardo Donati and his more famous brother, the knight Manno di Apardo Donati.

Manno and Pazzino Donati[1] spent almost their entire lives together. References to the activities and experiences of Manno Donati appear in several Florentine and Paduan chronicles from 1342 and 1370.[2] Like many other magnates at that time, Manno Donati supported the arrival of the Duke of Athens in 1342, but afterward he took part in the second conspiracy against him, led by his cousin Corso di

1 Manno di Apardo Donati was knighted by the Commune of Florence on 22 February 1337 (Provvisione 30, 147; Salvemini 1896, 106–7, doc. 14). Pazzino di Apardo Donati was knighted by King Ludwig of Hungary on 13 December 1347, in Forlì (G. Villani 1990–1, 12.107); Boccaccio may have been present on the occasion.

2 Ernest Hatch Wilkins lists these chronicles in his study of the friendship between Manno and Petrarch (Wilkins 1960, 381). For the life of Manno di Apardo Donati, beside Wilkins, see also Kohl 1992 and 1998, esp. 186–9.

Amerigo Donati. On that occasion, Manno was imprisoned by the duke, only to be freed again during the third and final conspiracy against the duke. When a new regime was about to be formed with the "fourteen good men" under the Bishop of Florence, Angelo Acciaiuoli, Manno Donati was supposed to be among the first priors, but the insurrection that brought the installation of the popular government did not allow him to take the position. He was again imprisoned, with his brother and other magnates, in December 1343, and later was released but forced to live outside the city. In this period, he enlisted as a *condottiero* at the service of Francesco I da Carrara, Lord of Padua. His successful military career made him appreciated in Florence as well, and he was hired by the Republic to fight against the Visconti in July 1357. This pattern of exile and welcome repeated itself. He was banned from Florence in 1361 together with Pazzino – Pazzino with a death sentence over his head for his involvement with the 1360 conspiracy.[3] They fled to Padua under Francesco I da Carrara, but in 1364 Manno came back to Florence to bring victory to the city during the battle of Cascina against Pisa on 28 July 1364; Matteo Villani wrote about the battle in his chronicle, and Antonio Pucci in his *cantare*, both exalting the decisive role of the *condottiero*. On 12 July 1364, thanks to the friendly intercession of Francesco I da Carrara ("amicabile petitur per partem domini Francisci de Carrara domini paduani"), the death sentence on his brother's head was lifted and Pazzino was pardoned, only sixteen days before winning the war against Pisa.[4] Manno kept fighting for the Florentine Republic and Francesco I da Carrara until the end of his life around 1374; his body is buried in the cathedral of Saint Anthony in Padua with an epitaph composed by Petrarch – the last of the nine epitaphs penned by the poet.

Manno and Pazzino di Apardo Donati were among those representatives of the old noble families still alive in Florence, knights whose ancestors had been invested with the rank of *cavaliere*. Hand in hand with the nobility of action and rank that came with knighthood was the nobility of spirit forged by beauty and appreciation of culture. The brothers were noble in this respect, too, as members of the Petrarchan circle in Padua (Billanovich and Pellegrin 1964, 230). Manno was "among the friends of Petrarch's later years" (Wilkins 1961, 136, 381; Zardo 1887, 112–24, 286–91) and was very close to Lombardo della Seta (Billanovich and Pellegrin 1964, 230); he was remembered with respect and affection by Coluccio Salutati in his letter addressed to Gregory XI (Witt 1976, 97). In 1366–7, Pazzino and Manno di Apardo Donati rented out a store and house in the neighbourhood of Santa Maria degli Alberighi ("unam apothecam cuiusdam domus posite in populo Sancte Marie Alberighi de Florentia") to the University of

3 Manno di Apardo Donati may have been banned in 1361 because of his brother's involvement in the conspiracy.

4 ASFi, *PR* 51, ff. 171v–172r.

Florence, denoting a certain connection with the official cultural environment of the city (*Statuti dell'Università* 1881, 146–7, 154–6, 500–1).

Another member, by marriage, of the Donati family is the protagonist of a novella in the *Decameron*. Thanks to the discovery of a parchment that was used to cover an accounting register of the sixteenth century, held at the Ospedali degli Innocenti in Florence, we know that in 1345 Manno di Apardo Donati married Lapa di Uberto de' Pulci.[5] Lapa was also known as Monna Nonna de Pulci, as we learn from another document, quoted in Branca's edition of the *Decameron*: "Monna Lapa, called Monna Nonna, daughter of Uberto de' Pulci, wife of the deceased Passe Passavanti and afterward wife of Messer Manno de' Donati" ("Domina Lapa vocata Domina Nonna filia Uberti de Pulcis uxor quondam Passe Passavantis et postea uxor Domini Manni de Donatis").[6] Monna Nonna de' Pulci is the protagonist of *Decameron* VI.3, in which she is described as

> a young gentle-woman, whom this present pestilence has taken from us, Monna Nonna de' Pulci by name, a cousin of Messer Alessio Rinucci, whom you all must know; whom, for that she was lusty and fair, and of excellent discourse and a good courage, and but just settled with her husband in Porta San Piero.

> (una giovane la quale questa pistolenzia presente ci ha tolta donna, il cui nome fu monna Nonna de' Pulci, cugina di messere Alesso Rinucci e cui voi tutte doveste conoscere: la quale essendo allora una fresca e bella giovane e parlante e di gran cuore, di poco tempo avanti in Porta San Piero a marito venutane.) (*Dec.* VI.3.8–9)

The novella is set at the time when Antonio degli Orsi was bishop in Florence and Diego della Ratta, grand seneschal of King Robert, was visiting the city. This narrows the time-frame to 1310–11 or 1317–18.[7] From this date, and from the fact that Lauretta, the narrator of the story, describes her as just married, we can infer that Monna Nonna de' Pulci was born around 1300 and at the time of her second wedding must have been in her early forties, but she brought a very good dowry.[8] Commemoration of Monna Nonna, who died in 1348 of plague, might be seen as an homage to the widower as well, Manno di Apardo Donati, and to a larger group of people, as Boccaccio suggests with the words "whom you all must know." The names cited by Lauretta – Pulci, Rinucci, and, by implication, Donati – indicate that Boccaccio was writing for this specific group of people, whose members were part of his entourage.

---

5 Florence, Ospedale degli Innocenti, doc. 12569.

6 BNCF, *Magliabechiano* XXXVII 299, f. 33 (*Decameron*, ed. Branca [1992], 728, n. 7).

7 See *Decameron*, ed. Branca (1992), 727, n. 2. In 1311, Diego della Ratta knighted Stoldo di Coppo de' Rossi, Bandino di Liscio de' Rossi, and Giovanni di Pino de' Rossi, the father of Boccaccio's friend Pino di Giovanni de' Rossi (Salvemini 1896, 102–3).

8 Monna Lapa de' Pulci's dowry, assigned in 1342, is recorded in the document Florence, Ospedale degli Innocenti, doc. 12569.

It is interesting that in the novella the narrator, Lauretta, presents Monna Nonna as the "cousin of Alessio Rinucci." Alessio Rinucci, a man of law, was very attached to Nonna, so much so that one of his own daughters bears her name: Nonna di Alessio Rinucci. At this point Boccaccio clearly wants to clarify that the Nonna referenced by Lauretta is the cousin of Alessio Rinucci, not his daughter. But in so doing, readers of the 1350s could not help but think about the living Nonna as well, the daughter of Alessio Rinucci.[9] Certainly Boccaccio knew her well, too: she was living no more than twenty paces from his home in Santa Felicita, and was the wife of his dear friend, the *popolano* and *lanaiuolo* Luca di Feo Ugolini: one of the conspirators of 1360 in exile with Pino de' Rossi, grandson of Bartolo de' Bardi and Tedalda di Bartolomeo degli Acciaiuoli, and nephew of Doffo de' Bardi (see appendix A1.5) – one of the major actionists of the Bardi Ccompany for which Boccaccio's father worked. When Lauretta states "whom you all must know," was she implying them as well? Certainly, the group of people with whom Monna Nonna de' Pulci and Monna Nonna de' Rinucci were acquainted was large, and Boccaccio was among them.

In *Decameron* VI.3 and IX.8, the strategy Boccaccio adopts seems clear: exalt characters of a previous generation in order to pay tribute to living persons in his own entourage. It seems reasonable to infer that these very friends, neighbours, and acquaintances might have been the first readers of his novellas and maybe, in some way, the commissioners. In some cases, as for Monna Nonna, it was a way to remember them and their world after the plague took their lives.[10] The fatal epidemic left the survivors to mourn the lost ones, and telling their story was a way to accomplish the funeral rites that were neglected when "all the laws were broken," as we know from the introduction of the *Decameron*. Boccaccio too lost family members and close friends – Branca mentions "Matteo Frescobaldi, Giovanni Villani, Ventura Monachi and Bruno Casini, Francesco Albizzi and soon afterwards Coppo di Borghese Dominichi" (1976, 76) – but none were remembered in his novellas, with the exception of Coppo di Borghese Dominichi. Boccaccio, however, did not write about his own losses, either in a memoir or in private writing: he was writing not for himself, but for others. He was writing for those living friends, neighbours, and acquaintances who wanted their ancestors or their loved ones who had died in the plague to be remembered and praised. In this respect, we might say that the *Decameron* is a work of encomiastic literature in which a precise group of people is represented and exalted.

Day Six of the *Decameron* is a peculiar example of what I am trying to demonstrate: Boccaccio was writing his novellas to remember old friends and exalt their

9 Monna Nonna (d. 1357), daughter of Alessio Rinucci, married Luca di Feo Ugolini on 23 January 1340, with whom she had three sons: Niccolo', Meo, and Feo. Their house was located at the corner of Via di Maggio and Via di Pozzo Toscanelli (ASFi, *Diplomatico*, Santo Spirito, 11 January 1360, Florentine date).

10 See the research by Sebastiana Nobili, in, e.g., "La consolazione della letteratura: Una proposta per il *Decameron*" (2013). See also Nobili 2017.

ancestors and families. In this way, he was paying homage to his entourage. The sixth is considered the "Florentine day": eight of its novellas are set in Florence, and almost all the characters are identifiable.

Decameron VI: The Florentine Day

At the end of Day Five of the *Decameron*, focused on happy love affairs and with most novellas situated in Romagna, the reader enters the second half of the one hundred novellas, set mostly in Tuscany.[11] As Giorgio Padoan (1978, 108–9) observed, Days Six, Seven, Eight, and Nine take place mainly in Tuscany and the most Florentine day in the *Decameron* is the Sixth: all of these novellas take place in Florence and the protagonists are all Florentine. Day Seven moves a short distance from Florence, to Prato, and Day Ten takes place in Certaldo. By contrast, Days Two and Ten contain no novellas set in Florence; Days One and Five contain only one each (I.6 and V.9); Day Four contains two (IV.7 and IV.8); and Days Three and Seven contain three each (III.3, III.4, III.7; VII.1, VII.6, VII.8). The novellas of Days Eight and Nine, on the other hand, contain respectively five (VIII.3, VIII.5, VIII.6, VIII.7, VIII.9) and four novellas (IX.3, IX.5, IX.7, IX.8) situated in Florence.

Another characteristic links the novellas of Day Six: nearly all their protagonists are citizens of Florence who can be easily identified in their historical context, as opposed to the characters in other novellas, who are frequently difficult to identify, either because they are unknown or because their identities were deliberately concealed, as occurs in III.3.5:

> In our city, where wiles do more abound than either love or faith, there dwelt, not many years ago, a gentlewoman richly endowed (none more so) by nature with physical charms, as also with gracious manners, high spirit and fine discernment. Her name I know, but will not disclose it, nor yet that of any other who figures in this story, because there yet live those who might take offence thereat, though after all it might well be passed off with a laugh.
>
> (Nella nostra città, piú d'inganni piena che d'amore o di fede, non sono ancora molti anni passati, fu una gentil donna di bellezze ornata e di costumi, d'altezza d'animo e di sottili avvedimenti quanto alcun'altra dalla natura dotata, il cui nome, né ancora alcuno altro che alla presente novella appartenga, come che io gli sappia, *non intendo di palesare*, per ciò che ancora vivono di quegli che per questo si caricherebber di sdegno, dove di ciò sarebbe con risa da trapassare.)

---

11 Daniela Branca Delcorno notes: "The novellas of the *Decameron* set in Romagna are gathered in the fifth day (4, 5, 8), in the sunniest and most positive day of all" (2015, 49). The move in the setting of the novellas, from Romagna to Tuscany, parallels Boccaccio's biography, as he moved from Romagna to Florence in 1348.

The same discretion is used for the female narrators of the *Decameron*, all from Florence, whose identities are camouflaged (*Dec.* I.Intr.50–1):

> Their names I would set down in due form, had I not good reason to withhold them, being solicitous lest the matters which here ensue, as told and heard by them, should in after time be occasion of reproach to any of them, in view of the ample indulgence which was then, for the reasons heretofore set forth, accorded to the lighter hours of persons of much riper years than they, but which the manners of today have somewhat restricted; nor would I furnish material to detractors, ever ready to bestow their bite where praise is due, to cast by invidious speech the least slur upon the honor of these noble ladies. Wherefore, that what each says may be apprehended without confusion, I intend to give them names more or less appropriate to the character of each. The first, then, being the eldest of the seven, we will call Pampinea, the second Fiammetta, the third Filomena, the fourth Emilia, the fifth we will distinguish as Lauretta, the sixth as Neifile, and the last, not without reason, shall be named Elissa.
>
> (Li nomi delle quali io in propria forma racconterei, se giusta cagione da dirlo non mi togliesse, la quale è questa: che io non voglio che per le raccontate cose da loro, che seguono, e per l'ascoltare nel tempo avvenire alcuna di loro possa prender vergogna, essendo oggi alquanto ristrette le leggi al piacere che allora, per le cagioni di sopra mostrate, erano non che alla loro età ma a troppo piú matura larghissime; né ancora dar materia agl'invidiosi, presti a mordere ogni laudevole vita, di diminuire in niuno atto l'onestà delle valorose donne con isconci parlari. E però, acciò che quello che ciascuna dicesse senza confusione si possa comprendere appresso, per nomi alle qualità di ciascuna convenienti o in tutto o in parte intendo di nominarle: delle quali la prima, e quella che di piú età era, Pampinea chiameremo e la seconda Fiammetta, Filomena la terza e la quarta Emilia, e appresso Lauretta diremo alla quinta e alla sesta Neifile, e l'ultima Elissa non senza cagion nomeremo.)

The protagonists of I.6 are hidden, although there are allusions to the presence of the inquisitor Fra Mino da San Quirino; the two novellas situated in Florence on Day Four (IV.7 and IV.8) have as their protagonists anonymous representatives of the lower classes of the city (only one is named: Girolamo di Leonardo Sighieri). Days Eight and Nine contain many Florentine novellas, but their protagonists are either explicitly comical types or representatives of a specific category of person: Calandrino, Bruno, Buffalmacco, and Maestro Simone resemble figures from a *commedia dell'arte* (VIII.3, VIII.6, VIII.9; IX.3, IX.5); Ribi and Matteuzzo are jesters, and Maso il Saggio a trickster (VIII.5); and the scholar Ranieri represents the whole class of intellectuals full of knowledge but with no awareness of what women are capable of (VIII.7). There are other novellas with names and surnames beyond Day Six – consider, for example, Tedaldo degli Elisei (III.7), Arriguccio dei Berlinghieri (VII.8), Gianni di Lotteringhi or Gianni di Nello (VII.1) – but the fact remains that in Day Six we find a conspicuous range of Florentine citizens who can be identified, which is unique in the *Decameron*.

There are thus many reasons to take a close look at the novellas and the protagonists of Day Six, in particular, in the context of this study: to consider specifically whether and what kind of relationship Boccaccio had with these people. Why include these people and not others? Is there some common denominator linking these historical characters? As Olson has demonstrated, Boccaccio adapted the accounts found in contemporary chronicles to present Corso di Simone Donati in a positive light; I have shown that this was done because Boccaccio was very close to the Donati family. Even Monna Nonna de' Pulci (*Dec.* VI.3) is celebrated, not just to commemorate her after her death as belonging to Boccaccio's community of Oltrarno but also to pay tribute to her widower, Manno di Apardo Donati, and not just him, but also the woman who shared her name (Monna Nonna, the daughter of Alessio Rinucci), her father (Alessio Rinucci), and her husband (who happened to be Boccaccio's dear friend and neighbour Luca di Feo Ugolini, in exile with Pino de' Rossi after the conspiracy, and related to the Bardi family). In order to understand why Boccaccio wanted to write about these people, it is necessary to understand their lives and their importance in Florentine society, economy, and politics of the time. Most of all, we need to acknowledge the close relationships Boccaccio had with the descendants of these protagonists.

Day Six opens with a kind of diptych, and this is a unique circumstance in the *Decameron*. It is, in fact, the only occasion in one hundred novellas that we find a pair of tales whose protagonists, inspired by real people, are husband and wife: Madonna Oretta del Marchese Obizzo Malaspina and Messer Geri di Manetto Spini (VI.1 and VI.2; see appendix A1.4).[12] This unusual strategem may be explained by the fact that they were the aunt and uncle of Margherita Spini, wife of Niccolò Acciaiuoli, Boccaccio's sometime friend and sometime enemy. It would not be the only time Boccaccio pays homage to one of Acciaiuoli's female relatives to ingratiate himself with "his friend": we may recall that the author is going to dedicate the *De mulieribus claris* to Acciaiuoli's sister, Andreina, in 1363. Boccaccio certainly knew Margherita di Vanni Spini well: along with Ugolini di Cambi and Coppo Stefani (father of the chronicler Marchionne), Boccaccio served as legal counsel for the Acciaiuoli in drafting a notary act, dated 8 February 1342, whose purpose was to guarantee that certain goods, wanted by Niccolò, would reach the Certosa di Firenze.[13] These goods were supposed to guarantee a substantial dowry to Margherita Spini, who ratified the donation in the presence of her husband, thus renouncing all claims to them (F.P. Tocco 2001, 52). Opening Day Six with Monna Oretta and Geri Spini is a way to honour Margherita Spini,

---

12 For the Spini family, see Tripodi's genealogical table (2013, 150), reproduced in the appendix.

13 ASFi, *Corporazioni religiose soppresse dal governo francese* 51, ff. 195r–198r. This is a copy of the first half of 1500.

pay homage to her husband Niccolò, and remember their loss. Exalting the Spini family was important for several reasons.

The Spini were one of the oldest houses in Florence, from a mercantile and banking tradition, *popolare* in origin, but their ostentation (*grandigia*) had them inserted into the lists of magnates. They became privileged bankers under Pope Boniface VIII, of whom they were trustees, reaching in this way their political and economic apex between the late thirteenth and early fourteenth centuries. They were aligned with the Donati faction as part of the citizen opposition in the late thirteenth century, engaging in particularly uncompromising and militant Guelf politics, together with the Visdomini, Tornaquinci, Buondelmonti, and most of the Bardi. The house was divided into two main branches, those of Ugo and of Manetto, who had initiated the knightly line of the family.[14] Nepo degli Spini was chosen among the eight counsellors of the priors after the expulsion of the Duke of Athens, along with Ridolfo de' Bardi (related to Luca di Feo Ugolini) and Beltramo de' Pazzi (another conspirator of 1360) – part of the clique that tried to regain power after the fall of the duke (see chapter 1).

Geri di Manetto Spini was part of the most extreme faction of Black Guelfism (he was captain of the Guelf Party in 1323 and 1325);[15] the Florentine chronicler Dino Compagni (1255–1324) lambasted him precisely on account of his intransigence.[16] But, despite his extreme political views, in Boccaccio's novella (*Dec.* VI.2) he is able to recognize the nobility of soul of the baker Cisti – a reminder for readers of the 1350s that true Guelfs do not believe in nobility of blood, as we shall soon see. He was the best-known member of the Spini at this time, not only because of his politics but also because of his close relationship with Pope Boniface VIII as his banker. He built the grand Palazzo Spini, still present in the Piazza di Santa Trinita; in this palace, according to Boccaccio's novella, he hosted the pope's ambassadors. Dino Compagni records that the purpose of this visit was to reconcile the Black and White Guelf factions (I.21), a meeting that took place in 1300:

> This man [Neri di Cambi] worked so hard to convince the pope to lower the prestige of the Cerchi and their followers that the pope sent to Florence the friar messer Matteo di Acquasparta, cardinal of Porto, to pacify the Florentines. But the cardinal accomplished nothing because the factions would not grant him the powers he wanted, and so he left Florence in anger. (Compagni 1986, trans. Bornstein)

> (Il quale tanto aoperò col Papa per abassare lo stato de' Cerchi e de' loro seguaci, che mandò a Firenze messer frate Matteo d'Aquasparta, cardinale Portuense, per

14 The Ugo branch included knights: Doffo di Lapo Spini had earned distinction with his death in the war against Castruccio Castracani, which conferred on the family an indisputable Guelf mark (Tripodi 2013, 1).

15 Mazzoni 2010, app. 39.

16 Compagni 1968, I, 21–3; II, 22, 34; III, 19, 41.

pacificare i fiorentini. Ma niente fece, perché dalle parti non ebbe la commessione volea, e però sdegnato si partì di Firenze.) (Compagni 1968)

As already noted, Geri Spini married Oretta, daughter of Marquise Obizzo Malaspina and Tobia Spinola and thus a noblewoman of the elite. With her he had seven children, three of whom eventually married members of the Peruzzi and Bardi families.[17] The Spini family had a number of ties through marriage to the Acciaiuoli as well,[18] most notably the marriage of the grand seneschal of the kingdom of Naples, Niccolò Acciaiuoli, to Margherita di Vanni Spini, niece of Geri Spini.[19] All these families, the Bardi, Peruzzi, and Acciaiuoli, were part of Boccaccio's circle.

So was the family of the protagonist of the third novella of Day Six, Monna Nonna de' Pulci, the wife of Manno di Apardo Donati and cousin of Alessio Rinucci.[20] She belonged to the de' Pulci, an ancient noble family that included many notable knights. The family was connected to the de' Rossi through business and marriage (Lisa, one of the daughters of Pino di Giovanni de' Rossi, had married Jacopo de' Pulci). They were bankers, too; the Pulci-Rimbertini Company was papal.

The protagonist of the fourth novella of the Sixth Day is Currado Gianfigliazzi, the son of Giovanni (Vanni) di Cafaggio, deceased between 1312 and 1315 (appendix A1.6).[21] Boccaccio was very close to the Gianfigliazzi family – Alinora or Dianora, daughter of Niccolò di Tello Gianfigliazzi (cousin of Luigi and niece of Currado)[22] and wife of Pacino Peruzzi, appears in the guise of Adiona in the *Comedia delle ninfe fiorentine* and in the *Amorosa visione*; the jurist Luigi Gianfigliazzi is warmly recalled in the poem dedicated to Zanobi da Strada (*Carm.* VII 62–5);[23]

17 The children were Anfrione (married Tessa Gherardi); Federico; Guglielmino (became *piovano* of Santa Maria a Peretola); Luigi (married Bartolomea Cocchi and later Isabella Peruzzi); Albizino; Nera (married Agnolo di Galterotto de' Bardi); and Giorgio (married Lena de' Bardi) (Tripodi 2013, 152).

18 Banco di Dardano Acciaiuoli married Agnese di Lapo Spini; Bartolomeo Acciaiuoli married Gemma di Geri Spini (F.P. Tocco 2001, 7).

19 For further details on the marriage between Niccolò and Margherita, see F.P. Tocco 2001, 292–3.

20 Alessio Rinucci was a lawyer and a judge, prior three times, and gonfalonier of justice in 1336, as we learn from Scipione Ammirato (1647, 152).

21 The information on Currado Gianfigliazzi and the Gianfigliazzi family is taken from Armando Sapori, esp. the chapter "Le compagnie bancarie dei Gianfigliazzi" (1955, vol. 2, 927–73), and his reconstruction of the family (972). See Arrighi 2000a and Davidsohn 1956–68, vol. 4, 696–703; 1018–19; 1030. He married Lagia di Accerito di Messer Ranieri Buondelmonti, a magnate family.

22 Niccolò Gianfigliazzi was the son of Castello Gianfigliazzi, hence the cousin of Currado Gianfigliazzi, protagonist of *Decameron* VI.4. Also, he was the sole heir of the business fortune of Castello Gianfigliazzi (Sapori 1955, 952).

23 On the jurist Luigi Gianfigliazzi, see Arrighi (2000b). He was the son of Neri di Catello de' Gianfigliazzi, nephew of Niccolò, and cousin of Alinora. He participated in diplomatic missions (embassies to the pope and to the emperor) and was also a man of culture (connected to Coluccio Salutati, Francesco Bruni, Paolo Dell'Abbaco, and Boccaccio). In 1367, he and Boccaccio were on a committee to decide whether to continue the work for the *tabernaculus* of Orsammichele, commissioned to the artist Orcagna.

Stoldo di Matteo de' Gianfigliazzi repaid a loan on behalf of Giovanni and Jacopo di Boccaccio da Certaldo from the Commune of Florence on 4 July 1364 (Regnicoli 2013a, 389, doc. 106–8). The Gianfigliazzi family was Black Guelf, magnate; many were bankers and merchants; several members were knights, others were *podestà* outside Florence; and they had strong connections with other important families through multiple marriages.

Currado was born probably in the last part of the thirteenth century in Florence or Avignon, near where his father and his uncle Castello (Tello) had a major banking business. At his father's death, Currado preferred not to continue this activity – a choice that makes him similar to Boccaccio, who decided not to follow his father's career – but lived a life as a knight (also traditional in the family) with the title of noble knight (*nobilis miles*). In this position, he distinguished himself for his valour several times. In 1312, the troops of Emperor Henry VII assaulted his castle, and, although Currado and his forces put up a valiant resistance, they were outnumbered and finally defeated. The exiled Ghibelline Florentines who were with the emperor wanted to put him to death, but Henry rejected this penalty, precisely for the valour Currado had showed in the battle. The emperor gave him freedom, provided he left behind his children as hostages, while he carried an embassy on Henry's behalf to Florence. The Florentines, led by the bishop Antonio degli Orsi, refused any kind of negotiation. (The bishop is represented in the tale before that of Currado, *Decameron* VI.3, in which he is reproached by Monna Nonna.) In 1314, Currado fought against Uguccione della Faggiuola, and in 1325 (with Pino de' Rossi) against Castruccio Castracani of Lucca in the terrible battle of Altopascio, in which many Florentines fought and lost their lives. In this defeat, several members of important Florentine families were captured by the victors and freed only after the payment of significant sums. Currado Gianfigliazzi and Guido Frescobaldi (the father of Niccolò, one of our conspirators) suffered among the harsher treatments: they were granted bail but forbidden to go back to Florence; their properties were destroyed, their relatives were imprisoned, and they had to attend Castracani's triumphant entry into Lucca. This was Currado Gianfigliazzi's last military endeavour. From what we read in the *Decameron*, he retired from the city and spent the rest of his life in the countryside, attending to rural occupations and hunting, before he died in 1353:

> Currado Gianfigliazzi, as the eyes and ears of each of you may bear witness, has ever been a noble citizen of our city, open-handed and magnificent, and one that lived as a gentleman should with hounds and hawks, in which, to say nothing at present of more important matters, he found unfailing delight.
>
> (Currado Gianfigliazzi sì come ciascuna di voi e udito e veduto puote avere, sempre della nostra città è stato nobile cittadino, liberale e magnifico e vita cavalleresca tenendo, continuamente in cani et in uccelli s'è dilettato, le sue opere maggiori al presente lasciando stare.) (VI.4.4)

The Spini, Pulci, and Gianfigliazzi families were all Black Guelfs, loyal to the Donati family and in some cases connected by marriage ties. They were bankers, and many of them were inscribed in the Arte del Cambio, the major guild of bankers and money changers, in which Boccaccio's father had been active. In particular, they were the bankers of popes, with businesses predominantly in France and at the Court of Anjou in Naples, where Boccaccio spent his youth. Many of them were knights who fought against Castruccio Castracani in the battle of Altopascio. This was the elite who controlled the Florentine government and economy until 1343.

Fortune and Nature: A Philosophical Debate

In Day Six, "discourse is had of such as by some sprightly sally have repulsed an attack, or by some ready retort or device have avoided loss, peril or scorn" ("si ragiona di chi con alcuno leggiadro motto, tentato, si riscosse, o con pronta risposta o avvedimento fuggì perdita o pericolo o scorno"). *Motti*, fine words, witty retorts are the main topic of the Day Six: as the heading states, the protagonists use words to escape from situations that could prove harmful, causing "loss, peril, or scorn." Words become redeeming, a civil solution in circumstances that could lead to dishonour or worse. For this reason, kind words must be used: "wherefore to that which has been said touching the nature of wit I purpose but to add one word, to remind you that its bite should be as a sheep's bite and not as a dog's; for if it bite like a dog, 'tis no longer wit but discourtesy" ("vi voglio ricordare essere la natura de' motti cotale, che essi, come la pecora morde, deono cosí mordere l'uditore e non come 'l cane: per ciò che, se come il cane mordesse il motto, non sarebbe motto ma villania"; *Dec.* VI.3.3). Words become the main weapon of defence for the weakest members of society: the lowest classes, as shown by the cook Chichibio (VI.4) and the baker Cisti (VI.2), and the whole female gender, shown by Monna Nonna's sharp wit (VI.3).[24] In this way, these protagonists manage to extricate themselves from unpleasant situations, and in their lightning-quick retorts, they allow their intelligence and noble character to shine. Their words make the interlocutor see the truth for the first time: beneath the surface of people previously considered inferior, either by class or by gender, lurks a spirit equal to one's own, if not superior. This truth underlies the entire *Decameron*, but

24 In this regard, see Picone 2004, 172–3. Noble words offered by women are a secondary theme, promoted by Filomena (VI.1), Lauretta (VI.3), and Filostrato (VI.7) in the introductions to their novellas. The topic has already been broadly discussed by Pampinea in I.10, whose words are recalled verbatim by Filomena, marking a clear intratextual cross-reference in the *Decameron*. Whereas in I.10 women were said be unable to use words correctly, in VI.1 Oretta teaches female narrators and readers the correct manner of speaking and conversing.

it is articulated extensively here on Day Six in the philosophical preambles of Pampinea (VI.2) and Panfilo (VI.5).[25]

Pampinea offers an explanation for why so often people of inferior social position can be able and wise; she's not sure, she says, which of the two, Nature or Fortune, is responsible, so she comes up with another hypothesis:

> Fair ladies, I cannot myself determine whether Nature or Fortune be the more at fault, the one in furnishing a noble soul with a vile body, or the other in allotting a base occupation to a body endowed with a noble soul, whereof we may have seen an example, among others, in our fellow-citizen, Cisti; whom, furnished though he was with a most lofty soul, Fortune made a baker. And verily I should curse Nature and Fortune alike, did I not know that Nature is most discreet, and that Fortune, albeit the foolish imagine her blind, has a thousand eyes. For 'tis, I suppose, that, being wise above a little, they do as mortals often times do, who, being uncertain as to their future, provide against contingencies by burying their most precious treasures in the basest places in their houses, as being the least likely to be suspected; whence, in the hour of their greatest need, they bring them forth, the base place having kept them more safe than the dainty chamber would have done. And so, these two arbitresses of the world not seldom hide their most precious commodities in the obscurity of the crafts that are reputed most base, that thence being brought to light they may shine with a brighter splendour.
>
> (Belle donne, io non so da me medesima vedere chi piú in questo si pecchi, o la natura apparecchiando a una nobile anima un vil corpo, o la fortuna apparecchiando a un corpo dotato d'anima nobile vil mestiero, sí come in Cisti nostro cittadino e in molti ancora abbiamo potuto vedere avvenire; il qual Cisti, d'altissimo animo fornito, la fortuna fece fornaio. E certo io maladicerei e la natura parimente e la fortuna, se

---

25 The same topic has already been addressed by Ghismonda: "Thou seest that in regard of our flesh we are all moulded of the same substance, and that all souls are endowed by one and the same Creator with equal faculties, equal powers, equal virtues. 'Twas merit that made the first distinction between us, born as we were, nay, as we are, all equal, and those whose merits were and were approved in act the greatest were called noble, and the rest were not so denoted. Which law, albeit overlaid by the contrary usage of after times, is not yet abrogated, nor so impaired but that it is still traceable in nature and good manners; for which cause whoso with merit acts, does plainly shew himself a gentleman; and if any denote him otherwise, the default is his own and not his whom he so denotes" ("tu vedrai noi d'una massa di carne tutti la carne avere e da uno medesimo Creatore tutte l'anime con iguali forze, con iguali potenze, con iguali vertù essere create. La vertù primieramente noi, che tutti nascemmo e nasciamo iguali, ne distinse; e quegli che di lei maggior parte avevano e adoperavano nobili furon detti, e il rimanente rimase non nobile. E benché contraria usanza poi abbia questa legge nascosa, ella non è ancor tolta via né guasta dalla natura né da' buon costumi; e per ciò colui che virtuosamente adopera, apertamente si mostra gentile, e chi altramenti il chiama, non colui che è chiamato ma colui che chiama commette difetto"; *Dec.* IV.1.39–40).

io non conoscessi la natura esser discretissima e la fortuna aver mille occhi, come che gli sciocchi lei cieca figurino. Le quali io avviso che, sí come molto avvedute, fanno quello che i mortali spesse volte fanno, li quali, incerti de' futuri casi, per le loro oportunità le loro piú care cose ne' piú vili luoghi delle lor case, sí come meno sospetti, sepelliscono, e quindi ne' maggior bisogni le traggono, avendole il vil luogo piú sicuramente servate che la bella camera non avrebbe. E cosí le due ministre del mondo spesso le lor cose piú care nascondono sotto l'ombra dell'arti reputate piú vili, acciò che di quelle alle necessità traendole piú chiaro appaia il loro splendore.) (VI.2.3–6)

In her reasoning, she begins with an important distinction: does the fault belong more to Nature, when she gives a noble spirit to an ugly body, or to Fortune, when she gives a noble spirit to a base occupation (and thus a low social status)? Pampinea illustrates the second possibility with her novella of the baker Cisti (VI.2), whereas the first underpins the novella of Giotto and Forese da Rabatta, offered by Panfilo (VI.5). With Pampinea's introduction, we begin to understand the distinction between Nature and Fortune: the former concerns only the physical appearance of people, and the latter is related to one's position in society. Both "ministers of the world" determine where the soul will fall: Nature decides which kind of soul (noble/not noble) combines with which kind of body (beautiful/ugly), and Fortune chooses the place on the social ladder (rich/poor, noble/not noble, magnate/*popolano*, and so forth). Although Nature and Fortune are cursed by many who are dissatisfied with their physical or social conditions, they themselves are nevertheless "most discreet," for they reflect within themselves the divine will.[26]

Pampinea's preamble has been studied by Giuseppe Velli (1991), who demonstrates the philosophical roots of this passage in letters 44 and 46 of Seneca's *Ad Lucilium epistulae morales*. Letter 44 is especially pertinent because Boccaccio copied part of it in his *Zibaldone Magliabechiano* under the title *De nobilitate generis* (Costantini 1974, 118), discussing what nobility is. Seneca writes: "The soul alone renders us noble and it may rise superior to Fortune, no matter what that condition has been" ("animus facit nobilem, cui ex quacumque condicione supra fortunam licet surgere"; letter 44.5). Therefore, the characteristic of nobility as something inherent in the person and not conveyed by his or her social status is realized through the narrative of the tale of Cisti the baker: by means of his spirit and intelligence, he is able to rise from the place given him by Fortune. Cisti is introduced as having "a lofty spirit" ("un altissimo animo"; VI.2.3), and his clever words prove it to everyone. In this way, he becomes the representative of the "modern man," whose worth lies not in his social class but in his internal characteristics, the nobility of his soul – the novella, in short, presents a victory of "real" nobility over the social structures that restrict it, even within the rigidly

26 For a more recent study on Fortune in the *Decameron*, see Bragantini 2016.

hierarchical late Middle Ages. The *Decameron* abounds with lower-class characters endowed with noble souls, as Pampinea stresses in tale VI.2, citing the case of "Cisti, our fellow citizen, and many other people" ("Cisti nostro cittadino e in molti ancora"; VI.2.3). Pampinea knows these townspeople well, for she narrates three more tales about them, though the theme is less prominent in those narratives.[27]

The novella that deals with Nature, on the other hand (narrated by Panfilo), is that of Giotto and Forese da Rabatta, two rustic and ugly men:

> Dearest ladies, if Fortune, as Pampinea has shown us, does sometimes hide treasures most rich of native worth in the obscurity of base occupations, so in like manner 'tis not seldom found that Nature has enshrined prodigies of wit in the most ignoble of human forms. Whereof a notable example is afforded by two of our citizens, of whom I purpose for a brief while to discourse. The one, Messer Forese da Rabatta by name, was short and deformed of person and withal flat-cheeked and flat-nosed, insomuch that never a Baroncio had a visage so misshapen but his would have showed as hideous beside it; yet so conversant was this man with the laws, that by not a few of those well able to form an opinion he was reputed a veritable storehouse of civil jurisprudence. The other, whose name was Giotto, was of so excellent a wit that, let Nature, mother of all, operant ever by continual revolution of the heavens, fashion what she would, he with his style and pen and pencil would depict its like on such wise that it shewed not as its like, but rather as the thing itself, insomuch that the visual sense of men did often err in regard thereof, mistaking for real that which was but painted.
>
> (Carissime donne, egli avviene spesso che, sì come la fortuna sotto vili arti alcuna volta grandissimi tesori di vertù nasconde, come poco avanti Paminea fu mostrato, così ancora sotto turpissime forme d'uomini si truovano maravigliosi ingegni dalla natura essere stati riposti. La qual cosa assai apparve in due nostri cittadini de' quali io intendo brievemente di ragionarvi: per ciò che l'uno, il quale messer Forese da Rabatta fu chiamato, essendo di persona piccolo e isformato, con viso piatto e ricagnato

27 In II.3, the daughter of the King of England (disguised as an abbot) falls in love with a Florentine by the name of Alessandro. She deems him a gentleman, even though his profession is a lowly one ("mestiere … servile"; II.3.22). In X.7, we have Lisa, the daughter of an apothecary from Florence living in Palermo, who falls in love with King Piero when she sees him jousting in a tournament. Pampinea tells her audience that Lisa's speech and bearing lead the king to have high regard for her; we are told that the king "several times inwardly swore at Fortune for making her the daughter of such a man" ("piú volte seco stesso maladisse la fortuna che di tale uomo l'aveva fatta figliuola"; X.7.35). Pampinea also tells the tale of Agilulf and his groom (III.3) (see Filosa 2014b). There are tales with similar themes narrated by others of the party. In IV.1, for example, Fiammetta gives us the story of Guiscardo, the object of Ghismonda's love: "a man of exceedingly humble birth, but noble in character and bearing" ("uom di nazione assai umile ma per vertú e per costumi nobile"; IV.1.6).

che qualunque de' Baronci più trasformato l'ebbe sarebbe stato sozzo, fu di tanto sentimento nelle leggi, che da molti valenti uomini uno armario di ragione civile fu reputato; e l'altro, il cui nome fu Giotto, ebbe un ingegno di tanta eccellenzia, che niuna cosa dà la natura, madre di tutte le cose e operatrice col continuo girar de' cieli, che egli con lo stile e con la penna o col pennello non dipingesse sì simile a quella, che non simile, anzi piuttosto dessa paresse, in tanto che molte volte nelle cose da lui fatte si truova che il visivo senso degli uomini vi prese errore, quello credendo essere vero che era dipinto.) (VI.5.3–5)

This novella portrays Giotto and Forese da Rabatta, two people from Florence's recent history, individuals of supreme virtue and intellect; they both came from the Mugello countryside[28] and were only recently immersed in the city life of Florence, *homines-novi*, who belong to the higher guilds. The notary Forese da Rabatta was enrolled in the guild of judges and notaries, and the artist Giotto was rather unexpectedly enrolled among the *lanaiuoli*.[29] Boccaccio most likely met Giotto while he was in Naples, where Giotto was resident at the court of King Robert, from 1328 to 1333. Giotto painted two chapels in Santa Croce: the Peruzzi chapel in 1315 with the cycles of Saint John the Baptist and Saint John the Evangelist, and the Bardi chapel, located at the right side of the altar, between 1325 and 1328 with the cycle of Saint Francis. These are burial places that belonged to two very important families in the economic history of Florence in the early fourteenth century, families of bankers who were enrolled in the bankers' guild and had founded large companies. The Bardi chapel had been commissioned by Ridolfo de' Bardi, known as Doffo. Boccaccino worked for the Bardi company while in Naples along with the young Giovanni; Doffo de' Bardi was one of the fourteen good men who were tasked with reforming Florence under the guidance of Bishop Angelo Acciaiuoli after the expulsion of the Duke of Athens in 1343; and finally, he was the uncle of Luca di Feo Ugolini, one of the conspirators and a friend of Boccaccio. The notary who drafted the document of the new regime that was supposed to rule just after the expulsion of the Duke of Athens was the Forese da Rabatta of the *Decameron*, "the treasure-chest of civil law" ("l'armadio di ragione civile"), who most likely succumbed to plague in 1348.

In the novellas that tell of the baker Cisti, who belonged to the lower guilds, and Giotto and Forese Rabatta, who belonged to the higher guilds and represented the new citizens of Florence, Boccaccio celebrates noble spirits and great

28 The Medicis also came from the Mugello (Brucker 1957).

29 For the biographies of Forese da Rabatta and Giotto, see Ciappelli 1997 and Boskovits 2001. Giotto supplemented his income as an artist by renting out looms to poor weavers who could not afford their own work tools. He is suspected of practising usury on his loans; on at least one occasion, when the debtor was unable to repay a loan, he took some of the man's property corresponding to the amount of the debt.

intellects that transcend social hierarchies and physical appearances, undermining deep-seated beliefs that nobility comes from one's social condition, and that unattractive rustic characters are incapable of having a sophisticated intellect. These themes are recalled repeatedly in the *Decameron*, clearly representing a major concern of Boccaccio – illegitimate son of a merchant, recently moved to Florence, originally from the countryside of Certaldo, who had grown up and was educated at the court of Anjou. As Pier Massimo Forni appropriately points out:

> I would like to suggest that these stories … represent another step: that of the author himself from one social sphere (the one allotted to him by virtue of his birth) into a more privileged one. They are stories about access, about the holes in the fabric of destiny that allowed the illegitimate offspring of a Florentine merchant to breathe the rarefied and gentle air of the aristocratic Neapolitan circles. (Forni 2003, 214)

Beside the personal reasons Boccaccio had for including these stories in the *Decameron*, we can add political reasons, given the historical reality of Florence of the time. The notions that intelligence and virtue can be conveyed by fortune or nature did not jibe with the assumptions of the extremist factions of the city, who used pedigree and political and class affiliations as criteria for selecting their governors.

Noble Blood versus Noble Soul: A Political Debate

The philosophical debate on the nobility of the soul has a long tradition, but in the Florentine context it took on a political nuance. Its origins were classical: influenced by Senecan Stoicism,[30] before being adapted by Boethius (*De consolatione Philosophiae*, III.7–9), and rekindled and reassessed in the third poem of *Le dolci rime* of Dante, which introduced the fourth treatise of the unfinished *Convivio*.[31] Invoking both classical and Christian traditions, Dante earnestly countered the arguments that endorsed the nobility of blood and wealth, a debate that resurfaced throughout the thirteenth century. In *Le dolci rime*, Dante championed antiaristocratic ideals, denying that riches or antiquity of bloodline conferred nobility on a person; he rejected the notion that a man of low condition could not be born noble. In his perspective, nobility is a gift from God, transcending imminent worldly

30 The idea goes back to Plato and was elaborated by Ovid with his *Epistulae ex Ponto* I.9.39–40: "Si modo non census nec clarum nomen avorum, / sed probitas magnos ingeniumque facit" ("if indeed not wealth or the glorious name of one's ancestors but rather honesty and character make people great").

31 For the many possible influences on *Le dolci rime*, including the troubadours Guido Guinizzelli and Guittone d'Arezzo, see the introductory note by Claudio Giunta in the Mondadori edition of the *Convivio* (2014a, 521–6).

circumstances: it is God who bestows "the seed of happiness" ("il seme di felicità") on a "well-disposed spirit," as could be proved by observing that individuals may demonstrate virtues above their family and social status.[32] Therefore, nobility of the soul was implanted directly by God, and there was no point reasoning in terms of the "ancient wealth" of a specific house: we all descend from Adam, and "if Adam himself was noble, then we all are noble, and if he was disgraceful then we all are disgraceful" ("se esso Adamo fu nobile, tutti siamo nobili, e se esso fu vile, tutti siamo vili").[33] Therefore nobility "does not befall a bloodline, but rather individual people" ("non cade in ischiatta, cioè in stirpe, ma cade ne le singulari persone").

Echoes of Dante's themes and arguments, as expressed in *Le dolci rime*, can be found in Boccaccio's definition of nobility in *De casibus virorum illustrium*, in the chapter "*Pauca de nobilitate*" (*De cas.* VI iii). Tellingly, the chapter follows the biography of Marius, who was always associated with the epithet of "new man," "homo novus":

> Indeed, I believe that nobility is nothing other than a certain resplendent honour that, through pleasantness and affability of character, gleams in the eyes of those who behold it righteously; and it arises from the willpower of some soul that has grown accustomed and directed, according to its strength, to execute the task of scorning vice and imitating virtue. And this cannot be bequeathed to one's descendants by some act of inheritance or legacy or any other legal practice any differently than may be bequeathed knowledge or intellect.
>
> Nobility does not dwell – as most people foolishly think – in royal palaces, nor does it enjoy wealth or sumptuous clothes, nor, because the statues of ancestors are famous, does it for that reason inhabit the homes of their descendants; it alone is attracted to purity of the soul, whoever's and wherever it is … Indeed, those who wish to possess nobility that is authentic and not superficial must cultivate virtues, live virtuously, and absolutely condemn, repel, and avoid vices.
>
> (Arbitror quippe nil aliud nobilitatem esse quam quoddam splendidum decus in recte prospicientium oculos morum facetia et affabilitate refulgens, surgens ex alicuius habituata animi voluntate et opere pro viribus executioni mandata spernendi vitia imitandeque virtutis, quod non aliter posteris hereditario vel legatario, seu quo mavis iure alio, linqui potest, quam scientia aut ingenium relinquatur.
>
> Hec non, ut rentur stolide plurimi, regias habitat domos seu divitiis et splendore vestium delectatur nec ob preteritorum famosas ymagines lares successorum incolit; sola quidem mentis puritate letatur in quocunque vel ubicunque sit … Virtutes quidem colere, virtuose agere, vitia omnino damnare repellere fugere necesse est volentibus nobilitatem certissimam, non umbratilem possidere.)

32 For a detailed analysis of *Le dolci rime*, see Borsa 2007 and the bibliography.

33 In the *De casibus virorum illustrium*, Boccaccio presents Adam in a distinctly negative light.

The debate over what constituted "true" nobility was present and recurring in mid-thirteenth-century Florence, as Boccaccio reminds us:

> 'Tis no long time since there dwelt in our city a young man, Michele Scalza by name, the pleasantest and merriest fellow in the world, and the best furnished with quaint stories: for which reason the Florentine youth set great store on having him with them when they forgathered in company. Now it so befell that one day, he being with a party of them at Mont' Ughi, *they fell a disputing together on this wise; to wit, who were the best gentlemen and of the longest descent in Florence.* One said, the Uberti, another, the Lamberti, or some other family, according to the predilection of the speaker.

> (Egli non è ancora guari di tempo passato che nella nostra città era un giovane chiamato Michele Scalza, il quale era il piú piacevole e il piú sollazzevole uomo del mondo e le piú nuove novelle aveva per le mani; per la qual cosa i giovani fiorentini avevan molto caro, quando in brigata si trovavano, di poter aver lui. Ora avvenne un giorno che, essendo egli con alquanti a Montughi, *si cominciò tra loro una quistion cosí fatta: quali fossero li piú gentili uomini di Firenze e i piú antichi*; de' quali alcuni dicevano gli Uberti e altri i Lamberti, e chi uno e chi un altro, secondo che nell'animo gli capea.) (*Dec.* VI.6.4–5; emphasis added)

Here, the young men of Florence discussing whether the Uberti or Lamberti are the oldest family in their city – as if this were the key point of the question – represent a common way of thinking, one that is about to receive an ironic lesson from Michele Scalza. He claims that the most noble family in the entire world (or at least in Maremma) are the Baronci: "Since the Baronci are more ancient than anyone else, they must necessarily be the noblest" ("I Baronci son più antichi che niuno atro uomo, sì che son più gentili"; *Dec.* VI.6.11).[34] The absurd demonstration is based on a syllogism that makes two assumptions: the first contradicts an objective fact, easily visible to everyone, that all the Baronci are far from noble in appearance but, on the contrary, hideously deformed; the second is a common misconception – that the noblest family is necessarily the oldest. Therefore, because the Baronci had been created while God was still learning how to draw[35] (that is, before Adam), they must be the most ancient and hence the most noble in the whole world. Those present listening to the "pleasant argument" put forth by Michele Scalza agreed with him with much laughter. To conclude the novella, Fiammetta adds: "And that is why, when Panfilo wanted to describe how hideous Messer Forese's face was, he was justified in saying that it would have looked ugly alongside one of the Baroncis" ("E per ciò meritamente Panfilo, volendo la

34 For an influential take on this novella, see Ferreri 1990.

35 This argument is derived from the *Saturnalia* of Macrobius (II, 2, 10); see Muscetta 1972, 250.

turpitudine del viso di messer Forese mostrare, disse che stato sarebbe sozzo a un de' Baronci"; *Dec.* VI.6.17). This final joke by Fiammetta serves to reiterate the greater nobility of Forese da Rabatta, who was indeed uglier than the Baronci and therefore even more noble. This joke, and the whole novella of Forese da Rabatta, reverses the notion that nobility shines mainly in individuals whose bodily appearance is perfect. (In this instance, Boccaccio deviates from Dante, who thought that a nobler soul corresponded to a better composed and more proportionate body.)

Of course, Michele Scalza's absurd argument ridicules the Baronci and especially the equation of antiquity of ancestry and nobility. In this novella, Boccaccio dramatizes Dante: there is no such thing as noble blood and we are all descended from the same Adam.[36] Nobility cannot be inherited, a point Dante makes in *Le dolci rime*:

> Someone, according to his wish and whim,
> imperiously has ruled
> that gentleness is ancient wealth of goods
> with gracious manners shown.
> Some other, in interpreting his phrase,
> proved of a lighter mind,
> for he removed the latter part of it,
> not owning it himself.
> After him come all those who simply call
> a person gentle, whose forefathers have
> dwelt in great riches many a century;
> and so within our midst
> is such a false opinion inured
> that only he is called
> a noble man, who so can boast, "I was
> grandson, or son, of such a might knight,"
> though a nonentity.
> Most pitiful to those who see the truth
> is he who's shown the way and loses it,
> just like a man who treads, though dead, the ground.

36 Boccaccio knew of the *Convivio* (he cites it in his *Life of Dante*), though he may not have read it. Among those who see an influence of the *Convivio* on the *Decameron*, see Ferreri 1990 and Forni 1996, 105–11. For the purposes of this discussion, it is not necessary that Boccaccio read the *Convivio*: all of Dante's ideas on nobility are clearly expressed in *Le dolci rime*, which is part of the fifteen *canzoni distese*, copied by his own hand in three codices: Toledano 104.6, Riccardiano 1035, and Chigiano L.V. 176. For more on Boccaccio's influence on the tradition of *canzoni distese*, see Arduini 2010 and 2012.

(Tale imperò che gentilezza volse,
secondo 'l suo parere,
che fosse antica possession d'avere
con reggimenti belli;
ed altri fu di più lieve savere,
che tal detto rivolse,
e l'ultima particole ne tolse,
ché non l'avea fors'elli!
Di retro da costui van tutti quelli
che fan gentile per ischiatta altrui
che lungiamente in gran ricchezza è stata;
ed è tanto durata
la così falsa oppinion tra nui,
che l'uom chiama colui
omo gentil, che può dicere: "Io fui
nepote" o "figlio di cotal valente",
benché sia da niente.
Ma vilissimo sembra, a chi 'l ver guata,
cui è scorto 'l cammino e poscia l'erra,
e tocca a tal ch'è morto e va per terra!) (ll. 21–37)

Why would Boccaccio want to challenge the idea of noble blood so strenuously? Why attack the Baronci? Who were the most visible members of the Baronci family at the time Boccaccio composed this novella, probably on or shortly after his return to Florence in summer 1348? The answers to these questions may be found in the identity of the man who brought so much amusement to the narrators: the man whose ugliness was apparent to everyone was Tommaso di Diodato Baronci. His patronymic in the context of the novella (Diodato, which literally means "given by God") adds hilarity to the narration: since Baronci was created by the Lord himself when he was learning how to draw, so he was indeed directly "given by God." Tommaso Baronci, who came from the Maremma (or perhaps Siena),[37] resident in

37 According to the heading of the novella, it would appear that the Baronci originally came from the Maremma: "Michele Scalza proves to some young men how the Baronci are the noblest men in the world or at least the Maremma, and he earns himself a dinner" ("Pruova Michele Scalza a certi giovani come i Baronci sono i più gentili uomini del mondo o di Maremma e vince una cena." Nevertheless, the reference to the Maremma in the novella may serve only as comic hyperbole (Tateo 1998, 163). The historical reality is that the sincere devotion of Tommaso di Diodato Baronci to Saint Ansanus, protector of Siena, may suggest an origin from that city: indeed, he commissioned frescoes with scenes from the life of Saint Thomas in the Chapel of Saint Ansanus in Santa Maria Maggiore in Florence and the triptych of the Madonna with child between Saint Mary Magdalene and Saint Ansanus, preserved today in the Rijksmuseum in Amsterdam. Both works were commissioned to Andrea di Cione, known as l'Orcagna.

Santa Maria Maggiore in Florence, was prior several times,[38] an important banker affiliated with the bankers' guild, and partner in 1350–3 of the company of Vieri di Cambio de' Medici. One of Vieri's daughters, Ginevra, married a Baronci, Chimenti di Buoncristiano, thus sealing a close link between the families. Vieri di Cambio de' Medici was one of the most unrepentant of the oligarchs in Florence, considered one of the champions of the Guelf Party (Stefani 1910, rubr. 775), for which he was sent into exile at the Ciompi Revolt in 1378; he was a strong supporter of the practice of *ammonizioni*.[39] His son-in-law, Chimenti di Buoncristiano Baronci, was prior in January 1347, exactly when the new anti-Ghibelline law was passed (Stefani 1910, rubr. 632 bis). In that year, among those successfully prosecuted for violating this law was Andrea di Tello da Lisca (Brucker 1962, 117–18), one of Boccaccio's friends and a future conspirator. Clearly, the Baronci were part of the oligarchic faction in the city, allied with the Albizzi and thus opposed to the more populist Ricci.

We cannot tell if Boccaccio was a partisan of either faction in the dispute (not every citizen in Florence took part),[40] but we can say that Dante's theory of the nobility of soul endorsed in the *Decameron* in this geographical and historical context is consistent with the need for politics that are more accessible to *gente nuova*, minor guilds, and an enlarged group of people in the ruling class. Ultimately, the *Decameron* seems to align with the Ricci faction – as does the *Consolatoria a Pino de' Rossi*. Therefore, when the *Decameron* was being composed, this debate about nobility and blood can be read beyond strictly philosophical terms, namely, as engaging the question of who had the right to actively participate in the political life of the Republic of Florence.

In Day Six, we read about a world in which the old nobility coexists with simple men of lofty spirit: Geri Spini is able to recognize the value of Cisti, the baker; Currado Gianfigliazzi is able to forgive Chichibio without making him pay for the offence of having stolen the crane's leg; Forese da Rabatta and Giotto are described as ingenious, intelligent, capable, knowledgeable men, albeit new

38 Tommaso di Diodato Baronci was prior May 1346–January 1347 and January 1357–January 1358; in 1350 and 1357 he was company gonfalonier; and in 1359 he was appointed to the main governing body of Florence (*Tratte*). According to novella 83 by Franco Sacchetti, Tommaso Baronci was no longer prior after 1361, because he had become convinced that the Priors' Palace was infested by the Devil as a result of three pranks by Marco del Rosso degli Strozzi and Tommaso Federighi. In fact, we know from the listings of the *Cronica fiorentina* by Stefani that all three were priors together between 1357 and January 1358.

39 Vieri di Cambio de' Medici was admitted to the bankers' guild in October 1348 (Brucker 1957, 6, n. 32). For Vieri di Cambio de' Medici, see Zaccaria 2009; Brucker 1957, 9–10; and Mazzoni 2010, 109; appendix II, 77.

40 The notary Ser Domenico di Jacopo da Certaldo (maybe a cousin of Boccaccio) during a council in July 1352 stated: "All citizens should be led back to unity" (ASFi, *CP* 1, f. 23r: Brucker 1962, 129). This refrain "appears with monotonous regularity in later protocols: *unitas civium*" (Brucker 1962, 129).

citizens of Florence and despite their ugliness and rustic origin. Boccaccio seems to envision a society based on harmony, in which distinctions of class disappear and people are led by virtues – a dream that was far from reality but that the narrators of the *Decameron* were building in the fiction of the overarching tale. The ten young narrators go back to Florence after the plague, which on one hand killed more than half of the population, but on the other made possible a resurgence, a new beginning on much better social bases. Once in Florence, the narrators will rebuild a new society based on the value of the nobility of soul, which allows citizens to look for improvements through virtue and to live in peace. They seek to re-found the subverted order and resuscitate the ethical and civic values of liberality, magnanimity, and loyalty that characterized the chivalric culture and distinguish the tales of the final day.[41]

This was Boccaccio's dream, and he wanted to imbue it in his readers, to whom he was representing the image of their best selves, the same readers who were called on to build a new society after the devastation of the plague. Boccaccio was not the only one who "postulated a visionary ideal" in Florence, as Brucker points out (1962, 131–2):

> When Matteo Villani and Donato Velluti deplored the rise of the *sette cittadinesche*, they emphasized that these factions were disruptive, that they added another dimension to the pattern of discord within Florence between individuals, families, and social classes. They postulated a visionary ideal that had never actually existed in the Arno city: of citizens motivated solely by desire to promote the public welfare, meeting together in harmony and concord to direct the affairs of state.

Founding the Utopian City

The ideal of harmony in the different social classes is achieved through words, resolving conflicts even within the patrician class. This is the case in novella VI.9,[42] whose two protagonists come from two early thirteenth-century families from opposing factions: Betto Brunelleschi, an ex-Ghibelline who later became an important leader of the Black Guelfs,[43] and Guido Cavalcanti, exponent of White Guelfism.

---

41 See also Cardini 2007.

42 I omit consideration of novellas VI.7, with a formidable Filippa, and VI.10, with an unforgettable Frate Cipolla, because they are not set in Florence. Also VI.8, because the protagonist, although of the Frescobaldi family, cannot be clearly identified. On *Decameron* VI.9, see Alfie 1995; Velli 1995, 218–21; Barański 2006; Olson 2014, 44–53.

43 For a biography of Betto Brunelleschi, see Cardini 1972. Dino Compagni is scathing on Betto Brunelleschi's conversion from Ghibelline to Black Guelf, underlining the casual, self-interested opportunism of his political choices, and accusing him of the murder of Corso Donati; Brunelleschi, according to Compagni, is "a terrible citizen" (1986, III.39).

As Cardini notes (*DBI*, 1972), Boccaccio's portrait of Betto Brunelleschi in the *Decameron* diverges considerably from what we read in the chronicles of the time and other historical materials: "From an examination of his political life, full of shadows and violence, we can see without a doubt a profile that is very different from the 'subtle and intelligent knight' ('sottile e intendente cavaliere') transmitted by Boccaccio." Betto Brunelleschi and Guido Cavalcanti each made an attempt on the life of Corso Donati, the leader of the Black Guelf faction. As noted previously, Boccaccio was closely linked by friendship to the Donati family. Why would he want to defend these two characters? I believe there are different motivations for doing so for each man.

As noted, the novellas of Day Six all take place in Tuscany, and eight out of the ten are in the city or its environs. The narrative time is a mythical Florence of the first three decades of the fourteenth century,[44] in which many nonetheless historically identifiable protagonists move. Many of these characters are ancestors of Boccaccio's entourage, Betto Brunelleschi among them. Betto had two sons, Ottaviano and Francesco; the latter is perhaps the son who confronted those who assaulted his father, killing one of them. We know nothing of Francesco, but we know that Ottaviano di Betto Brunelleschi, dead by 1342, had four children: a son named Boccaccio and three daughters who were all married by the end of that year. Giovanna married Albertozzo Alberti, Niccolosa married Bartolomeo di Alamanno de' Medici, and Tosa married Tili degli Adimari (appendix A1.7). It is important in our context to underscore how Niccolosa married Bartolomeo di Alamanno de' Medici (one of Alamanno de' Medici sons), who was for the Ricci faction and one of the ringleaders and an informant in the conspiracy of 1360.[45] According to Matteo Villani, it was his brother, Salvestro di Alamanno de' Medici, who convinced him to denounce the conspiracy to the Commune. Salvestro had a great influence in the Florentine councils in the late fourteenth century, and with Boccaccio's friends he took part in the war against the Ubaldini in Scarperia ("Petrarch's war"), making "the finest defence ever made" ("la più bella difesa si facesse mai"; Velluti 1914, 210).

Guido Cavalcanti, another of the protagonists in Day Six, is one of the most attractive figures in the whole *Decameron*. He is described by the narrator, Elissa:

> Besides being one of the best logicians in the world, and an excellent natural philosopher (qualities of which the company made no great account), he was without a peer for gallantry and courtesy and excellence of discourse and aptitude for all matters which he might set his mind to, and that belonged to a gentleman; and therewithal he was very rich, and, when he deemed any worthy of honour, knew how to bestow it to the uttermost.

44 On this point see Padoan 1978, 108–9; and Mineo 1994.

45 See Velluti 1914, 241–2; and Brucker 1957, 17.

(oltre a quello che egli fu un de' migliori loici che avesse il mondo e ottimo filosofo naturale (delle quali cose poco la brigata curava), si fu egli leggiadrissimo e costumato e parlante uom molto e ogni cosa che far volle e a gentile uom pertenente seppe meglio che altro uom fare; e con questo era ricchissimo, e a chiedere a lingua sapeva onorare cui nell'animo gli capeva che il valesse.) (*Dec.* VI.9.8)

Already through this presentation, Boccaccio reverses Dante's negative portrait of Guido di Cavalcante de' Cavalcanti,[46] presenting him instead as a paradigm of nobility. But Betto Brunelleschi's friends – as Elissa tells us immediately – underestimate his main quality as "one of the best logicians in the world, and an excellent natural philosopher."[47] Precisely this aspect allows him to best them, with intellect, virtue, and sophistication in rendering a quick retort to those who wished to "harass him" ("dargli briga"):

Now one day it so befell that, Guido being come, as was not seldom his wont, from Or San Michele by the Corso degli Adimari as far as San Giovanni, around which were then the great tombs of marble that are today in Santa Reparata, besides other tombs not a few, and Guido being between the columns of porphyry, that are there, and the tombs and the door of San Giovanni, which was locked, Messer Betto and his company came riding on to the piazza of Santa Reparata, and seeing him among the tombs, said: "Go we and flout him." So they set spurs to their horses, and making a mock onset, were upon him almost before he saw them. Whereupon: "Guido," they began, "thou wilt be none of our company; but, lo now, when thou hast proved that God does not exist, what wilt thou have achieved?"

Guido, seeing that he was surrounded, presently answered: "Gentlemen, you may say to me what you please in your own house." Thereupon he laid his hand on one of the great tombs, and being very nimble, vaulted over it, and so evaded them, and went his way.

(Ora avvenne un giorno che, essendo Guido partito d' Orto San Michele e venutosene per lo Corso degli Adimari infino a San Giovanni, il quale spesse volte era suo cammino, essendo arche grandi di marmo, che oggi sono in Santa Reparata, e molte altre dintorno a San Giovanni, e egli essendo tralle colonne del porfido che vi sono e quelle arche e la porta di San Giovanni, che serrata era, messer Betto con sua brigata a caval venendo su per la piazza di Santa Reparata, vedendo Guido là tra quelle

46 See Zygmunt Barański on this novella: "While Dante's Guido seems likely to be doomed to remain in this *arca* in perpetuity, Boccaccio's Guido, having fired off his cutting retort, gramatically escapes both from the clutches of the *brigata* and from the restrictions of the *arche grandi di marmo* (§10)" (2006, 285).

47 On the accusations of Epicureanism levelled at Guido Cavalcanti in this context, see Barański 2006 and 2020. On Boccaccio and Epicureanism, see Barański 2006, and Veglia 2000, 15–56.

sepolture, dissero: "Andiamo a dargli briga"; e spronati i cavalli, a guisa d'uno assalto sollazzevole gli furono, quasi prima che egli se ne avvedesse, sopra e cominciarongli a dire: "Guido, tu rifiuti d'esser di nostra brigata; ma ecco, quando tu avrai trovato che Idio non sia, che avrai fatto?"

A' quali Guido, da lor veggendosi chiuso, prestamente disse: "Signori, voi mi potete dire a casa vostra ciò che vi piace"; e posta la mano sopra una di quelle arche, che grandi erano, sí come colui che leggerissimo era, prese un salto e fussi gittato dall'altra parte, e sviluppatosi da loro se n'andò. (*Dec.* VI.9.10–12)

"Gentlemen, you may say to me what you please in your own house" are the only words Guido speaks in the novella, and they are followed by a leap of lightness and liberation.[48] He rises into the air and flies above the marble arches – where he had been relegated *in eternum* by his "friend" Dante Alighieri – and thus metaphorically rises above death; Betto's *brigata*, meanwhile, remain trapped among the tombs near San Giovanni – literally, if we consider that Betto Brunelleschi was buried in Santa Maria del Fiore next to the Baptistery.[49] Guido's parting words are not understood by the listeners, until they are interpreted by none other than Betto Brunelleschi:

"Nay but," quoth he, "'tis ye that have taken leave of your wits, if ye have not understood him; for meetly and in few words he has given us never so shrewd a reprimand; seeing that, if you consider it well, these tombs are the houses of the dead, that are laid and tarry therein; which he calls our house, to shew us that we, and all other simple, unlettered men, are, in comparison of him and the rest of the learned, in sorrier case than dead men, and so being here, we are in our own house."

("Gli smemorati siete voi, se voi non l'avete inteso: egli ci ha detta onestamente in poche parole la maggior villania del mondo, per ciò che, se voi riguarderete bene, queste arche sono le case de' morti, per ciò che in esse si pongono e dimorano i morti; le quali egli dice che sono nostra casa, a dimostrarci che noi e gli altri uomini idioti

48 On the lightness with which Guido Cavalcanti flies over the tombs, Italo Calvino wrote in his *Six Memos for the Next Millennium*: "If I had to choose an auspicious sign for the approach of the new millennium, I would choose this: the sudden nimble leap of the poet/philosopher who lifts himself against the weight of the world, proving that its heaviness contains the secret of lightness, while what many believe to be the life force of the times – loud and aggressive, roaring and rumbling – belongs to the realm of death, like a graveyard of rusted automobiles" (2016, 14).

49 Domenico Maria Manni writes that Betto Brunelleschi was "buried c. 1311, as far as we can tell, in the Chiesa di S. Maria del Fiore, since in an ancient list of its burials we find, among others who have been buried there, *D. Bettus de Brunelleschis*" (1742, 428). Franco Cardini in his biographical entry in the *DBI* (1972) writes: "The solemn funeral of B. gave way to a sad diatribe among the Dominicans of S. Maria Novella and the secular clergy of S. Reparata, who both contended for his luxurious ceremonial habit. The fallout of this episode dragged on, and only in 1321 did they reach a resolution."

> e non litterati siamo, a comparazion di lui e degli altri uomini scienziati, peggio che uomini morti, e per ciò, qui essendo, noi siamo a casa nostra.") (*Dec.* VI.9.14)

The incident proves that "elegant words" ("leggiardi motti") and the "prompt answer" ("le pronte risposte") require not only a nimble and crafty speaker but also a listener capable of understanding their significance.[50] Guido's retort to Betto and his friends works because it is not immediately intelligible, and the interval that occurs between the moment it is uttered and the moment it is understood gives him the time that he needs to lift himself up "lightly" ("leggerissimo") into the air and extricate himself from an unfortunate situation.

Betto realizes that Guido called the tombs "our house, to shew us that we, and all other simple, unlettered men, are, in comparison of him and the rest of the learned, in sorrier case than dead men." As Velli recalls, this assertion evokes Seneca's "Leisure without literature is death, a tomb for a living man" ("Otium sine litteris mors est, et hominis vivi sepultura"; *Ep. ad Luc.* 82.4).[51] The figure of Guido, drawn as logician ("loico") and philosopher, becomes the prototype for an entire category of people, namely, intellectuals like Boccaccio and perhaps also Maestro Alberto (*Dec.* II.10) and the scholar Ranieri (*Dec.* VIII.7) – other characters of the *Decameron* – whom it is risky to challenge. It is worth recalling that Boccaccio's authorial voice in the introduction to Day Four mentions Guido (along with Dante Alighieri and Cino da Pistoia) as *auctoritas*, a model in the literary field of love themes.[52] In this light, the character of Guido Cavalcanti helps us define the historical position of the writer in his times and his society.

Clearly in these novellas of Day Six, the society described by Boccaccio is idyllic and utopian, as all the characters who inhabit the city, whatever their social rank, birth, or education, manage to find a civil solution to every potential conflict by way of words. This is what apparently happened in the legendary Florence of the good old days:

> You are to know, then, that in former times there obtained in our city customs excellent and commendable not a few, whereof today not one is left to us, thanks to the greed which, growing with the wealth of our folk, has banished them all from among us. One of which customs was that in diverse quarters of Florence the gentlemen that there resided would assemble together in companies of a limited number, taking care to include therein only such as might conveniently bear the expenses, and to-day one, another tomorrow, each in his turn for a day, would entertain the rest of the company; and so they would not seldom do honour to gentlemen from distant parts when they visited the city, and also to their fellow citizens; and in like manner

50 See Renzo Bragantini's essay "Premesse sull'ascolto decameroniano" (2012, 69–87).

51 See Velli 1995, 219.

52 See Barański 2006.

they would meet together at least once a year all in the same trim, and on the most notable days would ride together through the city, and now and again they would tilt together, more especially on the greater feasts, or when the city was rejoiced by tidings of victory or some other glad event.

(Dovete adunque sapere che ne' tempi passati furono nella nostra città assai belle e laudevoli usanze, delle quali oggi niuna ve n'è rimasa, mercé della avarizia che in quella con le ricchezze è cresciuta, la quale tutte l'ha discacciate. Tralle quali n'era una cotale, che in diversi luoghi per Firenze si ragunavano insieme i gentili uomini delle contrade e facevano lor brigate di certo numero, guardando di mettervi tali che comportare potessono acconciamente le spese, e oggi l'uno, doman l'altro, e cosí per ordine tutti mettevan tavola, ciascuno il suo dí, a tutta la brigata; e in quella spesse volte onoravano e gentili uomini forestieri, quando ve ne capitavano, e ancora de' cittadini: e similmente si vestivano insieme almeno una volta l'anno, e insieme i dí piú notabili cavalcavano per la città, e talora armeggiavano, e massimamente per le feste principali o quando alcuna lieta novella di vittoria o d'altro fosse venuta nella città.) (*Dec.* VI.9.4–6)

These fictional groups of friends were gentle and courteous, and very different from the real "citizen sects" that were at the root of so many disagreements, factions, and internal battles within the Florence of their historical time (1290–1330), as they were in Boccaccio's.[53]

Through the fictions of the novellas of Day Six and its characters, Boccaccio gives a vision of a courteous and chivalric society that could be established in his own times, after 1348, immediately after the purification brought about by the plague. This is the intention of the company of narrators once they have returned to Florence: to found a new society, based on a prior utopia, whose values and virtues rest on the power of words and on the generosity, magnificence, and friendship set out in Day Ten of the *Decameron*.

In his choice of characters in Day Six, Boccaccio celebrates his friends' ancestors. There are two purposes to his strategy: to legitimate those who belong to his circle of friends and to encourage them to behave like their predecessors, if not better. The characters and their family relationships and connections to Boccaccio are shown in table 8.1. The people I list in the table are friends of Boccaccio that I have been able to identify directly; there were no doubt many others involved in these relationships. For example, the Rossi of Oltrarno were related to the Pulci family. As I show in part 1 of this book, in the immediate aftermath of the plague of 1348, Boccaccio and his friends played an important role in Florentine politics, if only for a little while. There was, for example, the war against the Ubaldini,

53 Cardini notes that the actual *brigate* "always had a political or at least an aggressive function" (1997, 94–5). See also Picone 1988 and Barolini 2012.

Table 8.1. The Protagonists of *Decameron*, Day Six, and their relationships to friends of Boccaccio

Novella	Protagonist	Relationship
VI.1	Monna Oretta	Aunt of Margherita di Vanni Spini, wife of *Niccolò Acciaiuoli*
VI.2	Geri Spini	Uncle of Margherita di Vanni Spini, wife of *Niccolò Acciaiuoli*
VI.3	Monna Nonna de' Pulci	Wife of *Manno di Apardo Donati* Sister-in-law of *Pazzino di Apardo Donati* Cousin of Alessio Rinucci, father of *Nonna di Alessio Rinucci*, wife of *Luca di Feo Ugolini*
VI.4	Currado Gianfigliazzi	Related to several members of the *Gianfigliazzi family* (e.g., Luigi Gianfigliazzi)
VI.9	Betto Brunellschi	Grandfather of Niccolosa, wife of *Bartolomeo di Alamanno de' Medici*

Note: The names of Boccaccio's friends are italicized

which William Caferro labels "Petrarch's War" precisely because it was inspired (if not actually desired) by the poet laureate; another example is the anti-Visconti campaign and the concomitant embassies, in which Luigi Gianfigliazzi, Pino de' Rossi, Uguccione de' Ricci, and Boccaccio were involved. Boccaccio also embraced the role of cultural promoter and intellectual, not to mention the public offices he held on behalf of the Commune of Florence: he arranged for a donation, requested by the Orsanmichele Company, for Sister Beatrice, Dante's daughter, and he attempted to bring Petrarch to the University of Florence. It would seem that Boccaccio and his circle really hoped to rebuild the Republic of Florence after the plague – or at least restore it after the mismanagement by the Duke of Athens and the popular government. Boccaccio, in good faith, used his collection of novellas to bolster the reputations of his friends by commemorating their ancestors, and he fantasized about a Republic capable of implementing justice, letting "no act of wrongdoing go unpunished" ("lasciare alcuno difetto commesso impunito"), and rewarding "every good deed" ("ben fatto remunerare"; *Trattatello*, incipit, red. 1, §1).[54] Indeed, in the few years after the plague, it seemed as if this dream might be fulfilled. But as we know, events turned out very differently: the Albizzi and the oligarchic faction seized power, and the last attempt by Boccaccio's friends to correct the city's course was crushed one day before New Year's Eve, 1360.

54 After an event in the winter of 1351, in the same period in which Boccaccio wrote the first version of *The Life of Dante*, Matteo Villani noted "the corrupt practices of the Commune of Florence, which does not punish wrongdoings or reward good deeds" ("la corrotta usanza del comune di Firenze di non punire le cose mal fatte, ne' meritare le buone"; 1995, 2.54); Boccaccio used the same words for the incipit of his *Life of Dante*.

Afterword

Boccaccio has been seen, first and foremost, as a writer, author of the *Decameron*, and, like Dante and Petrarch, a key figure in the great tradition of Italian literature in the vernacular. He is seen as a citizen of the great city of Florence, and a public servant. His decision to take religious orders later in his life is seen as a spiritual turn away from public life and its rewards to a life of greater interior and personal value. What is only now beginning to be understood in greater detail is just how deeply Boccaccio was involved in the turbulent politics of Florence, and the extent to which this involvement steered and inspired his work as a writer. Boccaccio, as we can now see, was also a profoundly political man. The evidence lies in the voluminous archives of the city as well as in his own works, contemporaneous accounts, and the commentaries of other writers. I began this undertaking with those records. Rather than starting with what is known about Boccaccio's life and work and going to archives for confirmation of various interpretations, I went the other way, searching the archives and uncovering facts that lead to new interpretations. This study, the result of that research, presents a richer and more textured picture of the man in his time, a microhistory, which, like a great tapestry, is intricately wrought of connections and interconnections that ramify well beyond their own spatio-temporal frame.

The well-documented financial, political, and social turbulence of mid-fourteenth-century Florence manifested itself also in a culture war, between the classical, elite literature, written in Latin and favoured by the Guelf Party, and the more populist literature written in the vernacular. Petrarch was the figure associated with the former, and Dante, whose poetry was memorized and recited even by the common people, was the champion of the new style. Boccaccio had to negotiate a life of letters that could exist within this split. He wrote not only imaginative, creative works of great popular appeal but also works in support of literature in the vernacular, and in support of his friends and the ideas they shared. He needed to be careful what he said and how, if he was to survive.

Boccaccio's life, over and over, demonstrates his belief in the power of language and literature, in friendship, honesty, civic and familial responsibility, and kindness. But these were not the only motivating factors in his life choices. Each of his decisions, to move from one place to another, to take on public responsibilities, to disseminate his poetry, fiction, and essays, even to turn to the Church, came in direct response to the conditions of this particular time and place. Each was an attempt to survive in an extraordinarily difficult and dangerous time, and it required intelligence, courage, diplomacy, and good judgment.

The material that I found in archives and contemporaneous accounts leads us to a new appreciation of an understudied aspect of Boccaccio's life and work. It demonstrates the extent to which intricate business and family connections were tied into politics, and how these interconnections played out in people's lives – specifically, in Boccaccio's. But there is still much to discover and relate. There are gaps in Boccaccio's life story, for which no documentation has yet been found. Avenues that could still be explored, for their own sake, and for what else they may tell us about Boccaccio, are the story of disease and mortality in that time, warfare and its effects, styles of governance, and church-state interactions. There is material in this study that points to a fruitful exploration of authors and audiences of the period, of vernacular literature versus institutional, refined literature (it is interesting that despite the Guelfs, Boccaccio and Dante and their vernacular writings have had much greater readership and influence than their nemesis, Petrarch, in his ambitious Latin works). The patterns we see in mid-fourteenth-century Florence may help us see other cities in Italy and Europe in a new light. We could reconsider reductive characterizations of other authors. This study presents Boccaccio's life and work in terms of intricately interconnected networks, as much political as social and artistic, but its findings and implications also open into many other areas of discovery.

Appendices

Appendix 1
Genealogical Tables

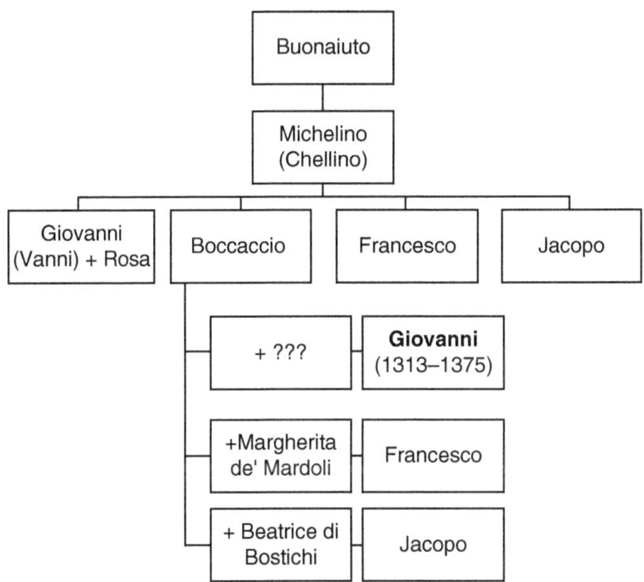

A1.1. Giovanni di Boccaccio da Certaldo

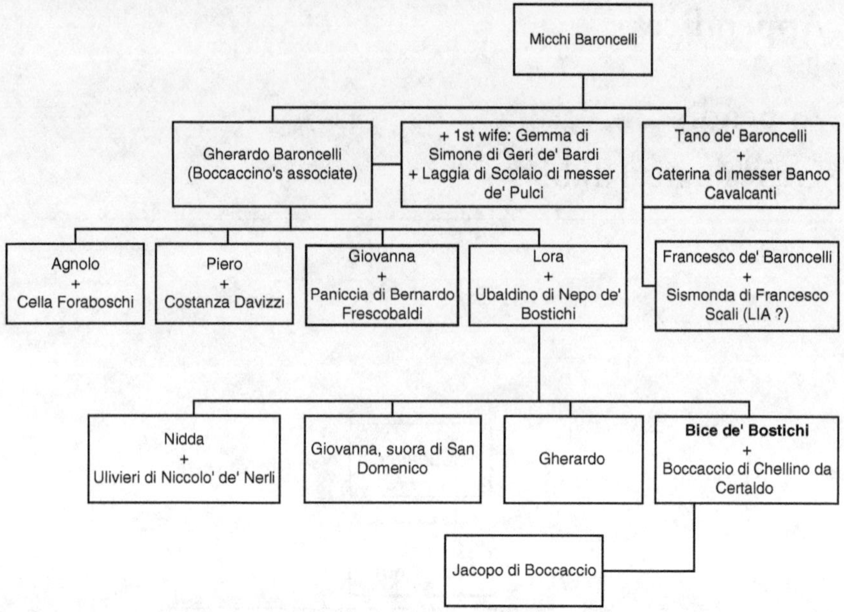

A1.2. Bice di Nepo de' Bostichi

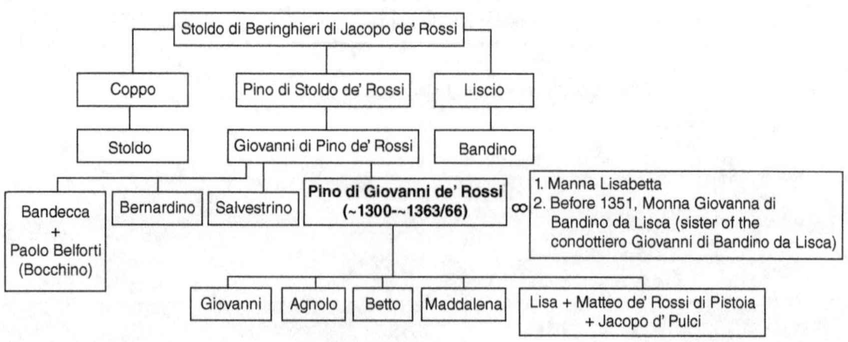

A1.3. Messer Pino di Giovanni de' Rossi

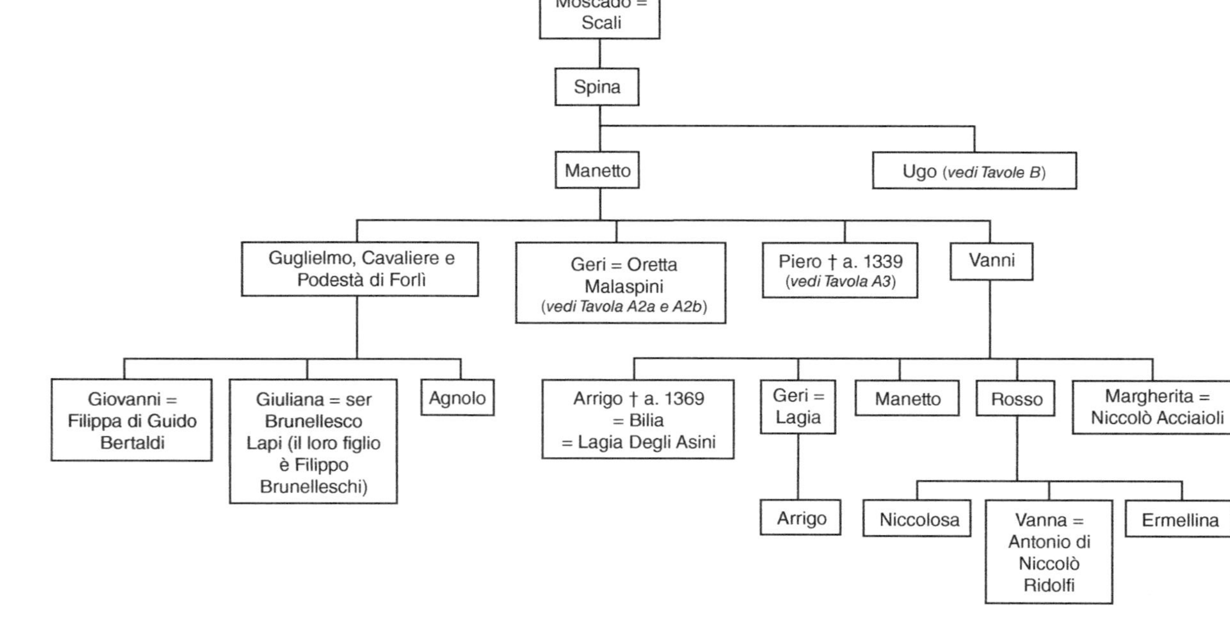

A1.4. Monna Oretta Malespini (*Dec.* VI.1) and Messer Geri di Manetto Spini (*Dec.* VI.2)

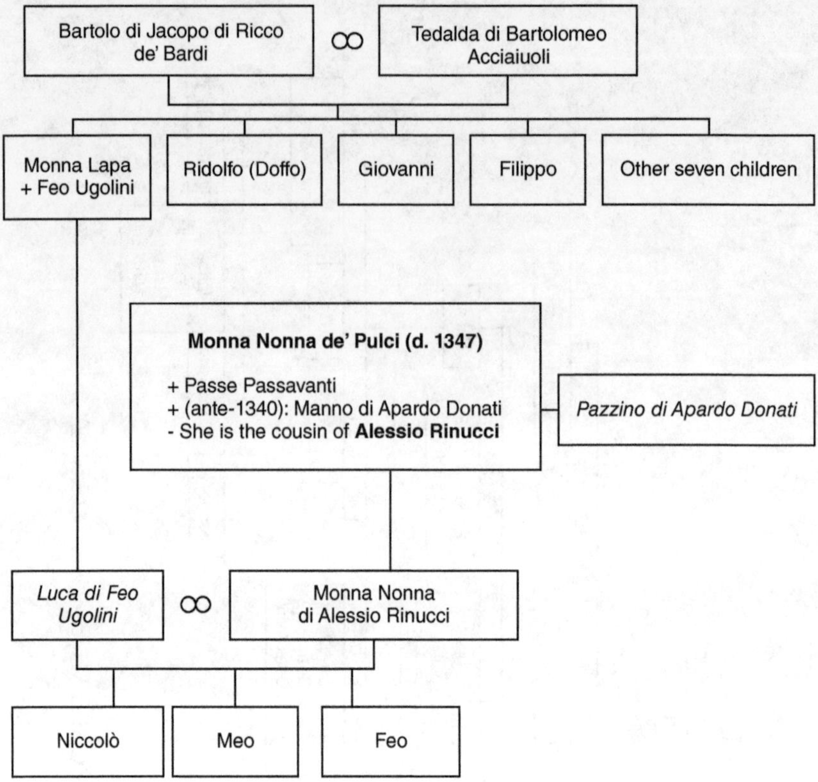

Bartolo di Jacopo di Ricco de' Bardi ∞ Tedalda di Bartolomeo Acciaiuoli

Monna Lapa + Feo Ugolini

Ridolfo (Doffo)

Giovanni

Filippo

Other seven children

Monna Nonna de' Pulci (d. 1347)

+ Passe Passavanti
+ (ante-1340): Manno di Apardo Donati
- She is the cousin of **Alessio Rinucci**

Pazzino di Apardo Donati

Luca di Feo Ugolini ∞ Monna Nonna di Alessio Rinucci

Niccolò

Meo

Feo

A1.5. Monna Nonna de' Pulci (*Dec.* VI.3)

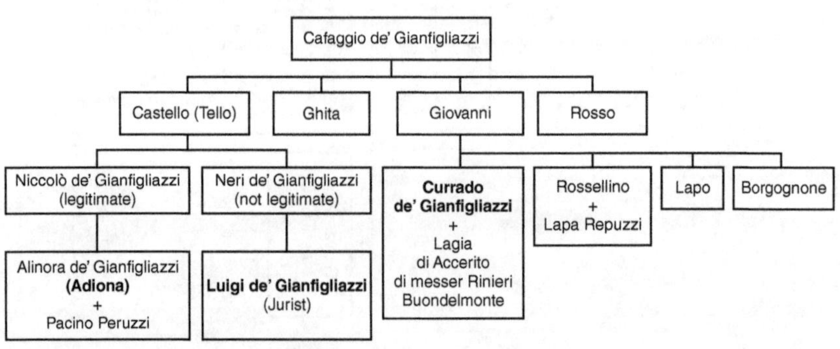

A1.6. Currado Gianfigliazzi (*Dec.* VI.4)

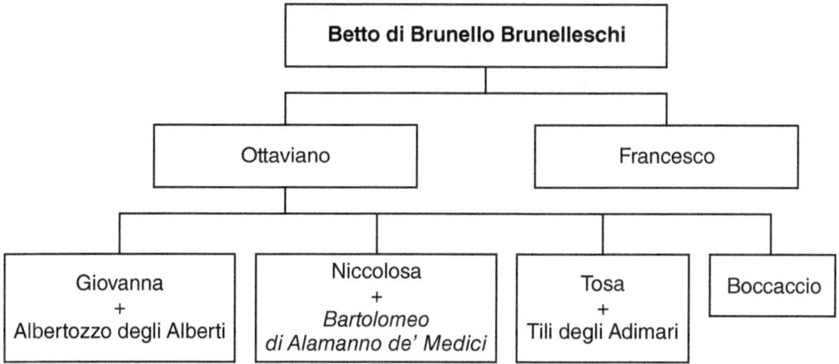

A1.7. Betto di Brunello Brunelleschi (*Dec.* VI.9)

Appendix 2
Transcriptions of Documents

1. The Death Sentence

ASFi, Atti del Podestà *1525, ff. 57r–58r*

[c. 57r] In nomine Domini, amen. Hec sunt condempnationes corporales et capitales[1] et sintentie dictarum condempnationum corporalium, date late et sintentialiter promulgate per mangnifichum et potentem militem dominum Lodovichum de Narnia, honorabilem Potestatem civitatis Florentie eiusque comitatus fortie et districtus, contra infrascriptos homines et personas pro infrascriptis nefandis scieleribus per eos et quemlibet ipsorum factis commissis et perpetratis in civitate Florentie, in publico et generali consilio dicte civitatis de consensu deliberatione presentia et voluntate omnium iudicum dicti domini Potestatis, et scripte et lecte per me Andream ser Francisci notarium infrascriptum, sub anno Domini millesimo tricentesimo sexagesimo, indictione XIIII[a], secundum consuetudinem dicte civitatis Florentie, tempore domini Inno<centi> Pape sexti, mense et die infrascriptis.

Nos Lodovichus de Narnia milex, Potestas civitatis Florentie eiusque comitatus fortie et districtus, pro tribunali sedentes ad ____ banchum iuris in sala _____[2] palatii nostre residentie,[3] ut moris est, in publico et generali consilio dicte civitatis ibidem de nostro mandato more solito congregato, infrascriptas condempnationes et sintentias contra infrascriptos homines et personas damus et sintentialiter proferrimus in his scriptis et in hunc modum, videlicet:

1 "Condempnationes corporales et capitales" is a judicial formula; it specifies that the person subject to the death sentence could also be subject to amputation of limbs or other parts of the body.

2 The two ruled lines are in the original (fig. A2.1a).

3 The Palazzo del Podestà, Via Proconsolo 4, Florence, known today as the Bargello.

Niccholaum Bartholi Boni quarterii Sancti Spiritus Dominichum Bandini populi Sancti Fridiani dominum Pinum domini Iohannis de Rubeis Ubertum Ubaldini Infangati populi Sancte Cicilie Bertramum Bartholomey de Pacçiis Andream Thelli populi Sancti Iacobi Niccholaum Guiddi Samontane de Frescobaldis Andream Pacchi de Alimariis Pacçinum domini Apardi de Donatis Pelliciam Bindi Sassi de Gerardinis Lucham Fey populi Sancti Felicis in Piacça et fratrem Christofarum Nucii de Florentia	ad hanc sententia audiendam coram nostra presentia personaliter constitutos

solitum morari in palatio dominorum Priorum Populi dicte civitatis, cives florentinos, et quemlibet ipsorum prodictores et sub statu pacificho et tranquillo dicte civitatis vivere non contentos,[4] homines in hac parte male condictionis vite et fame, contra quos et quemlibet ipsorum per viam et modum inquisitionis ex nostro et nostre curie offitio et arbitrio nobis in hac parte concesso per formam statutorum et ordinamentorum dic te civitatis processimus, in eo de eo et super eo, quod fama publica precedente et clamosa insinuatione referente, non quidem a malivolis, sed a veridicis et fide dingnis personis,[5] sepe sepius ad aures et notitiam nostram auditu pervenit quod supradicti omnes et singuli superius nominati et inquisiti, Deum pre oculis non habentes, sed potius humani generis inimicum,[6] videlicet predicti Niccholaus Bartholi, Dominichus, dominus Pinus, Ubertus, Bertramus, Andreas Telli, Niccholaus Guiddi, Andreas Pacchi, Paçcinus, Pellicia et Luchas, non advertentes quod presens pacificus et tranquillus status dicte civitatis Florentie in tranquillitate prosperitate et iustitia vigebat et viget, regebat et conservabat, ac etiam regit et gubernat sibi subditos et devotos, ac etiam fuit et est ad fundamentum regimen et gubernum etiam totius circumposite regionis et totius Tuscie; et quod ipsi et quilibet ipsorum ex dicto regimine cum iustitia permanebant in civitate et comitatu predictis, sicut alii cives dicte civitatis, sed potius

4 Being "not happy to live in the pacific and tranquil state of the state" is a formula commonly employed in cases of high treason: the phrase is repeated several times in the document.

5 The *fide digna persona* may be Salvestro di Alamanno de' Medici. According to Matteo Villani (1995, 10.25), he was the one who informed the Signoria in order to save his brother Bartolomeo di Alamanno de' Medici from death and the family from ignominy. Salvestro di Alamanno de' Medici was well respected in the Republic and was often called as councillor in the Signoria. According to Gene Brucker (1957, 16–17), he is the only Medici member in the fourteenth century with an important political role.

6 The "enemy of the human kind" is the devil: "Deum pre oculis non habentes, sed potius humani generis inimicum" is another judicial formula.

adtendentes contra libertatem civitatis predicte ad revolutionem et subversionem dicti pacifici status, maxime sumpta occasione, quod aliqui ex eis erant condepnati et aliqui admoniti pro gebellinis per offitiales Comunis predicti, et quod aliqui non habenbant in dicto Comuni nec habere poterant offitia sicut alii cives predicti, et ob hoc sub dicto pacifico statu vivere non contenti, animo et intentione dictum pacifichum statum subvertendi turbandi et removendi, et ipsum statum in alium commutandi, et reformationes dicti Comunis Florentie de gebellinis loquentes et contra eos removendi et cassandi et cancellandi, de facto insimul et vicissim inter se semel et pluries tamquam iniquitatis filii tractaverunt conspiraverunt, tractatum ratiocinium et conspirationem et confederationem fecerunt, per quem modum et viam et quo ordine predicta et ipsorum prava intentio in predictis possent executioni mandari, **[c. 57v]** et tandem dicto tractatu premisso et in eodem insistentes, firmaverunt posuerunt et declaraverunt inter se et sibi ad invicem, credentes et sperantes et sic inter se adfirmantes, habere supradictis favorem, auxilium et consilium plurimorum et diversorum civium mangnatum et popularium ac etiam artificum dicte civitatis per vim et violentiam et manu armata cum aliqua forensium peditum comitiva, noctis tempore, invadere, capere et occupare palatium Populi et residentie dominorum Priorum Populi dicte civitatis, et dicto palatio prehabito, ipsam civitatem capere et occupare ad rumorem, ita et talis quod ipse presens pacificus status civitatis predicte firmiter mutaretur; et quod novus modus teneretur et adhiberetur regimini supradicto, et maxime quod offitium dominorum Priorum esset de duodecim numero ultra et aliter quam modo persistat; et quod tamburum et Ordinamenta Iustitie, que nunc vigent contra nobiles dicte civitatis, elevarentur et cassarentur, et etiam deveta et multa alia tendentia ad predicta ultra et aliter quam nunc sint in dicto Comuni ordinata et stabilita pro salute et statu dicte civitatis et subiectores eius; et predicta fuerunt facta ratiocinata, pensata, dicta, tractata et ordinata semel et pluries inter eos superius nominatos causa et intentione implendi eorum pravam voluntatem et ut per vim et violentiam dicte reformationes tollerentur; et ipse pacificus status reciperet mutamentum, et adhiberetur novum regimen ad eorum beneplacitum ad mortem et confuxionem et perpetuum exterminium dicti presentis status et civium sub dicto statu viventium; et ad ipsius civitatis scandalum et turbationem, tumultum et rumorem, et etiam sedictionem; et per eos non stetit quoniam predicta secundum eorum intentionem tam pravam et iniquam effectui ducerentur; set quia pervenerunt ad notitiam civium civitatis predicte diligentius dictum presentem statum et ipsius domini Potestatis, ita quod dictum tractatum ad effectum perducere minime potuerunt, locis et temporibus in dicta inquisitione contentis, et dictus frater Christofarus, loco et tempore in dicta inquisitione contentis, dum sentiret dictum tractatum confederationem et seditionem et eisdem expresse consensisset, tanquam homo male condictionis et vite, inmemor a dicto Populo et Comune recepti honoris et offitii, per plura tempora ad predicta requisitus, maxime pro faciliori facultate habendi et occupandi palatium supradictum, ipse frater

Christofarus deliberate studiose et malo modo ad hoc ut ipse tractatus reciperet effectum, tanquam proditor dicti Comunis pro turbatione, scandalo et tumultu dicti pacifici status obtulit et promisit se daturum operam efficacem quod dictum palatium haberetur in hac forma, videlicet quia ipse frater Christofarus dixit quod, quando dictus tractatus deberet perfici, ipse adcederet de sero ad iacendum cum fratribus existentibus in dicto palatio, et cum ibi esset dixit se adcepturum claves porte palatii predicti, que nunc non aperitur, quas claves dixit se scire, et cum ipsis clavibus abseruit et firmavit se aperire dictam portam ipsis tractantibus et volentibus intrare per eam pro invasione palatii supradicti. Et costat nobis et nostre curie predicta omnia singula vera fuisse et esse, et fore commissa et perpetrata per predictos superius inquisitos et nominatos et quemlibet ipsorum per legitimam confessionem dictorum Niccholay Bartoli et Dominichi coram nobis in iudicio sponte factam; quibus et cuilibet eorum datus et adsignatus fuit certus terminus, iam elapssus, ad omnem ipsorum defensionem faciendam de predictis, et nullam fecerunt, et per contumaciam suprascriptorum aliorum in dicta inquisitione contentorum, quos et quemlibet ipsorum citari fecimus et requiri, ac etiam in bando poni et exbandiri de civitate comitatu et districtu Florentie per publicum bannitorem Comunis predicti in avere et persona; et non comparuerunt in terminis assignatis eisdem, sed potius contumaces fuerunt et sunt, prout hec et alia in actis nostris et nostre cure plenius continentur. Habita igitur dictorum citatorum et exbanditorum contumacia pro legitima probatione omnium predictorum, et ac si costaret de malefitiis supradictis secundum formam iuris et status dicte civitatis, ut dicta aborenda et nefanda fragitia penis debitis arceantur, et ipsorum malefactorum pene aliis transeant in exemplum, quod predicti Niccholaus Bartoli et Dominichus in nostra fortia constituti, et quilibet ipsorum, ducantur et duci debeant ad locum iustitie consuetum, et ibidem eis et cuilibet eorum capud a spatulis anputetur, ita quod penitus moriantur; et quod si quo tempore predicti alii suprascripti et in dicta inquisitione nominati pervenerint in fortiam Comunis predicti, quod ducantur et duci debeant ad dictum locum iustitie consuetum, et quod ibidem eis et cuilibet eorum capud a spatulis amputetur ita quod moriantur; et quod omnia et singula ipsorum superius nominatorum, tam presentium quam absentium, bona dicto Comuni Florentie confiscentur et adplicentur, et pro confiscatis et adplicatis eidem Comuni intelligantur habeantur et sint ex nunc, et quod in signum dicte confiscationis arma Populi dicte civitatis in his ipsis bonis et locis apparentibus ponantur et depingantur. Et insuper, ad perpetuam memoriam predictorum, **[c. 58r]** exempli gratia, ne alii quilibet presumant de cetero similia actentare vel facere, quod propter infamiam predictorum, ipsi inquisiti et quilibet ipsorum superius nominati et ipsorum inmagines omnes simul depingantur et depingni debeant in sala veteri suprascripti palatii dicte nostre residentie in loco patenti, ut ab omnibus videantur, sequentes formam iuris et statutorum et ordinamentorum Comunis et Populi dicte civitatis Florentie, et vigore nostri arbitrii, nobis in hac parte concessi, et consideratis qualitatibus dictorum mallefitiorum et

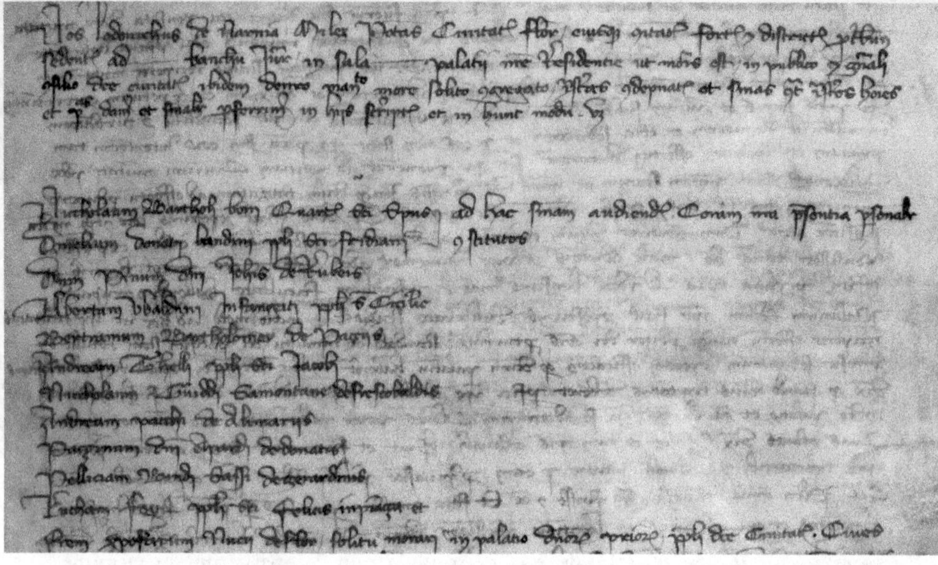

A2.1a. The Death Sentence, *Atti del Podestà* 1525, f. 57r

personarum dictorum delinquentium, et omnibus aliis que consideranda fuerunt, omni modo et iure quibus melius possumus, computato dictis exbanditis banno predicto in presente condepnatione in his scriptis sintentialiter condepnamus, et commictimus prudenti viro ser Hegideo de Tuderto nostro militi et sotio, ad hec presenti et intelligenti, quod contra predictos Niccholaum Bartholi et Dominicum Donati, iuxta formam dicte sententie, executionem faciat et fieri faciat diligenter.

Late date et sintentialiter promulgate fuerunt dicte condepnationes et sintentie per supradictum dominum Potestatem pro tribunali sedentem ad _____ banchum iuris in dicta sala _____ et in dicto consilio, ibidem de ipsius mandato ad vocem banditoris et sonum campane more solito congregato, de consensu presentia et voluntate dictorum suorum iudicum, absente tamen domino Iohanne de Amelia ipsius iudice et collaterale propter inpedimentum sue infirmitatis, et lecte et vulgaricçate fuerunt de ipsius Potestatis mandato per me Andream notarium infrascriptum, sub anno Domini indictione et pontificatu predictis, mense decembris die XXX[ta], presentibus ser Piero Banchini, Notario Camere Comunis Florentie [add. s. l.], Martino Lapi, Dominicho Nelli, Lupicino Gualberti, Gnuto Biagi et Antonio Pucii et pluribus aliis in dicto consilio existentibus testibus. Et facta fuit post predicta dicta commissio eidem ser Hegideo dicte executionis

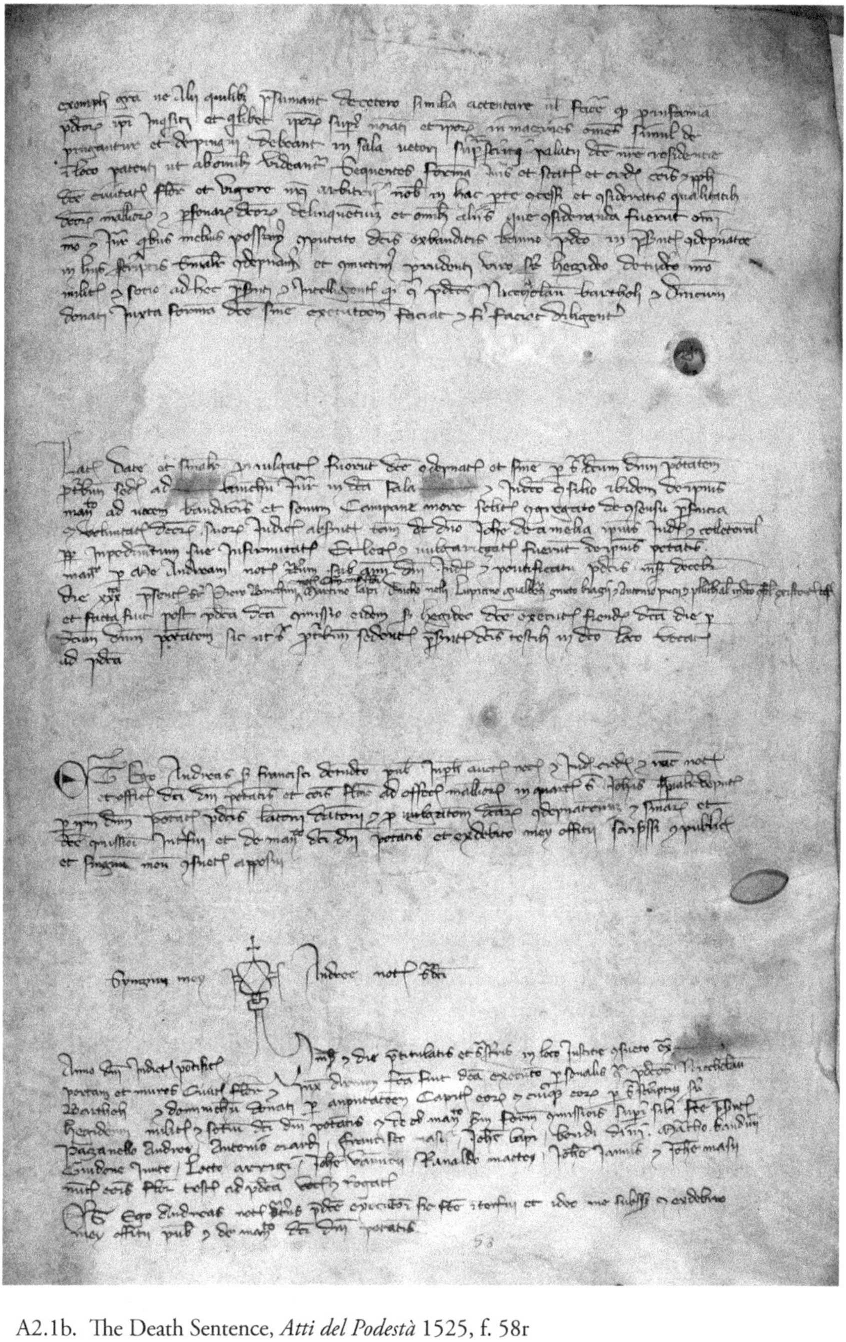

A2.1b. The Death Sentence, *Atti del Podestà* 1525, f. 58r

fiende dicta die per dictum dominum Potestatem, sicut supra pro tribunali sedentem, presentibus dictis testibus in dicto loco vocatis ad predicta.

Et ego Andrea ser Francisci de Tuderto, publicus imperiali auctoritate notarius et iudex ordinarius, et nunc notarius et offitialis dicti domini Potestatis et Comunis Florentie ad offitium mallefitiorum in quarterio Sancti Iohannis spetialiter deputatus per ipsum dominum Potestatem, predictis lationi dationi et promulgationi dictarum condepnationum et sintentiarum et dicte commissioni interfui, et de mandato dicti domini Potestatis et ex debito mey offitii scripssi et publicavi, et singnum meum consuetum apposui.

Syngnum mey (Signum tabellionatus) Andree notarii supradicti.[7]

Anno Domini, indictione, pontificatu, mense et die pretitulatis et suprascriptis, in loco iustitie consueto extra portam et muros civitatis Florentie et iuxta Arnum, facta fuit dicta executio personalis contra predictos Niccholaum Bartholi et Dominichum Donati per anputationem capitis eorum et cuiusque eorum per suprascriptum ser Hegideum militem et sotium dicti domini Potestatis, et de eius mandato secundum formam commissionis superius sibi facte, presentibus Paganello Andree, Antonio Ciardi, Francisco Masi, Iohanne Lapi, Bondi Dini, Marcho Bandini, Guidone Iunte, Locto Arrigi, Iohanne Vannuci, Ranaldo Mactey, Iohanne Iannis et Iohanne Masii, nuntio Comunis Florentie, testibus ad predicta vocatis et rogatis.

Et ego Andreas notarius suprascriptus predicte executioni sic facte interfui et ideo me subscripssi, et ex debito mey offiti publicavi et de mandato dicti domini Potestatis.

2. Document stating that Luca di Feo Ugolini is in Volterra

ASFi, Diplomatico, *Santo Spirito, 6 January 1360, Florentine dating*

In dei nomine, amen. Anno Domini incarnationis Eiusdem millesimo trecentesimo sexagesimo, indictione quartadecima, die sexto mensis ianuarii.

Pateat omnibus evidenter quod Lucas olim Fei Ugolini populi Sancti Felicis in Piaza de Florentia ut pater et legitimus administrator Barholomei vocati Mey et Fey suorum filiorum infantium renumptiavit maternam hereditatem delatam dictis Meo et Feo ab intestato, ac etiam suo proprio nomine renumptiavit et refutavit omni iuri usufructus, sibi mediante persona dictorum suorum filiorum et cuiuslibet eorum competenti vel in posterum competituro, in bonis et rebus dicte

7 *Signum tabellionatus* can be seen in fig. A2.1b. Also clearly visible are the spaces left between the different sections of the death penalty: sentence, execution, and validation.

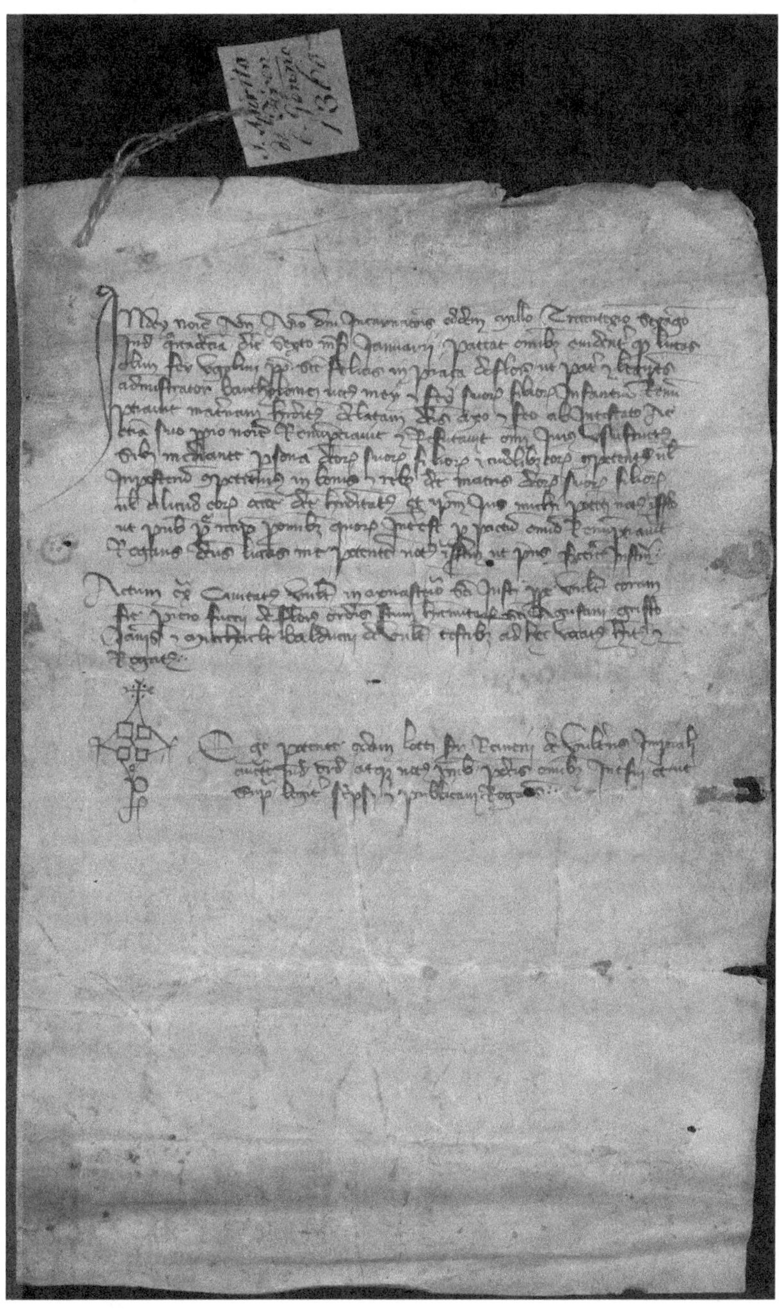

A2.2. Document stating that Luca di Feo Ugolini is in Volterra

matris dictorum suorum filiorum, vel alicuius eorum, occasione dicte hereditatis, et ipsum ius michi Potenti notario infrascripto, ut publice persone, recipienti pro omnibus quorum interest per pactum omnino renumptiavit. Rogans dictus Lucas me Potentem notarium infrascriptum ut presens conficere instrumentum.

Actum extra civitatem Vulterrarum in monasterio Sancti Iusti prope Vulterras, coram fratre Piero Fuccii de Florentia ordinis fratrum heremitarum Sancti Agustini, Griffo Iannis et Micchaele Balduccii.

3. The inheritance to be received by Niccolò di Luca di Feo Ugolini from his mother's estate

ASFi, Diplomatico, *Santo Spirito, 4 January 1360, Florentine dating*

Niccolaus adultus filius emancippatus luce olim fei populi sancti felicis ut de emancippatione constare dicitur manu Ser Bartoli ser Chermonteri notari una simul cum Piero olim Cennis Ugolini dicti populi sancti felicis constituiti in presentia sapienti et discreti viri domini Filippi domini Tomasi Corsini iudicis legis florentini et in matricula artis iudicum et notariorum civitatis Florentiae descripti proposerunt et exposuerunt dicto domino Filippo quod dictus lucas est absens a civitate Florentie tali causa et absentia quod ad presens ad curam dicti Niccolai attendere penitus non valeret et quod dictus Pierus est sibi proximior in gradu omnibus aliis agnatis et cognatis suis et quod ipse Niccolaus caret curatoris unde negotia sua propter etatis defectum agere non potest quare lesionem recipere nec remaneat indefensus petit ipse Niccolaus a dicto domino Filippo iudice supradicto quatenus autoritate qua fungitur per formam iuris vel statutorum et ordinamentorum comunis Florentie et omni modo via forma et iure quibus magis et melius possit eundem Pierum ibidem presentem volentem et illud petentem concederet daret decerneret et confirmaret in cura et pro curatore dicti Niccolai adulti et sibi Piero conmitteret gestum et administrationem persone et bonorum dicti Niccolai adulti

Appendix 3
The Conspirators: Prosopographical Notes

1. Niccolò di Bartolo del Buono[8]

Quartiere di Santo Spirito, Gonfalone del Nicchio, Popolo S. Jacopo Oltrarno

1336–42:	*Fattore* (employee) of the Peruzzi Company, at the Venice branch in 1338 and in Naples from 24 June 1338 to 1339 (when he met Giovanni Boccaccio) and again in 1342 [Sapori 1955, vol. 2, 727, scheda 104].
1344:	Niccolo's father, Bartolo di qd. Berto del Buono popolo S. Iacopo Oltrarno, was enrolled in the Guild of Por S. Maria [ASFi, *Manoscritti* 543, np].
1347:	1 July. Purchased the salt duty (*gabella del sale*) for four years, with Francesco di Piero del Buono, Niccolò del Bene, Maffeo di Lapo di Centellino, and Piero di Lapo da Castiglionchio [ASFi, *CCNCE* 1, ff. 3v, 10r, 23r–23v; *CCNCEU* 1, f. 4r; *CCSCE* 1, np; *CCSCE*, 2, np].
1349:	Enrolled in the Guild of Por S. Maria [ASFi, *Manoscritti* 543, np].
c. 1350:	Listed among the partners of the Uzzano Company, engaged in banking and the trade of wool, dyes, and wool clothes [Rutenberg 1957, 698].
1350:	Ambassador for Florence [*CCSCE*, 3, np].
1353:	18 April. Enrolled in the Cambio Guild [ASFi, *Manoscritti* 542, np].

8 Niccolò di Bartolo del Buono's biography is given in Mazzoni 2010, appendix, 108–81.

1354–8:	With the brothers Agostino and Giovanni di Mannuccio, became partner in a company of the Arte del Cambio [ASFi, *Arte del Cambio* 14, ff. 21r, 25v, 28v, 31r, 33v].
1358:	*Ammonito*. Accused of having been drawn and deputied as an officer of the Commune, and of having accepted and being sworn into said office, despite being Ghibelline. Condemned in absentia to a fine by the Commune of Florence [ASFi, *AEOG*, 278, ff. 16v–17r; Stefani 1910, rubr. 678; *Diario d'Anonimo fiorentino* 1876, 293 and 298; M. Villani 1995, 2.176].
1359:	25 February. Sworn in as *Consigliere del Popolo* [ASFi, *AP* 1217, np].
1359–60:	With Agostino di Mannuccio, a partner in a company of the Arte del Cambio [ASFi, *Arte del Cambio* 14, ff. 38v and 42v].
1360:	Condemned and beheaded for attempting to overthrow the regime, and for having negotiated to give Florence to the Visconti [ASFi, *AP* 1525, ff. 57r–58r; Stefani 1910, rubr. 685; *Diario d'Anonimo fiorentino* 1876, 298].
1378:	30 July. *Ammonizione* repealed [ASFi, *CPGNR* 5, f. 114r].

2. Domenico di Donato Bandini[9]

Quartiere di Santo Spirito, Gonfalone del Nicchio, Popolo S. Jacopo Oltrarno; then Gonfalone Drago, Popolo di San Frediano, "del Fondaccio"

1343–5:	Indication that he was married to a Madonna Filippa [*Prammatica* 2013, no. 3083].
After 1345–before 1354:	Married Dianora Gherardini, sister of Pelliccia Gherardini [Origo 1957, 47; State Archive of Prato, ASPo, D. 1114, 6101225, letters Avignon-Prato, Francesco di Marco Datini to Piera Pratese Boschetti, 28 August 1373, transcribed by Houssaye Michienzi 2013, 47, n. 41].[10]

9 Most of the information on Domenico di Donato Bandini is drawn from Mazzoni 2010, appendix 199, integrated with Origo 1957 and *Prammatica* 2013.

10 He had six children, three boys and three girls. He also had two sisters, named Caterina and Iohanna (*Prammatica* 2013, 1269, no. 1270), daughters of Donato di Bandino del popolo di San Frediano.

1352:	Enrolled through his father in the Guild of Por S. Maria [ASFi, *Manoscritti* 543, np].
1353:	September–December. Consul of the Guild of Por S. Maria [ASFi, *Mercanzia* 162, np].
1355:	One of the Five of the Mercanzia [ASFi, *Mercanzia* 163, np].
1358:	*Ammonito* [Stefani 1910, rubr. 678; *Diario d'Anonimo fiorentino* 1876, 293 and 298].
1358:	13 April. Sentenced in absentia, with Michele di Lapo, apothecary of the popolo S. Frediano, and Cambio di Nuccio, swordmaker of the popolo S. Lorenzo, to a fine to be paid to the Commune for having accepted, athough Ghibelline, the office of election scrutineer for the Signoria [ASFi, *AP* 1103, ff. 70r–70v].
1359:	2 May. Elected as *signore delle gabelle*; his name-slip was destroyed because Ghibelline [ASFi, *Tratte* 752, f. 62v].
1359:	29 August. Elected as *gonfaloniere di società*: his name-slip was destroyed for having been convicted as Ghibelline [ASFi, *Tratte* 753, f. 15v].
1360:	His brother, Aldobrando di Donato, quartiere di Santo Spirito, Gonfalone Drago, was subject to *ammonizione* [Stefani 1910, rubr. 686].
1360:	30 December. Condemned and beheaded for attempting to overthrow the regime, and for having negotiated to give Florence to the Visconti [ASFi, *AP* 1525, ff. 57r–58r].
1376:	Daughter Margherita married Francesco Datini in Avignon [Origo 1957, 47–9].
1378:	30 July. *Ammonizione* repealed [ASFi, *CPGNR* 5, f. 114r].

3. Messer Pino di Giovanni de' Rossi

Quartiere di Santo Spirito, gonfalone Nicchio, popolo di Santa Felicita

1300 approx.:	Born; father is Messer Giovanni di Pino de' Rossi.
1325:	One of the *feditori a cavallo* knights of the sesto d'Oltrarno in the battle of Altopascio [*Delizie degli eruditi Toscani* 1770–89, vol. 12, 262].
1337:	Podestà of Faenza [ASFi, *Sebregondi* 4578].
1340:	Members of the de' Rossi family joined the de' Bardi plot [G. Villani 1990–1, 12.119]. They were exiled

	but then pardoned by Walter of Brienne on 26 October 1342 [Paoli 1862, 76, doc. 57].
1341:	Podestà of Volterra [Tripodi 2011, 200].
1342:	The de' Rossi family supported the election of Walter of Brienne [Paoli 1862].
1343:	6 March. With the jurists Tommaso Corsini and Paolo di Neri Bordoni, represents Florence in a league formed to maintain a peace treaty between Florence, Pisa, and Lucca [Paoli 1862, 17–19].
1343:	Joined the first conspiracy against Walter of Brienne, together with the Bishop of Florence (Angelo Acciaiuoli), the Bardi, the Frescobaldi, and others from Oltrarno [Paoli 1862].
1343:	August/September. One of the fourteen *buoni uomini* charged with rebuilding the government in Florence after the banishment of the Duke of Athens, under the aegis of Angelo Acciaiuoli [Paoli 1862, 43–9]. Supported the change in city divisions in Florence from *sestieri* to *quartieri*.
1343:	The de' Rossi family petitioned to be considered *popolani*. The request was refused [Klapisch-Zuber 1988, 1214].
1345:	Indication that he was married to a woman named Lisa and had a daughter, Maddalena [*Prammatica* 2013, no. 1828–9].
1349:	Petitioned to be considered *popolano* [Klapisch-Zuber 2009, 202–3].
1349:	March and April. Captain of the Guelf Party [ASFi, *Capitani di Parte* 1, f. 2r; Mazzoni 2010, appendix 16].
1349:	*Podestà* of Faenza [BNCF, *Magl.* XVI 147, f. 122v].
1349:	Ambassador to King Charles IV of Bohemia, with Uguccione de' Ricci [BNCF, *Magl.* XVI 147, f. 122v].
1349:	Autumn. On the executive board that initiated the war against the Ubaldini clan (1349–50) [Caferro 2018a, 34].
1350:	November. Elected among the eighteen of the *balìa*, an office created to oppose the Visconti's expansionism [ASFi, *balie* 10, f. 1r; Regnicoli 2021a, 243].
1351:	Served on the committee in charge of overturning the convictions of Florentine exiles residing in

	Pistoia who had been of assistance to the city of Florence, at personal risk, in Florence's conquest of Pistoia. Among those readmitted was Francesco Benini [ASFi, *PR* 38, f. 206; P.G. Ricci 1959, 29–32].
1352:	May. Ambassador to King Charles IV of Bohemia [BNCF, *Magl.* XXVI 147, 122v; M. Villani 1995, 3.13], with Uguccione de' Ricci and others [Velluti 1914, 212–13; Canestrini 1849, 389–90].
1357:	Podestà of Perugia [ASFi, *Sebregondi* 4578].
1359:	8 October. Made a large donation to his sister Bandecca [*Lettere ed altre carte del secolo XIV spettanti alla famiglia Belforti* 2010, 48–9].
1360:	Joined the attempted coup of December 1360 [ASFi, *AP* 1525, f. 57r].
1363:	Pardoned and readmitted to Florence in 1363 [BNCF, *Magl.* XXVI, f. 12v].
1363:	Gave his daughter Lisa in marriage to Matteo de' Rossi di Pistoia [ASFi, *Spogli dell'Ancisa*, NN 180; *Manoscritti* 316; P.G. Ricci 1959, 24, n. 3].
1366:	Apparently deceased [Spogli della Rena: BNCF, *Magl.* 133, f. 12].
1376:	The Rossi family sold the chapel of Santa Felicita to the Barducci family [Fiorelli Malesci 1986, 159–62, 294, doc. 35; Richa 1972, 9: 322–35].
1378:	10 November. His son Giovanni di Pino di Giovanni de' Rossi became *popolano* and changed his name to "de Stoldis" [*Delizie*, vol. 14, 266].

4. Uberto di Ubaldino degli Infangati[11]

Quartiere di Santa Croce, Gonfalone del Carro, Popolo di Santa Cecilia

1326–36:	Employee (*fattore*) in the Bardi Company [Sapori 1955, vol. 2, 753, chart 333].
1332:	4 February. Arrested and imprisoned by the Signoria of Florence [Sapori 1955, vol. 2, 753, chart 333].
1342:	14 January. Without a partner, enrolled in the Arte del Cambio [ASFi, *Manoscritti* 542, np].

11 See Mazzoni 2010, appendix 230–1.

1342: May. All members of the Infangati family deemed *popolo* [ASFi, *Statuti* 19, f. 218r].

1343: 31 March. With his partner, Ubaldino di Fastello Petriboni, enrolled in the Arte del Cambio [ASFi, *Manoscritti* 542, np].

1343: Appointed *gonfaloniere di società* [ASFi, *CCCE* 4, f. 55r].

1343: September–December. Consul of the Arte del Cambio [ASFi, *Arte del Cambio* 12, f. f. 61r; *AP* 66, f. 2r; *Manoscritti*, 542, np].

1344: 1 October–31 December. One of the Five of the Mercanzia for the Arte del Cambio [ASFi, *Mercanzia* 148, np].

1345: 1 May–31 August. Consul of the Arte del Cambio [ASFi, *Manoscritti* 542, np; *Mercanzia* 149, f. 3r].

1346: 29 April. Acquitted of the charge of illegally holding goods belonging to Alessandro Agolanti, who had been convicted and exiled by the Commune, which were found to have been acquired legally and thus exempt from confiscation by the Commune [ASFi, *AEOG* 59, ff. 79r–82v and 96v–97v].

1347: 18 January. Enrolled in the Arte del Cambio, partner of Ubaldino di Fastello Petriboni [ASFi, *Manoscritti* 542, np].

1347: 17 April. Accused and convicted as Ghibelline [ASFi, *AEOG* 79, ff. 29r–29v; *CPGNR* 21, ff. 58r–58v].[12]

1347: 1 May–31 August. Consul of the Arte del Cambio [ASFi, *Mercanzia* 154, np].

1347: 28 August. Selected, with Primerano di Obriaco and Giovanni di Giraldo, as *gonfaloniere di società* [ASFi, *LF* 28, f. 57r; *CCNCE* 1, f. 19r].

---

12 See *Delizie*, vol. 13, 327–8: "Ubertum Ubaldini de Infangatis populi Sancte Cecilie, quarterio Sancte Crucis, quia dictus Ubertus sciens se esse Ghibellinus et non vere Guelfus, et se esse electum pro parte Communis Florentie, et per Consiliarios Mercatorum, et Mercantie, et per Capitudines, et Consules artium Civitatis Florentie in officium, et ad officium sexdecim bonorum Virorum popularium electorum contra cessantes, et fugitivos Civitatis, et Communis Florentie, et contra eorum bona, et debitores in favorem creditorum dictorum cessantium, et fugitivorum, et sciens se dictum officium debere iurare, vel acceptare non posse, dictus Ubertus sciens, se et malo modo dictum officium acceptavit, et iuravit." His family had been Ghibelline in the thirteenth century (*Delizie* 1779–89, vol. 9, 78).

1347: 8 September–7 January, 1348. *Gonfaloniere di società* [ASFi, *Tratte* 593, f. 11v].

1348: 4 September. Elected *gonfaloniere di società* for four months beginning 8 September [ASFi, *AP* 250, f. 44v].

1348: 1 November–31 December. Prior of the guilds [ASFi, *Priorista di Palazzo*, ad annum].

1348: Consul of the Arte del Cambio [ASFi, *Manoscritti* 542, np].

1349: 26 January. Chamberlain for the purchasers of the Salt Duty (*gabella del sale*) [ASFi, *PR* 36, f. 47v–48r; *CCSCE* 1, np; *CCSCE* 2, np].

1349: 15 September–14 December. Served as *buonuomo* [ASFi, *Tratte* 747, f. 4r].

1351: 13 February. With Ubaldino di Fastello, partner in a company of the Arte del Cambio [ASFi, *Arte del Cambio* 14, f. 6r].

1351: 1 May. Consul of the Arte del Cambio [ASFi, *Manoscritti* 542, np].

1351: 15 July. Guarantor, with Tommaso di Filippo Megalotti, Iacopo di Francesco Medici, and Francesco di Bernardo di Bacherello, for Baldinaccio and Giovanni di Caterina Infangati, who had been sentenced to a fine [ASFi, *AP* 700, f. 266v].

1351: 20 August. Consul of the Arte del Cambio [ASFi, *Mercanzia* 160, f. 8r].

1353: 18 February–26 May 1354. Sole proprietor of a company of the Arte del Cambio [ASFi, *Arte del Cambio* 14, ff. 17v and 22v].

1354: 1 September–31 January 1355. Consul of the Arte del Cambio [ASFi, *Mercanzia* 163, np].

1354: 21 October. Elected to the office of the governor of salt taxes (*gabella del sale*) [ASFi, *SCDFOA* 6, f. 31v; *AP* 942, ff. 83v–84r].

1360: 15 January. Appointed officer for the goods of rebels (Beni dei Ribelli) [ASFi, *AP* 1404, ff. 77v and 82v].

1359: 21 February. *Ammonito* [Stefani 1910, rubr. 681].

1360: 30 December. Sentenced to death in absentia for attempting to overthrow the regime, and for having negotiated to give Florence to the Visconti [ASFi, *AP* 1525, ff. 57r–58r].

5. Beltramo di Bartolomeo de' Pazzi

1343:	Participated in a plot against Walter of Brienne in the second failed coup and was imprisoned. Subsequently freed with the third and final conspiracy against the duke, when the Donati opened the Stinche Prison during the insurrection [de Vincentiis 2003, 211, n. 12].
1343:	Among the eight counsellors of the priors, during the regime of the fourteen under Bishop Angelo Acciaiuoli after the fall of the Duke of Athens [G. Villani 1990–1, 13.18].
1348:	24 July. Witness to a notary document by Antonio di Landi Albizzi [ASFi, *Diplomatico*, Santo Spirito, 24 July 1348].
1351:	19 September. Received payment for a troop transfer to reinforce the army in the Mugello against the Visconti [ASFi, *balie* 7 bis, f. 10r–10v: Caferro 2018b, 122].
1350:	With Geri de' Pazzi and Francesco di Ghinozzo de' Pazzi, implicated in a plot to discredit the *podesta'* and the communal administration (Brucker 1962, 113).
1360:	30 December. Sentenced to death in absentia for attempting to overthrow the regime and for having negotiated to give Florence to the Visconti [ASFi, *AP* 1525, ff. 57r–58r].

6. Andrea di Tello da Lisca

Quartiere Santo Spirito, gonfalone Nicchio, Popolo San Jacopo Oltrarno, wool merchant (Lanaioulo di Via di Maggio) [ASFi, *Lana* 20, ff. 2v, 27r, 80r, 82r]

1332:	5 December. Enrolled in the Wool Guild [ASFi, *Manoscritti* 540, np; Varanini 2002, 39, n. 39].
1334:	Married Giovanna Boscoli [Varanini 2002, 21; *Prammatica* 2013, no. 1438].
1347:	Investigated as a suspected Ghibelline, but defended himself successfully [ASFi, *ACP* 74, ff. 107r–113r; Brucker 1962, 118; Mazzoni 2010, 163–4; Campanelli 2003, 197–8].
1358:	Acquittal ratified by the executor of the ordinances of justice [Brucker 1962, 168, n. 80; Mazzoni 2010, 165].

1360:	30 December. Sentenced to death in absentia for attempting to overthrow the regime and for having negotiated the transfer of Florence to the Visconti [ASFi, *AP* 1525, ff. 57r–58r].
1365:	20 February. Deceased, as his son was enrolled in the Wool Guild as "Silvestro olim Andrea di Tello" [ASFi, *Manoscritti* 540, np; Varanini 2002, 39, n. 41]. At his death, he left a debt of 4,000 florins: his houses in the city and his lands in Santa Maria in Converciano were confiscated to pay the creditors [Varanini 2002, 21].

7. Niccolò di Guido de' Frescobaldi[13]

Quartiere Santo Spirito, gonfalone Nicchio

1340:	Took part in the Bardi plot, and was subsequently convicted and exiled [ASFi, *PR* 30, f. 27r–v].
1343:	Exiled by the popular government, together with many other magnates from Oltrarno [Bartolini 1998].
1360:	Took part in the plot of 30 December; died in exile [ASFi, *AP* 1525, ff. 57r–58r; Bartolini 1998].
1379:	28 February. His son "Leonardus quondam Niccolai de Frescobaldi" became *popolano* and changed his name to "Callerotta" [Bartolini 1998].

8. Andrea di Pacchio degli Adimari[14]

Quartiere San Giovanni, Gonfalone Vaio and then Gonfalone Drago, Popolo di San Cristoforo del Corso

1351:	Appears in a document with Manno and Pazzino di Apardo Donati [Ammirato 1647, 185]

13 He married Maddalena di Lapo di Fiorenzino de' Pulci. They had a son, Lionardo, who wrote the famous *Viaggio in Egitto e in Terrasanta*, and a daughter, Piera, who married Simone Orlandini. Lionardo travelled to the Holy Land with Giorgio Guccio Gucci and Andrea di Francesco Rinuccini, brother of the renowned Cino Rinuccini, the two sons of Francesco Rinuccini and Filippa de' Bardi celebrated in Boccaccio's *Contento quasi ne' pensier d'amore*. For this information, see Bartolini 1998.

14 Drawn from Mazzoni 2010, appendix, 140. It is interesting to note that his son Bernardo di Pacchio Adimari da Firenze is the possessor of a copy of Boccaccio's *Teseida* sold on 7–8 September 1936 in Lucerne, Switzerland, at the Antiquaria Hoepli (Branca 1991, 43).

1359:	2 May. Sworn in as officer of mercenary troops (*Ufficiale dei Difetti*) [ASFi, *AP* 1266, f. 7r].
1360:	30 December. Outlawed and sentenced to death in absentia for attempting to overthrow the regime [ASFi, *AP* 1525, ff. 57r–58r].
1365:	21 January. Pardoned by the Signoria [ASFi, *PR* 52, f. 96r–v].
1367:	26–7 October. Advised on the construction of Santa Maria del Fiore [*Documenti relativi a Santa Maria del Fiore* 1887, 199].
1972:	28 June. Became *popolano* and changed his name to "De Benziis" [*Delizie*, vol. 14, 264].
1373:	12 September. *Ammonito* [Stefani 1910, rubr. 743].
1378:	29 July. *Ammonizione* repealed [ASFi, *CPGNR* 5, f. 114r].
1382:	23 December. Plotted to overthrow the government of Florence [ASFi, *AP* 3113, np].

9. Pazzino di Messer Apardo Donati

Popolo Santa Maria Alberighi di Firenze

1343:	December. With his brother Manno Donati and other magnates, imprisoned for a short time by the new popular government [Kohl 1992].
1345:	For having pushed the wife of a Bordoni, sentenced to a fine of 300 lire as a magnate committing assault upon a *popolana*. Sentence overturned when it was learned that the woman too was a magnate [Klapisch-Zuber 2009, 29].
1347:	13 December. Knighted by Ludwig, King of Hungary, in Forlì at the court of Francesco Ordelaffi [G. Villani 1990–1, 13.107; Salvemini 1896, 151].
1351:	19 September. Received payment for troop transfer to reinforce the army in the Mugello against the Visconti [ASFi, *balie* 7 bis, f. 10r–v: Caferro 2018b, 122].
1351:	2 November. Witness payment received by Giovanni Boccaccio as ambassador [ASFi, *Libro del Camerlingo de' xviii*, Ufficiali sulla Lega e Taglia, MCCCL ecc., f. xviii; Imbriani 1882, 84; ASFi, *balìa* 7 bis, Caferro 2018b, 122].

1354: 18 April. Cleared of an earlier conviction through the "amicable intercession" of Can Grande II della Scala, Lord of Verona [ASFi, *PR* 41, f. 9v; Klapisch-Zuber 2009, 227–8, n. 43].

1360: 30 December. Outlawed and sentenced to death in absentia for attempting to overthrow the regime and for having negotiated to give Florence to the Visconti [ASFi, *AP* 1525, ff. 57r–58r].

1361: Exiled from Florence, returned with his brother Manno to the service of the *signore* of Padua, of the Carrara family.

1364: 12 July. Acquitted through the "amicable intercession" of Francesco I da Carrara, Lord of Padua [ASFi, *PR* 51, f. 171v; Klapisch-Zuber 2009, 227, n. 43]

1368: 23 March. Ambassador to Padua [Soldini 1780, 97].

1370: His brother Manno, before dying, asked the Commune of Florence for Pazzino to receive the same privileges he had: becoming *popolano* without changing either his name or his coat of arms [Klapisch-Zuber 2009, 227, n. 43].

1374: Tutor of Manno di Messer Manno d'Apardo Donati [Zardo 1887, 123].

1375: 15 June. Manno di Manno and Pazzino di Apardo Donati repaid a *prestanza* through intermediaries. On 20 November, the loans were repaid through Betto Tani on Pazzino's behalf and the "Heredes domini Manni" [ASFi, *Libro delle prestanze, Quartiere San Giovanni, Congalone Vaio*; Zardo 1887, 121–2; Wilkins 1960, 391].

1378: January. Together with Bonifacio Lupi, appointed to collect debts in Venice on behalf of Francesco I da Carrara [Kohl 1998, 189].

1382: September. Francesco I da Carrara made Pazzino his agent to sell a large house in Florence [Kohl 1998, 189].

1386: December. Francesco I da Carrara made Pazzino his proctor to recover a debt of 600 ducats owed him in Florence [Kohl 1998, 189].

1387: Completed the composition of his Strozziano codex XXXVII, 305 [Zardo 1887, 292].[15]

15 I tried to retrieve this codex with no success.

10. Luca di Feo Ugolini[16]

Quartiere Santo Spirito, gonfalone Ferza, popolo di San Felice in Piazza
Wool merchant (*lanaiuolo* in Via Maggio) [ASFi, *Arte della Lana* 20, ff. 2v, 27r, 80r, 82r]

1341:	Married Monna Nonna di Alessio Rinucci with a dowry of 550 florins, from properties and money, including the house in Via di Maggio.[17] [ASFi, *Diplomatico*, Santo Spirito, 11 January 1360; Monna Nonna is recorded as Nora in *Prammatica* 2013, no. 1654.]
1347:	28 April. *Gonfaloniere di compagnia* [ASFi, *Tratte* 742, 80].
1349:	Officer of the Gabella dei Contratti for the quartiere di Santo Spirito, together with Nicolas Gherardini Jannis [ASFi, *Manoscritti* 662, np].
1350:	29 October. Prior [ASFi, *Tratte* 747, 43; Stefani 1910, rubr. 143].
1355:	29 August. Prior [ASFi, *Tratte* 750, 1; Stefani 1910, rubr. 668].
1357:	*Gonfaloniere di Compagnia* [ASFi, *Tratte* 751, 16].
1357–8:	Monna Nonna deceased. His son Niccolò was emancipated and received his mother's inheritance [ASFi, *Diplomatico*, Santo Spirito, 4 January 1360].
1358:	Counsellor of the Arte della Lana [ASFi, *Diplomatico*, Santo Spirito, 11 March 1358].
1359:	June 12. Buonuomo [ASFi, *Tratte* 752, 72].
1360:	28 April. Prior [ASFi, *Tratte* 223, 77; Stefani 1910, rubr. 682].
1360:	30 December. Outlawed and sentenced to death in absentia for an attempt to overthrow the regime [ASFi, *AP* 1525, ff. 57r–58r].

16 Son of Lapa di Bartolo de' Bardi and Feo Ugolini, as the genealogical tree of Monna Nonna de' Pulci (A1.5) shows. His cousin Piero di Cenni Ubaldini was his partner in business, had a strong political life, and was *ammonito* in 1363. Piero di Cenni died in 1365. For details on Piero di Cenni Ugolini, see Mazzoni 2010, appendix, 258.

17 The brother of Monna Nonna was named Roberto. From Monna Nonna Luca di Feo Ugolini had at least three sons: Niccolò, Bartolomeo (called Meo) and Feo. See the genealogical tree of Monna Nonna de' Pulci (A1.5).

1361:	6 January. At the monastery of San Giusto, outside the walls of Volterra, he drew up a notary document [ASFi, *Diplomatico*, Santo Spirito, 6 January 1360].
1370:	12 March. His name-slip was destroyed [ASFi, *Tratte* 761, 61], because he had died.

11. Pelliccia de' Gherardini[18]

Quartiere di San Giovanni, popolo di San Simone

1293:	Born
1343–5:	Had a daughter named Maddalena [*Prammatica* 2013, no. 3209].
1349:	29 June. Together with his brother Cece, he asked to be separated "not only from the Gherardini, but more specifically from their cousins of the Vicchio branch" ("placeret esse per se et separatos nedum ab omnibus aliis de dicta domo de G. set etiam ab illis de ipsorum latere de Vicchio") [ASFi, *balie* 4, f. 5r; Klapisch-Zuber 2009, 288, n. 16].
1349:	29 June–21 July. Cece and Pelliccia formed a "domus per se," and they took the surname "da Vignamaggio" [ASFi, *balie* 4, f. 5r–v; Klapisch-Zuber 2009, 288–9].
1360:	30 December. Outlawed and sentenced to death in absentia for an attempt to overthrow the regime [ASFi, *AP* 1525, ff. 57r–58r].
1368:	23 February. He was pardoned, but the death sentence was commuted to exile for a period of five years [ASFi, *PR* 56, f. 161r–v; Brucker 1962, 187, n. 146; Klapish-Zuber 2009, 290, n. 27].

18 Francesco Datini writes of Pelliccia Gherardini: "This girl's mother is named mona Lianora, sister of Pelica Gherardini" ("La madre di questa fanciulla à nome mona Lianora, serocha del Pelica Gherardini") in a letter preserved in the State Archive of Prato (ASPo, D. 1114, 6101225, letters Avignon-Prato, Francesco di Marco Datini to Piera Pratese Boschetti, 28/08/1373, transcribed by Houssaye Michienzi 2013, 47, n. 41). According to Klapisch-Zuber (2009, 290), Pelliccia is the nickname of Cione Gherardini, who would be this Dianora Gherardini's father and Domenico di Donato Bandini's father-in-law. In either case, the family relationship between Pelliccia and Donato is very close.

1369:	17 February. Because of his old age ("decrepite etatis") he was granted residence in the Florentine countryside [ASFi, *PR* 58, f. 189r–v; Klapish-Zuber 2009, 290, n. 27].
1378:	25 October. Aged eighty ("homo senex videlicet octuantaginta annorum"), he finally managed to have his banishment repealed [ASFi, *PR* 67, ff. 63v–64r; Klapisch-Zuber 2009, 290, n. 27].
1405:	27 February. His sons, Amedeo and Accerito, returned to Florence [ASFi, *PR* 93, ff. 246v–247r; Klapisch-Zuber 2009, 291, n. 33].
1422:	Amadio di Pelliccia Gherardini sold the Vignamaggio estate, located between Greve, Lamole, and Panzano, to the Gherardi family [ASFi, *Catasto* 68, f. 211; *Gherardi* 324, f. 4; Pallanti 2004, 38].

12. Frate Cristofano di Nuccio

Monk of the Monastery of Settimo

1343–5:	Guardian of the Florentine Armoury (camararius Camere armorum palatii populi Florentine) [*Prammatica* 2013, 471].
1360:	30 December. Outlawed and sentenced to death in absentia for an attempt to overthrow the regime [ASFi, *AP* 1525, ff. 57r–58r].

Bibliography

Primary Sources

Works by Giovanni Boccaccio

Amorosa visione. Ed. Vittore Branca. In *Tutte le opere di Giovanni Boccaccio*, ed. Vittore Branca. Milan: Mondadori, 1974. Vol. 3. 1–272.

Boccaccio's Expositions on Dante's Comedy. Ed. and trans. Michael Papio. Toronto: University of Toronto Press, 2009.

Caccia di Diana. Ed. Irene Iocca. Rome: Salerno Editrice, 2016.

Carmina. Ed. Giuseppe Velli. In *Tutte le opere di Giovanni Boccaccio*, ed. Vittore Branca. Milan: Mondadori, 1998. Vol. 5.1. 493–878.

Comedia delle ninfe fiorentine. Ed. Antonio Enzo Quaglio. In *Tutte le opere di Giovanni Boccaccio*, ed. Vittore Branca. Milan: Mondadori, 1964. Vol. 2.

Concerning Famous Women. Ed. and trans. Guido Aldo Guarini. New Brunswick, NJ: Rutgers University Press, 1963.

Consolatoria a Pino de' Rossi. Ed. Giuseppe Chiecchi. In *Tutte le opere di Giovanni Boccaccio*, ed. Vittore Branca. Milan: Mondadori, 1998. Vol. 5.2. 617–87.

The Corbaccio. Ed. and trans. Anthony K. Cassell. Urbana: University of Illinois Press, 1975.

Corbaccio. Ed. Giulia Natali. Milan: Mursia, 1992.

Decameron. Ed. Vittore Branca. Turin: Einaudi, 1992.

Decameron. Trans. James M. Rigg. 2 vols. London: Navarre Society, 1903.

De casibus virorum illustrium. Ed. Pier Giorgio Ricci and Vittorio Zaccaria. In *Tutte le opere di Giovanni Boccaccio*, ed. Vittore Branca. Milan: Mondadori, 1964. Vol. 9.

De montibus, silvis, fontibus, lacubus, fluminibus, stagnis seu paludibus et de diversis nominibus maris. Ed. Manlio Pastore Stocchi. In *Tutte le opere di Giovanni Boccaccio*, ed. Vittore Branca. Milan: Mondadori, 1967. Vol. 8. 1816–2122.

De mulieribus claris. Ed. Vittorio Zaccaria. In *Tutte le opere di Giovanni Boccaccio*, ed. Vittore Branca. Milan: Mondadori, 1967. Vol. 10.

Diana's Hunt/Caccia di Diana: Boccaccio's First Fiction. Ed. and trans. Anthony K. Cassell and Victoria Kirkham. Philadelphia: University of Pennsylvania Press, 1991.

The Elegy of Lady Fiammetta. Ed. and trans. Mariangela Causa-Steindler and Thomas Mauch. Chicago: University of Chicago Press, 1990.

Epistole e lettere. Ed. Ginetta Auzzas. In *Tutte le opere di Giovanni Boccaccio*, ed. Vittore Branca. Milan: Mondadori, 1998. Vol. 5.1. 493–878.

Esposizioni sopra la Comedia di Dante. Ed. Giorgio Padoan. Milan: Mondadori, 1965.

Famous Women. Ed. and trans. Virginia Brown. The I Tatti Renaissance Library. Cambridge, MA: Harvard University Press, 2001.

Genealogie deorum gentilium. Ed. Vittorio Zaccaria. In *Tutte le opere di Giovanni Boccaccio*, ed. Vittore Branca. Milan: Mondadori, 1998. Vols. 7/8. 1–1813.

L'Ameto. Ed. and trans. Judith Serafini-Sauli. New York: Garland, 1985.

L'Ameto – Lettere – Il Corbaccio. Ed. Nicola Bruscoli. Bari: Laterza, 1940.

Le Rime. Ed. Antonio Lanza. Rome: Aracne, 2010.

The Life of Dante. Trans. Vincenzo Zin Bollettino. New York: Garland, 1990.

Ninfale Fiesolano. Ed. Armando Balduino. In *Tutte le opere di Giovanni Boccaccio*, ed. Vittore Branca. Milan: Mondadori, 1974. Vol. 3. 273–421.

Ninfale Fiesolano. Ed. Daniele Piccini. Milan: Biblioteca Universale Rizzoli, 2013.

Rime. Ed. Vittore Branca. In *Tutte le opere di Giovanni Boccaccio*, ed. Vittore Branca. Milan: Mondadori, 1992. Vol. 5.1. 1–374.

Rime. Ed. Roberto Leporatti. Florence: Edizioni del Galluzzo, 2013.

Trattatello in laude di Dante. Ed. Pier Giorgio Ricci. In *Tutte le opere di Giovanni Boccaccio*, ed. Vittore Branca. Milan: Mondadori, 1974. Vol. 3. 413–538.

Tutte le opere di Giovanni Boccaccio. Ed. Vittore Branca. 10 vols. Milan: Mondadori, 1964–98.

Other Primary Sources

Archivio delle Tratte. Introduzione e inventario. 1989. Ed. Paolo Viti and Raffaella Maria Zaccaria. Rome: Ministero per i beni culturali.

Boncompagno da Signa. 2012. *Amicitia*. Ed. Michael W. Dunne. Paris: Peeters.

Borghini, Vincenzo. 1974. *Storia della nobiltà fiorentina*. Ed. John R. Woodhouse. Pisa: Marlin.

Caterina da Siena. 1939. *Lettere*. Turin: Letteratura Italiana Einaudi. Rpt. *Lettere di Santa Caterina da Siena*. Ed. Pietro Masciatelli. Florence: Marzocco.

Chronica de origine civitate Florentie. 2009. Ed. Riccardo Chellini. Rome: Istituto storico italiano per il Medio Evo.

Commento alla Divina Commedia d'Anonimo fiorentino del secolo XIV. 1866. Ed. Pietro Fanfani. Bologna: Gaetano Romagnoli.

Compagni, Dino. 1968. *Cronica delle cose occorrenti ne' tempi suoi*. Ed. G. Luzzatto. Turin: Einaudi.

– 1986. *Dino Compagni's Chronicle of Florence*. Trans. Daniel E. Bornstein. Philadelphia: University of Philadelphia Press.

da Castiglionchio, Lapo e Bernardo. 2005. *Epistola al figlio Bernardo e due lettere di Bernardo al padre*. Ed. Serena Panerai. In *Antica possession con belli costumi: Due giornate di studio su Lapo da Castiglionchio il Vecchio*, ed. Franek Sznura. Florence: Aska. 323–445.

Dante Alighieri. 1965a. *Monarchia*. Ed. Pier Giorgio Ricci. Milan: Mondadori.

– 1965b. *Vita Nuova*. Ed. Fredi Chiappelli. Milan: Mursia.

– 1996. *Monarchy*. Ed. Prue Shaw. Cambridge: Cambridge University Press.

– 1999. *Dante's Lyric Poems*. Trans. Joseph Tusiani. Ottawa, ON: Legas.

– 2000. *The Divine Comedy*. Trans. Jean Hollander and Robert Hollander. New York: Anchor Books.

– 2004. *Monarchia con commentario di Cola di Rienzo e volgarizzamento di Marsilio Ficino*. Ed. Francesco Furlan. Milan: Mondadori.

– 2009. *Rime giovanili e della Vita nuova*. Ed. Teodolinda Barolini, notes by Manuele Grignolati. Milan: Biblioteca Universale Rizzoli.

– 2011. *Vita Nova*. Ed. Guglielmo Gorni. In *Opere I*, ed. Marco Santagata. Milan: Mondadori.

– 2014a. *Convivio*. Ed. Gianfranco Fioravanti and Claudio Giunta. In *Opere*, ed. Marco Santagata. Vol. 2. Milan: Mondadori. 5–805.

– 2014b. *Dante's Lyric Poetry: Poems of Youth and of the Vita Nuova*. Ed. Teodolinda Barolini. Toronto: University of Toronto Press.

– 2014c. *Monarchia*. Ed. Diego Quaglioni. In *Opere*, ed. Marco Santagata. Vol. 2. Milan: Mondadori. 809–1415.

Datini, Margherita. 2001. *Per la tua Margherita ..., lettere di una donna del '300 al marito mercante. Margherita Datini a Francesco di Marco 1382–1401*. CD-ROM. Ed. Diana Toccafondi and Gianni Cascone. Archivio di Stato di Prato: Quid Q121.

Delizie degli eruditi Toscani. 1770–89. Ed. Ildefonso di San Luigi. Florence: Gaetano Cambiagi stampator granducale. 24 vols.

Diario d'Anonimo fiorentino. 1876. Ed. Alessandro Gherardi. In *Cronache dei secoli xiii e xiv*. Florence: coi tipi di M. Cellini.

Documenti relativi a Santa Maria del Fiore. 1887. In Cesare Guasti, *Santa Maria del Fiore. La costruzione della chiesa e campanile secondo i documenti tratti dall'archivio dell'Opera secolare e da quello di Stato*, 144–230. Florence: Ricci.

Donato di Neri. 1931–9. *Cronaca senese di Donato di Neri e di suo figlio Neri*. In *Cronache senesi*, ed. A. Lisini and F. Iacometti. *Rerum Italicarum Scriptores: raccolta degli scrittori italiani dal cinquecento al millecinquecento*, ed. L.A. Muratori. Bologna: Zanichelli. Vol. 15, Part 6.

Frescobaldi, Lionardo. 2002. *Viaggio in Egitto e in Terrasanta*. In *Nel nome di Dio facemmo vela. Viaggio in Oriente di un pellegrinaggio medioevale*, ed. Gabriella Bartolini and Franco Cardini. Rome-Bari: Laterza. 124–86.

Gregorio Magno. 1877. *I Morali, volgarizzamenti nel sec. XIV da Zanobi da Strada*. Ed. Bartolomeo Sorio. Verona: Stabilimento tipografico eredi di Marco Moroni.

Guittone d'Arezzo. *Le Lettere di Frate Guittone d'Arezzo*. 1923. Ed. Francesco Meriano. Bologna: Angelo Gandolfi.

Il libro del chiodo. 1998. Ed. Fabrizio Ricciardelli. Rome: Istituto Storico Italiano per il Medio Evo.

Il libro del chiodo. Riproduzione in facsimile con edizione critica. 2004. Ed. Francesca Klein and Simone Sartini. Florence: Edizioni Polistampa.

Istorie pistolesi, ovvero delle cose avvenute in Toscana dall'anno 1300 al 1348. 1835. Ed. Antonio Maria Biscioni. Prato: Guasti.

Lancia, Andrea. 2001. *Ordinamenti, provvisioni e riformagioni del comune di Firenze volgarizzati da Andrea Lancia (1355–1357)*. Ed. Luca Azzetta. Venice: Istituto Veneto di Scienze, Lettere ed Arti.

Lettere ed altre carte del secolo XIV spettanti alla famiglia Belforti. Edizione del Manoscritto 8469 della Biblioteca Comunale "Mario Guarnacci" di Volterra. 2010. Ed. Roberto Abbondanza and Andrea Maiarelli. Volterra: Gian Piero Migliorini Editore.

Livy. 1938. *History of Rome, Volume XII: Books 40–42*. Trans. Evan T. Sage and Alfred C. Schlesinger. Cambridge, MA: Harvard University Press.

– 1949. *History of Rome, Volume VIII: Books 28–30*. Trans. Frank Gardner Moore. Cambridge, MA: Harvard University Press.

Morelli, Giovanni di Paolo. 1969. *Ricordi*. Ed. Vittore Branca. Florence: Le Monnier.

– 2015. *Memories*. In *Merchant Writers: Florentine Memoirs from the Middle Ages and Renaissance*, ed. Vittore Branca, trans. Murtha Baca. Toronto: University of Toronto Press. 98–253.

Nelli, Francesco. 1901. *Un amico di Petrarca – Le lettere del Nelli al Petrarca*. Ed. Enrico Cochin. Florence: Le Monnier.

Ordinamenti di giustizia 1293–1993. 1993. Florence: SP 44 Editore.

Ovid. 2009. *Heroides. Volgarizzamento fiorentino trecentesco di Filippo Ceffi*. Ed. Massimo Zaggia. Florence: SISMEL – Edizioni del Galluzzo.

Palmieri, Matteo. 2001. *La vita di Niccolò Acciaiuoli*. Ed. Alessandra Mita Ferraro. Naples: Società editrice il Mulino.

Petrarch, Francesco [Petrarca]. 1926. *Africa*. Ed. Nicola Festa. Florence: Le Lettere, 1926.

– 1933–42. *Le familiari*. Ed. Vittorio Rossi and Umberto Bosco. In *Edizione Nazionale delle opere di Francesco Petrarca*, vols. 10–13. Florence: Sansoni.

– 1964. *De viris illustribus*. Ed. Guido Martellotti. Florence: Sansoni.

– 1992a. *De vita solitaria*. Ed. Giorgio Ficara and Marco Noce. Milan: Mondadori.

– 1992b. *Letters of Old Age. Rerum senilium libri I–XVIII*. Trans. Aldo S. Bernardo, Saul Levin, and Reta A. Bernardo. Baltimore: Johns Hopkins University Press.

– 1994. *Lettere disperse*. Ed. Alessandro Pancheri. Parma: Guanda Editore.

– 1996. *The Complete Canzoniere*. Trans. Mark Musa. Bloomington: Indiana University Press.

– 2001. *Canzoniere*. Ed. Marco Santagata. Milan: Meridiani Mondadori.

– 2002. *Lettres de la vieillesse: Rerum senilium I–III*. Ed. Elvira Nota. Paris: Les belles lettres.

– 2005. *Letters on Familiar Matters*. Trans. Aldo S. Bernardo, 1975–85. Rpt. New York: Italica Press.

Prammatica sulle vesti delle donne fiorentine. 2013. Ed. Laurence Gérard-Marchant. *Draghi rossi e querce azzurre: elenchi descrittivi di abiti di lusso (Firenze 1343–1345).* Florence: SISMEL – Edizioni del Galluzzo.

Pucci, Antonio. 1770–89. *Il Centiloquio, che contiene la Cornica di Giovanni Villani in terza rima.* In *Delizie degli eruditi Toscani*, ed. Ildefonso di San Luigi. Florence: Gaetano Cambiagi stampator granducale. Vol. 4.

Rinuccini, Filippo di Cino. 1840. *Ricordi storici di Filippo di Cino Rinuccini dal 1282 al 1460 colla continuazione di Alamanno e Neri suoi figli fino al 1560.* Florence: dalla stamperia Piatti.

Sacchetti, Franco. 1970. *Il Trecentonovelle.* Ed. Emilio Faccioli. Turin: Einaudi.

– 2014. *Le Trecento Novelle.* Ed. Michelangelo Zaccarello. Florence: Edizioni del Galluzzo.

Salutati, Coluccio. 2014. *Political Writings.* Ed. Stefano Baldassarri and Rolf Bagemihl. I Tatti Renaissance Library. Cambridge, MA: Harvard University Press.

Sardo, Ranieri. 1963. *Cronaca di Pisa.* Rome: Istituto Storico Italiano.

Statuti della repubblica fiorentina. 1999. Ed. Giuliano Pinto, Francesco Silvestrini, and Andrea Zorzi. Florence: Olschki. 2 vols.

Statuti dell'arte del cambio di Firenze (1299–1316) con aggiunte e correzioni fino al 1320. 1955. Ed. Giulia Camerani Marri. Florence: Olschki.

Statuti dell'Università e dello Studio fiorentino dell'anno 1387, con un'appendice di documenti dal 1320 al 1472. 1881. Ed. Alessandro Gherardi. Vol. 7. In *Documenti di storia italiana.* Florence: Deputazione sopra gli studi di storia patria.

Stefani, Marchionne di Coppo. 1910. *Cronaca Fiorentina.* Ed. Niccolò Rodolico, in *Rerum Italicarum scriptores: Raccolta di Storici Italiani dal cinquecento al millecinquecento.* Ed. Ludovico Alessandro Muratori. Città di Castello: coi tipi della casa editrice S. Lapi. to. XXX, P. I, fasc. 1–9.

Tabarrini, Marco. 1846. "Cronache Volterrane, Cronichetta Anonima 1361–1478." *Archivio Storico Italiano*, Appendice 14: 317–32.

Varchi, Benedetto. 1803–4. *Storia fiorentina.* Milan: Società tipografica dei classici italiani. Vol. 5.

Velluti, Donato. 1914. *Cronica domestica di messer Donato Velluti con le addizioni di Paolo Velluti.* Florence: Sansoni.

Villani, Giovanni. 1990–1. *Nuova Cronica.* Ed. Giuseppe Porta. Milan: Guanda.

Villani, Matteo. 1995. *Cronica con la continuazione di Filippo Villani.* Ed. Giuseppe Porta. Milan: Guanda.

Secondary Sources

Agostini Muzzi, Oretta. 1978. "Per il Codice diplomatico boccaccesco." In *Il Boccaccio nelle culture e letterature nazionali*, ed. Francesco Mazzoni. Florence: Olschki. 627–99.

Alfie, Fabian. 1995. "Poetics Enacted: A Comparison of the Novellas of Guido Cavalcanti and Cecco Angiulieri in Boccaccio's *Decameron.*" *Studi sul Boccaccio* 23:171–96.

Ammirato, Scipione. 1647. *Istorie fiorentine.* Florence: Amador Massi.

Arduini, Beatrice. 2010. "Il desiderio naturale della conoscenza in *Le dolci rime d'amor ch'io solea.*" In *Le Rime di Dante (Gargnano del Garda, 25–27 settembre 2008)*, ed. Claudia Berra and Paolo Borsa. Milan: Cisalpino. 231–49.

– 2012. "Il ruolo di Boccaccio e di Marislio Ficino nella tradizione del *Convivio* di Dante." In *Boccaccio in America*, ed. Elsa Filosa and Michael Papio. Ravenna: Longo. 95–103.

Armstrong, Guyda, Rhiannon Daniels, and Stephen J. Milner. 2015. "Boccaccio as Cultural Mediator." In *The Cambridge Companion to Giovanni Boccaccio*, ed. Guyda Armstrong, Rhiannon Daniels, and Stephen J. Milner. Cambridge: Cambridge University Press. 3–19.

Arrighi, Vanna. 2000a. "Corrado Gianfigliazzi." In *Dizionario Biografico degli Italiani.* Rome: Treccani. Vol. 54.

– 2000b. "Luigi Gianfigliazzi." In *Dizionario Biografico degli Italiani.* Rome: Treccani. Vol. 54.

Artusi, Luciano. 2005. *Le arti e i mestieri di Firenze.* Florence: Newton & Compton.

Auzzas, Ginetta. 1967. "Studi sulle epistole. I. L'invito della Signoria fiorentina al Petrarca." *Studi sul Boccaccio* 4:203–40.

Azzetta, Luca. 2001. "Introduzione." In *Ordinamenti, provvisioni e riformagioni del comune di Firenze volgarizzati da Andrea Lancia (1355–1357)*, ed. Luca Azzetta. Venice: Istituto Veneto di Scienze, Lettere ed Arti. 9–49.

Azzetta, Luca, and Irene Ceccherini. 2016. "Filippo Ceffi volgarizzatore e copista nella Firenze del Trecento." *Italia Medievale e Umanistica* 56:99–156.

Baglio, Marco. 2013a. "*Avidulus gloriae*: Zanobi da Strada tra Boccaccio e Petrarca." *Italia Medioevale e Umanistica* 54:343–95.

– "Zanobi da Strada." 2013b. In *Autografi dei letterati italiani: Le origini e il Trecento*, ed. Giuseppina Brunetti, Maurizio Fiorilla, and Marco Petoletti. Rome: Salerno Editrice. Vol. 1. 321–40.

Baldasseroni, Francesco. 1902. "La guerra tra Firenze e Giovanni Visconti." *Studi storici* 11:361–407.

– 1903. "La guerra tra Firenze e Giovanni Visconti." *Studi storici* 12:41–94.

– 1909. "Relazioni tra Firenze, la chiesa e Carlo IV (1353–1355)." *Archivio Storico Italiano* 37:3–60.

Banella, Laura. 2015. "The Fortunes of an 'Authorial' Edition: Boccaccio's *Vita Nuova* in Antonio Pucci and il Saviozzo." In *Boccaccio 1313–2013*, ed. Francesco Ciabattoni, Elsa Filosa, and Kristina Olson. Ravenna: Longo. 237–47.

Barański, Zygmunt G. 2006. "'Alquanto tenea della oppinione degli Epicuri': The *auctoritas* of Boccaccio's Cavalcanti (and Dante)." In *Mittelalterliche Novellistik im europäischen Kontext: Kulturwissenschaftlische Prospektive*, ed. Mark Chinca. Berlin: Schmidt. 280–325.

– 2007. "Boccaccio and Epicurus." *Italianist* 27.2:10–27.

– 2009. "Petrarca, Dante, Cavalcanti." In *Petrarch and Dante: Anti-Dantism, Metaphysics, Tradition*, ed. Zygmunt G. Barański and Theodore J. Cachey. Notre Dame: University of Notre Dame Press. 50–113.

– 2020. *Dante, Petrarch, Boccaccio: Literature, Doctrine, Reality*. Cambridge: Legenda.

Barański, Zygmunt G., and Theodore J. Cachey, eds. 2009. *Petrarch and Dante: Anti-Dantism, Metaphysics, Tradition*. Notre Dame: University of Notre Dame Press.

Barbadoro, Bernardino. 1929. *Le finanze della Repubblica fiorentina: Imposta diretta e debito pubblico fino all'istituzione del Monte*. Florence: Olschki.

Barbi, Michele. 1913. "Qual è la seconda redazione della *Vita di Dante* del Boccaccio?" *Problemi di critica dantesca. I serie*: 395–427.

Barolini, Teodolinda. 2012. "Sociology of the *Brigata*: Gendered Groups in Dante, Forese, Folgore, Boccaccio – From 'Guido, i' vorrei' to Griselda." *Italian Studies* 67:4–22.

– 2015. "A Philosophy of Consolation: The Place of the Other in Life's Transactions ('Se Dio m'avesse dato fratello o non me lo avesse dato')." In *Boccaccio 1313–2013*, ed. Francesco Ciabattoni, Elsa Filosa, and Kristina Olson. Ravenna: Longo. 89–106.

Barsella, Susanna. 2013. "Tyranny and Obedience: A Political Reading of the Tale of Gualtieri (*Dec*. X.10)." *Italianistica* 42.2:67–77.

– 2015–16. "Boccaccio, i tiranni e la ragione naturale." *Heliotropia* 12–13:131–63.

Bartalini, Roberto. 2005. *Scultura gotica in Toscana. Maestri, monumenti, cantieri del Due e Trecento*. Milan: Silvana Editoriale.

Bartolini, Gabriella. 1998. "Frescobaldi, Lionardo." In *Dizionario biografico degli Italiani*. Vol. 50.

Bartuschat, Johannes. 2010. *Les "Vies" de Dante, Pétrarque et Boccace en Italie (XIV–XV siècles): Contribution à l'histoire du genre biographique*. Ravenna: Longo Editore.

Battaglia Ricci, Lucia. 2000. *Boccaccio*. Rome: Salerno Editrice.

– 2013. *Scrivere un libro di novelle: Giovanni Boccaccio autore, lettore, editore*. Ravenna: Longo.

Beardwood, Alice. 1931. *Alien Merchants in England, 1350 to 1377: Their Legal and Economic Position*. Cambridge, MA: Medieval Society of America.

Becker, Marvin B. 1955. "Gualtieri di Brienne e l'uso delle dispense giudiziarie." *Archivio Storico Italiano* 113:245–51.

– 1959. "Florentine Politics and the Diffusion of Heresy in the *Trecento*: A Socio-Economic Inquiry." *Speculum* 34.1:60–75.

– 1962. "Church and State in Florence on the Eve of the Renaissance (1343–1382)." *Speculum* 37.4:509–27.

– 1967–8. *Florence in Transition*. Baltimore: Johns Hopkins University Press.

Becker, Marvin, and Gene Brucker. 1956. "*Le arti minori* in Florentine Politics." *Mediaeval Studies* 18:93–104.

Bellandi, Riccardo. 2010. *I signori dell'Appennino*. Pisa: Pacini Editore.

Belloni, Annalisa, and Diego Quaglioni. 2014. "Un restauro dantesco: *Monarchia* I xii 6." *Aevum. Rassegna di scienze storiche, linguistiche e filologiche* 88.2:493–501.

Bendinelli Predelli, Maria, ed. 2006. *Firenze alla vigilia del Rinascimento. Antonio Pucci e i suoi contemporanei: atti del convegno di Montreal, 22–23 ottobre 2004, McGill University*. Florence: Cadmo.

Benedictow, Ole J. 2004. *The Black Death, 1346–1353: The Complete History*. Woodbridge, UK: Boydell Press.

Benvenuti, Anna. 1995. "Secondo che narrano le storie: il mito delle origini cittadine nella Firenze comunale." In *Il senso della storia nella cultura medievale italiana, 1110–1350*. Pistoia: Centro italiano di studi di storia dell'arte. 205–52.

Bernocchi, Mario. 1971. "Sulla presunta dote di Margherita Datini." *Prato Storia e Arte* 12:57–66.

Berté, Monica, and Marco Cursi. 2015. *Novità su Giovanni Boccaccio: un numero monografico di 'Italia Medioevale e Umanistica'.*" *Studi sul Boccaccio* 43:233–62.

Bettarini Bruni, Anna. 1980. "Un quesito d'amore tra Pucci e Boccaccio." *Studi di filologia italiana* 38:33–54.

Billanovich, Giuseppe. 1947a. *Petrarca letterato. Lo scrittoio del Petrarca*. Rome: Edizioni di Storia e Letteratura.

– 1947b. *Restauri boccacceschi*. Rome: Edizioni di Storia e Letteratura.

– 1994. "Zanobi da Strada e i i tesori di Montecassino." *Studi petrarcheschi* 11:183–99.

– 1996. *Petrarca e il primo umanesimo*. Padua: Antenore, 1996.

Billanovich, Giuseppe, and Elisabeth Pellegrin. 1964. "Una nuova lettera di Lombardo della Seta e la prima fortuna delle opere del Petrarca." In *Classical Medieval and Renaissance Studies in Honor of Berthold Louis Ullman*, ed. Charles Henderson Jr. Rome: Edizioni di Storia e Letteratura. Vol. 2. 215–36.

Biscione, Giuseppe. 2009. *Statuti del Comune di Firenze nell'Archivio di Stato. Tradizione archivistica e ordinamenti*. Rome: Ministero per i beni e le attività culturali direzione generale per gli archivi.

Bloom, Harold. 1997. *The Anxiety of Influence: A Theory of Poetry*. 2nd ed. Oxford: Oxford University Press.

Boccaccio autore e copista. 2013. Ed. Teresa De Robertis, Carla Maria Monti, Marco Petoletti, Giualiano Tanturli, and Stefano Zamponi. Florence: Mandragora.

Boccaccio e la Romagna. 2015. Ed. Gabriella Albanese and Paolo Pontari. Ravenna: Longo.

Boli, Todd. 2013. "Personality and Conflict (*Epistole, Lettere*)." In *Boccaccio: A Critical Guide to the Complete Works*, ed. Victoria Kirkham, Michael Sherberg, and Janet Leverie Smarr. Chicago: University of Chicago Press. 295–306.

Bologna, Corrado. 2006. "Un'ipotesi sulla ricezione del *De vulgari eloquentia*: il codice Berlinese." In *La cultura volgare padovana nell'età del Petrarca*, ed. Furio Brugnolo and Zeno Lorenzo Verlato. Padua: Il Poligrafo. 205–56.

Bonaini, F. 1857. "Statuto della Parte Guelfa compilato nel MCCCXXXV." *Giornale storico degli archivi toscani* 1:5–30.

Borsa, Paolo. 2007. "*Sub nomine nobilitatis*: Dante e Bartolo da Sassoferrato." In *Studi dedicati a Gennario Barbarisi*, ed. Claudia Berra and Michele Mari. Milan: CUEM. 59–121.

– 2014. "Le dolci rime di Dante. Nobiltà d'animo e nobiltà dell'anima." *Tenzone* 7:57–112.

– 2017. "Identità sociale e generi letterari. Nascita e morte del sodalizio stilnovista." *Reti medievali* 18:271–303.

Boskovits, Miklos. 2001. "Giotto di Bondone." In *Dizionario biografico degli italiani.* Rome: Treccani. Vol. 55.

Bowsky, William M. 1970. *The Finance of the Commune of Siena, 1287–1335*. Oxford: Clarendon Press.

Bragantini, Renzo. 2012. *Ingressi Laterali al Trecento Maggiore. Dante – Petrarca – Boccaccio*. Naples: Liguori.

– 2015. "L'amicizia, la fama, il libro: sulla seconda epistola a Mainardo Cavalcanti." In *Boccaccio 1313–2013*, ed. Francesco Ciabattoni, Elsa Filosa, and Kristina Olson. Ravenna: Longo. 107–18.

– 2016. "Invidie e favori della fortuna nel *Decameron*." In *Fortuna: Atti del quinto Colloquio internazionale di Letteratura italiana (Napoli, 2–3 maggio 2013)*, ed. Silvia Zoppo Garampi. Rome: Salerno Editrice. 87–107.

Brambilla, Simona. 2000. "Zanobi da Strada volgarizzatore di Cicerone: edizione critica del *sogno di Scipione*." *Studi petrarcheschi* 13:1–79.

Branca, Vittore. 1958. *Tradizione delle opere di Giovanni Boccaccio. Vol. I: un primo elenco dei codici e tre studi*. Rome: Edizioni di storia e letteratura.

– 1976. *Boccaccio: The Man and His Works*. New York: New York University Press.

– 1986. *Mercanti scrittori: Ricordi nella Firenze tra Medioevo e Rinascimento*. Milan: Rusconi.

– 1990. *Boccaccio medievale e nuovi studi sul Decameron*. Florence: Sansoni.

– 1991. *Tradizione delle opere di Giovanni Boccaccio. Vol. II: un secondo elenco di manoscritti e cinque studi sul "Decameron", con due appendici*. Rome: Edizioni di storia e letteratura.

– 1997. *Giovanni Boccaccio: Profilo Biografico*. Florence: Sansoni.

Branca Delcorno, Daniela. 2015. "La linea cortese di Boccaccio e dei suoi lettori tra Romagna ed Emilia." In *Boccaccio e la Romagna*, ed. Gabriella Albanese and Paolo Pontari. Ravenna: Longo. 47–66.

Bruni, Francesco. 1990. *Boccaccio: l'invenzione della letteratura mezzana*. Bologna: Il Mulino.

– 1997. "Between Oral Memory and Written Tradition in Florence at the Beginning of the XIVth Century: Coppo di Borghese Domenichi, Andrea Lancia and Giovanni Boccaccio." In *L'Histoire et les nouveaux publics dans l'Europe médiévale (XIIIe–XVe siècles): Actes du colloque international organisé par la Fondation européenne de la science à la Casa de Velasquez, Madrid, 23–24 avril 1993*, ed. Jean-Philippe Genet. Paris: Sorbonne. 113–25.

Brucker, Gene. 1957. "The Medici in the Fourteenth Century." *Speculum* 32:1–26.

– 1960. "The Ghibelline Trial of Matteo Villani (1362)." *Medievalia et Humanistica* 13:48–55.

– 1962. *Florentine Politics and Society (1343–1378)*. Princeton: Princeton University Press.

– 1969. "Florence and Its Universities." In *Action and Conviction in Early Modern Europe*, ed. Theodore K. Rabb and Jerrold E. Siegel. Princeton: Princeton University Press. 220–36.

– 1977a. *The Civic World of Early Renaissance Florence*. Princeton: Princeton University Press.

– 1977b. "Florence and the Black Death." In *Boccaccio: Secoli di vita*, ed. Marga Cottino-Jones and Edward Tuttle. Ravenna: Longo. 21–30.

Cachey, Theodore J. 2013. "Between Text and Territory (*De montibus, silvis, fontibus, lacubus, fluminibus, stagnis, seu paludibus ed de diversis nominibus maris*)." In *Boccaccio: A Critical Guide to the Complete Works*, ed. Victoria Kirkham, Michael Sherberg, and Janet Levarie Smarr. Chicago: University of Chicago Press. 273–82.

Caferro, William. 2006. "The Fox and the Lion: The Pisan-Florentine War, 1363–1364." In *John Hawkwood: An English Mercenary in Fourteenth-Century Italy*. Baltimore: Johns Hopkins University Press. 97–115.

– 2013. "Petrarch's War: Florentine Wages and the Black Death." *Speculum* 88.1:144–65.

– 2015. "*Le tre corone fiorentine* and War with the Ubaldini, 1349–1350." In *Boccaccio 1313–2013*, ed. Francesco Ciabattoni, Elsa Filosa, and Kristina Olson. Ravenna: Longo. 43–55.

– 2018a. *Petrarch's War: The Black Death in Context.* Cambridge: Cambridge University Press.

– 2018b. "The Visconti War and Boccaccio's Florentine Public Service in Context, 1351–53." *Heliotropia* 15:111–31.

Calvi, Giulia, and Isabelle Chabot, eds. 1998. *Le ricchezze delle donne: diritti patrimoniali e poteri familiari in Italia (XIII–XIX secc.).* Turin: Rosenberg & Sellier.

Calvino, Italo. 2016. *Six Memos for the Next Millennium.* Trans. Geoffrey Brock. Boston: Mariner Books.

Campanelli, Maurizio. 2003. "Quel che la filologia può dire alla storia: vicende di manoscritti e testi antighibellini nella Firenze del Trecento." *Bollettino dell'Istituto storico per il Medio Evo e archivio muratoriano* 105:87–247.

Canaccini, Federico. 2010. "Restano i termini, mutano i significati: Guelfi e Ghibellini. L'evoluzione semantica dei nomi delle fazioni medioevali italiane." In *Lotta politica nell'Italia medievale*, ed. Isa Lori Sanfilippo. Rome: Istituto storico italiano per il Medioevo. 85–94.

– 2012. "Battaglie di immagini tra Guelfi e Ghibellini nella Toscana comunale." *Studi medievali* 53.2:635–66.

– 2021. *1289. La battaglia di Campadino*. Bari: Laterza.

Canestrini, Giuseppe. 1849. "Alcuni documenti riguardanti le relazioni politiche dei Papi d'Avignone coi comuni d'Italia, avanti e dopo il tribunato di Cola di Rienzo e la calata di Carlo IV." *Archivio Storico Italiano* 7:349–430.

Cappelli, Eugenio. 1927. *La Compagnia dei Neri: L'arciconfraternita dei battuti di Santa Maria della Croce al Tempio*. Florence: Le Monnier.

Carabellese, Francesco. 1897. *La peste del 1348 e le condizioni della sanità pubblica in Toscana*. Rocca di San Casciano: Cappelli.

Cardini, Franco. 1972. "Betto Brunelleschi." *Dizionario biografico degli italiani*. Rome: Treccani. Vol. 14.

– 1981. "Il *Decameron*: un genere laico? Le dieci giornate della rifondazione cavalleresca del mondo." *Quaderno medievali* 12:105–19.

– 1997. *L'acciaiar de' cavalieri: Studi sulla cavalleria nel mondo toscano e italico (sec. XII–XV)*. Florence: Le Lettere.

– 2007. *Le cento novelle contro la morte. Giovanni Boccaccio e la rifondazione cavalleresca del mondo*. Rome: Salerno Editrice.

Carrai, Stefano. 2016. *Boccaccio e i volgarizzamenti*. Rome: Antenore.

Cassell, Anthony. 2004. *The Monarchia Controversy: An Historical Study with Accompanying Translations of Dante Alighieri's Monarchia, Guido Vernani's Refutation of the Monarchia Composed by Dante and Pope John XXII's Bull, Si Fratrum*. Washington, DC: Catholic University of America Press.

Castelnuovo, Guido. 2014. *Être noble dans la cité: Les noblesses italiennes en quête d'identité (XIIIe–XVe)*. Paris: Classiques Garnier.

Centanni, Monica. 2008. "*Hercules Gradivus* nel Tempio Malatestiano." *Engramma: La tradizione classica nella memoria occidentale* 61. http://www.engramma.it

Chabot, Isabelle. 1998. "La loi du lignage. Notes sur le système successoral florentin (XIV/XV–XVII siècle)." *Clio. Femmes, dots et patrimoines* 7:51–72.

Cheneval, Francis. 1995. *Die Rezeption der Monarchia Dantes bis zur Editio Princeps im Jahre 1559. Metamorphosen eines philosophiches Werks mit einer kritischen Edition von Guido Vernanis Tractatus de potestate summi ponteficis*. Munich: Fink.

Chiecchi, Giuseppe. 1979. "La lettera a Pino de' Rossi. Appunti cronologici, osservazioni e fonti." *Studi sul Boccaccio* 11:295–331.2013.

– 1994. *Giovanni Boccaccio e il romanzo familiare*. Venice: Marsilio.

– 2005. *La parola del dolore: primi studi sulla letteratura consolatoria tra medioevo e umanesimo*. Rome: Antenore.

– 2013. *Dante, Boccaccio, l'origine*. Florence: Olschki.

– 2014. "Sotto il magistero di Dante: la favola fiesolana e fiorentina nella letteratura di Giovanni Boccaccio." In *Le Lezioni di Vittore Branca*, ed. Cesare De Michelis and Gilberto Pizzamiglio. Florence: Olschki. 89–102.

– 2017. *Nell'arte narrativa di Boccaccio*. Florence: Olschki.

Ciabani, Roberto. 1992. *Le famiglie di Firenze*. Florence: Bonechi.

– 1998. *Firenze: di gonfalone in gonfalone*. Florence: Edizioni della Meridiana.

Ciampi, S. 1830. *Monumenti di un manoscritto autografo e lettere inedite di Giovanni Boccaccio*. Milan: Paolo Andrea Molina.

Ciappelli, Giovanni. 1997. "Forese da Rabatta." In *Dizionario biografico degli italiani*. Rome: Treccani. Vol. 48.

Clarke, Paula. 2007. "The Villani Chronicles." In *Chronicling History: Chroniclers and Historians in Medieval and Renaissance Italy*, ed. Sharon Dale, Alison Williams Lewin, and Duane J. Osheim. Philadelphia: Penn State University Press. 113–44.

Conti, Marco. 2012. "Il pozzo dei Toscanelli." *L'universo* 92:40–60.

Conti, Massimo. 2008. *Delitti e castighi: Itinerari nella Firenze dei crimini e della giustizia tra il XIII e il XVIII secolo*. Florence: Centro Di.

Contini, Gianfranco. 1970. *Letteratura italiana delle origini*. Florence: Sansoni.

Corazzini, Francesco. 1877. *Lettere edite ed inedite di Giovanni Boccaccio*. Florence: Sansoni.

Cortese, Albertina. 1964. "Un documento sulla condanna di Pino de' Rossi." *Studi sul Boccaccio* 2:15–24.

Costantini, M. Aldo. 1973. "Studi sullo Zibaldone Magliabechiano." *Studi sul Boccaccio* 7:21–58.

– 1974. "Studi sullo Zibaldone Magliabechiano. II. Il Florilegio senechiano." *Studi sul Boccaccio* 8:79–126.

– 1998. "Tra chiose e postille dello Zibaldone Magliabechiano: un catalogo e una chiave di lettura." In *Gli Zibaldoni di Boccaccio,* ed. Michelangelo Picone and Claude Cazalé Bérard. Florence: Franco Cesati Editore. 29–35.

Crabb, Ann. 2015. *The Merchant of Prato's Wife: Margherita Datini and Her World, 1360–1423.* Ann Arbor: University of Michigan Press.

Crescini, Vincenzo. 1887. *Contributo agli studi sul Boccaccio con documenti inediti.* Turin: Loescher.

Curti, Elisa. 2016a. "Le ninfe di Boccaccio. Osservazioni sulla tradizione toscana." In *Boccaccio in versi. Atti del Convegno di Parma, 13–14 marzo 2014.* Florence: Franco Casati Editore. 29–46.

– 2016b. "*Tutte eran ninfe a quel tempo chiamate.* Boccaccio e le ninfe: osservazioni sulla tradizione toscana." *Lettere Italiane* 68:246–65.

Curtius, Ernest Robert. 1940. "Theologische Poetik im italienischen Trecento." *Zeitschrift für Romanische Philologie* 60:1–15.

Dal Giglio al David. Arte Civica a Firenze fra Medioevo e Rinascimento. 2013. Ed. Maria Monica Donato and Daniela Parenti. Florence: Giunti.

Dameron, George. 1992. "Revisiting the Italian Magnates: Church Property, Social Conflict, and Political Legitimization in the Thirteenth-Century Commune." *Viator* 23:167–88.

– 2015. "Identificazione di un killer: recenti scoperte scientifiche e storiche sulla natura della peste nera." In *Boccaccio 1313–2013,* ed. Francesco Ciabattoni, Elsa Filosa, and Kristina Olson. Ravenna: Longo. 57–69.

– 2017. "Feeding the Medieval Italian City-State: Grain, War, and Political Legitimacy in Tuscany, c. 1150–c. 1350." *Speculum* 92.4:976–1019.

Dante e Boccaccio. Lectura Dantis Scaligera, 2004–2005. 2006. Ed. Ennio Sandal. Padua: Antenore.

Davidsohn, Robert. 1956–68. *Storia di Firenze.* Florence: Sansoni. 8 vols.

Delcorno, Carlo. 2015. "Boccaccio and the Literature of Friars." In *Boccaccio, 1313–2013,* ed. Francesco Ciabattoni, Elsa Filosa, and Kristina Olson. Ravenna: Longo. 161–86.

della Torre, Arnaldo. 1905. *La giovinezza di Giovanni Boccaccio (1313–1341). Proposta di una nuova cronologia.* Città di Castello: Casa tipografico-editrice S. Lapi.

De Robertis, Teresa. 2013. *Boccaccio copista.* In *Boccaccio autore e copista,* ed. Teresa De Robertis, Carla Maria Monti, Marco Petoletti, Giualiano Tanturli, and Stefano Zamponi. Florence: Madragora. 329–35.

de Vincentiis, Amedeo. 2003. "Politica, memoria e oblio a Firenze nel XIV secolo. La tradizione documentaria della signoria del duca d'Atene." *Archivio storico italiano* 161:209–48.

– 2013. "L'ultima signoria. Firenze, il duca d'Atene e la fine del consenso angioino." In *Le signorie cittadine in Toscana. Esperienze di potere e forme di governo personale (secoli XIII–XV),* ed. Andrea Zorzi. Rome: Viella. 83–120.

Diacciati, Silvia. 2011. *Popolani e magnati: società e politica nella Firenze del Duecento*. Spoleto: Fondazione Centro Italiano di Studi sull'Alto Medioevo.

Diacciati, Silvia, and Andrea Zorzi, eds. 2013. *La legislazione antimagnatizia a Firenze*. Rome: Istituto palazzo Borromini.

Donati, Claudio. 1988. *L'idea di nobiltà in Italia. Secoli XIV–XVIII*. Bari: Laterza.

– 2005. "L'*Epistola* di Lapo da Castiglionchio e la disputa sulla nobiltà a Firenze fino al consolidamento del Principato." In *Antica possessione con belli costumi: Due giornate di studio su Lapo da Castiglionchio il Vecchio*, ed. Franek Sznura. Florence: Aska. 30–45.

Donato, Maria Monica, and Umberto Montano. 2005. *Il cibo e la bellezza*. Florence: Giunti.

Dorini, U. 1914. "Contributi alla biografia del Boccaccio." *Miscellanea storica della Valdelsa* 22:73–91.

Edgerton, Samuel J. 1979. "A Little-Known Purpose of Art in the Italian Renaissance." *Art History* 2:45–61.

– 1985. *Pictures and Punishment. Art and Criminal Prosecution during the Florentine Renaissance*. Ithaca: Cornell University Press.

Eisner, Martin. 2013. *Boccaccio and the Invention of Italian Literature: Dante, Petrarch, Cavalcanti, and the Authority of the Vernacular*. Cambridge: Cambridge University Press.

Fabbri, Lorenzo. 2011. "Un esperimento di signoria familiare: i Belforti di Volterra (1340–1361)." *Rassegna Volterranea* 88:161–84.

– 2019. *Mater Florum: Flora e il suo culto a Roma*. Florence: Olschki.

Faibisoff, Leah, and William Robins. 2019. "Giovanni Boccaccio and Ventura Monachi." *Studi sul Boccaccio* 47:113–27.

Falkeid, Unn. 2017. *The Avignon Papacy Contested: An Intellectual History from Dante to Catherine of Siena*. Cambridge, MA: Harvard University Press.

Falsini, Alberto Benigno. 1971. "Firenze dopo il 1348: le conseguenze della peste nera." *Archivio Storico Italiano* 129:425–503.

Fenzi, Enrico. 2005. "Petrarca a Milano: tempi e modi di una scelta meditata." In *Petrarca e la Lombardia*, ed. Giuseppe Frasso, Giuseppe Velli, and Maurizio Vitale. Padua: Antenore. 221–63.

Feo, Michele. 1943. "Petrarca Francesco." In *Enciclopedia Dantesca*. Rome: Istituto della Enciclopedia Italiana. Vol. 4, 450–8.

Ferraro, Domenico. 2015. "Petrarca a Milano: le ragioni di una scelta." *Rinascimento* 55:225–55.

Ferreri, Rosario. 1970. "Una risposta di Antonio Pucci al Boccaccio." *Romance Notes* 12:189–91.

– 1990. "Appunti sulla presenza del *Convivio* nel *Decameron*. I. Il proemio del *Decameron*; II. La novella VI, 6 e la *quaestio* della nobiltà." *Studi sul Boccaccio* 19:63–77.

Ferretti, Massimo. 2007. "Pitture per condannati a morte del Trecento bolognese." In *Misericordie. Conversioni sotto il patibolo tra Medioevo ed età moderna*, ed. Adriano Prosperi. Pisa: Edizioni della Normale. 85–151.

Filosa, Elsa. 2007. "Modalità di contatto tra *Decameron* e *Corbaccio*: Giovenale nella novella di Monna Sismonda (*Dec.* VII 8)." *Modern Language Notes* 122.1:123–32.

– 2012. *Tre studi sul De mulieribus claris*. Milan: LED edizioni universitarie di Lettere Economia Diritto.

– 2013. "To Praise Dante, to Please Petrarch (*Trattatello in laude di Dante*)." In *Boccaccio: A Critical Guide to the Complete Works*, ed. Victoria Kirkham, Michael Sherberg, and Janet Leverie Smarr. Chicago: University of Chicago Press. 213–20.

– 2014a. "L'amicizia ai tempi della congiura (Firenze 1960–61): *A confortatore non duole capo*." *Studi sul Boccaccio* 42:195–220.

– 2014b. "The Tale of King Agilulf and His Groom (*Dec.* III.2)." In *The Decameron: Third Day in Perspective*, ed. Pier Massimo Forni and Francesco Ciabattoni. Toronto: University of Toronto Press. 22–43.

– 2016. "La condanna di Niccolò di Bartolo del Buono, Pino de' Rossi, e gli altri congiurati del 1360 (ASFi, *Atti del Podestà*, 1525, 57r–58r)." *Studi sul Boccaccio* 44:235–50.

– 2017. "Pino de' Rossi." In *Dizionario Biografico degli Italiani*. Rome: Treccani. Vol. 88.

– 2018. "Messer Pino di messer Giovanni de' Rossi." *Heliotropia* 15:133–59.

– 2019. "History of Virginia: Livy, Boccaccio, and Botticelli." In *Botticelli: Heroines and Heroes*, ed. Nathaniel Silver. London: Paul Holberton Publishing. 78–93.

Fiorelli Malesci, Francesca. 1986. *La chiesa di Santa Felicita a Firenze*. Florence: Cassa di risparmio di Firenze.

Foresti, Arnaldo. 1931. "Il Boccaccio a Ravenna nell'inverno del 1361–62." *Giornale storico della letteratura italiana* 98:73–83.

Forni, Pier Massimo. 1996. *Adventures in Speech: Rhetoric and Narration in Boccaccio's Decameron*. Philadelphia: University of Pennsylavia Press.

– 2003. "The Tale of the King of Cyprus and the Lady of Guascony." In *The Decameron: First Day in Perspective*, ed. Elissa B. Weaver. Toronto: University of Toronto Press. 207–21.

Foscolo, Ugo. 1953. "A Parallel between Dante and Petrarca." In *Saggi e Discorsi Critici*, ed. Cesare Foligno. Florence: Le Monnier.

Franceschi, Franco. 2015. "Medici Economic Policy." *The Medici: Citizens and Masters*, ed. Robert Black and John Law. Florence: Villa I Tatti, Harvard University Center for Italian Renaissance Studies. 129–54.

Fredona, Robert. 2010. "Political Conspiracy in Florence (1340–1382)." PhD diss., Cornell University.

Freedberg, David. 1989. *The Power of Images: Studies in the History and Theory of Response*. Chicago: University of Chicago Press.

Friedman, David. 1988. *Florentine New Town: Urban Design in the Late Middle Ages*. Cambridge, MA: MIT Press.

Fryde, E.B. 1949–50. "Materials for the Study of Edward III's Credit Operations, 1327–48." *Bulletin of the Institute of Historical Research* 22:105–38 and 23:1–30.

– 1952. "Edward III's Wool Monopoly: A Fourteenth–Century Trading Venture." *History* 37:8–24.

– 1955. "Loans to the English Crown, 1328–31." *English Historical Review* 70:198–211.

Fubini, Mario. 1970–8. "Catone." In *Enciclopedia dantesca*. Rome: Istituto della Enciclopedia Italiana. 876–82.

Fubini, Riccardo. 2005. "Lapo da Castiglionchio tra Niccolò Acciaiuoli e Petrarca. Lineamenti introduttivi a una biografia." In *Antica possession con belli costumi: Due giornate di studio su Lapo da Castiglionchio il Vecchio*, ed. Franek Sznura. Florence: Aska. 11–29.

Furlan, Francesco. 2015. "Da Cola al Rinascimento: letture 'umanistiche' del *Monarchia*." *Letture classensi* 42:175–200.

Gargan, Luciano. 2015. "Un nuovo profilo biografico di Giovanni Conversini da Ravenna." In *Dante e la sua eredità a Ravenna nel Trecento*, ed. Marco Petoletti. Ravenna: Longo. 177–233.

Gaston, Kara. 2018. "History of Writing after Coppo di Borghese Domenici: *Decameron* V 9." *Le Tre Corone* 5:121–36.

Gérard-Marchant, Laurence, ed. 2013. *Draghi rossi e querce azzurre: elenchi descrittivi di abiti di lusso (Firenze 1343–1345)*. Florence: SISMEL – Edizioni del Galluzzo.

Gerola, G. 1898. "Alcuni documenti inediti per la biografia del Boccaccio." *Giornale storico della letteratura italiana* 32:355–60.

Gherardi, Alessandro. 1885. "L'antica Camera del Comune di Firenze e un quaderno d'uscita de suoi Camarlinghi dell'anno 1303." *Archivio Storico Italiano* 16:313–61.

Ghisalberti, Carlo. 1960. "La condanna al bando nel diritto comune." *Archivio giuridico* 158:3–75.

Giuliani, Marco. 2006. *Le arti fiorentine*. Florence: Scramasax.

Goldthwaite, Richard A. 2009. *The Economy of Renaissance Florence*. Baltimore: Johns Hopkins University Press.

Green, Monica. 2015. *Pandemic Disease in the Medieval World: Rethinking the Black Death*. York: Arc Medieval Press.

Grendler, Paul F. 2002. *The Universities of the Italian Renaissance*. Baltimore: Johns Hopkins University Press.

Guidi, Guidubaldo. 1981. *Il governo della città-repubblica di Firenze del primo Quattrocento*. 3 vols. Florence: Olschki.

Guidotti, Paola. 1930. "Un amico di Petrarca e del Boccaccio: Zanobi da Strada." *Archivio Storico Italiano* 7.13:249–93.

Hankins, James. 2019. "Boccaccio and the Political Thought of Renaissance Humanism." In *A Boccaccian Renaissance*, ed. Martin Eisner and David Lummus. Notre Dame: Notre Dame University Press. 3–36.

Hankins, James, ed. 2000. *Renaissance Civic Humanism: Reappraisals and Reflections*. Cambridge: Cambridge University Press.

Henderson, John. 1994. *Piety and Charity in Late Medieval Florence*. Chicago: University of Chicago Press.

Herlihy, David. 1964. "Direct and Indirect Taxation in Tuscan Urban Italy, c. 1200–1400." In *Finances et comptabilité urbaines du 13e au 16e siècle*. Brussels: Centre pro civitate. 385–405.

Hortis, Attilio. 1875. *Giovanni Boccaccio ambasciatore in Avignone e Pileo da Prata proposto da' Fiorentini a Patriarca di Aquileia*. Trieste: Tipografia di Hermanstorfer.

– 1879. *Studi sulle opere latine del Boccaccio: con particolare riguardo alla storia della erudizione nel medio evo e alle letterature straniere*. Trieste: A. Polla.

Hoshino, Hidetoshi. 1980. *L'arte della lana in Firenze nel basso Medioevo. Il commercio della lana e il mercato dei panni fiorentini nei secoli XII–XV.* Florence: Olschki.

Houssaye Michienzi, Ingrid. 2013. *Datini, Majourque et le Maghreb (14e–15e siècles): Réseaux, espaces méditerranéens et stratégie marchandes.* Leiden: Brill.

Houston, Jason. 2010. *Building a Monument to Dante: Boccaccio as Dantista.* Toronto: University of Toronto Press.

– 2018. "Boccaccio on Friendship (Theory and Practice)." In *Reconsidering Boccaccio: Medieval Contexts and Global Intertexts*, ed. Olivia Holmes and Dana E. Stewart. Toronto: University of Toronto Press. 81–97.

Hunt, Edwin S. 1994. *The Medieval Super-Companies: A Study of the Peruzzi Company of Florence.* Cambridge: Cambridge University Press.

Hunt, Edwin, and James M. Murray. 1999. *A History of Business in Medieval Europe 1200–1550.* Cambridge: Cambridge University Press.

Imbriani, Vincenzo. 1882. "La pretesa Beatrice, figliuola di Dante Allaghieri." *Giornale napoletano di Filosofia e Lettere, Scienze morali e politiche* 7.19:55–87.

Kelly, John. 2005. *The Great Mortality: An Intimate History of the Black Death, the Most Devastating Plague of All Time.* New York: HarperCollins.

Kelly, Samantha. 2003. *The New Solomon: Robert of Naples (1309–1343) and Fourteenth-Century Kingship.* Leiden: Brill.

Kirkham, Victoria. 1998. "Iohannes de Certaldo: La firma dell'autore." In *Gli Zibaldoni di Boccaccio: Memoria, scrittura, riscrittura. Atti del Seminario internazionale di Firenze-Certaldo (26–28 aprile 1996)*, ed. Michelangelo Picone and Claude Cazalé Bérard. Florence: Franco Cesati Editore. 455–68.

Klapisch-Zuber, Christine. 1988. "Ruptures de parenté et changements d'identité chez les magnats florentins du XIVe siècle." *Annales. Économies, Sociétés, Civilisations* 43.5:1205–40.

– 2009. *Ritorno alla politica: I magnati fiorentini.* Rome: Viella.

Klein, Francesca. 1988. "Niccolò del Buono." In *Dizionario biografico degli Italiani.* Rome: Istituto della Enciclopedia Italiana. Vol. 36.

Kohl, Benjamin G. 1977. "Francesco da Carrara, il Vecchio." In *Dizionario biografico degli italiani.* Rome: Istituto della Enciclopedia Italiana. Vol. 20.

– 1992. "Manno Donati." In *Dizionario biografico degli italiani.* Rome: Istituto della Enciclopedia Italiana. Vol. 41.

– 1998. *Padua under the Carrara: 1318–1405.* Baltimore: Johns Hopkins University Press.

Kolsky, Stephen. 2003. *The Genealogy of Women: Studies in Boccaccio's "De mulieribus Claris."* New York: Peter Lang.

Lansing, Carol. 1991. *The Florentine Magnates: Lineage and Faction in a Medieval Commune.* Princeton: Princeton University Press.

L'arme segreta. Araldica e storia dell'arte nel Medioevo. 2015. Ed. Matteo Ferrari. Florence: Le Lettere.

La Roncière, Charles-Marie de. 1968. "Indirect Taxes or 'Gabelles' at Florence in the Fourteenth Century: The Evolution of Tariffs and the Problems of Collection." In

Florentine Studies: Politics and Society in Renaissance Florence, ed. Nicolai Rubinstein. Evanston: Northwestern University Press. 140–92.

– 2005. *Firenze e le sue campagne nel Trecento: mercanti, produzione, traffici*. Florence: Olschki.

Latini, Angiolo. 1913. "Il fratello di Giovanni Boccaccio." *Miscellanea storica della Valdelsa* 2–3:32–43.

Léonard, Emile G. 1932–6. *Histoire de Jeanne Ière Reine de Naples, comtesse de Provence (1343–1382)*. Monaco and Paris. 3 vols.

– 1934. "Victimes de Petrarque et de Boccace: Zanobi da Strada." *Etudes Italiennes* 4:5–19.

Leoncini, Gaetano. 1869. *Illustrazione sulla Cattedrale di Volterra*. Siena: Lazzeri.

Leoni, L. 1875. "Breve di Clemente VI in favore di Gualtieri di Brienne, duca d'Atene." *Archivio Storico Italiano* 22:181–2.

Litta, Pompeo. 1819–83. *Famiglie celebri d'Italia*. Milan. Vol. 16.

Little, Lester. 2011. "Plague Historians in Lab Coats." *Past & Present* 213:267–90.

Lummus, David. 2011. "Boccaccio's Three Venuses: On the Convergence of Celestial and Transgressive Love in the *Genealogie Deorum Gentilium Libri*." *Medievalia et Humanistica* 37:65–88.

– 2012. "Boccaccio's Hellenism and the Foundations of Modernity." *Mediaevalia* 33:101–67.

Macrì-Leone, Francesco. 1890. "La politica di Giovanni Boccaccio." *Giornale storico della letteratura italiana* 15:79–110.

Maffei, Elena. 2005. *Dal reato alla sentenza: il processo criminale in età comunale*. Rome: Edizioni di storia e letteratura.

Magna, Laura. 1982. "Gli Ubaldini del Mugello: Una signoria feudale nel contado fiorentino." In *I ceti dirigenti dell'età comunale nei secoli XII e XIII*. Pisa: Pacini. 13–66.

Manni, Domenico Maria. 1742. *Istoria del Decamerone di Giovanni Boccaccio*. Florence: Antonio Ristori.

Marchesi, Simone. 2009. "Petrarch's Philological Epic (*Africa*)." In *Petrarch: A Critical Guide to the Complete Works*, ed. Victoria Kirkham and Armando Maggi. Chicago: University of Chicago Press. 113–30.

– 2013. "Boccaccio on Fortune (*De casibus virorum illustrium*)." In *Boccaccio: A Critical Guide to the Complete Works*, ed. Victoria Kirkham, Michael Sherberg, and Janet Smarr. Chicago: University of Chicago Press. 245–54.

Martinez, Ronald L. 2000. "Cato of Utica." In *The Dante Encyclopedia*, ed. Richard Lansing. New York: Garland. 146–9.

Marzi, Demetrio. 1910. *La Cancelleria della Repubblica Fiorentina*. Rocca S. Casciano: Cappelli.

Masi, Gino. 1931. "La pittura infamante nella legislazione e nella vita del comune fiorentino (sec. XIII–XVI)." In *Studi di diritto commerciale in onore di Cesare Vivante*. Rome: Società editrice del Foro Italiano. Vol. 2. 625–57.

Massera, Aldo Francesco. 1913. "Il serventese boccaccesco delle belle donne." *Miscellanea storica della Valdelsa* 21:55–67.

– 1927. "Di tre epistole metriche boccaccesche." *Giornale dantesco* 30:31–44.

Matteini, Nevio. 1958. *Il più antico oppositore politico di Dante: Guido Vernani da Rimini. Testo critico del "De Reprobatione Monarchiae."* Padua: CEDAM.

Maxson, Brian J. 2014. *The Humanist World of Renaissance Florence.* Cambridge: Cambridge University Press.

Mazzoni, Vieri. 2005. "Lapo e la famiglia da Castiglionchio nella politica fiorentina fino ai Ciompi." In *Antica possessione con belli costumi: Due giornate di studio su Lapo da Castiglionchio il Vecchio*, ed. Franek Sznura. Florence: Aska. 80–120.

– 2010. *Accusare e proscrivere: Il nemico politico. Legislazione antighibellina e persecuzione giudiziaria a Firenze (1347–1378).* Pisa: Pacini Editore.

– 2015. "Nuovi documenti su Giannozzo e la famiglia Manetti." *Bullettino dell'Istituto Storico Italiano per il Medio Evo* 117:339–56.

– 2016. "Uguccione de' Ricci." *Dizionario biografico degli italiani.* Rome: Treccani. Vol. 87.

Mazzoni, Vieri, and Alessandro Monti. 2013. *Il Libro dell'imposta di Montaccianico (1306): Fiscalità discriminatoria e liste di proscrizione nella Firenze del Trecento.* Florence: Aska.

Mazzoni, Vieri, and Francesco Silvestrini. 1999. "Strategie politiche e interessi economici nei rapporti tra la Parte Guelfa e il Comune di Firenze: La confisca patrimoniale ai 'ribelli' di San Miniato (ca. 1368–ca. 1400)." *Archivio Storico Italiano* 579:3–61.

Mazzotta, Giuseppe. 1979. *Dante, Poet of the Desert: History and Allegory in the "Divina Commedia."* Princeton: Princeton University Press.

– 1986. *The World at Play in Boccaccio's "Decameron."* Princeton: Princeton University Press.

– 2007. "Life of Dante." In *The Cambridge Companion to Dante*, 2nd ed., ed. Rachel Jacoff. Cambridge: Cambridge University Press. 1–13.

– 2015. "Boccaccio's Way." In *Boccaccio 1313–2013*, ed. Francesco Ciabattoni, Elsa Filosa, and Kristina Olson. Ravenna: Longo. 29–41.

Melis, Federigo. 1962. *Aspetti della vita economica medievale: Studi sull'Archivio Datini di Prato.* Siena: Monte dei Paschi di Siena.

Meloni, Giuseppe. 1998. "Il mercante Giovanni Boccaccio a Montpellier e Avignone: Un documento inedito (1355)." *Studi sul Boccaccio* 26:99–126.

Mésoniat, Claudio. 1984. *Poetica theologia: La "Lucula Noctis" di Giovanni Dominici e le dispute letterarie tra '300 e '400.* Rome: Edizioni di Storia e Letteratura.

Milani, Giuliano. 2003. *L'esclusione dal Comune. Conflitti e bandi politici a Bologna e in altre città italiane tra XII e XIV secolo.* Rome: Istituto Storico per il Medioevo.

Mineo, Nicolò. 1994. "La sesta giornata del Decameron o del potere delle donne." *Rassegna europea di letteratura italiana* 3:44–69.

Minnis, Alastair J. 1988. *Medieval Theory of Authorship*, 2nd ed. Philadelphia: University of Pennsylvania Press.

Misericordie: Conversioni sotto il patibolo tra Medioevo ed età moderna. 2007. Ed. Adriano Prosperi. Pisa: Edizioni della Normale.

Molho, Anthony. 1971. "Communal Income: Taxes on the Contado and the Gabelles." In *Florentine Public Finances in the Early Renaissance, 1400–1433*. Cambridge, MA: Harvard University Press. 22–59.

Mommsen, Theodore E. 1953. "Petrarch and the Story of the Choice of Hercules." *Journal of the Warburg and Courtauld Institutes* 16:178–92.

Monti, Carla Maria. 2016. "La *Genealogia* e il *De montibus*: due parti di un unico progetto." *Studi sul Boccaccio* 44:327–66.

Morpurgo, Salomone. 1881. *Antonio Pucci e Vito Biagi, banditori fiorentini del secolo XIV. Dodici strambotti di Luigi Pulci*. Rome: Forzani.

Murray, Alexander. 1998. *Suicide in the Middle Ages*. 2 vols. Oxford: Oxford University Press.

Muscetta, Carlo. 1972. *Boccaccio*. Bari: Laterza.

Najemy, John M. 1982. *Corporatism and Consensus in Florentine Electoral Politics: 1280–1400*. Chapel Hill: University of North Carolina Press.

– 2006. *A History of Florence 1200–1575*. Oxford: Blackwell.

Naphy, William G., and Andrew Spicer. 2004. *Plague: Black Death and Pestilence in Europe*. Stroud: Tempus.

Nelson, Jonathan. 2010. *Storie di Lucrezia e di Virginia Romana*. In *Virtù d'amore. Pittura nuziale nel Quattrocento fiorentino*, ed. Claudio Paolini, Daniela Parenti, and Ludovica Sebregondi. Florence: Giunti. 194–7.

Niccoli, Ottavia. 2011. *Vedere con gli occhi del cuore. Alle origini del potere delle immagini*. Bari: Laterza.

Nobili, Sebastiana. 2013. "La consolazione della letteratura. Una proposta per il *Decameron*." In *Boccaccio e i suoi lettori: Una lunga ricezione*, ed. Gian Maria Anselmi, Giovanni Baffetti, Carlo Delcorno, and Sebastiana Nobili. Bologna: Il Mulino. 209–42.

– 2017. *La consolazione della letteratura. Un itinerario fra Dante e Boccaccio*. Ravenna: Longo.

Novati, Francesco. 1889. "Luigi Gianfigliazzi, giureconsulto ed oratore fiorentino del sec. XIV." *Archivio Storico Italiano* 5:440–7.

Nuzzo, Armando. 2010. "Osservazioni sulla figura dell'Ercole nel sigillo del Comune di Firenze." In *Le strade di Ercole: Itinerari Umanistici e altri percorsi. Seminario internazionale per i centenari di Coluccio Salutati e Lorenzo Valla (Bergamo: 25–26 Ottobre 2007)*, ed. Luca Carlo Rossi. Florence: SISMEL – Edizioni del Galluzzo. 343–52.

Olson, Kristina M. 2014. *Courtesy Lost: Dante, Boccaccio and the Literature of History*. Toronto: University of Toronto Press.

Origo, Iris. 1957. *The Merchant of Prato: Francesco di Marco Datini*. Oxford: Alden Press.

Ortalli, Gherardo. 2015. *La pittura infamante nei secoli XIII–XVI*. Rome: Viella.

Ottokar, Nicola. 1962. *Il comune di Firenze alla fine del Duecento*. Turin: Einaudi.

Padoan, Giorgio. 1959. *L'ultima opera di Giovanni Boccaccio: Le "Esposizioni sopra il Dante."* Florence: Olschki.

Padoan, Giorgio. 1978. *Il Boccaccio, le Muse, il Parnaso, e l'Arno*. Florence: Olschki.

– 1997. "*Habent sua fata libelli.* Dal Claricio al Mannelli al Boccaccio." *Studi sul Boccaccio* 25:141–212.

– 1998. "Alcune riflessioni sul testo critico della *Consolatoria a Pino de' Rossi.*" *Studi sul Boccaccio* 26:265–74.

– 2002. *Ultimi studi di filologia dantesca e boccacciana.* Ed. Aldo Maria Costantini. Ravenna: Longo.

Pagnin, Beniamino. 1974. "Poggetto, Bertrando." *Enciclopedia Dantesca.* Rome: Treccani. Vol. 4. 572.

Palermo, Luciano. 2013. "Di fronte alla crisi: l'economia e il linguaggio della carestia nelle fonti medievali." In *Crisis alimentarias en la Edad Media: modelos, explicaciones y representaciones,* ed. Pere Benito i Monclùs. Lleia: Editorial Milenio. 47–67.

Pallanti, Giuseppe. 2004. *Monna Lisa: mulier ingenua.* Florence: Edizioni Polistampa.

Pampaloni, Guido. 1964a. "Gherardo Baroncelli." In *Dizionario Biografico degli Italiani.* Rome: Treccani. Vol. 6.

– 1964b. "Tano Baroncelli." In *Dizionario Biografico degli Italiani.* Rome: Treccani. Vol. 6.

Panella, Antonio. 1913. "Politica ecclesiastica del comune fiorentino dopo la cacciata del Duca d'Atene." *Archivio Storico Italiano* 71.2:271–365.

Panofski, Erwin. 1939. *Studies in Iconology: Humanistic Themes in the Art of the Renaissance.* Oxford: Oxford University Press.

Paolazzi, Carlo. 1983. "Petrarca, Boccaccio e il Trattatello in laude di Dante." *Studi Danteschi* 55:165–249.

Paoli, Cesare. *Della Signoria di Gualtieri duca d'Atene.* 1862. Florence: Coi tipi di M. Cellini e C.

Paparelli, Gioacchino. 1979. "Due modi di leggere Dante: Petrarca e Boccaccio." In *Giovanni Boccaccio editore e interprete di Dante.* Florence: Olschki. 73–90.

Papio, Michael. 2009. "Introduction: Boccaccio as *lector Dantis.*" In Giovanni Boccaccio, *Boccaccio's Exposition on Dante's Comedy,* trans. Michael Papio. Toronto: University of Toronto Press. 3–37.

– 2015–16. "Sulla povertà politica e filosofica del Boccaccio." *Heliotropia* 12–13:213–32.

Pérez Carrasco, Mariano. 2016. "Poesìa y filosofìa en la primera recepciòn de Dante: Graziolo de' Bambagioli, Guido Vernani, Cecco d'Ascoli." *Tenzone* 16:229–55.

Pertusi, Agostino. 1964. *Leonzio Pilato tra Petrarca e Boccaccio. Le sue versioni omeriche negli autografi di Venezia e la cultura greca del primo umanesimo.* Venice and Rome: Istituto per la collaborazione culturale.

Petoletti, Marco. 1998. "Alberico da Rosciate lettore della *Commedia.*" In *Maestri e traduttori bergamaschi fra Medioevo e Rinascimento,* ed. Claudia Villa and Francesco Lo Monaco. Bergamo: Biblioteca Civica Angelo Mai. 78–80.

– 2013. "Gli Zabaldoni di Giovanni Boccaccio." In *Boccaccio autore e copista,* ed. Teresa De Robertis, Carla Maria Monti, Marco Petoletti, Giualiano Tanturli, and Stefano Zamponi. Florence: Madragora. 291–326.

Piacentini, Angelo. 2014. "La novella bresciana del *Decameron.*" *Studi sul Boccaccio* 42:93–141.

– 2015. "*Hic claudor Dante*. Per il testo e la fortuna degli epitaffi di Dante." In *Dante e la sua eredità a Ravenna nel Trecento*. Ravenna: Longo. 41–70.

Piattoli, Renato. 1970. "Donati." *Enciclopedia Dantesca*. Rome: Treccani.

Picchio Simonelli, Maria. [1979] 2000. "L'inquisizione e Dante: alcune osservazioni." *Dante Studies* 97: 129–49. Rpt. *Dante Studies* 118:303–21.

Piccini, Daniele. 2002. "Franceschino degli Albizzi, uno e due." *Studi petrarcheschi* 15:129–86.

Picone, Michelangelo. 1988. "La brigata di Folgore fra Dante e Boccaccio." In *Il gioco della vita bella: Folgore da San Gimignano*. San Gimignano: Studi e Testi San Gimignano. 25–40.

– 2004. "Leggiadri motti e pronte risposte: La sesta giornata." In *Introduzione al Decameron*, ed. Michelangelo Picone and Margherita Mesirca. Florence: Franco Cesati Editore. 163–85.

Pirani, Francesco. 2019. *Con il senno e con la spada: Il cardinale Albornoz e l'Italia del Trecento*. Rome: Salerno Editore.

Pirillo, Diego. 2018. *The Refugee-Diplomat: Venice, England and the Reformation*. Ithaca: Cornell University Press.

Pistolesi, Elena. 2014. "Il *De vulgari eloquentia* di Giovanni Boccaccio." *Giornale Storico della Letteratura Italiana* 191.2:161–99.

Piur, Paul. 1925. *Petrarcas "Buch ohne Namen" und die Päpstliche Kurie*. Halle: Niemeyer.

Pontari, Paolo. 2015. "Boccaccio a Ravenna tra Dante e Petrarca: novità sulla *Vita Petri Damiani*." In *Boccaccio e la Romagna*, ed. Gabriella Albanese and Paolo Pontari. Ravenna: Longo. 119–48.

Porta Casucci, Emanuela. 2015–16. "'Un uomo di vetro' fra corti e cortile. Giovanni Boccaccio, i Del Buono, i Rossi e gli altri." *Heliotropia* 12–13:189–212.

Preto, Paolo. 2003. *Persona per hora secreta*. Milan: Il Saggiatore.

Prosdocimi, Luigi. 1960. "Alberico da Rosciate." In *Dizionario Biografico degli Italiani*. Rome: Treccani. Vol. 1. 656–7.

Prosperi, Adriano. 1982. "Il sangue e l'anima. Ricerche sulle Compagnie di giustizia in Italia." *Quaderni storici* 51:959–99.

– 2013. *Delitto e perdono. La pena di morte nell'orizzonte mentale dell'Europa Cristiana (XIV–XVIII secolo)*. Turin: Einaudi.

Quaglio, Antonio E. 1976. "Antonio Pucci: primo lettore-copista-interprete di Giovanni Boccaccio." *Filologia e critica* 1:15–79.

Quaglioni, Diego. 1979–80. "*Nembrot primus fuit tyrannus*. 'Tiranno' e 'tirannide' nel pensiero giuridico-politico del Trecento italiano: il commento a C. i, 2, i 6 di Alberico da Rosate (c. 1290–1360)." *Annali dell'Istituto Italiano per gli Studi Storici* 6:83–104.

Quaglioni, Diego. 1983. *Politica e diritto nel Trecento italiano. Il "De tyranno" di Bartolo di Sassoferrato (1314–1357) – con l'edizione critica dei trattati "De Guelphis et Gebellinis", "De regimine civitatis" e "De tyranno."* Florence: Olschki.

Rao, Ida Giovanna. 1995. "Il Gran siniscalco Nicola Acciaioli e la vendita di Prato ai Fiorentini." In *Studi in onore di Arnaldo D'Addario*. Lecce: Conte editore. Vol. 3. 799–808.

Raveggi, Sergio. 2000. "I Rettori fiorentini." In *I podestà dell'Italia comunale*, ed. Jean-Claude Maire Vigueur. Rome: Sede dell'istituto Palazzo Borromini. 595–643.

Regnicoli, Laura. 2013a. *I documenti su Giovanni Boccaccio*. In *Boccaccio autore e copista*, ed. Teresa De Robertis, Carla Maria Monti, Marco Petoletti, Giuliano Tanturli, and Stefano Zamponi. Florence: Mandragora. 385–402.

– 2013b. "Codice diplomatico di Giovanni Boccaccio: i documenti fiscali." *Italia medioevale e umanistica* 54:1–80.

– 2014. "La *cura sepulcri* di Giovanni Boccaccio." *Studi sul Boccaccio* 42:25–79.

– 2018. "Per la biografia di Giovanni Boccaccio: L'*Elegia di Madonna Fiammetta* attraverso i documenti." In *Aimer ou ne pas aimer: Boccaccio, Elegia di madonna Fiammetta, et Corbaccio*, ed. Anna Pia Filotico, Manuele Gragnolati, and Philippe Guerin. Paris: Presses Sorbonne Nouvelle. 15–34.

– 2021a. "Il Codice diplomatico di Boccaccio." In *Boccaccio*, ed. Maurizio Fiorilla and Irene Iocca. Rome: Carocci Editore. 235–51.

– 2021b. "Boccaccio e la consorteria fiorentina de' Rossi." In *Échanges épistolaires autour de Pétrarque et Boccace*, ed. Sabrina Ferrara. Paris: Champion. 275–305.

Rezasco, Giulio. 1881. *Dizionario del linguaggio italiano storico ed amministrativo*. Florence: Le Monnier.

Ricci, Corrado. 1910. "I Boccacci e il Boccaccio a Ravenna." In *Miscellanea di studi in onore di Attilio Hortis*. Trieste: Caprin.

Ricci, Pier Giorgio. 1959. "Studi sulle opere latine e volgari del Boccaccio." *Rinascimento* 10.1:3–32.

– 1965. "Il commento di Cola di Rienzo alla *Monarchia* di Dante." *Studi medioevali* 42:665–708.

– 1974. "Le tre redazioni del *Trattatello in laude di Dante*." *Studi sul Boccaccio* 8:197–214.

– 1976. "Vernani, Guido." In *Enciclopedia Dantesca*. Rome: Treccani. Vol. 5. 967–68.

– 1985. *Studi sulla vita e le opere del Boccaccio*. Milan and Naples: Riccardo Ricciardi Editore.

Ricciardelli, Fabrizio. 2007. *The Politics of Exclusion in Early Renaissance Florence*. Turnhout: Brepols.

Richa, Giuseppe. 1972. *Notizie istoriche delle chiese fiorentine, divise ne' suoi quartieri*. Vol. 9. Rome: Multigrafica Editrice.

Rinoldi, Paolo. 2016. "La *Caccia di Diana* e la critica delle fonti: una ricognizione." In *Boccaccio in versi: Atti del Convegno di Parma, 13–14 marzo 2014*, ed. Pantalea Mazzitello, Giulia Raboni, Paolo Rinoldi, and Carlo Varotti. Florence: Franco Cesati Editore. 47–60.

Robiglio, Andrea. 2006. "The Thinker as a Noble Man (bene natus) and Preliminary Remarks on the Medieval Concepts of Nobility." *Vivarium* 44:205–47.

Robins, William. 2000. "Antonio Pucci, Guardiano degli atti della Mercanzia." *Studi e problemi di critica testuale* 61:29–70.

Robins, William, and Leah Faibisoff. 2020. "The Jokesters and the Judge (VIII.5)." In *The Decameron: Eighth Day in Perspective*, ed. William Robins. Toronto: University of Toronto Press. 108–28.

Rombach, Ursula. 1977. "Francesco Petrarca ed Ercole al bivio." In *Petrarca e la cultura europea*, ed. L. Rotondi Secchi Tarugi. Milan: Nuovi Orizzonti. 55–70.

Ronconi, Giorgio. 1976. *Le origini delle dispute umanistiche sulla poesia (Mussato e Petrarca)*. Rome: Bulzoni.

Rossi, Luca Carlo. 2010. "La 'vita di Ercole' del Petrarca." In *Le strade di Ercole: Itinerari Umanistici e altri percorsi. Seminario internazionale per i centenari di Coluccio Salutati e Lorenzo Valla (Bergamo: 25–26 Ottobre 2007)*, ed. Luca Carlo Rossi. Florence: SISMEL – Edizioni del Galluzzo. 169–87.

Rostagno, Enrico. 1913. "Per la storia degli studi boccacceschi." *Miscellanea storica della Valdelsa* 21:1–25.

Rutenberg, Viktor J. 1957. "La compagnia di Uzzano (su documenti dell'Archivio di Leningrado)." In *Studi in onore di Armando Sapori*. Milan. Vol. 1. 687–706.

Saiber, Arielle. 2013. "The Game of Love (*Caccia di Diana*)." In *Boccaccio: A Critical Guide to the Complete Works*, ed. Victoria Kirkham, Michael Sherberg, and Janet Leverie Smarr. Chicago: University of Chicago Press. 109–17.

Salvemini, Gaetano. 1896. *La dignità cavalleresca nel comune di Firenze*. Florence: Tipografia Ricci.

– 1899. "Gli ordinamenti di giustizia del 6 luglio 1295." In *Magnati e popolani in Firenze dal 1280 al 1295. Appendice documentaria*, appendix 12. Florence: Tipografia Carnesecchi e Figli. 384–432.

Sanesi, Ireneo. 1893. "Un documento inedito su Giovanni Boccaccio." *Rassegna bibliografica della letteratura italiana* 1:120–4.

Santagata, Marco. 1990. *Per moderne carte: La biblioteca volgare di Petrarca*. Bologna: il Mulino.

– 2016. *Dante: The Story of His Life*. Cambridge, MA: Harvard University Press.

– 2019. *Boccaccio: Fragilità di un genio*. Milan: Mondadori.

Sapori, Armando. 1926. *La crisi delle compagnie mercantili dei Bardi e dei Peruzzi*. Florence: Olschki.

– 1955. *Studi di Storia Economica. Secoli XII – XIV – XV.* Florence: Sansoni. 2 vols.

– 1958. "La gabella delle porte di Firenze." *Miscellanea in onore di Roberto Crespi* 1:321–48.

Saxonhouse, Arlene. 1985. *Women in the History of Political Thought: Ancient Greece to Machiavelli*. New York: Praeger.

Sestan, Ernesto. 1972. "Brienne Gualtieri." In *Dizionario biografico degli italiani*. Rome: Treccani. Vol. 14.

Soldini, Francesco. 1780. *Delle eccellenze e grandezze della nazione fiorentina*. Florence: Stamperia Vanni e Tofani.

Steinberg, Justin. 2017. "Mimesis on Trial: Legal and Literary Verisimilitude in Boccaccio's *Decameron*." *Representation* 139:118–45.

– 2020. "The Artist and the Police (VIII.3)." In *The Decameron Eighth Day in Perspective*, ed. William Robins. Toronto: University of Toronto Press. 59–88.

Swanson, Jenny. 1989. *John of Wales: A Study of the Works and Ideas of a Thirteenth-Century Friar*. Cambridge: Cambridge University Press.

Sznura, Franek. 1975. *L'espansione urbana a Firenze nel dugento*. Florence: La Nuova Italia.

– 2013. "La *Prammatica fiorentina.* Note sulla redazione e contenuto." In *La prammatica sulle vesti delle donne fiorentine*, ed. Laurence Gérard-Marchant. *Draghi rossi e querce azzurre: elenchi descrittivi di abiti di lusso (Firenze 1343–1345).* Florence: SISMEL – Edizioni del Galluzzo. 39–74.

Tangheroni, Marco. 1973. *Politica, commercio, agricoltura a Pisa nel Trecento.* Pisa: Pacini.

Tanturli, Giuliano. 2013. "Consolatoria a Pino de' Rossi." In *Boccaccio, autore e copista*, ed. Teresa De Robertis, Carla Maria Monti, Marco Petoletti, Giuliano Tanturli, and Stefano Zamponi. Florence: Mandragora. 153–6.

Tanzini, Lorenzo. 2018. *1345. La bancarotta di Firenze. Una storia di banchieri, fallimenti, e finanza.* Rome: Salerno Editrice.

Tateo, Francesco. 1998. *Boccaccio.* Bari: Laterza.

The Art of Executing Well: Rituals of Execution in Renaissance Italy. 2008. Ed. Nicholas Terpstra. Kirksville, MO: Truman State University Press.

Tocco, Felice. 1909. *Studii francescani.* Naples: Perella.

Tocco, Francesco Paolo. 2001. *Niccolò Acciaiuoli. Vita e politica in Italia alla metà del XIV secolo.* Rome: nella sede dell'Istituto Palazzo Borromini.

Tognetti, Sergio. 2016. "La mercatura fiorentina giura fedeltà al Duca d'Atene. Dai rogiti di ser Bartolo di ser Neri da Ruffiano." *Ricerche storiche* 45.3:415–37.

Tordi, Domenico. 1923. *Gl'inventari dell'eredità di Jacopo Boccaccio ed altri documenti riguardanti anche il suo grande fratello Giovanni Boccaccio raccolti ed annotati da Domenico Tordi.* Orvieto: Tipografia Rubeca e Scaletti.

Trexler, Richard C. 1978. "Honor among Thieves: The Trust Function on the Urban Clergy in the Florentine Republic." In *Essays Presented to Myron P. Gilmore*, ed. Sergio Bertelli and Gloria Ramakus. Florence: La Nuova Italia Editrice. 317–34.

Tripodi, Claudia. 2011. "Dalla signoria di Volterra al catasto del 1429: la parabola della famiglia Belforti." *Rassegna volterranea* 88:185–207.

– 2013. *Gli Spini tra XIV e XV secolo. Il declino di un antico casato fiorentino.* Florence: Olschki.

Trotta, Stefania. 1995. "L'*Elegia di madonna Fiammetta* di Giovanni Boccaccio e un volgarizzamento delle *Epistulae heroidum* di Ovidio attribuito a Filippo Ceffi." *Italia Medioevale e Umanistica* 38:217–61.

Tufano, Ilaria. 2021. *Boccaccio e il suo mondo.* Soveria Mannelli: Rubettino.

Tylus, Jane. 2013. "On the Threshold of Paradise (Comedia delle ninfe fiorentine, or Ameto)." In *Boccaccio: A Critical Guide to the Complete Works*, ed. Victoria Kirkham, Michael Sherberg, and Janet Leverie Smarr. Chicago: University of Chicago Press. 133–43.

Valeri, Nino. 1965. *Le origini dello stato moderno in Italia (1328–1450).* Vol. 1. *Storia d'Italia.* Turin: UTET.

Vannucci, Marcello. 1993. *Le grandi famiglie di Firenze.* Rome: Newton Compton editori.

Varanini, Gian Maria. 2002. "Tra Firenze e Verona. La famiglia da Lisca nel Tre e Quattrocento." In *Domus illorum de Lischa: una famiglia e un palazzo del Rinascimento a Verona*, ed. Stefano Lodi. Vicenza: Neri Pozza Editore. 15–42.

Vecchi Galli, Paola. 2009. "Dante e Petrarca: Scrivere il padre." *Studi di problemi e critica testuale* 79:57–82.

Veglia, Marco. 2000. *La vita lieta: una lettura del Decameron*. Ravenna: Longo.

– 2014. *La strada più impervia. Boccaccio tra Dante e Petrarca*. Padua and Rome: Antenore.

Velli, Giuseppe. 1991. "Seneca nel *Decameron*." *Giornale Storico della Letteratura Italiana* 168:321–34. Rpt. *Petrarca e Boccaccio*, 209–21.

– 1995. *Petrarca e Boccaccio: Tradizione – Memoria – Scrittura*. Padua: Antenore.

– 2002. "Petrarca, Dante, la poesia classica: *Ne la stagion che'l ciel rapido inchina* (*RVF*, L), *Io son venuto al punto de la rota* (*Rime*, C)." *Studi Petrarcheschi* 15:81–98.

– 2004. "Il rapporto Petrarca-Boccaccio: a proposito (anche) della Griselda." *Levia Gravia* 6:215–25.

– 2005. "Petrarca e Boccaccio: l'incontro milanese." In *Petrarca e la Lombardia*, ed. Giuseppe Frasso, Giuseppe Velli and Maurizio Vitale. Padua: Antenore. 145–64.

– 2007. "Petrarca, i classici, i preumanisti padovani (e l'ombra di Dante)." In *Francesco Petrarca: da Padova all'Europa. Atti del convegno internazionale di studi – Padova, 17–18 giugno 2004*, ed. Gino Belloni, Giuseppe Frasso, Manlio Pastore Stocchi, and Giuseppe Velli. Padua: Antenore. 3–18.

– 2019. "Memory." In *The Decameron: A Critical Lexicon*, ed. Pier Massimo Forni, Renzo Bragantini, and Christopher Kleinhenz, trans. Michael Papio. Tempe: Arizona Center for Medieval and Renaissance Studies. 183–210.

von Roon-Bassermann, Elizabeth. 1964. "Die Rossi von Oltrarno. Ein Beitrag zur mittelatlerlichen Sozial- und Wirtshaftsgechichte von Florenze." *Vierteljahrschrift für Sozial- und Wirtshaftsgechichte* 51:235–48.

Weisz, Jean S. 1984. *Pittura e Misericordia: The Oratory of S. Giovanni Decollato in Rome*. Ann Arbor: UMI Research Press.

Wilkins, Ernst Hatch. 1960. "Petrarch and Manno Donati." *Speculum* 35.3:381–93.

– 1961. *Life of Petrarch*. Chicago: University of Chicago Press.

Witt, Ronald G. 1976. *Coluccio Salutati and His Public Letters*. Geneva: Librairie Droz.

– 2012. *The Two Latin Cultures and the Foundation of Renaissance Humanism in Medieval Italy*. Cambridge: Cambridge University Press.

Yunn, Amee. 2015. *The Bargello Palace: The Invention of Civic Architecture in Florence*. London: Harvey Miller.

Zaccaria, Raffaella. 2003. "Guadagni, Migliore." In *Dizionario biografico degli italiani*. Rome: Treccani. Vol. 60.

– 2009. "Vieri de' Medici." In *Dizionario biografico degli italiani*. Rome: Treccani. Vol. 73.

Zaccaria, Vittorio. 1963. "Le fasi redazionali del *De mulieribus claris*." *Studi sul Boccaccio* 1:253–332.

– 1986. "La difesa della poesia nelle 'Genealogie' del Boccaccio." *Lettere Italiane* 38.3:281–311.

– 2001. *Boccaccio narratore, storico, moralista e mitografo*. Florence: Olschki.

Zafarana, Zelina. 1968. "Boccaccio di Chellino." In *Dizionario biografico degli italiani*. Rome: Treccani. Vol. 10.

– 1971. "Gherardo Bordoni." In *Dizionario biografico degli italiani*. Rome: Treccani. Vol. 12.

Zardo, Antonio. 1887. *Petrarca e i Carraresi*. Milan: Hoepli.

Zorzi, Andrea. 1988. *L'amministrazione della giustizia penale nella Repubblica fiorentina. Aspetti e problemi*. Florence: Olschki.

– 1994. "The Judicial System in Florence in the Fourteenth and Fifteenth Centuries." In *Crime, Society, and the Law in Renaissance Italy*, ed. Trevor Dean and K.J.P. Love. Cambridge, MA: Cambridge University Press. 40–58.

– 1995. *Politica e giustizia a Firenze al tempo degli ordinamenti antimagnatizi*. Florence: Edifir.

– 2000. "I rettori di Firenze. Reclutamento, flussi, scambi (1193–1313)." In *I Podestà dell'Italia comunale*, ed. Jean-Claude Maire Vigueur. 2 vols. Rome: Sede dell'Istituto Palazzo Borromini. 595–643.

– 2010. *Le signorie cittadine in Italia (secoli XIII–XV)*. Milan: Mondadori.

Index of Names